IRISH REBEL

İRISH REBEL

John Devoy
and America's Fight

for

Ireland's Freedom

TERRY GOLWAY

ST. MARTIN'S PRESS ❦ NEW YORK

Frontispiece: The standard portrait of John Devoy in his later years.
(Courtesy of the McLoughlin family)
Page 320: John Devoy's funeral procession makes its way through Dublin.
(UPI/Corbis-Bettmann)

Design by MAUREEN TROY

Library of Congress Cataloging-in-Publication Data

Golway, Terry.
    Irish rebel : John Devoy and America's fight for Ireland's freedom /
by Terry Golway.
        p.   cm.
    ISBN 0-312-18118-3
    1. Devoy, John, 1842–1928. 2. Revolutionaries—Ireland—
Biography.—3. Ireland—History—1837–1901—Biography. 4. Fenians—
Biography. I. Title.
DA954.G64   1998
941.5081—dc21   97-40277
                                                           CIP

First Edition: March 1998

10 9 8 7 6 5 4 3 2 1

This book is for Eileen Duggan

CONTENTS

contents

THIS BOOK IS THE PRODUCT OF A CONVERSATION I HAD ON ELLIS Island with Angela Carter, who runs Irish Books in New York and who is one of Irish America's great treasures. Angela's encouragement—and her insistence that John Devoy's story was a tale worth telling—provided me with the inspiration to go forward. In the early stages of my research, a dozen people insisted that I meet Peter Quinn, the chief speechwriter for Time Warner, who, they said, knew something about John Devoy. As it transpired, Peter knew a great deal about a great many things, and he conveyed them with wit and elegance. His help has been almost as invaluable as his friendship.

I would never have considered such a project, or, indeed, have ever heard of John Devoy, were it not for the Reverend Maurice Burke, my parish priest for a quarter century in Tottenville, Staten Island. Father Burke's love of Ireland and his strong sense of social justice have made a lasting impression.

During the four years of researching and writing this book, many friends, acquaintances, and colleagues have made polite inquiries about my progress and then listened patiently as I shared with them, in numbing detail, my latest observations on the life and times of John Devoy. I thank them all for their interest, particularly the staffs of the *New York Observer* and the Jesuit weekly, *America*.

As a journalist, I'm used to dealing with political officials whose job it is to prevent information from seeing the light of day. Imagine, then, my astonishment when I found myself talking to librarians and archivists who consider it their solemn duty to help writers obtain the information they need as quickly as possible. My thanks and admiration go to the staffs of the National Library of Ireland, the National Archives in Dublin, Glasnevin Cemetery in Dublin, the Public Records Office in London, the New York Public Library, the Municipal Archives of New York City, the Museum of the City of New York, the Bureau of Vital Statistics in Atlantic City, the Library of Congress and the National Archives in Washington. In addition, I received immeasurable help from Chris Cahill, Paul Ruppert, Bill O'Connor, Rosa Meehan, and Alec Omsby at the American Irish Historical Society; John Ridge and Marion Casey of the New York Irish History Roundtable; the staff at the McManus Collection at Seton Hall University; and the archival staff at Catholic University of America. Thanks, too, to Michael Kenny of the National Museum of Ireland, Mary Holt Moore, Dave Burke, Father Sean McManus, James McDermott, and Charlie and Jeanne McLoughlin for their help with photos.

A number of people offered their advice and support along the way, and I'm grateful for both. Among them were Patty O'Connell, Mitchell Moss, Tom Quinn, Dermot McEvoy, Rob Walsh, Sean Cronin, Dermot Brangan, Eamon Delaney, and a trio of Scanlons: John, Michael, and Dan. Thanks, also, to Seamus and Marie Heaney for their hospitality in Dublin in 1995, and to Kieran Scully for his knowledge of Dublin.

John Devoy has taken me away from my old friends, and for this I ask their forgiveness, in particular Amy Doerzbacher, Deborah Hartnett, Mike Hammer, Phil Russo, Kevin Davitt, Jim Hughes, Dan Janison, and Anne Silverstein. We have some catching up to do. And I wish Al Brumme was here to read this.

It has been my good fortune to work with several wonderful editors at the New York Observer. Three especially deserve thanks: Ken Paul, for his integrity; Peter Kaplan, for his humanity; and Joe Conason, for his interest.

Arthur Carter, the Observer's publisher, could well be the answer to what ails the newspaper business in America. He is fiercely independent, he welcomes writing with a sharp point of view, and he insists that those lucky enough to work for him get on with the business of speaking truth to power. I'm lucky to work for him, and I'm even luckier to consider him a friend.

Veronica Kinane of the Kildare Historical Society generously allowed me to examine her fascinating collection of local history, including her copy of a picture John Devoy sent his onetime fiancée, Eliza Kenny. Thanks, also, to a pair of young scholars: Karel Kiely, who allowed me to quote from her study of the Poor Law Union in Naas, County Kildare, and Ed O'Donnell of Hunter College, whose study of the New York Irish during the Gilded Age provided this manuscript with many telling details.

My editor, Diane Higgins, has been a wonderful source of encouragement. Her sharp eye helped fashion what was an unspeakably wieldy tome into something direct and pointed. Her assistants, Becky Davis and Lisa Paradis, and copy editor Steve Boldt also helped make this book a lighter load on the shelves. John Wright, my agent and friend, has been and will continue to be that rarest of combinations: a nurturing nudge. This book could not have been written without his help and skill.

Eileen Duggan, my wife, has spent four years listening to a verbal (and unedited) version of this book. During that time we have had two children, Katherine and Conor. I'm not sure what the connection is, but there you have it. Without her love and friendship, all would be in vain.

Terry Golway
Maplewood, New Jersey
August 12, 1997

CHAPTER ONE

A Land Beyond the Waves

JOHN DEVOY WAS PLAYING POKER WITH FOUR FELLOW GRADUATES of British jails as they sailed across the Atlantic, bound for New York, in mid-January 1871 aboard the Cunard steamship *Cuba.* After five years of a meager prison diet, Devoy's short, husky frame showed few signs of deprivation. His hands, however, were tough and calloused from years spent breaking stones.

In return for their early release from prison, Devoy and his playing partners, Irish rebels all, agreed to live anywhere but in the United Kingdom of Great Britain and Ireland. Collectively, they chose New York, the burgeoning capital-in-exile of an Irish Republic that existed only in the minds of John Devoy and his friends. From New York, they would continue the work of bringing revolution and independence to Ireland.

In Devoy's pocket was a half-written letter to his long-suffering father, an extraordinary Dublin brewery clerk who lost his small farm in the Irish potato famine, his oldest son during a Famine-era cholera epidemic, and his wife when she was just forty-two, leaving him with seven children to rear. William Devoy's third child, John, was a stubborn, headstrong, but brilliant young man who was forever at odds with teachers, priests, civil authorities, and sometimes William himself. When he was nineteen, John ran away from home and joined the French Foreign Legion after a row with his father over politics. William Devoy, a gentle and intensely religious man, was helpless in the face of his son's ferocity.

Though William himself once tramped the hills near his family's farm on behalf of Irish political crusades, he feared that the eternally doomed struggle for an independent Irish nation would be his son's ruin. To be sure, John Devoy, now twenty-nine, had long ago succumbed to the call of Ireland's ancient martyrs, and for it he had sacrificed job prospects, material advancement, and the woman he loved. Her name was Eliza Kenny, and she was the attractive daughter of a farm family who lived near the old Devoy homestead in Naas, County Kildare. They became engaged just before Devoy was arrested in 1866 while helping to organize a rebellion in Ireland. In a long letter smuggled out of his prison cell, he released Eliza from the engagement, but promised to marry her if she were still single when he was free again. His time of freedom had arrived at last, and Eliza was patiently waiting in her parents' little cabin. But there were no half-written letters to Eliza in Devoy's pocket as he sailed to his new home. She would wait fifty-four years before hearing from her fiancé again.

As the ship drew ever closer to New York, Devoy and three of his colleagues scrutinized their cards and cast bemused glances at the inscrutable, haggard features of the fifth of their number, Jeremiah O'Donovan Rossa. When their journey to freedom began in Liverpool in early January, Rossa told his friends he had never played a game of poker in his life. Now, after a week on the high seas, Rossa was winning hand after hand. But neither Devoy nor the other ex-prisoners, Charles O'Connell, John McClure, and Henry Mulleda, were about to complain about Rossa's suspicious good fortune. For the first time since the mid-1860s they were free men, free from Britain's prisons, and free from the weight of Ireland's tortured history. In America, they believed, they would find a clean slate, a future rather than a past, and most of all, a chance to succeed where they had so recently failed.

The card games had been put aside, and Rossa was counting his winnings—seven pounds sterling—when the *Cuba* made its way past Sandy Hook and into the embrace of New York Harbor on January 19. The view from the ship's deck was similar to that which had greeted the hundreds of thousands of starving Irish exiles who fled the great famine some quarter century before. To the west rose the gentle hills of Staten Island, whose distance from the cities of New York and Brooklyn made it a perfect location for an immigrant quarantine station. Many disease-ridden Irish men, women, and children were taken off coffin ships and brought to the island's green shores, where they died and were buried in short order. Eventually, the native islanders objected to this unwanted influx of starving, exhausted, and poor immigrants, so they burned down the quarantine station. It was rebuilt, and it would be the *Cuba*'s first stop in America.

The tall masts lining Manhattan's bustling eastern shore came into view as the ship sailed through the narrow strait separating Staten Island from Brooklyn. The sight was breathtaking, something the well-read but provincial Irish exiles had never seen before. It was grandeur on a grand scale, the loading dock from which the young American republic was planning its long march westward to the Pacific. Here, in this bustling port city, vibrant and powerful and rich, John Devoy planned to summon the great mass of Irish America on behalf of the impoverished and oppressed people he had left behind. From the *Cuba*'s decks on this January day, anything seemed possible in New York, in America.

But there was a grittier reality to New York invisible to Devoy's faulty eyes. The stench from the waterfront was such that the city was about to dredge the East River dock areas in hopes of removing an offensive and potent buildup of toxic silt. And that was hardly the end of the hidden assaults on public health in the winter of 1871. Smallpox was ravaging the city's poor neighborhoods, causing some residents to flee, as the *New York Herald* delicately put it, "like rats [abandoning] a sinking ship." The city may have defeated Philadelphia and Boston in the race to become the nation's leader in population, wealth, culture, and commerce, but it also led the nation in mortality rates, infectious diseases, and poor housing. In the heavily Irish Tenth Ward on the Lower East Side, the population lived in conditions unheard of in human history—276,000 to a square mile. The streets were filled with the stench of slaughterhouses, outdoor privies, and gasworks.

Still, whatever its problems, New York had a reputation as a place of refuge and exile for the Irish, despite the best efforts of a few of the natives. Some twenty-eight years before the *Cuba* sailed into New York Harbor, the city elected an avowedly nativist mayor, James Harper, who had campaigned on an overt anti-immigrant—which meant anti-Irish and anti-Catholic—platform. The Catholic bishop of New York, John Hughes, showed up at the new mayor's doorstep and told him that if even one Catholic church was burned down as a result of the mayor's rhetoric, he, Hughes, would see to it that his flock put a torch to the city. No churches were burned in New York, but there was at least one close call. The seat of Hughes's power, the original St. Patrick's Cathedral near the notorious Five Points slum, was spared only when the Ancient Order of Hibernians fought off a torch-bearing nativist mob intent on scaling the churchyard's ten-foot walls, which had been built for exactly such an occasion.

As a sign of how much had changed since Harper's time, the city's leading politicians were preparing a civic reception for Devoy and his friends. In the mass democracy that was New York, there was power in numbers, and in this city of nearly 1 million people, 20 percent were Irish-born and 37 percent claimed at least one Irish-born parent. By contrast, in 1870 there were but 2,800 Italian immigrants in New York and 80,000 Jews. So Gaelic was this Anglo-Dutch city becoming that one of its leading newspapers referred to the metropolis as "New Cork," after Ireland's second-largest city. And so Catholic was the mass of immigrants that an editorial in the New York Times wondered, "How Long Will Protestants Endure?" It was a fair question: in 1840, New York was 64 percent native-born and predominantly Protestant, and by the time of Devoy's arrival, it was 47 percent foreign-born and, stunningly, 50 percent Catholic.

This dramatic transformation repulsed the city's middle classes, who believed they were losing their city to feckless foreigners who brought with them alien customs, terrible diseases, and a despised religion, complaints that would sound familiar to anyone living in New York or indeed anywhere in America in the late twentieth century.

The Irish had a few complaints of their own. Theirs was a miserable existence, with male laborers earning about $300 a year, some $400 less than what was considered a subsistence salary. Skilled in nothing but the rudimentaries of agriculture, they nevertheless flocked to America's cities, where they settled for hard and menial work. The men worked on the docks, in stables, and dug foundations for the city's great buidings; the women worked as domestics and garment workers. Remarkably, they managed not only to send some money home, often to bring relatives over, but also financed the building of a great cathedral, St. Patrick's, and dozens of lesser churches.

Those who lived in the city's squalor actually were not nearly the worst off. If an Irish immigrant wished to hear the music of his homeland, he need only take a rowboat ride to Blackwell's Island off Manhattan's shore in the East River. There, the city had built a complex consisting of a workhouse, an almshouse, a charity hospital, a prison, and a lunatic asylum. The Irish were overrepresented in each, and in every category depicting poverty, violence, and pathology. The Irish were five times more likely to be arrested than German immigrants, the group to which the Irish were inevitably compared and always unfavorably. Irish natives held 50 percent of the city's worst-paid jobs at a time when the Irish-born made up about 20 percent of the city's population.

A contemporary observer, visiting an Irish neighborhood, remarked that "the effect produced on the mind . . . a vehement desire to pull down and raze to the ground the vast system which holds in bondage thousands and thousands of men, women, and children. These . . . houses tower up to heaven, each flat holding from five to ten families, and one building numbering . . . a population of six hundred souls. To their credit be it said, the condition of the Irish is by no means the worst, but the atmosphere of the place is death, morally and physically."

From these suffering souls, Devoy proposed to build a movement to set free a land three thousand miles away. It seemed not merely audacious, but hopelessly romantic. In the coming decades he would take for himself the role of Irish America's conscience, referee, and most of all, chief organizer. Using the education his father had demanded he receive, he would manipulate American opinion and demonize his opponents, using his extraordinary gift for language and invective. He would form alliances, brittle and combustible though they often were, with a generation of other remarkable Irish exiles, such as the poet and editor John Boyle O'Reilly, Devoy's boyhood friend James J. O'Kelly, the rebel-turned-humanitarian Michael Davitt, newspaper publisher Patrick Ford, an inventor named John Holland, a physician from Philadelpia named William Carroll, and an astonishing array of politicians. He would advise presidential candidates James Blaine and William Henry Harrison, challenge the likes of Andrew Carnegie and Woodrow Wilson, and throw Irish America's support behind an aristocratic, Anglo-Irish landlord named Charles Stewart Parnell. Late in his life, when he was deaf and nearly blind, he would seek a place for himself on the firing line during the Easter Rising in Dublin in 1916. As an old man who had spent a lifetime with romantics seeking a martyr's death, he would find the conspirator he had sought all his life in the young, dashing Michael Collins, hero of Ireland's War of Independence, only to mourn him when he was slain by his own brethren in a bloody, awful quarrel that was a lifetime in coming.

With such allies—and sometimes without them—Devoy would see to it that the historical grievances of a small country off the European mainland would find a voice through the power and influence of America's first exile political movement. And of the movement's founders, only Devoy would live to see the flag of a free Ireland flying in peace over Dublin.

AS THE *CUBA* DREW within a few miles of the city, politicians, journalists, and Irish-American dignitaries scurried about to prepare for the long-awaited moment. In the chaotic offices of the *New York Herald* near Park Row in downtown Manhattan, the paper's city editor, Mike Kelly, had just discovered a major crimp in his plans to cover the festivities. His reporter was drunk. Kelly turned to the paper's corps of freelancers, called space men because they were paid according to how much of what they wrote got into the paper, and chose Joseph I. C. Clarke, a broke, twenty-nine-year-old poet new to the *Herald's* newsroom. Clarke was an admirable choice, for he, too, was once an Irish revolutionary and was a friend of Devoy's closest friend, James J. O'Kelly, another revolutionary turned journalist who would find work at the *Herald.* Some six years before, Clarke himself had nearly joined Devoy and the others in a British prison, but a tip allowed him to escape to New York just ahead of Scotland Yard. Now, like Kelly, Clarke was part of a fledgling Irish-Catholic immigrant foray into jobs and professions that would serve as a point of contact with mainstream, Protestant New York.

Clarke arrived at the piers near South Street in time to climb aboard a U.S. government cutter taking Thomas Murphy, the collector of the Port of New York, into the harbor to greet the *Cuba* as it docked off Staten Island. Murphy bore with him a letter from his boss, President Ulysses S. Grant, offering the former prisoners the White House's kind regards and an official invitation to board the federal cutter for the last leg of their long journey. The president's gesture would appall the British, and that was exactly Grant's intention. He and his onetime soldiers hadn't forgotten Britain's cooperation with the Confederates during the Civil War. Twisting the British lion's tale was official Washington policy in Reconstruction America, a development that greatly pleased the competing factions of Irish-American nationalism.

Once in the harbor, Murphy and his delegation of Republicans quickly realized that theirs would not be a leisurely, late-afternoon cruise. In the distance came another small boat, this one carrying the Democratic representatives of Tammany Hall. And yet another boat was racing toward the *Cuba*. This one carried no competing politicians, but a group representing the Knights of St. Patrick, one of the dozens of Irish fraternal groups and benevolent societies in the city. All three boats were determined to be the first to greet the conquering heroes.

As torches blazed along the waterfront and cannons fired a welcoming salute, the Knights pulled alongside the *Cuba* first, followed by Murphy and the federal ship, with Tammany finishing last. Murphy scrambled aboard to seek out the heroes and hustle them into his boat for the short journey to Manhattan. Clarke wandered off in search of a story. He stumbled into the *Cuba*'s smoking room, where he found John Devoy conducting an interview with a Spanish journalist. Devoy was fluent in French and knew a little Spanish; the Spanish journalist knew some French, so the interview was conducted haphazardly in both languages, and in Devoy's prematurely aged growl. Clarke had never met Devoy, but apparently he recognized him even without the beard Devoy wore before his arrest. He also knew of Devoy's linguistic prowess. "I see you didn't forget your French," Clarke said by way of introduction.

Devoy was charmed to hear an Irish accent, and coming from a fellow rebel-in-exile, no less. When Clarke dropped O'Kelly's name, Devoy sat down with the young *Herald* reporter and proceeded to give him the inside story of the exiles' prison ordeal and their ten-day trip across the Atlantic. The rookie space man had a scoop. He would earn the astounding sum of $48 for this day's work.

In the meantime, however, things were not quite so convivial on the *Cuba*'s decks. The Tammany boat had arrived, and its party was not pleased with its last-place finish. The delegation's leader, Richard O'Gorman, burst onto the scene just as Murphy was reading President Grant's greeting and his invitation to board the federal boat. The exiles, Devoy included, gathered round to hear Murphy, and they concluded that the letter from Grant was fake. After all, they had spent their young lives in defiance of authority figures—who were they that the president of the United States should greet them?

O'Gorman seized the moment and demanded the right to greet the prisoners on behalf of the City of New York, whose hospitality should take precedence over dubious messages from Washington. As Devoy and his friends looked on with horror, the two political delegations then staged an impromptu reenactment of the Civil War, with the various civic worthies pushing and shoving each other along the ship's slippery decks.

Finally, the former prisoners assembled in the *Cuba*'s cabin and agreed to allow O'Gorman to read an address from the city fathers. But Murphy's party had second thoughts about this compromise, and they burst into the cabin in midaddress, led by a maverick Irish-born veteran of the Mexican Army and a onetime Irish revolutionary leader, F. F. Millen. Millen one-upped O'Gorman: "Unlike this gentleman," he said, gesturing toward his Tammany rival, "I don't offer you a reception at the hands of the city government, but I extend to you the hospitality of the United States." It was reported, and later denied, that Millen's address was made all the more hospitable by an offer of cold cash if only the exiles agreed to steam to Manhattan in the federal boat. Rossa would later write that "I myself might have been a lord today—or a Sing Sing convict—had I grasped the treasures laid before me."

Tammany's operatives were not about to surrender. The city's health commissioner challenged Millen, "Are you the United States, sir?" Millen replied, "No, but I desire to save the men from being made the tool of Tammany tricksters."

Those were fighting words, and O'Gorman's men knew an insult when they heard one. The two parties turned on each other yet again. The health commissioner said he might have reason to order the ship and all aboard it into indefinite quarantine, unless, of course, the guests of honor decided to accompany the Tammany delegation. The exiles, whose affections were so hotly contested, withdrew from the cabin in disgust. Devoy growled to Clarke, the young reporter, "Do they think that by dangling the dollars before us they can influence us? We are not children nor have we been in prison for the cause . . . to fall into the hands of buyers." The *Herald* correspondent took note of Devoy's words, as well as his physical appearance: "Though not over five feet six in height, [he] has the square, strong shoulders of a young Hercules. His head is large, and rests on a short, thick neck. His hair is cropped . . . close and surmounts a square, massive forehead under which a pair of small, deep-set blue eyes give the expression of shewdness. . . . He complains of shortness of sight, the worst result of his five years' incarceration."

At midnight, after hours of negotiations, Devoy and his colleagues withdrew to the ship's salon, where they drew up a written statement and presented it to their Irish-American suitors:

"It is painful for us to-night to see so much disunion among our-selves . . . as you have not united cordially to receive us, we will . . . remain on board the ship tonight, and go to a hotel to-morrow."

The competing parties returned to their cutters with nothing to show for their exertions. The *Cuba* Five had gotten their first glimpse of Irish America, and it was not a flattering view. Still, the absurd display did nothing to discourage Devoy from believing that Ireland's salvation would one day come from Irish America.

Devoy and company set sail for Cunard's docks in Jersey City the morning after the debacle—in a decidedly neutral Cunard tug. From Jersey City, the exiles took a ferryboat to New York just like any other travelers seeking to spend a Saturday afternoon in the city. But New York's Irish population was not to be denied its celebration, and awaiting the exiles' arrival were a battalion of the Knights of St. Patrick and legions of Irish immigrants, who formed a spontaneous parade to escort the *Cuba* Five to Sweeney's Hotel in downtown Manhattan. Some three thousand callers, including Boss Tweed himself, paid their respects at a daylong reception in one of the hotel's parlors.

"All day long . . . Sweeney's Hotel and the approaches to it were the scene of the most lively excitement, caused by the congregation of numerous sympathizers," the *Herald* reported. "The green flag was flying from the highest flagstaff on the roof of the hotel." Tweed met privately with Devoy and the others, and he was told in firm but polite terms that he should postpone a planned parade in the exiles' honor until a second Cunard ship, the *Russia,* landed with nine more newly freed prisoners. Tweed reluctantly agreed. He had raised $26,000 for the occasion—and had named himself the parade's grand marshal.

At one point in these first few days in New York, the *Cuba* Five gathered for a group photograph that would be widely reprinted in American's Irish community. The unsmiling image of Devoy framed the photograph's left corner. He stood ramrod stiff, while his colleagues adopted more casual poses. Devoy was clean-shaven, although he would soon grow back the fine, thick beard he had worn before his arrest. As the *Herald* noted, he looked younger than his twenty-nine years, even in the formal bow tie and vest he wore. His right hand dangled from arm bent at the elbow. This big and gnarled hand was that of a man intimate with the hard labor that was a Victorian prisoner's lot.

The celebrations went on for the better part of two weeks, and the promised parade did finally take place once the *Russia* arrived in late January. On January 30, Sweeney's Hotel was still alive to the joyful noise of receptions and parties—the *Herald* said the "excitement was worth a hundred dollars a day to Sweeney's in drinks alone." Delegations from the heavily Irish cities of the Northeast poured into New York to present the exiles with windy proclamations paying tribute to everything from their long years of self-sacrifice to their as-yet-undisplayed, but naturally assumed, Irish wit. A resolution of welcome was introduced on the floor of Congress by former Union general Benjamin Butler, now a maverick Republican congressman from Massachusetts.

The gaudy receptions culminated in a weeklong visit to Washington, D.C., and a meeting at the White House with President Grant on February 22. But on the eve of their White House visit, which the Republicans arranged as a highly public snub of British sensitivities, the former prisoners found themselves on the edge of public humiliation. Patrick "Pagan" O'Leary, who arrived in New York aboard the *Russia*, had been telling Washington well-wishers that one of his fellow exiles, a friend of Devoy's named William Roantree, was a British spy. The Pagan, so called because he had renounced both his Catholic faith and St. Patrick—the latter because he had preached the virtues of forgiveness to the ancient Celts—was given to wild talk and speculation, but he was indulged because he was a born eccentric and because he became even odder after taking a bullet to the head during the Mexican War (fighting on the Mexican side). This time, however, the Pagan's ramblings threatened public embarrassment.

With the exiles' triumphant tour of the nation's capital hanging in the balance, it was left to the levelheaded Devoy to devise a scheme to silence the Pagan and then get on with the business of accepting America's salute. Understanding that the Pagan was not somebody given to reasonable discourse, Devoy offered O'Leary the following, seemingly cold-blooded proposition: the exiles would convene a trial to hear the charges, and if they believed them, Roantree would be sentenced to death and O'Leary would be the executioner. If they rejected the charges, however, O'Leary himself would be put to death for making false charges. O'Leary agreed to it immediately.

As Devoy planned, the panel chose not to believe O'Leary's charge, but in its mercy the panel's members decided to spare the Pagan's life if he promised never again to repeat the charges. "We could hardly keep ourselves from laughing during the proceedings," Devoy wrote, "but The Pagan took them as seriously as he did his grandmother's stories about the fairies . . . and he was most discreet" during the remainder of the visit.

Devoy would play an arbiter's role many more times in the coming years. Few such occasions would end with Devoy fighting back laughter.

The meeting with Grant on the White House steps went off without a hitch, with Grant shaking hands with the fourteen former prisoners in attendance and muttering a few words of small talk with each one. Devoy thought Grant's arm looked like a pump handle as the president mechanically walked through his paces.

Not all of the exiles who gathered at the White House on that winter's day in 1871 would resist America's siren call of assimilation and the pursuit of material glory. Some preferred to start a new life, to put the agonies of Ireland behind them. But of those who gladly remained in the Irish ghetto, who regarded America as little more than a staging area for another try at rebellion in Ireland, none was so single-minded, ferocious, divisive, and driven as John Devoy.

He decided that Ireland would find its long-sought salvation in America. And he would, somehow, make it happen.

CHAPTER TWO

A Most Distressful Country

JOHN DEVOY'S FIRST RECORDED ACT OF REBELLION TOOK PLACE A few years after his family was forced to move from County Kildare to Dublin city in the last, dying days of the Great Irish Famine. The family crowded into a flat in the city's Summerhill section and then into a bigger house in the Liberties neighborhood, hard by the River Liffey and the city's brewing district. Young John was sent off to a primary school on Marlborough Street, across from the procathedral where he would receive the childhood sacraments of First Communion and Confirmation. The school's instructors and its curriculum had but one goal in mind, and that was to turn Irish-Catholic children into good and loyal citizens of the British Empire.

One morning when he was nine or ten—when he told this story in his old age, he could not remember the exact year—Devoy decided that he would no longer join his classmates when they rose to sing "God Save the Queen." Even at this early age, he thought of himself as an Irish patriot, and Irish patriots did not pay homage to people they viewed as foreign rulers.

The young Devoy took politics seriously. He grew up on tales of the bloody and failed Irish rebellion of 1798, which its leaders had hoped would match the American and French revolutions in spreading the cause of republicanism. His grandfathers fought in '98, or so family legend had it. So did his mother's uncle, who was born in the same cabin Devoy was born in. And Devoy's father, born in the shadow of the failed rebellion, was no stranger to Irish nationalism.

The cause seemingly grew from the freshly watered graves of each new generation's patriots.

So determined was young John to follow this well-worn path of sorrows, and so earnest was his effort to reclaim his ancient heritage, that he tried to teach himself the Irish language, the tongue of his great-grandparents. Irish had long ago begun to disappear from Ireland's Anglicized capital, Dublin, and its surrounding counties. In rural districts where the bulk of the country's population lived, children were punished if they were heard speaking Irish. The Irish language was associated with shame, failure, and ruin, the tongue of illiterate farmers who lived at the mercy of the fickle potato. But for a literate, educated Dubliner such as young John, the purchase of an Irish primer for a penny in a neighborhood shop seemed to be an act of cultural rebellion, albeit one only the well-fed son of Dublin could afford.

The passion he brought to his politics could be traced to the hearth of his old family home in the small townland of Kill in County Kildare, some twelve miles to the southwest of Dublin. It was there, under a well-kept thatched roof, that John Devoy lay awake at night and listened to his father reading aloud from a fiercely nationalist newspaper called *The Nation*. The paper was the work of a group of college-educated, middle-class intellectuals, most of them Protestant, intent on ridding Ireland of British rule either by argument or by force. Eventually, they would try both and would fail miserably. But their remarkable words left many legacies, not the least of which were the images that danced in John Devoy's head as he watched his father in front of the fireplace, reading sedition out loud to illiterate but appreciative farmers dressed in corduroy knee breeches, dragging thoughtfully on their pipes.

William Devoy's politics were not exclusively of the passive, fireside sort. He had spent the early summer of his years campaigning in a peaceful but vain quest to break the legislative bond that had held Britain and Ireland together since 1801. William also was a member of a mass temperance movement aimed at freeing some Irishmen from another sort of bondage—and as a member of Father Theobald Mathew's Total Abstinence League, William Devoy was a steadfastly sober man. He was a nationalist, all right, but he believed in constitutional politics and not confrontation and rebellion.

William's son was already a different case entirely, as was made clear on the morning he refused to sing "God Save the Queen."

From his seat in front of the classroom—he couldn't see the blackboard from the back of the room, for his eyes were poor even at this young age—the young John Devoy informed his instructor that he would not sing the foreigner's anthem. The instructor, sensing trouble, called for the school's superintendent, a burly Irishman named Sheehy.

The superintendent bore a fine Irish name, but Sheehy was a teacher in a British-run school system, paid to inculcate in his charges the British view of things. So Sheehy was not pleased to find a little rebel in his classroom, and teachers in Irish schools were allowed great latitude in expressing their displeasure.

Sheehy took the measure of his challenger, a short, dark-haired, nearsighted son of a brewery clerk. Devoy returned Sheehy's glare, his blue eyes flashing defiance.

"Sing, sir!" Sheehy ordered, paying reverence to Victorian manners even as he fingered a slab of slate in his hand.

Devoy refused.

Sheehy summoned the slate to action, smashing it against the stubborn boy's skull. "The blow sent a hundred stars into my head and hurt me badly," Devoy would write more than a half century later.

The young rebel was absent from his front-row seat for days, complaining of "lightness in the head." The school's rules, lately installed during a rash of absences the authorities traced to the large number of young boys frolicking in Dublin's Phoenix Park, demanded that a parent show up in person to explain a student's prolonged absence. Such chores generally fell to mothers, but Elizabeth Devoy had to attend to the demands of her other children. The long walk from the family home on Newmarket, a high street with a fine view of the Wicklow Mountains, to Marlborough Street in the city's commercial center would occupy the better part of a morning. Elizabeth Devoy sent her son back to school on his own, with no parent to vouch for his ailment.

Once again, Sheehy was not pleased.

He ordered the boy to put out his hand so that it might be slapped. Devoy refused. He had clearly learned nothing in the intervening days. So Sheehy produced a cane, which promised another hard-earned lesson in conformity. But before too many blows were struck, the young rebel summoned all the strength he could, approaching Sheehy's thighs at ram speed, pushing him back and then delivering a swift kick to the superintendent's knees.

The school was scandalized, and John Devoy was expelled. But, in his own way, he had cast his first blows for liberty. In a foreshadowing of his future role as Irish America's chief arbiter, disciplinarian, and ideologue, Devoy's energetic blows were directed at a fellow Irishman.

JOHN DEVOY, THE THIRD child and second son of William and Elizabeth Devoy, was born on September 3, 1842, in a small house on a tiny patch of land amid the rolling hills and great green fields of County Kildare. James and Bridget preceded him. After John, there would be two more girls followed by three more boys.

Fortuitously, John was born at the very moment when Ireland's grievances were about to boil over in a historic experiment in popular politics. A barrel-chested, golden-voiced Irishman named Daniel O'Connell was organizing the great mass of Irish peasants as they had never been organized before, an achievement that would mark him as one of the great European statesmen of the nineteenth century. Under his peaceful leadership, huge masses of ordinary Irish people gathered in open-air meetings throughout the countryside in support of O'Connell's proposal to repeal the hated Act of Union, which wedded Ireland to Britain in a legislative marriage to which the mass of the Irish people never consented. The gatherings were huge affairs—one drew a million people, this at a time when Ireland's population was about 8 million. The size of O'Connell's crowds and their disciplined and peaceful demeanor made for a frightening spectacle when viewed from the Houses of Parliament.

William Devoy was one of O'Connell's repeal wardens, which meant that he helped organize his neighbors and kept order at O'Connell's huge meetings. The movement was about to reach its zenith on that September day in 1842 when William Devoy became a father again.

The Devoy cottage in which John was born was set just off the main road to Dublin, on a holding of a mere half acre, well short of the two or three acres that were considered the minimum necessary to raise a family. So William, literate, well read, and politically active, was forced to sell his labor where and when he could. He broke stones for the local roadbuilders, worked as a navvy when the Great Southern and Western Railroad extended its lines outside of Dublin, and went into business as a self-employed contractor.

All the furniture in the cabin was homemade, as were the partitions that divided the cottage into separate rooms. William even repaired his children's shoes and made the family's kitchen utensils.

It was the family's garden, however, that was William's crowning glory. Though small and unable to feed the Devoys on its own, every inch of the plot was cultivated. A row of hedges screened the cottage from the busy Dublin road beyond the cabin's front door. Within the tract itself, William planted strawberries, cabbage, and of course potatoes—the crop upon which fully 3 million Irish men, women, and children depended for their daily existence. Elsewhere on the holding, William planted cherry trees, rosebushes, laurels, hollies, and flower beds.

Elizabeth Devoy's family, the Dunnes, gave William and Elizabeth the plot rent-free after their marriage in 1834. The story of Ireland's miseries, based so much on land and its ownership, was written in the Devoy family's history and the very dirt they relied on for their potatoes: John Devoy's grandfather, for whom the young rebel was named, was raised on an expansive, 235-acre holding. His father, William, and his seven brothers and sisters made ends meet on a nine-acre farm. By the time of John's birth, the Devoys essentially were landless. The half acre that William tended to with such care wasn't his. It belonged to the great landlord, the Earl of Mayo, from whom Elizabeth Dunne's family rented thirty-five acres.

Land was fate in Ireland, and while the Devoys and Dunnes were far better off than the mass of their countrymen, even they felt the insidious effects of British laws intended to take land out of the hands of Irish Catholics and put it into the possession of settlers from England and Scotland. The settlers were regarded as more reliable and more loyal to the Crown because they were Protestant, and Protestantism and the British Crown were knitted together with threads of blood and kinship. Land in Catholic Ireland was regarded as the post-Reformation spoils of victory for Britain's Protestants.

If William and Elizabeth's little garden was a metaphor for a chunk of Irish history, their cottage actually was at the center of a small historical drama that took place less than a half century before John was born. On a dangerous morning in 1798, it served as a refuge for a mud-splattered, bloodstained young rebel named Johnny Dunne—John Devoy's great-uncle on his mother's side.

Ireland was alive with cries and the crash of battle in 1798 as an army of impoverished Irishmen bearing pikes battled a British Army that had so recently been embarrassed in North America. The rebellion was the work of an affluent Anglo-Irish Protestant barrister named Theobald Wolfe Tone, who was neither the first nor the last unlikely figure around whom the Irish-Catholic peasantry rallied. It was Tone who gave Irish nationalism its ideology: an independent Ireland would be a republic, Tone pronounced, and it would find common cause with the two great revolutionary governments of the day—France and the United States.

Tone formed an organization that he called, optimistically, the Society of United Irishmen, for he believed that in an independent Irish Republic, Protestant and Catholic, or colonist and colonized, would put aside ancient differences and join together in the coming great age of democracy and equality. Such inclusion threatened the very texture of British rule in Ireland, dependent as it was on the assurance that Irish Protestants would never make common cause with Ireland's Catholics and, in fact, would continue to think of themselves as British, because of their Protestantism.

Among the thousands of Catholics who joined Tone's society was a teenager named John Devoy, grandfather of the bruised and battered rebel of Marlborough Street School.

Through force of personality, Wolfe Tone persuaded the revolutionary government of republican France to support the fledgling United Irishmen, and, on December 16, 1796, a fleet of forty-five ships carrying fourteen thousand soldiers set sail for Ireland under the command of the young French general Lazare Hoche. It was a supreme moment, for a mere eleven thousand British soldiers were garrisoned in Ireland at the time.

But a sudden storm swept the ships from their landing areas in Bantry Bay near Cork, and the threat disappeared. It would go down in Irish nationalist lore as a great and tragic might-have-been.

In the imagination of Irish nationalists born in the shadow of 1796, there was a moment where it was forever December 16, and General Hoche is aboard his ship, the *Fraternité*, watching the sails of his armada billow in the wind. A fog has rolled in to cover their departure from France, and Wolfe Tone is dressed in his French admiral's uniform, standing side by side with Hoche and ready to take on the might and power of the British Army. The sea offers a limitless horizon, and the storm is far, far away.

The storm postponed the rebellion for almost two years, and by the time it came, Hoche was dead of natural causes, the French were a great deal less interested in exporting their revolution, and the British were a great deal more prepared for it. The fighting was sporadic, unorganized, memorable, and terribly bloody. In six months of warfare, the Rebellion of '98 cost the lives of twenty-five thousand people, more than double the number of dead in the American Revolution's eight long years.

It was after one such bloody night that Johnny Dunne burst into his little cabin near the main road to Dublin. He threw off his bloody clothes and collapsed into bed, exhausted, leaving his wife to hide the evidence before she trudged to the fields for her morning chores. The couple had but one pair of shoes, however, and Johnny Dunne's wife was forced to put on her husband's bloodstained shoes for her field work.

It's not clear exactly which battle Johnny Dunne fought in, but many brutal engagements were fought in and around the Dunne and Devoy homesteads during the spring and summer of '98. Johnny Dunne might have been part of a five-hundred-strong force of local farmers who attacked the nearby British outpost of Prosperous, killed sixteen of the fifty-seven soldiers stationed there, and celebrated the victory by burning the body of the garrison's commander. Or he could have been part of a peasant column that marched on the market town of Naas, charging cannons with pikes. Most of the farmers escaped with their lives; three who didn't were strung up in the streets of the town as a reminder of the fate that awaited Irish rebels.

A party of British yeomen showed up at the Dunne cottage not long after Johnny made his dramatic return. The yeomen were a ruthless lot, willing to hang a peasant on mere suspicion of being a rebel. And Johnny Dunne was very much a suspect, and his wife, out in the field, was wearing the only bit of evidence the soldiers would need—the bloody shoes.

A short standoff between Johnny and his would-be captors was broken only when a member of the local gentry happened by and assured the yeomen that Johnny was a fine lad who couldn't possibly be a rebel. The yeomen withdrew. Johnny Dunne was free to fight another day.

While Johnny Dunne was doing his best for Ireland, John Devoy's paternal grandfather was doing his best to persuade a young woman named Mary Brennan of his charms. The young couple was upwardly mobile, in the limited sense that it was possible for Catholics in eighteenth-century Ireland. They were English-speakers, an important class distinction, although John was born to Irish-speaking parents, both of whom would live more than a century. The young John Devoy had secure employment as a groom to the Duke of Leinster, while Mary was the daughter of a prosperous farmer and a maid to a member of the local gentry, Lady Cecilia Fitzgerald. The lady's cousin was Lord Edward Fitzgerald, who had gained immortality—and an early death—while fighting side by side with the Catholic peasantry during the Rebellion of 1798.

John Devoy eventually won over Mary Brennan, but not her family, whose members no doubt expected Mary to find an eligible member of the small Catholic aristocracy. Mary would have none of it, and one night she tossed her clothes out a back window and crept through an unwatched door, where Devoy awaited. The two eloped, moved to London and then back to County Kildare, finally settling in the townland of Kill, where many years later John Devoy's namesake entered the world just when Daniel O'Connell was promising that the following year, 1843, would see Ireland free from the weight of a political union it neither requested nor supported.

The Ireland of John Devoy's birth was poor and fertile. The island's population grew from 6.8 million to 8.1 million in the twenty years before Devoy's birth. Though Catholics like the Devoys and the Dunnes were beginning to make inroads into the middle classes, most were relegated to poverty. Some three miles down the road that ran outside the Devoy cottage, the authorities were finishing up construction of a workhouse in the town of Naas. Designed to give shelter and labor to the poorest of the poor, it would soon become a busy, crowded place.

As midcentury approached, the potato—cheap, efficient, and easy to grow—loomed all the more important in the daily life of the Irish people. Though the potato gave periodic warnings of its fickle nature, Ireland's overseers and landlords gave little thought to the peasantry's growing dependence on this single crop. In fact, some considered it the natural order of things. Why, after all, would the feckless Irish want anything else? The Anglo-Irish writer Anthony Trollope noted that in Ireland "there were plenty of beggars . . . but it never struck me that there was much distress. . . . The earth gave forth its potatoes freely, and neither man nor pig wanted more."

Trollope miscalculated. Even as John Devoy entered the world, Daniel O'Connell was announcing that the simple Irish were capable of more sophisticated yearnings. O'Connell was determined, after more than a decade of working within British constitutional politics, to regain for Ireland the home-rule parliament it had had before the Rebellion of '98. O'Connell's crusade envisioned nothing less than the dissolution of the union that combined Ireland and Britain into one nation, but if the goal seemed elusive, history argued on O'Connell's behalf. Once before, in the 1820s, O'Connell had set the heather blazing on behalf of Ireland's disenfranchised and had won the day by forcing Britain to concede what was, significantly, called Catholic Emancipation.

Ireland's Catholics early in the nineteenth century suffered systematic discrimination that was the legacy of a particularly insidious set of statutes known as the Penal Laws, which were designed to demoralize and indeed to demonize Catholics as outcasts in land ruled by Protestants. Among other strictures, the laws prohibited Catholics from inheriting land whole, which meant that Catholic-owned farms were split up rather than passed down to the oldest son, leading to a class of small and desperate farmers. While some of the more egregious Penal Laws had been repealed by the time William Devoy and Elizabeth Dunne were born, one hadn't. Catholics were barred from admission to the House of Commons through the neat trick of demanding that members swear an oath stating that they believed that "the invocation or adoration of the Virgin Mary or any other saint, and the sacrifice of the Mass, as they are now used in the Church of Rome, are superstitious and idolatrous." No Catholic could swear such an oath, of course, and that was exactly the intent.

But in 1829, Britain reluctantly lifted the religious test after O'Connell was elected to the House for the second time. The prime minister, the Duke of Wellington, told King George IV that the only alternative was all-out war in Ireland. George IV agreed with great reluctance.

More than a decade after his famous victory, O'Connell, now approaching age seventy, decided to mount one last crusade. Blessed with a powerful voice, an easy eloquence, and an enormous stage presence, he moved the Irish masses with sentimental word pictures that sound today like overblown passages from a clumsy tourist come-on. "The sun never shone upon a lovelier or greener or brighter land," he said to an audience all too familiar with the land and its less romantic traits. "Oh, it is a land to fill one with patriotism, its picturesque beauties please and delight the eye, its majestic mountains rise to the heavens." With such words, O'Connell set out to organize the hundred thousand Catholics eligible to vote in parliamentary elections and the great mass of unfranchised but potentially dangerous peasants. He combined in a precarious alliance with the Protestant writers of *The Nation*, brilliant men such as Thomas Davis and John Mitchel who would collectively be known as Young Ireland. Together, they cast the shadow of yet another rebellion in Ireland during John Devoy's first five years of life.

John was just over a year old when O'Connell's movement swept through County Kildare for a memorable meeting near the town of Mullaghmast, near the Devoy home. William Devoy left his wife and three children behind to join his five brothers in a straw-lined cart that took them to the great meeting. The six men were so cramped they decided to leave behind their father, the elder John Devoy, still very much alive at age sixty-three and intent on seeing the great Irish hero. His sons, however, locked the old man in a back room before setting off for Mullaghmast.

Apparently William and his brothers forgot what determined people their parents were. Just as Mary Brennan defied her family by sneaking out a back door, the elder John Devoy crawled out a back window, took a shortcut to the meeting, and arrived there before his sons.

They joined some 750,000 people in watching O'Connell put on a memorable show. O'Connell was dressed in the scarlet cloak of an Irish alderman, and he wore a cap that was fashioned to resemble a crown—not the English crown, but the one worn by the high kings of Ireland before the English invasions.

England, O'Connell told the massive crowd, "could not long resist these demonstrations of . . . peaceful resolve." Even the Irish-born soldiers serving in the British Army broke out in cheers.

Shortly after the Devoy clan returned to Kill, British authorities banned O'Connell's next monster rally, this one scheduled for Clontarf, where the great Irish hero Brian Boru defeated the Vikings in 1014. O'Connell, a deeply conservative man for all his rhetoric, chose not to defy the ban. His crusade and Young Ireland's agitation did not cease, as is commonly thought, but the campaign never was quite the same. Besides, the day was coming fast when political crusades would seem tragically and terribly irrelevant.

John Devoy's early years were, by his own sketchy account, happy and uneventful, which made his childhood blessed by the standards of many other Irish-Catholic children. The Devoy cottage grew cramped with two more additions, Catherine in 1845 and Mary in 1847, but a few miles to the south, in the Naas workhouse, conditions were a good deal worse. Attracted by the promise of work and shelter, no matter the indignities imposed by government overseers, the poor of County Kildare were streaming into Naas, increasingly desperate, increasingly hungry.

There is no record of John missing a meal. William's casual labor was enough to supplement his garden's small harvest. The main concern in the Devoy household was not food, but education. William assumed the role of tutor, particularly on matters of religion, instructing his children nightly in the mysteries of the Roman Catholic Church. He expected his young offspring to sit through not one but several masses on Sundays. The lessons did not go unheeded, for when John was quizzed by a local priest about some rudimentary bit of Catholic dogma, he was amazed by the child's complex answers. "It's not the Catechism he knows, but theology," the priest told William.

William's devotion to his faith never flagged even in old age. Many years later, he would describe his Sunday routine in a letter to his son in America: "I rise at six o'clock on Sunday and go to seven o'clock mass . . . and wait for the eight o'clock mass . . . go to breakfast, then 11:30 and 12 o'clock masses, and on to the park as far as I have time to walk and [be] home by 3 o'clock. Sometimes I sleep an hour, then to vespers at 7:30 and that ends the day's amusements." William Devoy was a formidable figure.

After being prepared for the world of letters and numbers at home, the Devoy children were sent to a new national school in Kill, one of many the government built throughout Ireland at the time of John's birth. The schools, seemingly a sign of a more enlightened government policy, pleased neither the Catholic hierarchy nor Irish nationalists. The Church objected to the mixing of Catholic and Protestant children, leading Ireland's Cardinal Paul Cullen to order his priests to refuse absolution to parents who sent their children to such dens of heresy—parents such as the devout William and Elizabeth Devoy.

Nationalists despised the schools because of such customs as the daily singing of "God Save the Queen" as well as the schools' emphasis on British history. Devoy himself would write that the national schools were "established for the express purpose of denationalizing the children of Ireland."

John started at the Kill school in 1847, following in the shadow of his brilliant older brother, James. The eldest child of William and Elizabeth was the star of a school that clearly had high standards, whatever its presumed failings as an incubator of Irish nationalism. James, not yet a teenager in the mid-1840s, was already well-versed in geometry.

Young John, however, did nothing for the family's academic reputation. He had great difficulty learning the alphabet, leading his father to consult with school officials. They decided to move John closer to the blackboard, at which point they realized the child was nearsighted. "At that time, giving spectacles to a young boy or girl was never thought of," the nearly blind Devoy would write eighty years later. "If I had got them then and been coaxed to wear them perhaps I shouldn't have so much difficulty in writing this."

Not much more is recorded of the Devoy family's years in Kill, although it is clear that John's early childhood was not the sort that would haunt many of his future colleagues in revolution. While James Devoy was studying Euclid and John was studying the alphabet, the parents of a child named Michael Davitt were being evicted, half-starved, from their small farm in County Mayo. In County Kerry, a youthful Jeremiah O'Donovan Rossa was watching his father die of starvation, leaving behind a large family. Rossa would write of his childhood that he felt "something that was worse than the hunger . . . and that was the degradation into which want and hunger will reduce human nature."

Ireland's pain was brought home to the Devoy household only after a comical fit of absentmindedness left William without work and without prospects. In 1848, William was still active in nationalist circles, though O'Connell was dead and Young Ireland scattered. He was also trying to establish a contracting business, and the two came together in one unfortunate circumstance when William was bidding for work on the estate of Lord Mayo, one of the local aristocrats and the man who owned the plot of land on which the Devoys lived. Instead of mailing the Lord a bid, William mistakenly sent his report on nationalist activities in his community. The bid was sent to his nationalist allies in Dublin. Devoy's friends were amused, but Lord Mayo wasn't. William didn't get the job.

It was an awful blow. William and Elizabeth were forced to give up their rent-free plot in Kill and move the family to Dublin, the destination for many others seeking to flee the ruined Irish landscape.

As the Devoys loaded a borrowed cart with their few earthly possessions, leaving behind a garden now black with ruined potatoes, nearly a million of their countrymen were dead of starvation, and another 2 million vanished, gone to lands beyond the sea.

The Great Famine was in its fourth year.

CHAPTER THREE

A Great Hunger

IN THE SUMMER OF 1845, SOME 5 MILLION OF IRELAND'S 8 MILLION people depended on agriculture, which meant the potato, for their daily subsistence. So it was with understandable relief that the Irish took to the fields in July of that fateful year to discover that the season's crop was coming along fine and promised a plentiful harvest.

But the bounty was not to be. On September 11, the *Freeman's Journal* newspaper included the following dispatch, phrased in appropriately fearful language:

"We regret to have to state that we have had communications from more than one well-informed correspondent announcing the fact of what is called 'cholera' in potatoes in Ireland, especially in the north. In one instance the party had been digging potatoes—the finest he had ever seen—from a particular field, and a particular ridge of that field up to Monday last; and on digging in the same ridge on Tuesday he found the tubers all blasted, and unfit for the use of man or beast."

The "cholera" was in fact a fungus called the *Phytophthora infestans*, although it was years before the disease was diagnosed. The fungus crept across Ireland's potato fields in the late summer and early fall of 1845, turning the crop black, putrid, and inedible almost overnight. "The leaves [of the potato] had been blighted, and from being green, parts of them were turned black and brown, and when these parts were felt between the fingers they would crumble into ashes," wrote O'Donovan Rossa, a teenager during the Famine years. "The air was laden with a sickly odor of decay, as if the hand of Death had striken the potato field." In fact, it had.

Alarm was immediate. The blight of '45 was followed by even more disastrous failures in 1846. By then, it was clear that this was not the standard blight to which Ireland had become accustomed. It persisted, terribly, for five years. Even after the Famine was over, the flight of the hungry continued. In the decade following the first potato failure, one-eighth of the Irish nation stumbled ashore on South Street in lower Manhattan. From this exiled nation, Irish nationalism would take on a new, and utterly defiant, form.

Between death and diaspora, the Ireland of John Devoy's birth was wiped out before he was ten years old. Entire villages ceased to exist; the roads were littered with the dead and were clogged with starving exiles. The Gaelic language, the tongue of half the Irish population before the Famine, soon became a relic, as did the rural culture that had sustained it.

O'Donovan Rossa, growing up near Skibbereen, recalled that his family, already struggling, had given shelter to an evicted family of husband, wife, six children, and their donkey. A few days afterward, "I heard my father and my mother whispering, and looking inquiringly at each other; the donkey was the subject of their conversation," Rossa wrote. "The donkey had disappeared. Where was the donkey? It had been killed and eaten." Rossa's father died several months later of starvation.

Survivors like Rossa would see to it that their children and their children's children never forgot such scenes, repeated a thousand times over. All that would come later, the bloodshed and the bitterness and the fury; the ravenous appetite for revenge, justice, and independence would follow from the appalling calamity known as the Great Irish Famine.

There was, in fact, no such thing as a famine, at least as the word suggests the absence of food. For in the ravaged Irish countryside of the late 1840s, the crops did not fail. The blight ruined only the potato. Barley and oats were plentiful, and livestock blithely grazed on grieving pastures. But Irish society had been built on the premise that the peasantry required only potatoes for their daily existence, and that the grains and livestock of the country were raised to pay the landlord his rent. When the potato failed, nothing stood between the peasant and the grave save the charity of strangers and the whim of politicians held hostage by free-market fundamentalists. In this defining crisis of the tortured Anglo-Irish relationship, Britain held fast to the principles of free trade, and so the produce of Ireland was transported elsewhere, mainly to Britain, while the Irish peasantry ate grass and died on the roadside.

Exactly what caused the blight was a mystery to educated civil servant and uneducated farmer alike, so much so that both saw the hand of God wreaking some sort of terrible vengeance on the Irish peasantry. The farmer's reliance on ethereal explanations was understandable enough; the civil servant's, however, was unforgivable, for it excused neglect and inaction. The chief administrator of famine relief, an officious, thirty-nine-year-old civil servant named George Edward Trevelyan, saw the famine as a sure sign from Providence that the Irish ought to do something to improve their lot. "I think I see a bright light shining in the distance through the dark cloud which at present hangs over Ireland," he wrote in fall of 1846, when the dying had only just begun. "The deep and inveterate root of social evil [remains], and I hope I am not guilty of irreverence in thinking that, this being altogether beyond the power of man, the cure has been applied by the direct stroke of an all-wise Providence in a manner as unexpected and unthought of as it is likely to be effectual. God grant that we may rightly perform our part and not turn into a curse what was intended as a blessing."

Trevelyan's curiously optimistic view of Ireland's mass starvation came to symbolize Britain's attitude toward the disaster in its midst. Never mind that Trevelyan worked extemely hard in overseeing early attempts at relief; never mind that some government-sponsored relief projects probably saved lives. The Irish understandably concluded that Britain didn't much care whether or not Ireland starved. When Daniel O'Connell, in his dying days, rose to the floor of the House of Commons to plead for England's help in 1847, Benjamin Disraeli was unmoved by the aging orator's pathetic pleas. "Ireland is in your hands," O'Connell told his colleagues in a feeble whisper. "If you do not save her, she cannot save herself." The House listened in respect-

ful awe, save for Disraeli, who could see only "a feeble old man muttering before a table."

The question of English culpability has long been argued and
remains unresolved. It can be argued that when the blight first appeared, English politicians reacted with some sympathy. Robert Peel,
prime minister during the first few months of the Famine, took extraordinary steps to relieve suffering. He set up a network of com-
mittees to coordinate public works projects, a sort of Works Progress
Administration of its day. And he ordered the expediture of £100,000
of public money to buy supplies of American corn. The measure was
not as philanthropic as it might seem, for the corn was not meant to
be given away to the starving, but as a means of controlling the
supply, and therefore the price, of food in Ireland. However well-
intentioned, Peel's scheme did nothing for those who couldn't buy
food no matter how low the price might be.

Unfortunately for Ireland, Peel's government fell when the prime
minister did away with long-cherished laws protecting England's domestic agricultural markets—laws that seemed curiously at odds with
the Victorian belief in free trade. In place of Peel came a Whig government headed by Lord John Russell, a tiny, even dwarflike, man
with a large head who had once been thought of as a dangerous
radical.

In 1847, when the potato seemed returned to health, Lord Russell's government pronounced an end to the crisis and wrapped up its
relief operations. Any further help would have to come from the Irish
property owners themselves. At the time, more than seven-hundred-
thousand people, the vast majority of them heads of households, were
employed on public-works projects, and 3 million were receiving some
sort of government relief. Ireland's gentry could not afford to pay for
such a huge undertaking. And so the public works were abandoned,
and relief was wound down. But the potato's newfound health was a
mirage. The crop failed again, and the Irish continued to die in horrifying numbers.

Even as Britain was withdrawing from Famine relief in favor of
what might be called a gentrification of the crisis, it saw fit to take
one last proactive measure. On the off chance that the Irish should
awaken from their hunger-induced stupor, Parliament passed legislation imposing restrictions on civil liberties, allowing the Queen's rep-

resentative to place selected areas under martial law. Called a Coercion Bill, it was the seventeenth time since the Act of Union that London had seen fit to suspend civil liberties in Ireland.

It was here, then, that the decisive point was reached, allowing nationalists to point to the Famine as the ultimate expression of England's cruelty toward the Irish. In place of relief, the Irish were given coercion. In the fall of 1847, Trevelyan began writing his history of the crisis, as if it were over. Alas for Trevelyan's literary aspirations, his history was too little, too early. And as the Irish peasants were being driven from their lands and were dying in beds of straw, Trevelyan wrote that "the great evil with which we have to contend is not the physical evil of the famine, but the moral evil of the selfish, perverse and turbulent character of the people."

The problem with the starving Irish, then, was not their poverty but their character.

Midway through the Famine a section of the Young Ireland movement, calling itself the Irish Confederation, rose in what amounted to little more than a token show of force against British rule. The rising was supported by some of the same middle-class Protestant journalists who had contributed so mightily to Ireland's literature of rebellion through their work on *The Nation*. William Devoy, the assiduous *Nation* reader, supported the Confederation, although he apparently did not take part in the several skirmishes that would go down in nationalist history as the Rising of '48.

It is curious that the most formidable Irish revolutionary to emerge from the shattered Ireland of the mid–nineteenth century barely mentions the Famine in his memoirs, and then only to note that his family left County Kildare as the death and upheaval were ending. John Devoy's family was fortunate enough live in a part of the country where a rudimentary cash economy allowed them to buy food and supplies with the money William earned as a laborer—that is, until his fatal postal mishap put an end to his contracting business.

The townland of Kill and the larger village of Naas, however, did not entirely escape the devastation, even if the Devoy family did. The workhouse in Naas, whose jurisdiction included Kill, began to fill up with the starving and impoverished in the fall of 1845, just after the first potato failure. Designed to house 550 people, the workhouse sheltered 762 at the beginning of 1847, when icy winds added to the starving peasantry's trials, covering Ireland in a rare winter's blanket of snow. Commissioners in charge of poor relief hired carpenters to build platforms in the workhouse stables to accommodate the overflow.

Workhouses, the homeless shelters of the Victorian era, were built throughout Ireland beginning in 1838. Solid as fortresses and just as inviting, they still stand in many Irish villages, a grim reminder of a time when government relief was given grudgingly and then only to those deemed deserving of assistance. Conditions on the outside were horrifying, but those within the workhouse's formidable walls were terrible, too. By the middle of 1847, the inmates in the Naas workhouse were cut to two meals a day, the first consisting of oatmeal and rice, and the second of corn and oatmeal. At the same time, workhouse officials put in an order for more coffins.

Just a short distance from the workhouse, John Devoy and his four siblings were enjoying what amounted to a privileged life, at least in the relative terms of famine Ireland. Had William Devoy not mixed up his letters and sent the wrong one to Lord Mayo's home, the family might have gotten through the crisis intact. Instead, they borrowed a cart from the Dunne family, set off to Dublin, and settled on the city's north side in Summerhill.

Dublin had been spared the worst of the Famine; indeed, the journalist John Mitchel wrote that during the Famine Dublin "had never before been so gay and luxurious . . . theaters and concert-rooms had never been filled with such brilliant throngs."

But the splendor of Ireland's capital was already fading when the Devoys made their journey from Kill as the city's aristocracy abandoned the central city for more fashionable outposts such as Ballsbridge and Donnybrook. Devoy's neighorhood in Summerhill, to the east of the city center, would later become one of Dublin's most notorious tenement districts. And the neighborhood known as the Liberties, where the Devoys moved after four years in Summerhill, was then and is yet known as a rough-and-tumble district far removed from the theaters and concert-rooms of Mitchel's memory.

Misery was not long in visiting the Devoy household. The family arrived in the city just as a fearful new epidemic was about to add to Ireland's horrors. Cholera, among the most dreaded of nineteenth-century diseases, had been sweeping across Europe through the turbulent 1840s. It is unclear whether James Devoy contracted the disease in Kildare or after the family settled in the Summerhill section of Dublin. But on August 14, 1849, the eldest child of William and Elizabeth Devoy, renowned in his hometown for his fledgling genius, died at the age of fourteen and was buried in Dublin's Glasnevin Cemetery. He was one of more than eleven-thousand Dubliners who died in the epidemic; most are buried together in the south section of the cemetery.

After James's death, William, the family patriarch, assembled his brood every night on the floor of their home, and together the Devoy family prayed the rosary for the repose of James's soul. Often, William would add his own prayers to the litany, and afterward, John and his siblings were expected to add theirs. So long did these sessions last that John developed welts on his knees from constant kneeling.

Skilled and blessed with a wealth of relatives, William Devoy had little trouble making a living in Dublin. Through a brother-in-law, he found work driving a coal cart, and later one of his brothers got him work as a drayman in Watkins Brewery on the south side of the city, near St. Patrick's Cathedral. Eventually, William put his literacy and other skills to good use at the brewery and worked his way to managing clerk.

John and his sisters were joined by three brothers after James's death. Joseph, Michael, and James—the latter named in memory of the Devoys' oldest child—completed Elizabeth Devoy's childbearing.

Devoy's memoirs give only occasional hints of what his family's struggle must have been like. He notes that welts and all, he took over the chores as leader of the nightly rosary when his father's work kept him overnight at the brewery office, an indication of the sacrifices both William and Elizabeth had to make to feed and care for their family of seven children. On any further details, he is silent.

But it would be wrong to assume that the silence indicates any lack of suffering, for Devoy was silent on a great many matters, not the least of them personal tragedies. In his old age, he, like many of his exile contemporaries, may have chosen silence as the only weapon against bitterness and despair.

DEVOY'S EXPERIENCES IN IRELAND'S schools didn't improve much after his expulsion from the Marlborough Street school. After his run-in with Sheehy, he was sent off to a private school at a cost of eight pence a week, compared to the penny a week other schools charged. There, a schoolmaster named Murphy kept his young charges at bay with a strong leather strap, which he used indiscriminately. "I whipped me boys all around each day to make them Spartans," the teacher noted with satisfaction.

Within a few months, John transferred to a school on the appropriately named School Street, a few blocks from the family home on Newmarket in the Liberties district. There, finally, John prospered. But even though he did well enough to be appointed a school monitor for a salary of ten shillings a week, his relations with authority figures were as stormy as they would remain for the rest of his long life. Murphy was yet another classroom sadist fond of wringing his students' ears. He indulged his habit one afternoon with two of John's friends who had gotten their sums wrong. Young John's was correct, but he got his ears wrung, too. John was no more ready to accept this undeserved punishment than he was Sheehy's, so he drove his elbow into Murphy's body, then picked up a slate and threw it at his teacher. He missed by an inch.

Though he was a prodigious reader and a frequent visitor to the nearby library at the Catholic Young Men's Society, John left school at age seventeen to take a job with a firm that sold hops to Watkins Brewery, where his father worked. Even then, however, John could not escape the awful practices of Ireland's classrooms. His young brother James, a prodigy like his dead namesake, found himself behind in his lessons, despite being as avid a reader as John. For his lethargy, he was beaten by John's tormentor, Murphy, who used a stick across James's back. "When the boy came home from school, he said nothing, but went into his bedroom, took off all his clothes except his trousers and shoes, and stepped out backwards, saying, 'Do you see that?' His back was one hideous mass of cuts and bruises," Devoy recalled.

John, enraged, showed up on Murphy's doorstep determined to exact revenge. Fortunately for the schoolmaster, his wife, known in the neighborhood as a kind woman, talked the hotheaded rebel out of assaulting her husband.

He never forgot the beatings and his rage; more than a half century later, he recorded it all in his memoirs, seemingly as fresh in his memory as the triumphs and failures of his adult life. It would be hard to imagine that John Devoy's famous venom and unceasing rage had nothing to do with blows administered by fellow Irishmen named Sheehy and Murphy.

THE TEENAGED JOHN DEVOY suffered another blow just before leaving school, but this one goes unrecorded in his recollections. On April 14, 1858, when John was fifteen years old, Elizabeth Devoy died at the age of forty-two. She left William with the challenge of rearing their seven surviving children.

While there is little question that William Devoy was the overwhelming influence in the Devoy household, Elizabeth clearly was a formidable woman. Devoy never forgot the fury and defiance in his mother's face when the reactionary Archbishop Paul Cullen ordered priests to refuse absolution to parents who continued to send their children to National schools rather than Catholic schools. Cullen couldn't abide the thought of Catholics and Protestants mixing in the same classroom, as was the practice in the National schools. Despite Cullen's chilling order, Elizabeth Devoy refused to obey, an example young John never forgot.

THE SAME YEAR OF his mother's death, John enrolled in an Irish-language class held in a room on Middle Abbey Street in Dublin and, later, in the Jervis Street editorial offices of a revived *Nation* newspaper. To his father's despair, he became ever more deeply involved in nationalist politics, to the neglect of his education. The language class may have seemed as innocent an exercise as John's sneaking out of mass early to join his friends for an afternoon of singing nationalist ballads, but William Devoy understood the course of Irish nationalism as well as anybody. In polarized and politicized Ireland, the study of Gaelic language was as much an exercise in politics as it was a scholarly pursuit. (And John never did become fluent in Irish.) Sure enough, John's involvement deepened when in 1859 he joined the National Petition Movement, which was collecting signatures to demand a plebiscite on self-determination in Ireland at a time when

British politicians and the *Times* of London were calling for greater self-government in Italy.

The campaign started in the very office in which Devoy was taking his Irish instruction, and soon it spread across the Irish countryside like no political movement since the glory days of Daniel O'Connell. Remarkably, five hundred thousand people signed the petitions, and they were delivered to the floor of the House of Commons. Barely a decade after the Famine, Irish nationalist feeling was again rising from the ruins. John Devoy was determined to be a part of it. And so were his young friends.

One of them was named James J. O'Kelly, an educated, well-read son of a Dublin blacksmith whom Devoy met at his language class. O'Kelly's father wanted James to join him in the forge; his mother dreamed that James would become a sculptor. James was more inclined to his mother's aspiration, but his father won the argument. Devoy recalled seeing James's well-muscled father use a saber to cut an iron bar in half as it hung from the ceiling.

In his late teens, Devoy was a frequent visitor to the O'Kelly family forge, assisting James in the business and also in some mischief-making. The two of them took to making pikes, like those used by the rebels of 1798. One day, they believed, their time would come.

On St. Patrick's Day in 1858, a month before John Devoy's mother died, a single-minded, self-centered veteran of the aborted 1848 rebellion gathered some friends together in a room in Dublin. There, James Stephens and his comrades swore an oath pledging to bring about an independent Irish republic. The group would become known as the Irish Republican Brotherhood (IRB), forerunner to the Irish Republican Army.

Stephens's attempt to revive a national movement less than a decade after the Famine seemed preposterous, but the man had done homework of a most arduous sort. Obsessed with a sense of his own mission as well as with Irish national identity, he set out on a three-thousand-mile walking tour of Ireland in 1856 to gauge for himself the chances of sowing revolution in the country's recently devastated fields. The journey, perhaps not surprisingly given the human tendency to see and hear what one wants to see and hear, persuaded Stephens that the land was fertile.

Not long after Stephens's fateful St. Patrick's Day meeting, an

Irish immigrant in New York named John O'Mahoney established an
American counterpart to the IRB. O'Mahoney was a prosperous Catholic and an Irish-language scholar. Immersed as he was in Celtic mythology, he called his American-based organization the Fenian
Brotherhood, named for the legendary warriors called the Fianna who
fought under the leadership of the chieftan Finn MacCool. The rubric
Fenian stuck as a shorthand description of the international conspiracy that the Irish national movement became.

The Stephens-O'Mahoney alliance was a redefining moment in
the long history of Irish national struggle. Ireland, a small, impoverished nation on the western outpost of Europe, living in the shadow
of the world's foremost military and economic power, would no longer
labor on its own. From now on, British and Irish alike had to contend
with a third party—the United States, the world's ascendant nation
with its millions of exiled Irish ready, willing, and increasingly able
to use their votes, and their spare pennies, on behalf of the people
they left behind and the cause they didn't.

Both the IRB and the Fenian Brotherhood were organized in
small, well-disciplined circles—a twentieth-century revolutionary
would call them cells. Each circle was designed for up to eight hundred members and was commanded by men identified not by title but
by letters. At the head of each circle was a center, referred to in
Fenian parlance simply as A; assisting the center were nine captains,
or B's, who in turn had a staff of sergeants, or C's. O'Mahoney was
designated the "head center" in America, with Stephens accorded
the title of "chief organizer" of the Irish republic.

All of this activity did not pass without John Devoy's notice,
much to his father's chagrin. In his middle years, William Devoy had
come to believe that his youthful involvement in the O'Connell and
Young Ireland movements had cost his family dearly, perhaps recal-
ling the tragedies that followed the fateful postal mix-up that revealed
his politics to a royally displeased Lord Mayo. He believed his oldest
living son was about to make a similar mistake. Father and son had
a series of rows over John's political activity, and perhaps as a sop to
his father's admonitions, John joined William in enrolling in night
classes at Dublin's Catholic University.

In early 1861, when Devoy was eighteen years old, he and his
friend James J. O'Kelly joined the fledgling Fenian movement. Con-

firming William's suspicions about his son's innocent-sounding Irish-language classes, young John and his friend James were sworn into the Irish Republican Brotherhood in the very office in which those classes took place. An IRB man named James Joseph O'Connell O'Callaghan had joined the class, not to learn the language—he never learned a word of it—but to identify possible recruits. O'Callaghan told Devoy that the IRB was infiltrating the country, which, to a limited extent, it was. IRB membership was growing, and members were beginning to drill and train for the moment when the exiles in America would join them on the battlefield. O'Callaghan, however, swore to Devoy that the IRB already had twenty-thousand members in Cork and fifteen-thousand in Tipperary alone. "Evidently," Devoy wrote dryly, O'Callaghan multiplied "the actual number by five."

Devoy knew full well that by joining the IRB he was committing himself to a violent overthrow of British rule in Ireland. But what did he know of soldiering? What, in fact, did any of the Fenians in Ireland know of tactics and strategy? Devoy and O'Kelly soon settled on the same solution. In Devoy's case, the answer suggested itself after yet another bitter argument with his father.

Devoy had been an IRB member no more than a few weeks when William warned him that his next political meeting would be his last. William said he would enforce his edict with that ultimate parental threat: he'd show up and personally drag John home should he dare defy the rules of the Devoy house.

Headstrong as ever, and already wondering how he might obtain a soldier's expertise, John saw only one way out of his dilemma. In March of 1861, he decided he would leave the Devoy household in pursuit of a soldier's life in the uniform of the French Republic.

He didn't tell his father of his plan, but he felt duty-bound to explain himself to his superiors in the IRB. In early March, he met none other than the chief organizer of the Irish republic himself, James Stephens, who was holding regular meetings of the IRB in his spartan Dublin lodgings. Stephens did his best to persuade Devoy that if it was a soldier's training he wanted, he'd be better off in America. The cannons of South Carolina were about to fire on Fort Sumter, and the Union and Confederate armies would soon offer any young man training aplenty in the art of modern warfare. Stephens offered

Devoy a letter of introduction to O'Mahoney, who was raising an Irish regiment in the New York National Guard, and to another Irish-American named Thomas Francis Meagher, who would soon command the Union Army's Irish Brigade. Devoy would have none of it. The American Civil War, he said, would be over in a few months.

In his short but thus far successful career as a revolutionary organizer, James Stephens was used to winning arguments. But the brewery clerk's son was unmoved. "That young man is very stubborn," Stephens said of his young recruit.

After spending St. Patrick's Day in Dublin, the eighteen-year-old John Devoy left behind the quarrels with his father and boarded a steamer for London, the first leg of his journey to France. James J. O'Kelly saw him off and gave him the address of relatives in London, with whom he stayed before setting sail for France. He carried with him a letter of introduction, written by a mutual acquaintance, to journalist John Mitchel, who had taken up residence on the rue de l'Est in Paris. Stephens, who had taught French in Dublin before taking up Fenianism full-time, gave Devoy a slip of paper with a single sentence in French, which he no doubt practiced on the way across the English Channel: *Ayez la bonté m'indiquer la rue de l'Est.* "Have the goodness to show me the way to the rue de l'Est." Armed with the two pieces of paper and two pounds sterling that one of his brothers gave him, the stubborn young man headed off to join the French Army, unaware that, as a non-Frenchman, he could do so such thing. He would have to join the Foreign Legion.

The terrible reality of what he had done made itself plain as soon as he landed in Boulogne, across the Channel from Dover. He was told he couldn't enlist in the Legion there, that he would have to journey to a provincial capital to do so. Devoy hadn't anticipated the red tape, and he had spent nearly all of the meager funds his brother had sent. He booked a room in the city's Hôtel de New York, where the hostess spoke English, and sent desperate word to his brother to send more money. In the meantime, he was penniless, unable to afford a meal of any sort. After two days without eating, he wandered off to the site of Napoleon's former camp along the beaches of Boulogne, from which the Frenchman had hoped to cross the Channel and invade Britain in the heady days of 1805.

But not even Bonaparte's memory and thoughts of what might

have been could shake the suffering from John Devoy's bones. As he moved among the shadows, his thoughts returned to Ireland, to his home and his family. It was, he thought, dinnertime in Dublin.

The young man who had terrorized teachers and been the despair of his patient father, who had lost his brother and mother in a matter of a few years and watched as his country sank ever more into decline, could no longer suppress his agonies. As he walked with the ghosts of Napoleon's never-launched invasion, the starving young Fenian broke down and wept.

CHAPTER FOUR

Bold Fenian Men

A FEW WEEKS BEFORE JOHN DEVOY RAN OFF TO FRANCE, AN EX-
iled Irishman named Terence Bellow McManus died in San Francisco,
impoverished and forgotten. He had sacrified a promising career in
the shipping business to take part in the Young Ireland rising of 1848
and had paid dearly for it. He was arrested, convicted, and transported
to Tasmania, eventually escaping and making his way to northern
California.

He died on January 15, 1861, and might have gone to his grave
in the same obscurity in which he spent his last years but for the
ingenuity of Ireland's exiled revolutionaries in America. Showing a
deft appreciation for the power of symbols, the leader of the American
Irish, John O'Mahoney, proposed to send McManus's corpse back to
Ireland after a long, cross-country tour of the United States. In death,
McManus would serve to strengthen the link between the two Irish
communities.

It is a measure of Irish America's isolation from the cultural mainstream of its adopted country that O'Mahoney dared carry out such
a demonstration just as the American republic was about to be ripped
apart. At a time when civil war was breaking out, the McManus
funeral processions must have seemed a curious and even ridiculous
exercise, confirming the Yankees' worst suspicions of the true loyalties
of this alien immigrant group and perhaps hardening Southern attitudes toward the chaotic and foreign urban centers of the industri-
alized North.

The procession ended finally in late summer with a requiem mass in New York's old St. Patrick's Cathedral presided over by none other than the ranking cleric in New York, Bishop John Hughes. In a sermon that sounded for all the world like a blessing of the Irish-American agitations, Hughes noted that "some of the most learned and holy men of the Church have laid it down . . . that there are cases in which it is lawful to resist and overthrow a tyrannical government."

McManus's body was shipped to Ireland in November, and thousands turned out to escort it through Cork city. A similar reception was held in Dublin, but the city's primate, Cardinal Paul Cullen, didn't share Bishop Hughes's appreciation for acts of rebellion. He barred the city's churches from receiving McManus's moldering remains. The contrast between Cullen's cool contempt and Hughes's passion was obvious. The rage of the Famine Irish in America was making its presence felt.

In coordinating the McManus affair, the American Irish pulled off a spectacular public relations coup. The spirit of rebellion flared anew, its sparks floating on winds from the west.

John Devoy followed these proceedings from a tent in the Algerian desert. Through his Fenian contacts he met the Paris correspondent of *The Nation,* a professor at the Sorbonne named J. P. Leonard. Leonard took the eager young Irishman to the Ministry of War, where John Devoy was sworn into the French Foreign Legion on May 2, 1861.

Devoy was assigned to an engineering corps under the command of a Colonel Faidherrbe, and he was dispatched to Algeria to be part of the French colonial garrison in North Africa. The would-be revolutionary apparently gave little thought to the irony of a Fenian wearing the uniform of an army of occupation. The French, after all, weren't in North Africa because they were particularly fond of sand and sun. As a Legionnaire, he was in the service of European imperialism, and while he might have convinced himself that French rule in Algeria was not the same as English rule in Ireland, the difference might well have been lost on the North Africans.

For all of his martial enthusiasm, Devoy learned little about war and combat in Algeria. His battalion saw no action during the year Devoy spent in uniform. In fact, so few shots did Devoy fire that he earned a reprimand for allowing rust to gather in his rifle.

He was discharged under the signature of his commanding officer, although later chroniclers of the period suggested that he deserted. Though he returned home untested, Devoy's time in Algeria was hardly a waste and may in fact have saved him from a far worse fate. Had he followed Stephens's advice and traveled to America for military experience, he might well have found himself on the killing fields of the American South, places where Irishmen wearing American uniforms fell in piles. Instead, he came back whole, with at least some claim to expertise in military matters. And he came back with a greater fluency in French than the single phrase he had learned from James Stephens. Upon his return to Dublin, he presented himself to Stephens, and the itinerant teacher immediately quizzed the stubborn young man in French. Devoy passed his first test as a Fenian. He continued to study French and attended readings in French at the Royal Dublin Society.

The John Devoy who presented himself to Stephens in Dublin was no less stubborn, but clearly more mature and confident. With the IRB expanding throughout the countryside, Stephens needed officers who knew local conditions and who could be trusted with the illegal organization's closely guarded secrets. Who better to organize the area around Naas than the Foreign Legion veteran who hailed from the neighborhood? The twenty-year-old Devoy was promptly given orders to bring the organization to the place where he was born.

Devoy was living in Dublin with his father and his siblings until Stephens ordered him to Naas in late 1862. He recorded nothing about his reunion with his father and family, but it seems they reconciled. When Devoy moved to Naas, he found work in the Watkins Brewery office in town, an arrangement his father, who also worked for Watkins, no doubt had a hand in.

Devoy took rooms in the Cork Coach Company's offices in the center of town, not far from the brewery's warehouse on the road to the railroad hub town of Sallins. His work was one part of a three-pronged strategy Stephens employed to bring the country to a war footing. First, and most obvious, was the recruitment of the nation's young men, who would eventually be trained in rudimentary military tactics for the promised rebellion. Devoy was one of dozens of junior officers charged with recruitment and training.

Secondly, and most ingeniously, Stephens understood that Britain's 26,000-strong garrison in Ireland constituted not an insurmountable obstacle to rebellion but, in fact, the weakest link in the Crown's defenses. Fully 60 percent of the soldiers were of Irish blood, at least by Devoy's reckoning. If they could quietly be subverted, the British Army in Ireland could be rendered ineffective before the first shot was fired.

The third part of the conspiracy lay overseas, in America, home to hundreds of thousands of Irish emigrants and their offspring. The Fenian presence in America was already conspicuous, for it was an open, legal organization whose members left no doubt about what they were planning.

Devoy's organizing had to be done on the sly, and he had to judge for himself whether the young men he was recruiting would remain true to their oath when the call for action came. He also had to be mindful of infiltration, for just as the Fenians were subverting the British Army, so the Crown was infiltrating the Fenians. Devoy was careful to note and recognize members of Dublin Castle's special detective force, known as the G Division.

For all the required discretion, he did not lack for enthusiasm, nor was he hampered by a lack of salesmanship. He even swore in the poor, bedraggled young man from whom he bought turf for his fire. On occasional Sundays, he took the men under his command on a twelve-mile march into Dublin for drilling, with the men packing bread-and-butter sandwiches to eat along the journey. On the Dublin road, Devoy and his entourage passed the Catholic church in Kill, where Devoy was baptized. Devoy and the secret soldiers often trooped into the church to hear mass, then continued on their journey to Dublin.

In fall of 1863, with the IRB well on its way to the fifty thousand or so members it would claim at its zenith, Fenians on both sides of the Atlantic were preparing in earnest for the rebellion Stephens promised. On the American side in particular, the Fenians under O'Mahoney—now a colonel in the Ninty-ninth New York Regiment, which guarded Confederate prisoners in upstate Elmira—were growing impatient, even as they were dodging bullets and cannon shot on the battlefields of the South. Nearly 150,000 Irish-born soldiers wore the blue and gray; how many of them were sworn Fenians is uncertain.

There is little doubt, however, that for thousands of Fenians in the Union and Confederate armies, the great struggle that would define the American republic was but training for the struggle to bring about an Irish republic.

IN NOVEMBER 1863, THE very month Abraham Lincoln traveled to Gettysburg, America's Irish rebels—including many Union officers on leave—assembled in convention in Chicago to prepare for the coming battle across the Atlantic. John O'Mahoney, the head center, had issued a summons to America's Fenians in an article in the *New York Mercury* in September. In it, he stated that the Brotherhood had the support of Secretary of State William Seward. Though it sounds like so much idle boasting, relations between the Union and Great Britain were near the breaking point thanks to London's granting of belligerent status to the Confederacy and Britain's complicity in the building of rebel blockade runners.

James Stephens himself came to America in spring of 1864, touring Union encampments in an effort to recruit soldiers and officers for the Irish Republican Brotherhood. He estimated that one hundred thousand Irish-Americans were sworn to fight for Irish freedom. Of course, Stephens was prone to exaggeration.

Upon his return to Ireland in August 1864, Stephens summoned his young lieutenant from County Kildare, John Devoy, for a private meeting in Dublin. Devoy found the man he called "the Captain" in excellent spirits, so much so that Stephens couldn't sit still as he regaled Devoy with stories about the movement's growing strength in America. Finally, he told Devoy the purpose of this unusual audience: the Irish would take to the battlefield in 1865.

As the promised year of action began, Devoy and other local IRB leaders stepped up their illicit drilling and training. With new demands on his time, and the rebellion supposedly only a matter of months away, Devoy thought it time to put his affairs in order. On January 2, 1865, he wrote a discreet letter to his employers at Watkins Brewery, advising them that they ought to start looking for a new clerk, although, of course, he didn't explain why he would be leaving. "I will remain till such time as the person who replaces me is thoroughly acquainted with the business—that is, if you wish it so," he wrote. They did wish it so, and in fact, they were in no hurry to replace him.

Around this time—the exact date is uncertain—one of the brewery's managers, John Cahill, introduced his young clerk to a pretty teenager named Elizabeth Kenny, whom everybody called Eliza. She lived with her sister, Mary Hannah, and her parents on a small farm in the townland of Tipper, about a mile outside of Naas. Like the Devoy family, the Kennys were comfortable enough by the standards of midcentury Ireland, although the family patriarch, like William Devoy, couldn't support his family off their small holding. Christopher Kenny worked at a nearby flour mill while sending his two girls to the convent school in Naas.

What the Kenny family thought of Eliza's budding relationship with the handsome, dark-haired rebel from Naas is unknown, but based on later events, the Kennys did nothing to discourage their daughter from what must have seemed, and indeed what ultimately was, a hopeless situation. Devoy during these years was hardly the single-minded rebel of his later years. There is from this period a tale of his going to the wedding of an acquaintance during which thirty-two couples, possibly including John and Eliza, danced the night away and came away engaged to be married.

Nevertheless, Ireland and the revolution came first, and Eliza must have understood that and may, indeed, have relished the idea of becoming the wife of an Irish rebel. Her father, like Devoy's, had joined the militant Irish Confederation in the famine year of 1848, when the Young Irelanders were preparing their ill-fated rebellion. No doubt Christopher Kenny and John Devoy got along well.

As the IRB made ready for the coming fight, the American Civil War was winding down, and O'Mahoney and the Fenians were preparing to bring their hard-won experience to Ireland. At the Fenian Brotherhood's annual convention in Cincinnati in January 1865, O'Mahoney proclaimed that the organization was "virtually at war with the oligarchy of Great Britain." It sounded preposterous, but no less an authority than Queen Victoria believed that a Fenian-inspired war was in danger of breaking out between the victorious Union and the Union of Great Britain and Ireland. She noted in her diary on February 12, 1865, that she had been talking that day "of America and the danger, which seems approaching, of our having a war with her as soon as she makes peace; of the impossibility of our being able to hold Canada."

As winter faded into spring, couriers from New York began bringing a steady supply of cash to the IRB, and British intelligence noted the sudden appearance in Ireland of men wearing felt hats and square-toed shoes—fashions that marked the men as Americans. In August, O'Mahoney issued a final call for money and raised $30,000 in two weeks—the total amount of money sent to Ireland in 1865 alone was more than $250,000. The IRB's membership reached its peak, and members were being instructed in the art of military engineering and musketry. Meanwhile, Ireland's legions in America were being mustered out of their blue and gray uniforms by the thousands, freeing them for combat across the Atlantic.

In Ireland, the most dangerous part of the conspiracy was well in place. By Devoy's count, eight thousand of the twenty-six thousand British troops in Ireland were sworn Fenians, as were another seven thousand British soldiers stationed outside Ireland. The time was ripe. Sensing that the fight was imminent, Devoy wrote yet another letter to his employers, who were in no hurry to lose their clerk despite his stated intentions in January. On August 17, 1865, Devoy wrote:

"As I am about to immigrate to America, I beg to inform you that I intend to leave your employment as soon as you can find it convenient to get another in my place. I do not wish to give you the slightest inconvenience, and shall therefore wait till whatever time it suits you to replace me, but I would feel greatly obliged by you making that time as short as possible."

Devoy, of course, was not going to America—the flow in human traffic in 1865 was the reverse of the usual custom. Irish-Americans were arriving in Ireland by the dozens during the summer of '65. Everything seemed in place.

Government officials, having penetrated the Fenians in several places, decided they had had enough. On September 14, 1865, constables raided the offices of the *Irish People*—a newspaper that served as the IRB's propaganda arm—arresting everybody in the office. Meanwhile, John Devoy's activity in Naas had come to the attention of the constabulary. On the night of September 28, an Irish printer with the unlikely name of John Podesta—his parents were Italian immigrants to Ireland—delivered to a Fenian friend of his an advance copy of the official police bulletin, *Hue and Cry*. Podesta worked in the Government Printing Office in Dublin and managed to sneak home a copy of the bulletin because he was the only Catholic in the plant who wasn't searched before leaving the office. He was, after all, Italian. He was also a friend of John Devoy's. The ink was still wet on the page when Devoy received it.

The *Hue and Cry* dated September 29 contained a list of persons against whom arrest warrants had been sworn. On page 2 of the four-page broadsheet, the paper ran a list of wanted men from County Kildare. Included among them was John Devoy, "who stands charged with being a Fenian, and associated with others in a treasonable conspiracy against the Queen's authority in Ireland." The notice inaccurately described him as twenty-seven years old—he was twenty-three—and more accurately noted that he was "5 feet, 6½ inches high, stout make, dark complexion, thin face, grey eyes, regular nose, short dark hair, short dark moustache and beard; wore a black silk hat, dark cloth trowsers [*sic*], dark plaid vest." As a final touch, *Hue and Cry* noted that the suspect was "rather sullen in appearance."

John Devoy was now a wanted man.

Eliza Kenny and her family didn't withdraw their affections, and William Devoy, who had always feared for the worst for his hotheaded son, stood by John as the police closed in. Devoy left the brewery and moved his base of operations from Naas to Dublin. Foolishly, he moved in with his father and siblings, and he was there no more than a few days when there was a knock on William Devoy's door. Proving himself worthy of his family's lineage, John escaped by leaping out a back window and fleeing across the roof of a neighboring house while his siblings created a distraction.

From now on, Devoy was more discreet in his choice of lodgings. When in Dublin, he stayed in a loft on Dorset Street with several hard-bitten Fenians, including Michael Cody, one of Devoy's deputies who would go on to become part of an assassination committee formed to shoot detectives and informers. Shaken by his narrow escape at his father's flat, and perhaps influenced by the men with whom he now lodged, Devoy began carrying a revolver.

That Devoy lodged with desperate men after his escape is certain.

The question is to what extent he, too, was a member of the Fenian assassination committee, or if there even was such an entity. Its existence was alleged in court during Fenian trials in Dublin in 1867, when a government informer took the stand in the prosecution of Devoy's deputy Cody. The informer, John Joseph Corydon, had served as a lieutenant in the Union Army during the Civil War and was among the thousands of Irish soldiers who took the Fenian oath in hopes of fighting for Ireland one day. After the war, he was a trusted confidant of Stephens's and was a courier between New York and Dublin. He started giving information to the British in late 1866 and was the government's star witness at a number of trials.

In this starring role, Corydon revealed the existence of a Fenian committee impaneled to assassinate detectives and informers. Cody, he said, was the chief organizer, but Devoy was one of the committee's members beginning in January 1866. Corydon said that Cody told him "there was a body of men, five or six or more, banded together for the purpose of shooting informers and detectives." Under a relentless cross-examination by Cody's lawyer, the Irish statesman Isaac Butt, Corydon said he had never actually told police of the existence of the committee per se, an admission Butt found hard to accept from a paid government informant. Butt asked Corydon to identify leading Fenians who were in league with Cody's assassination committee. "John Devoy was one," he replied.

Corydon went on to mention Devoy several times in connection with the assassination committee, asserting that an American-born IRB leader, Col. Thomas Kelly, gave Devoy money to carry out the committee's hits. If true, the money was wasted. While an informer named George Clarke was killed in 1866 along the banks of the Royal Canal, Devoy had nothing to do with it.

In October of 1865, Stephens appointed Devoy to the post that would win him fame in Fenian annals. Though a wanted man, Devoy was named the IRB's chief organizer of the British Army, a post that would entail the highly dangerous work of continuing the subversion of the British garrison begun by Pagan O'Leary, who was now in prison. In a letter to Devoy in late October, Stephens allotted Devoy an expense account of three pounds a week and authorized him to appoint a staff of eight men to assist him. In a postscript, the Captain advised Devoy, "Be prudent now. You owe me this, to justify the appointment of so young a man to so responsible a post."

Young though he was, Devoy was well suited for the job. On at least one occasion, he took full advantage of the military bearing he had learned in the Foreign Legion by donning a British Army uniform and actually marching into a barracks to collect information about troop strength and to further the Fenian seduction of Irishmen wearing British scarlet. He managed this despite the twice-weekly reminder in *Hue and Cry* that he remained a fugitive from justice.

But Devoy's thoughts, even now, were not entirely of the battle to come. Wanted man though he was, he still managed to slip away from Dublin to visit Eliza. He made the journey from Dublin only at night, and only after getting off the train seven miles away from the Kenny Farm to avoid being spotted by ever-vigilant constables. He walked the rest of the way, cutting through the fields of his boyhood in Kill and Naas to make his way to the townland of Tipper, where the Kennys lived in a small farmhouse.

John Devoy was a welcome guest in the Kenny household even though it entailed their risking arrest for hiding a fugitive. When Devoy showed up at the farmhouse, exhausted from his journey from Dublin, Eliza's mother would vacate her place in the main bedroom, joining her daughters in their room while the fugitive bunked with Eliza's father.

Eliza herself became a full partner in Devoy's shadowy life. She served as her fiancé's courier, taking messages from Devoy to his Fenian subordinates in Naas under the unsuspecting eye of the constables who were now a constant presence in and around the town.

During one of Devoy's secret sojourns to the Kenny farmhouse, he once again had a narrow escape. Agents for the landlord who owned the estate on which the Kenny farmhouse stood showed up unexpectedly one day with an order to evict the household. The agents were probably accompanied by constables, a common practice. Devoy was in the Kenny house when the agents arrived, putting both himself and the entire family at risk of instant arrest. Quickly exiting, he hid behind a haystack while the agent removed every bit of furniture from the Kennys' home. After doing so, the agent then reinstated the tenants, for the purpose of this exercise was nothing more than routine harassment.

DESPITE THE INCREASED GOVERNMENT vigilance, the Fenian conspiracy was unbroken. Stephens was in hiding, but very much in touch with his high command, Devoy included. In America, O'Mahoney was trying to fend off his so-called men of action, who wondered why Stephens hadn't called for an insurrection immediately after the government suppressed the *Irish People*. Ireland was tense, and men like Devoy were on the run, but the moment hadn't yet passed. It was in Stephens's hands.

He did nothing, and he lost America. In October, the dissidents in the Fenian Brotherhood across the Atlantic split with O'Mahoney and set out on an independent course of action. An increasingly important American Fenian named Thomas W. Sweeny wrote of his doubts in October 1865. His opinion was not to be ignored, for he was a legitimate Union hero, having risen to the rank of brigadier general despite the loss of his right arm. He was still in the Union Army in October 1865 when he was appointed the shadow Irish government-in-exile's secretary of war. Upon his appointment, he wrote his colleague William Roberts:

"The most reliable accounts from Ireland have convinced me that our friends there are totally unprepared with the martial means necessary to contend, with any show of success, against the British troops, and that to incite an insurrection, at present, would be but to provide a wholesale massacre in which thousands of brave lives would be sacrificed in a useless stuggle." Sweeny then made a suggestion that would soon tear apart the American movement and fatally wound Stephens's strategy: "The Canadian frontier, extending from the north of the St. Lawrence to Lake Huron, a distance of more than 1,300 miles, is assailable at all points."

Thus was born one of American history's most curious episodes: the raising of a private army within the borders of the United States to threaten a country with which the United States was at peace.

Meanwhile, the British government again took the offensive. Stephens was arrested on the evening of November 11, 1865. He was in prison no more than two weeks when a rescue party that included Devoy on the outside and an IRB operative named John Breslin on the inside set him free in a dramatic and attention-grabbing rescue. Devoy was among the first to help Stephens after he leaped from the top of the prison wall. The next morning, the Queen's viceroy in Ireland reported back to London, "All our work is undone." Overstatement was hardly confined to enthusiastic Fenians.

The newly liberated Stephens, now among the world's most wanted men, was not in a mood to capitalize on his sensational escape. Devoy and others were summoned to a round of meetings in late December. The word was delivered: 1865 would not, in fact, be the year of action.

All the while, Devoy was continuing to strengthen the Fenian hold in the British garrison, particularly in Dublin, where the heaviest Fenian blows would fall. Of the six thousand troops stationed in the city, Devoy figured sixteen hundred were Fenians, and three thousand of the total were Irish-born. Each of the infiltrated regiments had a center, and Devoy personally chose men to command various companies of infantry and cavalry. As the new year dawned, the Fenian organization in the army was itching for battle.

The government was beginning to understand how close it was to the brink. The result, not surprisingly, was a huge upsurge in arrests and the beginning of a mass transfer of the British Army garrison in Ireland, infected as it was with Fenian fever. By the end of January, the tables had been turned, and now the movement was on the brink. On February 17, 1866, the government moved in for the kill. The Habeas Corpus Act was suspended, meaning wholesale arrests could be made without regard to the niceties of evidence, and the suspects held for weeks. American officers who had come over for the fight were especially targeted, and all but a dozen of the 150 or so in Dublin were arrested in just two days. Increasingly desperate men such as Devoy fumed while Stephens and the IRB watched the organization disintegrate.

To keep the police guessing, Devoy moved from room to room in cheap lodging houses along narrow alleys near Francis, Patrick, Nicholas, and Bride Streets in Dublin. The rooms were had for four pence a night, and nearby, some bad but filling meals could be had for the same price. Devoy and his friends, nearly all of them wanted men, found a measure of daytime freedom only in the morning, when they trooped to a nearby restaurant for breakfast when the police were changing shifts. Otherwise, Devoy's daytime existence consisted of careful walks around the city and occasional visits to friendly public houses.

Two nights after the suspension of habeas corpus, Devoy discussed the IRB's desperate straits with Colonel Kelly, the American, in the back room of a public house on Camden Street in Dublin. A body-guard of Fenians was deployed outside the pub, fully prepared to fend off any police incursion.

As Devoy and Kelly tried to put the damaged pieces back to-gether, one of Devoy's contacts burst into the room with news that two Fenian-infiltrated regiments in Dublin's Richmond Barracks were preparing to start the rebellion on their own, never mind what Stephens or Kelly had to say. In an instant, then, the damaged-but-viable conspiracy was threatened with destruction. Devoy reckoned that he had to act quickly. In another room was one of his subverted soldiers, and as luck would have it, he actually was in army uniform, having just been granted a short furlough. Even luckier, the soldier Fenian was about Devoy's size. So Devoy and the soldier exchanged clothes, and Devoy cut off his beard at the chin, leaving a mustache and sideburns in the fashion of most British Army troops. So dressed—but wearing his own boots, as the soldier's didn't fit him—he began a walking tour of the pubs near the barracks, gathering intelligence along the way. He arranged to meet some of the soldier Fenians at the barracks gate, fully prepared to enter the barracks if necessary. It wasn't. More than fifty soldier Fenians met him outside, under the full view of the guards—who were also sworn Fenians—and Devoy persuaded them to call off their mutiny and await orders from Stephens, Kelly, and himself.

A disaster was averted, but Devoy understood how close the conspiracy was to collapse. In his recent travels, he had been hearing muttered complaints of Fenians grown impatient with Stephens. The most vocal dissenters were those private citizens who had quit their jobs to train full-time, living on the bare subsistence money the IRB paid to a few hundred such men. Two hotheaded Fenians urged Devoy to lead a coup against Stephens and call out the Fenian soldiers into action. Devoy was horrified and refused.

Stephens required Devoy to file regular written reports on his activities, a task Devoy considered absurd, considering that he had complete access to Stephens anyway and anything on paper could fall into the wrong hands. He complied nevertheless, and on February 20, the day after he put an end to the mutiny in Richmond Barracks, Devoy found a friendly pub and prepared to write a long memo telling Stephens that the conspiracy required either immediate action or a definite postponement, instead of a vague promise of action in the future.

He then met with colleagues, all of whom were as impatient as he was. The meeting adjourned at 9:30 P.M., and Devoy left encouraged by the support he had received. At this late hour, he realized he hadn't eaten since breakfast, so he ducked into a grocery, bought some spiced beef and a roll, and ate his dinner while walking the streets of Dublin. He planned to spend the night with his father's oldest sister, who had offered her house as a refuge several times when Devoy was trying to elude the police.

He was barely on his solitary journey when he heard footsteps behind him. It wasn't the police, but an emissary from Colonel Kelly. James Stephens himself wished to see Devoy.

Devoy's report had shaken the Captain from his doldrums. From all over Dublin came the IRB's top command, assembled in Stephens's rooms across from the Kildare Street Club, the fashionable meeting place of the pro-English establishment. Stephens was in a subdued mood, wearing a pair of slippers and pacing the floor with his hands in his pockets. The rest of the Fenian high command, nine men including Devoy, sat around a table. Stephens told Devoy that he had read his report, considered it, and thought it should be considered then and there, by the IRB's leaders. This night, Devoy thought, might well be the night when action would at last be ordered.

They talked until three in the morning. Opponents of quick action argued that the IRB had only two thousand rifles and a few hundred revolvers. Devoy countered by reminding them of the vast stores of weapons available in lightly guarded depots such as Athlone, a place he knew well. Stephens remained silent during most of the discussion, but clearly he favored a delay of at least two or three weeks.

The hours of conversation produced only an agreement to reconvene later. Devoy went to his aunt's house, slept for three hours, and returned to the deliberations with something nobody had had the night before—a plan.

Kelly opened the proceedings with an accounting of the Fenian circles in Dublin. Surprisingly, they were very much intact and eager to commence the fight. That was the good news. The bad news was the number of arms: only eight hundred rifles in the capital for an estimated eight thousand men. Stephens reckoned that he could get two thousand rifles from England, and other commanders, including Devoy, threw in a few hundred here and there.

The Americans in the group, no doubt influenced by the slaughter they had witnessed on Southern battlefields, believed the lack of guns ruled out an immediate insurrection. That appeared to be the final word, until a stubborn young man with but a year's experience in the Foreign Legion spoke up.

Devoy was hesitant at first, realizing that he had nothing to compare with the experience of the Americans. But, he said, the situation was desperate, and perhaps desperate means ought to be considered. With that, he outlined a plan to raid army installations in Dublin and in Athlone, all of them well infiltrated with Fenians, to capture the tens of thousands of rifles stored within.

The American officers, while impressed, decided that neither the Dublin nor the Athlone assaults could take place until more arms were landed from Liverpool. A vote was taken. Four of Devoy's colleagues voted for postponement of the fight; Devoy and two others voted for immediate war. Devoy, exhausted and disconsolate, left the room in disgust for an appointment with his staff at a restaurant on George's Street. There, he broke the bad news. Despite his lack of sleep, he spent the rest of the day roaming the streets of Dublin, meeting with lower-level IRB men to explain the changed circumstances. As sunset on February 22 approached, he made his way to a meeting with several British Army turncoats at Pilsworth's public house on James's Street, a frequent meeting place for IRB men.

Devoy and several other disappointed Fenians were gathered in the pub's back room when word reached them that two detectives were lurking outside the pub. Calmly, Devoy advised the soldiers in the room—who were the most vulnerable, since they would be considered traitorous—to leave quietly through a back door. Several did. But before Devoy himself could make a dramatic escape, the detectives burst into the room. Devoy reached for a revolver, trying to make a quick calculation of the odds. One of his colleagues, however, glanced out the window and shouted, "Don't fire! There are a hundred policemen outside!" Devoy took his hand out of his pocket. It was over. The detectives placed John Devoy under arrest.

Some nights earlier, he had visited Naas for what was to be one last time. He and Eliza arranged to meet alone in a field near the family farmhouse, far from the eyes of parents and friends. There, they said good-bye, never guessing that they would not see each other again for fifty-eight years.

CHAPTER FIVE

On the Cause Must Go

A POLICE PHOTOGRAPH OF JOHN DEVOY TAKEN AFTER HIS ARREST shows a stern, angry young man with long, thin sideburns and dark, disheveled hair. His woolen jacket appears to be very worn. His dark eyes look away from the camera, unwilling to cooperate in this new, state-of-the-art bit of criminology that would become known as the mug shot. Some hours or days later, he was brought before a camera again, this time shorn of sideburns, his hair closely cropped. And this time, he looked directly into the camera, his face set in a stern challenge.

He was assigned a number, clapped into North Dublin's Mountjoy Jail, then taken to Kilmainham Jail. His revolution was over. A prisoner at age twenty-three, John Devoy had seemingly confirmed the worst fears of his long-suffering father. The best he could hope for was a sentence that would allow him to spend his middle years as a free man; at worst, he could have been sent to the prison colonies of Australia or Van Diemen's Land, which would likely have ensured that William would never again see his prodigal child.

During those first few days in prison, Devoy wrote Eliza a seventeen-page letter on paper torn out of books in the prison library. He released her from their engagement, but promised to marry her if she were still single when he was a free man again. It was a promise he would not keep, and Eliza would wait seventeen years before marrying an acquaintance of Devoy's.

Just a few days before Devoy's arrest, a Masonic hall in downtown

Pittsburgh was alive with all the pageantry of a nineteenth-century American political convention. But it was hardly that. The dissident branch of America's Fenian Brotherhood had assembled for a prewar conclave under the full gaze of the press and the government. Spies and infiltrators, while present, were superfluous, since the Fenian private army was nothing if not open about its ambition. It was preparing to wage war upon a country, British-ruled Canada, with which the United States was at peace.

President Andrew Johnson and his advisers displayed little concern about this remarkable gathering in Pittsburgh. Washington was indebted to the Irish after so many of them had shed blood for the Union cause. In fact, in the South, many of the defeated rebels held the Irish collectively responsible for the Union's triumph. One Fenian organizer reported back to New York that he was having a hard time recruiting in places such as Alabama and Texas because "there is much bitterness against the Irish of the North on account of their being regarded by the Southern people, Irish included, as the chief cause of the destruction of the Confederacy."

But Washington's willingness to look the other way as the Irish built their private army also had more than just a tinge of calculation. At the very moment the Irish were parading their warlike intentions, the Johnson administration was pressing London for millions of dollars in compensation for shipping lost to Southern commerce raiders built in British ports, most prominently the CSS *Alabama*. Postwar public opinion in the North was decidedly, even rabidly, anti-British, thanks to London's decision early in the war to grant the Confederacy status as a belligerent—one step away from full diplomatic recognition. Confederate raiders had used Canada as a staging area for an attack on New York City late in the war. So it was with a certain sly smile that the American public greeted rumors of a Fenian military buildup along the Canadian border.

Not only was Washington ignoring the Fenians as they sold bonds and marched through the streets in military formation, the Johnson administration was actually selling weapons to the Fenian army. From the headquarters of the dissident wing of the movement at 706 Broadway in lower Manhattan, the organization's secretary of war, Thomas Sweeny, coordinated the purchase of thousands of rifles from government arsenals in Pennsylvania and upstate New York. Sweeny would later write that "the United States government, in selling their stores to my Agents, was perfectly well aware of the purposes for which they were intended." He, like other Fenians, insisted that high government officials approved the plan to invade Canada, noting that "individuals in eminent positions at Washington" had expressed "sympathy . . . for us."

Sweeny submitted to the Pittsburgh convention a plan to invade lower Canada with at least ten thousand men who would cross the frontier in winter, when the "lakes and rivers are bridged with ice." The invasion force would consist of three wings, from Detroit and Chicago to the west, Buffalo in the center, and St. Albans, Vermont, in the east.

The British consulate in New York was on the verge of a collective nervous breakdown. It had penetrated the Fenians in New York with several informers, but the information it was receiving might well have been coming from the likes of James Stephens or his excitable propagandists. Edward Archibald, the British consul in New York whose chief duty was to keep on eye on the American Irish, wrote to London that "from two or three different informants I received the report that systematic arrangements are being made to set fire to London in several hundred places at the same time. . . . It is expected that, in the confusion that will ensue, the Fenians may be able to attack the prisons, and penitentiaries, as well as plunder the Banks. I am told that the phrase 'strike at the heart of the enemy,' sometimes used by the leaders, means the burning of London." There is nothing in the Fenians' record of such a plan.

The press, particularly the *Herald*, speculated freely about the date and location of the Fenians' eventual invasion, and gossiped about which wing, O'Mahoney's or Roberts-Sweeny's, would be first to send the troops into action. On March 9, the Fenians were discussed at a cabinet meeting in Washington. Navy Secretary Gideon Welles proposed that the Johnson administration call in General Grant for consultations, while the scheming Secretary of War Edwin Stanton insisted that the president immediately crush the Fenians. Welles believed Stanton wished to see the weak Johnson embarrassed, since such a move was likely to cost the president politically. "The Irish element . . . is a strong one and clannish, and if a movement against an organization of theirs was to be made, I wished to see others besides the President moving," Welles wrote in his diary. For the time being, nothing was done, even though the *Toronto Globe* pleaded that Washington "interfere and bring to an end the proceedings of the Fenian Society."

Ultimately, though, the division of the American Fenian movement into the O'Mahoney wing and the Roberts-Sweeny wing was playing into the hands of mainstream American opinion, which was not particularly pro-Irish even if it was, at least in the North, anti-English. The impoverished Irish of the Northeast's cities were associated in the minds of native-born Americans with Saturday-night brawls and vicious street gangs, and the feuding men in command of the Fenian armies movement were doing nothing to broaden the Irish image in the United States.

Meanwhile, at the headquarters of the Roberts-Sweeny wing on Broadway, the *Herald* reported that no less than $3,000 had been collected within twenty minutes on March 16, the day before St. Patrick's Day. New York was filled with talk that one or both of the Fenian armies would soon be on the march northward. Anxiety was at fever pitch in parts of Canada, so much so that Montreal's St. Patrick's Day parade was canceled for fear that it might be used as a signal for invasion. Seward, the American secretary of state, was moved to announce that the Johnson administration would permit no violation of American neutrality within its borders.

As March gave way to April, the press reported signs of a Fenian military buildup in Portland and Eastport in Maine, near the offshore Canadian island of Campobello. The reports were correct; O'Mahoney had decided he would not let his rivals be the first to strike. Roberts and Sweeny were stunned to discover that the man they thought incapable of action was apparently about to take the lead on the battlefield. Sweeny's plans for an invasion in winter were in danger of being made irrelevant.

Throughout early April, small groups of O'Mahoney's men left their homes and jobs and made their way to Maine in civilian clothes. In mid-April, a Fenian steamer—part of what some hoped would be a Fenian navy—arrived in Eastport with five hundred weapons for the hundreds of Fenians encamped in and around the town. Also arriving at about the same time were U.S. marshals dispatched from Washington and British consular staff sent to Eastport from Portland.

The marshals and the diplomats booked rooms in the only large hotel in Eastport, the Maybee Hotel, the very place where the Fenians' top commanders were staying. "It is very amusing to see them scowling at each other across tables," wrote one observer.

O'Mahoney's army made its first move on April 15, descending on Indian Island, a small bit of Canada off the Eastport coast. The Fenians exulted, "The spirit of liberty is abroad!"

O'Mahoney's rivals were in a quandary. Sweeny's plan called for an invasion across frozen lakes and rivers, but by the time winter arrived, the flag of the Irish republic might well be flying in Canada already, planted there by O'Mahoney. On April 16, lower Manhattan was furious with Fenian activity, with O'Mahoney's men scurrying around Union Square and the Roberts-Sweeny loyalists parading into headquarters on Broadway for an emergency convention. Once impaneled, the Roberts-Sweeny faction passed a resolution urging their commanding general to order immediate action. Sweeny was aghast, but was told that his objections would mean the end of the organization. "I reluctantly yielded, preferring the chances of an honorable failure in the field to the disintegration of the organization," he wrote. The plan of campaign would have to be revised, and soon.

With O'Mahoney's move on Indian Island, however, Washington finally cracked down. The Johnson administration dispatched to Eastport no less a personage than General George Gordon Meade, a hero of Gettysburg, along with federal troops and some artillery. Meade immediately ordered the seizure of the Fenian steamer, with its arms still aboard. O'Mahoney's Fenians were no match for the show of force, and they immediately withdrew when it became clear that Meade meant business. What had started out as a bold adventure ended meekly.

The Roberts-Sweeny wing was ecstatic. O'Mahoney had been disgraced and discredited, leaving a void in the Irish-American movement that the dissident Fenians intended to fill. But Sweeny himself had little reason for cheer, for O'Mahoney's blunder meant that Sweeny's hastily revised plans had better succeed, for another fiasco was likely to make the Fenian movement an American laughingstock.

From his office on lower Broadway, Sweeny took command of a sprawling military enterprise. The dissident Fenian militia was organized into regional departments, with regiments as far afield as Davenport, Iowa, Portsmouth, Virginia, and Chattanooga, Tennessee. Sweeny's unenviable assignment was to whip the scattered regiments into a legitimate fighting force and have them in position, armed and ready, by June. In the meantime, Sweeny was still negotiating with agents to purchase weapons from U.S. government arsenals. More than four thousand muskets were distributed to Fenian agents at the government's arsenal in Bridesburg, Pennsylvania, on May 3, and in the following days Sweeny carried on negotiations with an arms agent in New York to get 2 million rounds of ammunition from government stores.

A thousand-mile Fenian front extended from Chicago to St. Albans, with troops representing nearly two dozen states prepared to stike a blow for Ireland's liberty and avenge the starvation and exile of the Famine. Throughout May, Irish-Americans began filtering into Cleveland, Chicago, Buffalo, Toledo, and a handful of smaller towns along the border, often under the watchful eye of U.S. marshals.

At this climatic moment, things started to fall apart. The *New York Times* reported in late May that the Sweeny faction had been infiltrated by British spies. The Fenians disregarded the report as evidence of the newspaper's hostility and contempt, which it may well have been. But it was also correct. No sooner was Sweeny dispatching his orders than they were in the hands of at least three informers, who passed them on to Canadian and British officials. Some of the information the informers were gathering, however, wasn't entirely accurate. One spy in Buffalo told Canadian officials that the Fenians had one hundred thousand men ready to send over the border. In fact, to Sweeny's chagrin, the number was about one-tenth that figure.

As invasion day approached, Sweeny learned that the Midwest and Plains states regiments could raise only half the three thousand troops that had been expected, and worse yet, the transport he had been promised to ferry troops across Lakes Michigan and Huron was nonexistent. The left wing of the Army of the Irish Republic was out of action before the invasion began. Meanwhile, the Johnson administration, under pressure from Canadian and British officials, carried out several sporadic raids on Fenian arms depots in upstate New York, a sign that Washington might not be as neutral as Sweeny had hoped.

And it was becoming clear that the Fenians simply were not mustering the kinds of numbers Sweeny required.

Only in Buffalo and St. Albans were troops prepared, armed, and ready to go into combat. The left wing was paralyzed by lack of transport, and the staging areas in Ohio and parts of western New York were in disarray. James Stephens, touring the country on behalf of the old O'Mahoney wing, was doing his best to discourage Sweeny and Roberts. On May 26, speaking at Cooper Union in Manhattan, he lashed out at his rivals, saying an invasion of Canada was no more sensible than an assault on Japan.

Under cover of night on May 31, eight hundred soldiers of the Irish Republic in exile took the field, crossing the Niagara River in Buffalo under the command of John O'Neill, a Civil War veteran like many of the soldiers under his command. In fact, many of the officers wore the blue of their former Union regiments; enlisted men wore green and black. Upon landing in the village of Fort Erie on the Canadian side of the river, the troops planted American and Fenian flags, claiming the land for the Irish Republic in exile. The *Herald* greeted the news with a one-word headline: "WAR." The battle for an Irish Republic had begun in the unlikeliest of fields.

It was, at first, a one-sided battle, for Canadian officials were caught off guard. The Fenian success was in large measure a tribute to the skills of O'Neill, who didn't hesitate even when an American gunboat appeared on the river, jeopardizing his supply lines and reinforcements. O'Neill marched his men toward the town of Ridgeway, where, in midmorning on June 2, the first blood was spilled. O'Neill's Civil War veterans found themselves faced with 840 young, part-time militiamen mustered in haste to meet the Fenian threat. They were no match for the invaders, and after a fierce firefight, the defenders beat a hasty retreat toward the town. The Canadians suffered a dozen killed and forty wounded, while eight Fenians were killed and twenty wounded. A jubilant *Herald*, after noting that the cause of Fenianism and Irish freedom had brought together "the most active fighting men in the cause of Jefferson Davis hand in hand with some of the bravest Irish soldiers of the Union," reported that Canadians were entertaining fearful visions of "Sherman's legions on another march to the sea."

Though the Johnson administration maintained a conspicuous silence while the Fenians rushed across the border, the president quickly dispatched both Meade and Grant to upstate New York to get a look at the situation for themselves. Grant arrived in Buffalo on June 2, and he ordered Meade to tell the governors of border states that their militias ought to be activated to prevent any further invasions from American soil.

Meanwhile, O'Neill, anticipating a British counterattack, requested reinforcements. Three thousand Fenians were massed in Buffalo awaiting orders to cross into Canada to join O'Neill's men. But with Grant, Meade, and a federal cruiser now patrolling the Niagara River, O'Neill was cut off from supplies and reinforcements. O'Neill had little choice but to fall back closer to the border, and on the morning of June 3, he decided to return to Buffalo after fighting a minor skirmish near Fort Erie. The Fenians boarded two canal boats on the Canadian side of the river and were halfway across when an armed federal tug, the *Harrison*, pulled alongside. O'Neill and his men were placed under arrest.

President Johnson's official silence ended on June 6, when, to the relief of Canadian and British officials, he issued a proclamation forbidding any American citizens from taking part in any further raids. A day later, acting on Grant's orders, Meade's men confronted Sweeny in St. Albans and placed the former Union general under arrest.

The destruction of the Fenian invasion was a devastating blow to the Irish-American national movement. Immediately the cry went up that Seward and the Johnson administration had double-crossed the Irish. In an interview with a bitter Fenian leader, Meade was told that "we have been lured on by this Cabinet, and used for the [purposes] of Mr. Seward. They encouraged us on to this thing. We bought our rifles from your arsenals, and were given to understand that you would not interfere."

Instead, some seven thousand Fenian soldiers were now in the custody of General Meade, who had once commanded some of them. They were allowed to return home, bitter but mostly unbloodied, after a few days. Those who had journeyed to the border staging areas from New York City were given free rail passage home when Boss Tweed and New York mayor William Hoffman agreed to pick up the tab.

The Fenians would try one more invasion, in 1870, and would meet with an equally ignominious end. Canada, in the meantime, was so startled by this threat from the south that its leaders hurried to complete a confederation that would unite its vast provinces into a single nation.

By the end of 1870, the Irish-American movement was in shambles. It would be revived only when a ship filled with exiles sailed into New York Harbor in January 1871.

JOHN DEVOY SIGNED HIS name on the first page of his prison-issue Book of Common Prayer and dated it January 6, 1871, the day his five-year torment came to an end. With an aroused Irish populace vehemently protesting on behalf of the imprisoned Fenians, British prime minister William Gladstone saw valor in discretion and conceded to Ireland's demands that Devoy, Rossa, and other, lesser-known guests of the Queen be released. On December 16, 1870, Gladstone wrote to the prisoners from Downing Street, informing them of their imminent return to freedom.

Devoy survived his prison ordeal with his health intact, but his was a fearsome struggle with hunger, boredom, and his rebellious nature. During Devoy's stay of two months and twenty-four days in Portland Prison, one of several institutions he stayed in during his prison years, eight of the fifteen hundred prisoners died, one by suicide. So common were prisoners' deaths that they were simply noted in the prison governor's daily journal along with observations about the day's weather conditions and a summary of the number of lashings administered to recalcitrant inmates.

After Devoy was taken by surprise in Pillsworth's taproom in February 1866, he spent a year awaiting indictment and trial. His routine was broken only by the limited exercise he was allowed in a fenced-off section of the prison yard designed exclusively for the incarcerated Fenian rebels. The Fenians were allotted cells no more than ten feet by seven, with a hammock bed that Rossa compared, unfavorably, to a coffin. Food was passed through a trapdoor into which guards with lanterns peered hourly through the night, adding the torture of sleep deprivation to the jail's other indignities.

Devoy's one regular visitor was the Catholic chaplain, a rather earnest man named Father Cody who was known for his pedestrian sermons during Sunday's masses in the prison chapel. Cody and Devoy got along well enough, primarily because they didn't discuss Irish politics. Finally the priest suggested that Devoy make his confession. Cody had strayed onto a sensitive point, for duplicitous priests were infamous for asking suspected Fenians about their politics in the intimacy of the confessional box. Devoy hadn't been to confession in five years for that very reason, but he had come to trust Father Cody and so he enumerated his sins of five years—"my long story," he called it. Upon its completion, Father Cody asked, "Did you take the Fenian oath?"

"I thought you promised not to ask me that question," Devoy snapped.

"Oh, I have to ask it," the priest replied.

Devoy informed the priest that he would no longer discuss politics while on his knees.

The case of the *Queen vs. John Devoy* was called in Dublin's Green Street courthouse on February 19, 1867. When the judge read the charge and asked Devoy how he would plea, the young Fenian rose and said simply, "Guilty, my lord." Among his enemies in time to come, those three words would haunt him even in his old age, for Irish nationalists were (and are) legendary for displaying their contempt for the British justice system. Pleading guilty, or so the myth goes, just wasn't, and isn't, done, for it explicitly recognizes the authority of the court. Devoy later insisted that the Fenian high command ordered him to plead guilty because the Fenians were planning to rescue him in much the same way that Devoy had helped rescue James Stephens in 1865. In his last years, Devoy changed his story slightly, saying he was ordered to plead guilty in the hope that he would receive a light sentence and would then return to reorganize the movement.

Some three weeks after Devoy's plea, on the evening of March 5, the sentries in Mountjoy Jail were put on alert. In his dreary prison cell, Devoy could hear the guards' "deep, sonorous voices" as they patrolled the prison with a sudden urgency in their step. Through one of his sisters, who visited him in February, Devoy had heard that his onetime Fenian comrades, the few who were left, were planning a rebellion in early March. The unmistakable strain in the guards' voices persuaded Devoy, correctly, that the rebellion was under way.

He climbed up to his small cell window and looked out on a bleak winterscape of snow, ice, and sleet. The Fenian rising already had no chance of success, what with the rebels' leaders in prison, their arms seized, and their morale broken. The awful weather added to the indignities. As he gazed out the window forlornly, Devoy later recalled, "I said to myself sadly: 'God help the poor fellows who are out tonight without overcoats or warm clothing. And what are they going to fight with?" As it turned out, there was very little fighting.

The Fenian Rising was crushed in a day. Devoy heard the bad news from a chaplain in Mountjoy the following morning. But word of the rising and its quick end did not cross the Atlantic for weeks, too late to stop a boatload of forty Civil War veterans and eight thousand rifles from leaving New York in hopes of aiding a risen Ireland. The ship, *Erin's Hope*, set sail in mid-April. By the time it arrived off Sligo in May, the history of the rebellion was being written.

JUST AFTER ST. PATRICK'S Day, Devoy was transported to Millbank prison on the banks of the Thames, close enough to the Houses of Parliament to hear Big Ben chime the monotonous hours. Millbank was one of two probation prisons where convicts spent the first nine months or so of their sentence, forbidden to communicate with anyone either outside or inside. After enduring such a stretch, prisoners were then dispatched to various public works prisons, where the rules were not so strict.

Jeremiah O'Donovan Rossa was among the prisoners' leaders in Millbank. He had already created trouble for prison officials by smuggling out a letter to the home secretary documenting conditions in places where Irish rebels were held. When Devoy was marched into Millbank, O'Donovan Rossa was a walking skeleton. His continual defiance of authorities led to a steady diet of bread and water—the regimen ordered for those placed in special punishment cells. Rossa's astounding ability to procure writing material was a particular embarrassment, since he not only wrote to government officials, but to the press as well. After one such literary exercise, Rossa was sentenced to solitary confinement for twenty-eight days, his hands tied behind his back even at mealtime.

In Millbank, Devoy was shown to a cell nine feet by eight with a stone floor and whitewashed walls that would play havoc with his eyes. The cell was unheated, and the only furniture was a plank bed and a water bucket, which doubled as a stool. Devoy and the other prisoners sat on their overturned buckets eight hours a day while they performed their single chore—the tedious work of tearing old tar ropes to strands of floss for use in mats. In prison parlance, the job was known as "picking oakum," and each prisoner was expected to pick three pounds of rope a day.

Even when Devoy was not on punishment rations, a regular occurrence, his meals were so sparse that he would later write that he was hungry his entire imprisonment.

The prisoners were bathed once every two weeks, four men to a trough. The last four to bathe sat in the same water the first four used. At night, the Irish prisoners communicated with one another by tapping on walls and floors, a practice that encouraged authorities to move the Fenians frequently. Devoy tapped out messages one night and discovered that Rossa was in an adjacent cell. The two of them communicated in this fashion for several weeks, and on Christmas Eve, 1867, they tapped Christmas prayers to each other.

Devoy tried to escape several times, once by wrestling a guard for his keys. After he had been in Millbank for nearly a year—well over the usual nine-month span—his frustrations got the better of him and he attacked two warders who were monitoring him as he swept out his cell. He knocked one down with the broom handle, but he missed the other, allowing him to scramble away to summon the guards. Devoy realized that escape was impossible, so he helped the injured warder to his feet, dressed the wound he had inflicted, and allowed the wounded man to escort him back to his cell. He was soon dispatched to the prison's penal cells for a four-month stretch of bread, water, and isolation.

After serving eleven months and three days in Millbank, Devoy was transferred in February 1868 to the island prison of Portland, where conditions were somewhat less cruel. Here, at least, Devoy was put to work outdoors, breaking stones and working on docks. His diet improved a bit, and on Sundays, he was allowed to associate freely with his fellow Fenians during exercise. But Devoy's time in Portland was short-lived. After a mere twelve weeks, he led a strike to protest bread-and-water punishments and was sent back to Millbank.

Devoy saw few visitors during his second stretch in Millbank, which ended with his transfer to Chatham prison on March 15, 1869. His father visited him once during his first term in Millbank, but there is no record of a return visit. The prison's governor wrote at least two letters to Devoy's family, informing them that John was in his "usual state of health" but that they could not see him for themselves.

But before leaving Millbank for good, Devoy managed one last act of defiance. He found a way to carve his name in block letters into the wooden trim above his cell door. This minor act of rebellion would soon inspire another young Irish rebel named Michael Davitt, a one-armed member of the Irish Republican Brotherhood who was assigned Devoy's former cell in Millbank after his arrest in 1870.

Devoy's removal to Chatham was hardly a step forward in the march toward rehabilitation. His new residence was reserved for what he called "the hard men." The monotonous labor—darning endless pairs of socks, among other chores—the punishments, and the skimpy diet were fearsome.

During Devoy's final months in prison, a British commission was impaneled to investigate conditions in Chatham and other places where Fenians were incarcerated. The panel, headed by Lord Devon, interviewed Devoy during his last summer of captivity, 1870. He went on record with a characteristically blunt statement:

"Five years bitter experience, to say nothing of the record of seven hundred, have made me look with suspicion on everything emanating from the quarter in which your commission had its origin. . . . I never asked for an inquiry because I believed that a complete and impartial one would not be granted; and that if friends of mine, or of the other prisoners, did ask, it was for a public one."

Four months after the commission finished its work, Gladstone's letter of good tidings arrived in Chatham. Devoy was on his way to America. The Irish diaspora was about to get the leader it so desperately needed.

CHAPTER SIX

Bound for Western Australia

For all his voracious reading, eclectic education, minor celebrity, and natural intelligence, the best that John Devoy could do in the heart of American capitalism was a $700-a-year clerk's job with a sugar trader on Wall Street. His new home was a single room in a flophouse owned by his fellow exile Jeremiah O'Donovan Rossa, who had managed to cash in on his fame as England's most ferocious ex-prisoner. Rossa's business, the Northern Hotel, was a two-story structure near Chatham Square in the middle of New York's notorious Five Points neighborhood.

The cause of Irish freedom, and of the Irish in America, lay dormant as Devoy adjusted to his new life. The failed invasions of Canada had turned militant Irish-American nationalism from a potentially powerful and disruptive conspiracy into a source of ridicule. At many points in Devoy's long life few would have condemned him for giving up the fight, and surely the early years of his exile offered little promise. His prospects in life were dim, and all he had to show for his decade of service in the Irish Republican Brotherhood was a failed rising, five years in prison, and ignominious exile. The Fenians were in disarray and the Irish-Americans were so poor and miserable that they could hardly spare the energy, never mind the money, for a fight that increasingly seemed hopeless and quite remote from the daily concerns of life in America.

The admonitions of Devoy's friend from Boston, the poet, editor, and ex-Fenian John Boyle O'Reilly, seemed wisdom itself: "The great mass of the Irish people have never belonged to any organization for

National revolution," O'Reilly wrote realistically, but with regret, too. "They have held aloof because they saw dissension and chicanery. . . . John, no matter what organization you join, you have a right, a duty, to make your means of living a primary consideration. Ireland can best be helped by men who have helped themselves. Go into business, old man." What's more, Eliza Kenny was three thousand miles away, still single and wondering when her fiancé would make good on his promise to marry her.

72

In fact, none of this mattered to Devoy. Not the flophouse nor the lack of prospects nor his promise to Eliza. There was, Devoy believed, work to be done, and he devoted every waking hour to rebuilding Irish America as the voice and muscle of the Irish at home. By day, he added his columns of figures and performed his mundane chores in the city's financial district; by night, he conspired with equally hardy souls in his solitary room or theirs. When the meetings were over, he turned his attention to his astonishing correspondence, which kept him in touch with like-minded Irishmen from the copper mines of Montana to the gold fields of northern California to the teeming cities of Philadelphia, Boston, and Chicago. Already the afflictions that would leave him nearly blind in his old age had begun to appear, as the nights spent hunched over a desk in the inadequate glow of candlelight began to take their toll.

He joined an obscure New York–based organization called the Clan na Gael, or Family of the Irish. This secretive, oath-bound group with Masonic-type rituals had been founded in 1867 by yet another Irish-American revolutionary on staff at the *New York Herald*. Jerome Collins was the paper's meteorological and science editor, and he created the first weather forecast in the annals of American journalism. He also was an Irish exile who, like Devoy, saw America as the promised land from which to torture Britain.

Under Collins, who would later die on an infamous expedition to the North Pole, the Clan remained in the shadows of New York's Irish-American subculture. But Devoy saw it as the foundation upon which he could build a new, competent conspiracy. What he needed was a victory of some sort, something to purge the memory of failed Canadian invasions and internecine squabbling. Until the opportunity presented itself, he would continue the tedious work of organizing.

Devoy's agitations in the early 1870s were not confined merely to the goal of Irish freedom, although that cause certainly remained uppermost in his mind. In these early years in New York, he joined the Marx-inspired International Workingmen's Association—the First International—was elected as the group's Irish delegate to its North American convention, and attended meetings of the group's Central Committee in the 10th Ward Hotel in Manhattan. Irish America was growing impatient for the promise of its new country, and that discontent was manifesting itself in the burgeoning trade-union movement. Condemned by the clergy, as Fenianism was, the union movement found no shortage of recruits among the immigrant Irish-Catholics. From the coal mines of Pennsylvania to the factories of the Northeast, Irish-Americans were organizing for a battle that would resonate with themes from Ireland, but was more immediate and perhaps held out even greater hope of success.

In a measure of just how far-flung Devoy's contacts were, E. M. Sorge, the First International's North American secretary, received a letter from Karl Marx in 1871, asking Sorge to "hand over the enclosed letter from our Irish Secretary MacDonnell to J. Devoy." Tellingly, this letter doesn't appear among the thousands Devoy preserved for posterity nor, in fact, is there any mention in his memoirs of his short-lived membership in the IWA.

Some time in late 1873 or early 1874, Devoy received a letter from a man he had last seen in Ireland before his arrest. James Wilson had been a soldier in the British Army and a sworn Fenian, subverted to the cause of Irish freedom by John Devoy himself. Like other Irish-born soldiers found guilty of treason in the mid-1860s, Wilson was sentenced to life in prison and was transported to the prison colony of Western Australia, which would quickly become the final resting place for many of the soldier Fenians.

Wilson was thin, sick, and nearly worked to death when he learned, through a newspaper clipping, that John Devoy and his colleagues not only had been released from prison, but had been welcomed as conquering heroes in America. For the Fenians in Australia, however, there was no such prospect of eventual release. Instead, they would die in one of the world's great wastelands, their suffering ignored or forgotten, even, Wilson thought, by his former comrades.

More in desperation than in hope, Wilson wrote a letter to Devoy and had it smuggled out of the colony and sent to New York:

"Dear friend, remember this is a voice from the tomb. For is not this a living tomb? In the tomb it is only a man's body [that] is good for worms, but in this living tomb the canker worm of care enters the very soul. Think that we have been nearly nine years in this living tomb since our first arrest and that it is impossible for mind or body to withstand the continual strain that is upon them. One or the other must give way. It is to aid us in this sad strait that I now, in the name of my comrades and myself, ask you to aid us. . . . We ask you to aid us with your tongue and pen, with your brain and intellect, with your ability and influence. We think if you forsake us, then we are friend-less indeed."

Devoy began forming in his mind a plan whose success promised the reward of a galvanized and united Irish race at home and abroad, and one that would assure him of unquestioned leadership among the Irish in America. But first, he would need money, a ship, and a strong wind.

It took months for Devoy to persuade his Clan na Gael colleagues to undertake the aid James Wilson had so poignantly requested. De-voy's plan was breathtaking in its simplicity: get me a boat and a crew, he said in so many words, and I'll bring back our men from Australia.

The Clan's reluctance to act was based on two bitter realities. The Panic of 1873 played havoc with the Clan's fund-raising, for it was hard enough to get commitments of even a dollar or so a year in good times, never mind in a long recession. Added to the economic condition was an understandable fear that such an audacious under-taking might be doomed to yet another failure, one that might well ruin the Clan's attempt to succeed the Fenian Brotherhood as the premier Irish-American revolutionary group.

Finally, though, Devoy prevailed. On July 15, 1874, nearly sev-enty members of the Clan gathered in Baltimore for a three-day con-vention. Devoy's personal prospects were slightly better than they had been two years before. He had gotten work as a reporter with the *New York Herald*, no doubt with the assistance of his childhood friend and fellow exile James J. O'Kelly, who was the paper's chief drama critic.

Before leaving for the Baltimore convention, Devoy placed in his pocket some of the letters he had recently received from the Australian exiles. One of the letters, from Martin Hogan, was read aloud from the convention floor. "It is not my hard fate I deplore," Hogan wrote, "for I willingly bear it for the cause of dear old Ireland, but I must feel sad at the thought of being forgotten and neglected by those more fortunate companions . . . who have succeeded in eluding the grasp of the oppressor. If I had the means I could get away from here at any time. I therefore address you in the hope that you will endeavor to procure and send me pecuniary help for that purpose. . . . Believe me that even though it should be my fate to perish in this villainous dungeon of the world, the last pulse of my heart shall beat 'God Save Ireland.' "

Devoy argued forcefully that the Clan was morally bound to help men such as Hogan, whose courage and eloquence could be so valuable in the propaganda war in America. He was met with skepticism, but his appeal to conscience and honor finally won the day. A resolution authorizing the formation of a ten-man rescue committee passed unanimously. Devoy was appointed chairman of the committee and chairman of the Clan itself. He had the assignment he wanted. Now all he had to do was make it work.

Throughout the summer of 1874, Devoy began sketching the details of his plan in his spare time at night and on weekends, for his days were spent scurrying around the city as a reporter on the *Herald*. In early 1875, he dispatched a vague circular to the Clan's eighty-four branches (or camps, as they were called):

"By instructions from the Convention, the F.C. (the Clan's code for Executive Board) has determined to undertake the release of the Australian Prisoners by means of a special subscription. The project is one that should enlist the active sympathy and support of every man who really has the cause of Ireland at heart, and no member is so poor that he cannot subscribe something toward it. . . . The rescue of these men would be an act of humanity in itself, and could be the first victory gained over England in our day. We can imagine nothing that would act as a greater stimulus to the work we are engaged in."

During the next four months, Devoy would think of almost nothing else but the rescue. When he finished his workweek at the *Herald* on Friday nights, he often boarded a train that took him to Boston and O'Reilly's office by way of New Haven, where he parlayed with another ally, James Reynolds, and New Bedford, where he visited the bustling shipyards crowded with whaling men from across the globe. Through John Boyle O'Reilly he met a New Bedford police captain named Henry Hathaway, the former whaler who had helped O'Reilly escape from Western Australia. Hathaway wasn't Irish, but he proved more than willing to help Devoy, who took the unusual step of taking this police officer into his confidence. The policeman and the former convict met frequently in late January, when Devoy stayed in New Bedford for days at a time. Hathaway recommended that the Clan purchase its own ship for the mission, estimating that it would cost about $12,000 to buy a ship, hire a crew, and supply the vessel for the long journey, which Hathaway reckoned would take a year.

The captain's cost estimate might as well have been a million dollars for all that Devoy's circular was bringing in, for the recession-struck Irish were in no mood to part with their money. Devoy, however, was not about to allow mere dollars to get in the way of a plan he believed would excite the world's imagination. The Clan, which had to be browbeaten into supporting the project, had a reserve of $42,000 dedicated exclusively for what were termed "revolutionary purposes." When the Baltimore Convention approved Devoy's rescue plan, it was understood that the attempt would be self-financing, that there would be no dipping into the revolutionary till. With his special appeal on its way to raising a disappointing $7,000, Devoy proposed that he borrow from the revolutionary fund, promising to pay it back by having the rescue ship do some whaling on its way to and from Australia. The captured oil would be shipped to America and sold to cover the project's expenses.

With characteristic tenacity, Devoy dispatched letters to the nine other members of the rescue committee and lobbied local officials in the Clan. The work was difficult and consuming enough, but it was doubly hard on Devoy, who was doing it all in his spare time or whatever time off he could arrange with the *Herald*. In addition to his meetings with Hathaway and O'Reilly, Devoy was organizing new Clan na Gael camps in eastern Massachusetts and Rhode Island. "I have not a solitary minute to myself," he wrote to Reynolds, his friend from New Haven. "This thing must be made a success at all hazards."

One of those hazards was Devoy's eyesight, which was failing under the strain. On February 10, he wrote to Reynolds, apologizing for having been out of touch. "I ought to have written before," he admitted, "but I have been writing to the [rescue committee] and my eyes were bad for some time, and it was painful to write."

In mid-March 1875, Devoy bought a ship called the *Catalpa* for $5,600. The *Catalpa* would require a complete overhaul, as it had been converted from a whaler to a merchant vessel. But the price seemed right, and Devoy journeyed to New Bedford to complete the deal.

The vessel was ready by mid-April, with a crew of Portuguese and African sailors headed by Capt. George Anthony, the twenty-nine-year-old son-in-law of the agent who had arranged for the ship's sale, James Richardson. Before the ship set off, Hathaway arranged for Devoy to address Richardson and Anthony to explain the true purpose of the *Catalpa*'s mission. Devoy began his presentation with the first Saxon invasions of Ireland in the eleventh century and concluded with the story of the prisoners in Australia and the part they had played in Ireland's long freedom struggle. Anthony was aghast when Devoy asked him if he would help the American Irish in their trans-oceanic crusade. For a moment he was silent, but he finally accepted.

The *Catalpa*, refitted and ready, sailed back to New Bedford from Boston, and on the afternoon of April 29, 1875, a clear day with a calm sea, it sailed out of New Bedford harbor with John Devoy and two associates aboard for the first forty miles. Devoy shared a meal of hardtack, salt beef, and cheese with his colleagues before scrambling into a whaleboat that took him back to New Bedford. He was in no mood to sleep after his long day—he spent the evening corresponding with his associates.

Devoy expected the *Catalpa* to reach Australia by January 1876. There was no time to lose, for the *Catalpa* was only one part of the plan.

Having dispatched the first unit of his rescue team eastward from New York, Devoy devoted himself to the second. Obviously someone had to coordinate tactics and strategy on the ground in Australia, a task as critical and potentially perilous as Captain Anthony's. Whoever drew the assignment, Devoy figured, would have to get to Australia by way of California, where there were funds to be had through a former Fenian—and former prisoner in Australia—named John Kenealy, now a prominent businessman. Once in Australia, the Clan's agent would pose as a rich Irish-American with an interest in Australian gold mines, courtesy of Kenealy's money. Under this cover, he would scout the territory, set up communication with the prisoners, and await the appearance of the *Catalpa* offshore.

Devoy nominated another exile, John Breslin, to go to Australia. Tough and resourceful, that rare sort of man in whom Devoy had almost complete confidence, Breslin was well suited to the task. He had played a key role in the rescue of James Stephens from prison in 1866. Once again, though, Devoy had to coerce his colleagues into agreement, for some objected to Breslin because he was not a Clan na Gael member. Devoy arranged for a quick oath-taking, then sent Breslin and another ally, Thomas Desmond, on a train due west.

After some delays, Breslin and Desmond boarded their ship to Australia on September 13, carrying with them false documents attesting to Breslin's alleged wealth. An Irish-American judge in Sacramento provided a notary's seal for the bogus papers, which detailed nonexistent, but seemingly fantastic, real estate holdings. Devoy instructed Breslin to keep the papers in full view of strangers once he reached Australia.

AFTER THE EXCITEMENT AND stress of organizing the rescue mission, Devoy suffered an emotional letdown, and by June 1875 he complained to Reynolds that he was "bored to death," although he had no time to "sit down to do anything." Days after his letter to Reynolds, he voluntarily surrendered the chairmanship of the Clan at its annual convention, turning the chair over to a remarkable Irish-born Presbyterian and onetime surgeon in the Union Army, Dr. William Carroll, who would preside for five tumultuous years.

Devoy's departure as the Clan's chairman hardly changed anything, for he remained the organization's driving force as he continued to set policy, recruit new members, and establish new branches. As the Clan sought to spread its influence and prepare for the day when it would provide Ireland with the men and material in the next rebellion, there was no shortage of ideas crossing Devoy's desk. Perhaps the most creative came from James O'Kelly, who proposed using West Point as a stealth training program for future officers in the army of the Irish Republic. "I am going to try to get about half a dozen of real good fellows appointed to West Point from the different States—fellows that may be useful to us afterwards. . . . This means of providing ourselves with thoroughly trained officers has hitherto been, stupidly, overlooked," O'Kelly wrote to Devoy.

The scheme was not as far-fetched as it might seem, for the Clan was beginning to infiltrate American politics at its highest levels. The senior senator from Florida, B. L. Conover, the grandson of Irish Presbyterian rebels in 1798, had taken the Clan's oath. Conover used his position to promote the Clan's various schemes, including a plan, soon aborted, to send Devoy to St. Petersburg to meet with the czar's representatives when war between Russia and Britain seemed imminent. Conover played a critical role in Devoy's rescue plan—through his Senate office, Conover made arrangements for the *Catalpa* to land secretly in Florida on its way home from Australia.

As the American centennial year of 1876 approached, Devoy received sporadic reports from both the *Catalpa* and from Breslin—who had set up shop in Australia under an alias—indicating that all was going smoothly. In the meantime, Devoy moved the Clan into a formal alliance with the Irish Republican Brotherhood, a development that would give the Clan, and thus Devoy, moral claim to speak as the sole American agent of the Irish revolutionary movement. In January 1876, as Devoy was holding regular meetings of his rescue committee in the Merchants Hotel in New York and other places, an agent of the IRB arrived in New York to discuss the formation of an international Revolutionary Directory to coordinate and plan the next rebellion. Three members would come from the Clan, three from the IRB, and one from among the Irish exiles in Australia. Negotiations dragged on for a year, but eventually the directory was formed, with Devoy one of the three American representatives.

Though it was often strained in the coming years, the alliance would become a powerful influence on Ireland's revolutionary politics, formalizing the Irish revolutionary movement as an international conspiracy and assuring the American Irish of a role in any prospective rebellion. For Devoy, the new alliance was yet another personal triumph in his determined journey to rally the American Irish behind one organization—his. He soon found out how difficult the task would be.

Devoy was suffering through one of his periodic bouts of insomnia when the leading Irish newspaper in New York, the *Irish World*, published a sensational letter from the ever-unpredictable Jeremiah O'Donovan Rossa. In it, he proposed the establishment of what he called, rather bluntly, a Skirmishing Fund, designed to bring war and destruction to Britain's shores with the help of American money. "England will not know where or how she is to be struck," he wrote. He nominated himself to be the collector of skirmishing funds, because "anyone who has ever known . . . me will not challenge the safekeeping of a few thousand dollars."

The sleepless Devoy was livid. From his desk at the *Herald* on March 1, he wrote a "Dear Friend" letter—the usual secretive salutation when writing to a fellow Clan member—condemning Rossa's public declarations and wild promises. Devoy added, however, that he had "always . . . been in favor of a public revolutionary fund to be placed in the hands of a committee which would have full control of it." He thought it absurd, however, to give such a fund so melodramatic a name as Skirmishing Fund. "I have argued this point over and over again with Rossa, but he thinks the whole thing depends on the word 'skirmishing' being left in," Devoy wrote. "That is just what most of us object to. We don't see why on earth we should announce our intentions to the world." Making a veiled reference to the *Catalpa* rescue mission, Devoy contrasted his stealth and vision with Rossa's. "We have one 'skirmish' on foot now. If that succeeds it will give us an immense lift and we can then tackle the same job in England."

Despite Devoy's objections, Rossa and the *World* went forward with the Skirmishing Fund. Every week for the next four years, the *Irish World* presented an update on collections and expenses, letters from those who wished death and destruction on England via the United States, and a list of every person who contributed even a few pennies to the cause. The British asked Washington to shut down the *World* and Rossa. The U.S. government, still very much in the hands of Union Civil War veterans with long memories, replied that it was helpless.

Eventually, Devoy gave up his attempt to rein in Rossa and, cleverly, agreed to become a trustee of the fund, a position that gave him a chance to supervise expenses.

Meanwhile, the first skirmish was about to reach its climax.

Half a world away, near the town of Freemantle in Western Australia, John Breslin was marking the days and fearing the worst. According to Devoy's timetable, the *Catalpa* should have pulled into the port of Bunbury, 120 miles to the south, in January. But there was no news of her.

Finally, on March 29, Breslin checked on ship arrivals posted in a telegraph office in Freemantle. A new notice was pinned up on a bulletin board, announcing the arrival of the whaler *Catalpa* in Bunbury. Breslin set out for the port on a mail car the next morning. Soon he and Captain Anthony were discussing the next phase of the rescue in Anthony's quarters on board the *Catalpa*.

Breslin knew the six prisoners were allowed to work outside the prison's walls without supervision. Freemantle was surrounded by ocean and desert; geography, more than the prison walls, kept Freemantle's convicts in chains. Wilson worked as an assistant to a local clergyman, while Hogan labored as a carpenter. The others were assigned such tasks as filling in swamps along the beachfront. So there would be no need to breach Freemantle's prison walls. With two wagons and four pairs of horses, Breslin and Desmond would simply spirit the prisoners away and hope that their absence wouldn't be noticed until the party was out to sea.

As the harbor waves lapped against the *Catalpa*'s hull, Breslin laid out the more delicate part of the rescue. The *Catalpa*, he told Anthony, should proceed to Rockingham Beach, some twenty miles south of Freemantle, and remain offshore after dispatching a whaleboat to the beach to pick up the prisoners.

Breslin smuggled a message to the prisoners on Good Friday, April 14, advising them to be ready in the morning. "We have money, arms and clothes; let no man's heart fail him, for this chance can never occur again," he said. Stirring though the words were, Breslin was wrong, for this chance would have to occur again. A telegram reached Breslin late Good Friday afternoon that the *Catalpa* had dragged its anchor and would need repairs before setting out for Rockingham Beach. Breslin managed to get word back to the prisoners that the rescue would have to be postponed. Later that night, another message reached his rooms at the Emerald Isle Hotel; the *Catalpa* had been repaired, and Anthony was off for Rockingham and would be in place by Easter Sunday.

Saturday morning Breslin rose early and wandered out to a jetty in Freemantle town, where the prisoners were at work. He caught Wilson's eye and delivered a hand signal indicating that the rescue would take place the following morning. Wilson returned a puzzled glance; the next day was Sunday, the only day in the week when they would not be dispatched to their outdoor labors. Breslin nearly panicked, but composed himself, walked closer to the prisoners, and mouthed a message that the rescue would be Monday.

By eight o'clock Monday morning, Breslin and Desmond were in position on a road leading away from the prison. Their traps held hats and coats for the prisoners to wear, and weapons in case they were pursued. A few minutes after eight, Breslin spotted the first group of three prisoners, led by Wilson, approaching the traps along the prison road. Wordlessly, the three men drew near, then leaped into Desmond's trap. Desmond cracked his whip and they were off in a veritable cloud of dust. Minutes later a second group, led by Hogan, appeared. They were not nearly as discreet as the first. One of them was carrying a spade for his assigned work duty. When he spotted Breslin, he threw it like a javelin into the bush. Another was carrying a kerosene can; he drop-kicked it into the woods before they jumped aboard. Now Breslin was off to the races, too. Nobody had seen them leave.

On the beach at Rockingham, Anthony and his men awoke early, cooked breakfast, and waited. In taking personal command of the rescue whaleboat and its crew, Anthony was defying Devoy's explicit orders to remain on board the *Catalpa*. Devoy didn't want Anthony involved in case something went terribly wrong on the beach. The young captain had no political quarrel with British authorities, so there was no reason to involve him in risky business. Anthony decided otherwise.

Sometime in midmorning a group of workers approached Anthony and his rescue party and struck up a conversation. Anthony tried his best to seem interested, but his attention was diverted by puffs of smoke in the distance. One of the workers said matter-of-factly that the steamer *Georgette*, a small gunboat, was patrolling the coast, hence the smoke. Anthony was not a happy man.

In the midst of this chatter, Breslin and Desmond, their horses sweating profusely, arrived in a clatter of hooves and shouts. Anthony quickly assured his crew that they were not about to be robbed by marauding convicts. Relieved, they hurriedly helped the men and their cargo into the whaleboat and shoved off without bidding their newfound friends in the work party a farewell.

Ninety minutes passed before prison officials realized that the six men were missing. When police arrived at Rockingham, they found two empty wagons and two idle teams of horses.

The wave-lashed journey from the beach to the *Catalpa* was supposed to take five hours. It took fifteen, with the mother ship often disappearing beyond the horizon. The rescue party rowed and partly sailed through the night, relying on Anthony's sense of direction once the *Catalpa* disappeared in the darkness. Finally, with the crew nearing exhaustion, the whaleboat returned to its mother, with the prisoners scrambling on board, wet and cold.

A day into the journey toward Florida and Senator Conover's welcoming party, the sky was once again puncuated with white, cloudlike puffs. The *Georgette* had a full head of steam and was sailing toward them. The *Catalpa*, powered by sails only, couldn't hope to flee. Anthony ordered an American flag hoisted atop the mainmast.

In a few hours, the *Georgette* was within hailing distance. It fired a shot across the *Catalpa*'s bow, and its captain demanded that Anthony allow a boarding party to retrieve the prisoners. Anthony replied that since there were no prisoners aboard, he could entertain no such request.

While the two captains carried on their loud poker match, Breslin went below and began distributing weapons to the *Catalpa*'s crew. He saw several scattered pieces of timber and ordered them to be placed in the ship's portholes as battering rams.

The *Georgette* was better prepared for hostilities. "You have fifteen minutes to surrender the prisoners," its captain told Anthony. "If you don't, we'll commence firing."

Anthony was unmoved. He pointed to the top of his mainmast. "We sail under the protection of the flag of the United States," he replied. "Fire on us and you fire on the American flag."

Anthony had played all of his cards. The men on his ship took up positions. After fifteen minutes, however, no shots were fired. The

Georgette lingered for a while, then abruptly changed course and steamed back to its port.

AT THE *HERALD*'S OFFICE on Park Row, John Devoy was scanning the morning's newspapers on April 23. The London newspapers carried a short item reporting that the telegraph cable connecting Australia with Java, and thus the rest of the world, had been cut.

Though known as a grim and matter-of-fact man, Devoy no doubt allowed himself a satisfied smile. The cut wires were a prearranged signal that Breslin had made good his escape, and that the *Catalpa* was on its way home. The New Zealand IRB men had done the job after they learned that the *Georgette* had returned without its quarry.

The rest of the world found out about the daring rescue in early June. Dublin erupted. Torchlight parades snaked through the city's narrow streets, and British prime minister Benjamin Disraeli, who had refused pleas to pardon the prisoners, was burned in effigy. The London *Times* thundered that America once again was to blame, and that its government was responsible for a gross violation of international law. Devoy received a letter from Boyle O'Reilly: "All credit belongs to you, old man. Soon the world will know what you have brought about." American newspapers were filled with talk of a shadowy Irish-American organization that had tugged the lion's tail with great effect. Devoy had won his victory.

On the high seas, the six former prisoners were appalled to learn that their journey home would be interrupted so that Anthony and his crew could catch a few whales. Their disgust turned to anger when Breslin insisted that the whaling expedition in the North Atlantic go forward despite the ex-prisoners' anxieties. The prisoners confronted Anthony with a petition demanding that he change course and head immediately to New York—not Florida. Anthony complied over Breslin's protests.

In early August, Devoy packed a few bags and took a train south to Philadelphia for the Clan na Gael's annual convention. It promised to be a triumphant affair. The *Catalpa* was expected in Florida within a month's time. Devoy had achieved exactly what he had intended—the first practical, revolutionary victory over the English in years, and one that seemed destined to inspire renewed interest among Irish-Americans. The convention was but a day old, however, when a telegram arrived for Devoy from O'Donovan Rossa in New York:

"*Catalpa* sailed into Harbor today. Men crazy to get off. Please send instructions."

Devoy repacked his bags. Other Clan officials wired Rossa: "John on his way. Don't let them off until then."

Devoy was back in Rossa's hotel the next day. The two of them headed to the piers of South Street, where they found a tender to take them aboard the *Catalpa*. There, he was stunned to hear of the near-mutiny and the failure to follow his well-laid plans to finance the rescue's mounting costs. He hid his anger, however, and welcomed his onetime Fenian comrades.

The next day, the prisoners were brought off the *Catalpa* and were greeted with a hastily organized but well-publicized reception. Tammany Hall, treated so rudely when Devoy and Rossa arrived in New York in 1871, was more than happy to order the streets cleared for an impromptu parade in downtown Manhattan. The prisoners were escorted to Sweeney's Hotel near City Hall—just as Devoy and Rossa had been five years before—and they registered as guests of the city.

As Devoy watched the proceedings from Broadway, a young Irishman from County Clare elbowed his way through the crowd and introduced himself. His name was John Holland, and he was a former Christian Brother who had been forced to leave Ireland on account of poor health. Healthy now, he was earning his living as a teacher in Paterson, New Jersey. Teaching, however, was merely how he paid his bills. An inventor, he was obsessed with the possibilities of undersea navigation. Holland's brother, a member of Clan na Gael, told him that Devoy might be interested in hearing about the military possibilities of submarine warfare. Instantly intrigued, Devoy promised to meet with Holland as soon as possible. Holland returned home to New Jersey pleased to have found a potential sponsor, particularly one with access to cash.

THE STORY OF THE *Catalpa* didn't end with the prisoners' triumphant return. Questions about the rescue's finances dragged on for years, with one of Devoy's colleagues, John Goff, among those charging that money was either misappropriated or wasted. The Clan would eventually decide it was satisfied with Devoy's accounting, especially since the failure to whale on the return trip left a $12,000 gap in the committee's finances. Still, grumblers were not satisfied, and some of their complaints reached Hogan's ear. Devoy had promised each former prisoner $5,000, but they received only about half that figure. The others were content enough and defended Devoy in public. Still, the controversy lingered nearly as long as the journey had taken.

Devoy and Breslin agreed to meet Hogan on New Year's Eve, 1876, to discuss his complaints about misappropriated money. Hogan showed up just before midnight and appeared to be drunk. Within minutes Devoy and Hogan were shouting at each other across a table. Hogan reached into a bag and pulled out two revolvers, which he dumped onto the table.

"There's only one way to resolve this," he told Devoy, rising from the table and glancing at the guns.

Devoy rose from the table, too, but Breslin grabbed both guns. Hogan lunged and was met with a gun butt to his face. The police were called.

That evening, Martin Hogan was carted off to a jail cell.

CHAPTER SEVEN

Fetters Rent in Twain

As A REPOSITORY OF IRISH AMERICA'S FONDEST WISHES IN THE 1870s, there was no more unlikely place than the rugged terrain of Bosnia-Herzegovina. But even as the *Catalpa* sailed triumphantly into New York, John Devoy's gaze was fixed on the Balkans, where war and atrocity seemed to foreshadow a great apocalypse involving Europe's grasping empires.

An uprising in Bosnia against the Turks, who had been in the Balkans longer than the English had been in Ireland, turned the region into a killing ground in the summer of 1876. Soon, insurgents in Serbia and elsewhere took up arms against their Ottoman overlords. From his desk at the *New York Herald*—where he was rising through the reportorial ranks to become foreign editor—Devoy monitored events during his long overnight shifts with but one question in mind: What did it mean for Ireland?

A parochial question, it was born of the wide-ranging interests characteristic of Devoy and other well-educated and well-read leaders of Clan na Gael. And unlike his landlord, Rossa, whose wild threats of bombs and fire in British cities were taking on a lunatic tone, Devoy viewed the next Irish revolution as the long and final product of cold calculations that might well span the globe. His gaze was drawn to the Balkans, but his eyes occasionally glanced elsewhere, too. Spanish politics were taking a republican turn, and the Spanish government was glowering at the Union Jack that flew defiantly in Gibraltar. Devoy sensed an opportunity there. Meanwhile, the Zulus were showing signs of restlessness under Britain's colonial rule. Devoy had visions of supplying them with weapons from America. The old Irish maxim—England's difficulty is Ireland's opportunity—meant that opportunity could present itself anywhere and at any time.

The man responsible for war fever in Britain was the very man who had offered Devoy amnesty in 1871, the once and future British prime minister William Gladstone. Out of office but seeing a chance to regain the premiership, Gladstone issued a mass-produced pamphlet demanding that the government of Benjamin Disraeli intervene on behalf of the Balkan Christians. The pro-Turk Disraeli resisted his rival's call to arms, arguing, without a hint of irony, that the Balkans simply were Turkey's Ireland, an incomprehensible and querulous place whose passions could not be understood by an outside power. But British public opinion was with Gladstone.

If Gladstone's argument prevailed, Devoy reckoned, an Anglo-Russian war would likely follow, for in the Byzantine world of nineteenth-century imperial politics, the Balkans were Russia's backyard, and the Russians would resist a British military intrusion in the region. If a great-power war did break out, one of the sacred tenets of Irish republicanism would be fulfilled. Devoy and his colleagues in Clan na Gael agreed that Ireland and its exiles in America could strike for Irish freedom only when Britain was preoccupied with events elsewhere. The might of the Empire was far too great to consider anything else.

All the while, though, visions of a premature rising, one sparked by a half-cocked revolutionary like Rossa or an unforeseen and uncontrollable event—another famine, perhaps—haunted Devoy's always sporadic sleep. While his public image was, and would continue to be, one of implacable resistance to British rule in Ireland, Devoy privately feared that the wrong signal would send the Irish peasantry marching to slaughter. Discipline, enforced ruthlessly and sparing nobody, would therefore be Devoy's watchword as events unfolded, and the Clan na Gael was to be the vehicle for policing the movement and discrediting those Devoy referred to as "butters-in."

In the fall of 1876, Devoy and the Clan, fresh from their headline-grabbing *Catalpa* adventure, set out to prepare an Irish-American response to the Balkan crisis. Dr. Carroll, the Philadelphia surgeon who succeeded Devoy as chairman of the Clan, wrote Devoy on October 19, 1876, with a contingency plan to begin drilling young Irish-

Americans in case their services were needed in Ireland. "We must be ready to send off 5 to 10,000 men within a month, if required," Carroll wrote, even while expressing, correctly, a guess that Britain would not involve itself in a war on behalf of suffering Bosnians. ("She will bluster, and muster . . . order all hands to be ready for immediate service" and then do nothing, he predicted.)

The Clan had only recently ordered the formation of a General Military Board to train a private militia of Irish-American volunteers for duty in Ireland if and when the time came. But the American wing of the Irish Liberating Army consisted of a mere 39 officers and 552 enlisted men, along with 545 rifles. Another 9 officers and 65 enlisted men were learning the art of war in the U.S. Army or various National Guard units.

At the board's head was an Irish-born Mexican War veteran named F. F. Millen, who fancied himself a general. He had another role that even Devoy, who found him insufferable, never suspected: in the mid-1860s, he had become a paid informant for the British, one of at least two spies who successfully infiltrated the Clan na Gael's highest counsels. His role as a spy was not uncovered for nearly a century.

In the meantime, Devoy and Carroll decided to revisit high international intrigue, no doubt thinking it worked well enough for the *Catalpa* rescue. They once again called on the services of Florida's Senator Conover, who arranged for a Clan delegation to meet with the Russian ambassador to the United States, Shiskin, in Washington.

Devoy, Carroll, and several other Clan members, including the spy Millen and the Clan's founder, *Herald* meteorologist Jerome Collins, trooped to the embassy on November 1, 1876, to discuss the possibility of an Irish-Russian alliance if Russia and Britain went to war. The ambassador's English was poor, so the interview took place in French, giving the French-speaking Devoy the most prominent role as he acted as spokesman and translator. Devoy presented Shiskin with a memoradum outlining the help Ireland could give Russia if the czar's ministers agreed to assist a rebellion in Ireland. The ambassador offered the customary courtesies, promising to send the document to St. Petersburg and offering to continue negotiations through Senator Conover's office.

But he could not resist adding his own analysis, perhaps hoping that this would be the last time he would have to parley with these amateur conspirators. How could they expect Russia to act in the name of Irish independence, he asked, when the Irish themselves gave no indication that they wished separation from Britain? He pointed out that Ireland's members of parliament all swore allegiance to the Queen, and that the loudest demands in Ireland were not for independence but a devolved, federal-style relationship with mainland Britain. With that to consider, Devoy and his colleagues were excused.

It was a moment of utter humiliation, all the more because Devoy had no reply. All of his cold calculations melted in the relentless heat of Shiskin's observation. To an outsider's eye, post-Famine Ireland was not a caldron of revolutionary conspiracy, but a rather content province willing to settle for a few reforms and status within the United Kingdom not unlike that of American states, with their own legislatures and well-defined powers. At the head of Ireland's delegation to Parliament was the gentle Isaac Butt, who won the affections of Devoy and his young Fenian colleagues when he served as their lawyer during the mass arrests of 1866 and 1867. Although he gladly defended Fenians, he was an utterly respectable member of the Anglo-Irish aristocracy who loved the traditions of the House of Commons. In fact, one of Butt's young colleagues, Charles Stewart Parnell, was beginning to lose patience with the grand old man's respectability.

The Clan leaders went home and presumably searched their souls. Devoy certainly did. The visit to the Russian embassy was an epiphany. Devoy concluded that he would have to adjust the Irish-American movement's sails and tack into an utterly unpredictable wind.

As 1876 drew to a close, Devoy's mission in America was becoming clearer than at any other time since the beginning of his exile. The two-year saga of the *Catalpa* rescue concluded in triumph for the Clan, but the movement operated in such shadows that even public victories brought little recognition, thanks in part to the Clan's obsession with secrecy. (When the *Boston Pilot*, edited by Devoy's friend and confidant John Boyle O'Reilly, celebrated the *Catalpa's* victory, it was conspicuously mysterious: "To one devoted man, more than to any other, the whole affair is creditable," the paper wrote of Devoy without mentioning his name.)

To observers such as the Russian ambassdor, then, the Irish

showed no outward signs of discontent. The Irish revolution, in Devoy's own words, existed in "ratholes" of conspiracy at a time when Britain was expanding the voting franchise in Ireland and introducing the secret ballot—freeing voters from the glare of Church and landlord on election day. All the while, newly born public movements were breaking free of the shackles of secrecy and respectability on both sides of the Atlantic. The young landlord Parnell, whose mother was an American and an ardent Irish nationalist, was finding a way to make himself a thorn in British sides using the rules of the House of Commons as his weapon. And in America, voices with Irish accents were speaking out on behalf of their fellow immigrants, huddled in appalling urban slums or risking life and limb in dangerous coal mines. Devoy himself lived amid the squalor that was most Irish immigrants' lot in America. What did the promised freedom of America, and the goal of bringing such freedom to Ireland, mean to the slum dwellers Devoy passed every day in the streets of New York?

It was the Galway-born editor of the New York *Irish World*, Patrick Ford, who first enunciated Irish America's complaints with America's social order. Ford's aggressive belief in Jeffersonian and republican ideals made him, if anything, more American than many of the native-born Anglo-Protestants who regarded Ford's fellow immigrants as aliens. Commenting on the sumptuous wedding of General William T. Sherman's daughter in 1874, the *World* noted that "these elaborate and gorgeous ceremonies are not quite suited to our taste. Nor is the atmosphere surrounding them of a wholesome and vigorous kind. Pomp and pageantry are perfectly in keeping with the customs of monarchial countries . . . but they are not consonant with the genius of the Republic, whose acts are plain and whose airs as ever simple and unpretentious."

As the depression of the 1870s deepened, Ford experienced an epiphany of his own. He turned the *World*'s columns over to sweeping critiques of American society, suggesting that the struggle of working people in America was but an extension of the struggle in Ireland. The newspaper's bile was turned against both American political parties, condemned as tools of Wall Street. "The curse of the whole country now is . . . the Money Lords," the paper announced. "Shall this great country be owned and ruled by and for the whole people, or shall it be controlled by an oligarchy who will devour our sub-

stance?" The *Irish World* soon became not only the preeminent Irish-
American newspaper, with a circulation of thirty-five thousand, but
a trans-ethnic voice of American labor.

Devoy, the onetime member of the First International, was hardly
a stranger to this sort of social activism. His extensive reading list
included the journalism of James Fintan Lalor, a fiery Irish economic
theorist who linked political revolution to the cause of social justice,
specifically land reform. As the Irish in America began to articulate
a worldview of the society around them, Lalor's words, written at the
height of the Famine, took on a new resonance. "Political rights are
but paper and parchment," Lalor wrote in *The Nation* in 1847. "It is
the social constitution that determines the condition and character
of a people." Lalor died when Devoy was a child, but Devoy remembered seeing the funeral and recalled hearing his father expound on
the agitator's genius.

Increasingly, property owners and other princes of capital and
entitlement were assuming for Irish-Americans the same role they had
played for their Irish-born ancestors. The labor organizer P. J. Maguire
noted of the urban poor, Irish and otherwise, that "the majority of
these people have paid by way of rent enough to purchase for themselves not only one house but several, and still after this outlay they
are at the cruel mercy of landlords, who, on failure to pay the month's
rent, will cast them out into the streets homeless and houseless."
Devoy himself was in dire financial straits, later confessing that he
was unable to save so much as a dollar. It was, to say the least, an
ironic position, particularly after he had managed the thousands of
dollars the *Catalpa* rescue had cost.

As Irish-American political thought evolved, and as public men
like Parnell sought a place in Ireland's national debate, Devoy and
his fellow denizens of conspiracy's ratholes were in danger of being
left behind. Evidence of Devoy's disillusionment with traditional revolutionary tactics is evident in a letter from his father in the fall of
1877. "You say you are soberer now and cured of many delusions,"
William wrote, after first expressing his joy that John had ended a
long silence. "I believe that if you were here [in Ireland], the change
could have come sooner. Time and reflection I well know would do
something in that way. I myself have held out hoping nearly as long
as you but Ireland's hour is a long way off." For once, it appeared that

father and son were of one mind, a fact that might have eased William's anxieties as he slipped comfortably into old age, his children scattered across Ireland, Britain, and America. (John's brother Michael emigrated to New Mexico in 1877 to take up ranching.) William told his son that he simply wished "that God will grant me life until your exile is over [so] that I may see you before I go. I have no one that I care to talk with . . . but I won't be alone although my boys and girls are leagues and miles distant. I am always in their midst, thinking of the past, hoping for the future and praying for their temporal and eternal welfare."

Of Devoy's temporal welfare, the best that could be said was that though his hotel room may have been spartan, at least it wasn't one of the thousands of fearsome, unhealthy tenements that housed the bulk of Irish America and fully two-thirds of the city's population in the late 1870s. In the slums of urban America on the eve of the Gilded Age, tiny, airless boxes often housed families of six, seven, or more people in just a couple of rooms. One landlord agent noted that he had charge of two tenements for three years, "and during that time [I] have felt like a man that was committing murder." The streets in these already unhealthy communities were cleaned no more than once a week, an appalling breach of public health in a city of sixty thousand horses producing 2.5 million pounds of manure and sixty thousand gallons of urine every day.

The economic depression that began with the Panic of 1873 had not disappeared with the centennial fireworks. The Carpenters and Joiners union reported that it existed in name only in 1876, owing to the economic inactivity of the trade. Up to 75 percent of the coopers in Brooklyn were out of work in 1876. Hard times brought the classic American reaction—immigrants, who made up 40 percent of New York's 1 million people, were blamed for lower wages, disease, and a general disintegration of cultural and civic life.

Meanwhile, a new class of American royalty was about to take its place in the national pantheon of achievement. Marble mansions were rising along the city's fashionable avenues, and the newly rich—spurned by the old-money crowd that flocked to the Academy of Music on Fourteenth Street—pooled their resources to build the Metropolitan Opera House on Thirtieth and Fifth Avenue as a fitting monument to their wealth. The Vanderbilts, Whitneys, Morgans, and others were staking their claim as the city's new aristocrats, and even as carpenters and coopers and day laborers struggled for work, one sector in the U.S. economy was booming: silk production.

BEGINNING IN THE MONTHS after his humiliation at the Russian embassy, Devoy began to plot out how he might deliver traditional Irish nationalism out of its shadowy existence and link it to the broader agitations that were percolating on both sides of the Atlantic. It was heresy of the first order, and it was bound to create a firestorm of protest from his fellow Fenians wedded to the notion that violence, and only violence, would set Ireland free. As secretary of the seven-member Revolutionary Directory, which linked the Irish Republican Brotherhood in Ireland with the Clan na Gael in America, Devoy himself was a physical-force nationalist of the traditional sort. But unlike Rossa and particularly unlike the aging, infirm IRB leaders, Devoy saw that mere conspiracy was getting nowhere. He continued to carry on an erudite correspondence with Charles Kickham, the novelist and chairman of the IRB's Supreme Council who had been left nearly deaf and blind by a childhood accident, and John O'Leary, the grouchy literary man who chose Paris rather than America as a place of exile. All the while, though, Devoy was planning a strategy that would make the two aging writer-revolutionaries irrelevant.

But first, he had to shore up the movement in places where torrents of embarrassing words and actions had eroded Irish-American credibility. And that meant dealing with the man who remained the most public Irish exile in America, Jeremiah O'Donovan Rossa.

Rossa's weekly list of contributors to the Skirmishing Fund, published in Patrick Ford's Irish World complete with fiery letters and Rossa's equally intemperate annotations, was becoming a public embarrassment, especially in light of the changes Devoy saw coming. The sentiments of Rossa's correspondents no doubt represented a view held by sections of the Irish-American community, but their bluster sounded ridiculous. A Thomas Helen of Texas wrote to Rossa: "England once boasted that she was getting rid of us 'with a vengeance.' Enclosed find $4 to help you send vengeance back."

As the Skirmishing Fund's coffers grew to some $23,000—a sizable sum, and one raised in increments rarely larger than a few dollars—so did Devoy's uneasiness about the unstable Rossa's intentions. The *Irish-American* newspaper described Rossa's ravings as "a series of vague, bombastic and silly propositions for the blowing up of English prisons with dynamite [and] the burning of English cities." Dr. Carroll, the Clan's chairman, wrote that Rossa's rashness "may well give us pause before engaging in anything requiring strict and inviolate secrecy." So when two of the Skirmishing Fund's five trustees resigned in March of 1877, Devoy ruthlessly seized the opportunity, arranging with Dr. Carroll—one of the remaining trustees—to win an appointment to one of the vacant positions. Two of Devoy's allies were added to an expanded trusteeship, so that control of the fund effectively passed into the hands of Clan na Gael, with Rossa retaining the title of secretary of the fund.

In a statement printed in the *Irish World* in April, the new trustees announced that henceforth the Skirmishing Fund would be called the National Fund, which not only was less lurid, but also was more truthful in its advertising. In the coming months, the fund would be used to sponsor lecture tours, secret trips to Ireland, and other public relations and organizing efforts, including a stillborn plan to purchase a daily newspaper in Ireland. These were hardly the uses Rossa had had in mind, though Devoy would soon be funneling thousands of skirmishing dollars to something the Clan's leaders referred to as a "salt-water enterprise." On the banks of the Passaic River in New Jersey, the young inventor John Holland was tinkering with models for an oceangoing submarine that would soon be dubbed the *Fenian Ram*.

With Rossa chastened and, more important, removed from control over the ever-increasing fund, Devoy believed the crisis in America had passed. He turned his attention to Ireland, where the inaction of the Irish Republican Brotherhood's leadership and the gentle ineptness of Isaac Butt's Home Rule Party posed problems of a quite different sort.

In July 1877, Devoy's friend James J. O'Kelly traveled to France after resigning his post at the *Herald* amidst a scandal. For the second time in a matter of a few years, his wife, Harriet, was suing him for divorce, charging him with "unlawful relations" with a woman named Edith Gertrude Bowes, the mother of his son born before his marriage. The divorce received a Victorian-era version of tabloid treatment, thanks in part to O'Kelly's prominence in New York's journalistic community. To his mistress, O'Kelly wrote in 1877 that Harriet "has definitely abandoned me," a curious way of describing the turn of events. "Yesterday in my absence she went to the house and removed all of her property without even leaving a note to say goodbye." He conceded that he felt like "a very bad boy for causing so much sorrow," but insisted that, "after all, I did her no wrong, that is, no great wrong."

O'Kelly's first destination in Europe was Paris, where Edith was living and where their child had been born in 1876, and together the couple sought to establish their son's legitimacy through French law. In the meantime, O'Kelly met with another Irish visitor to the City of Lights, Charles Stewart Parnell, the member of parliament whose own personal complications lay very much in the future. The landed Protestant aristocrat, so often portrayed as aloof from the Irish-Catholics who adored him, apparently connected with O'Kelly, the Irish-Catholic blacksmith's son. Parnell confided to O'Kelly his dream of finding a way to link conservative Irish nationalists with the radical movement in Ireland and America. Whether O'Kelly revealed himself to be a onetime agent of Clan na Gael (he later claimed to have left the movement at this point, only to return to it two years later) is simply one of the dozens of unanswered variations on the question of what Parnell knew and when he knew it.

In a letter to Devoy, O'Kelly sized up his new acquaintance: "[He] is a man of promise, I think he ought to be supported. . . . He has many of the qualities of leadership—and time will give him more. He is cool—extremely so and resolute. With the right kind of support behind him and a band of real nationalists in the House of Commons he would so remould Irish public opinion as to clear away many of the stumbling blocks in the way of progressive action." O'Kelly followed up with another letter after a second meeting with Parnell in London. "I hope the American Irish will extend help and encouragment to Parnell and his co-workers," he wrote.

Devoy took O'Kelly's advice to heart, especially after Dr. Carroll, furnished with Skirmishing Fund money, traveled to Ireland and found the IRB sedentary. Carroll met with Parnell in Dublin on January 15, 1878, after an eventful and tragic morning. Earlier, Parnell had hosted a breakfast for four Fenians newly released from British prisons. One of them, Charles McCarthy, had suffered enormously in prison from heart disease. As the prisoners mingled with Parnell and several colleagues in Morrison's Hotel, McCarthy staggered, then dropped dead, apparently of a massive heart attack.

How much the shock of McCarthy's death affected Parnell is unknown. Within a few hours, however, Parnell made his way to Dr. Carroll's hotel room, where he persuaded the chief agent of the Irish-American revolutionary party that he supported nothing short of national independence for Ireland. Four days later, Parnell took the House of Commons floor to denounce the prison system that had forced McCarthy to work despite his illness. Indignant, he told the House that while Ireland was obliged to help Britain resolve the ongoing crisis in the Balkans, England itself was obliged to offer Ireland self-government—a purposely ambiguous phrase but one whose meaning was capable of inflaming passions. Parnell's speech did not pass without notice.

Back in New York, Devoy was following events closely. He decided great changes were coming, and he was determined to lead the way.

IF FENIANISM WAS TO take on a new and more complex character, however, several obstacles had to be overcome. Their names were Isaac Butt, spokesman for out-of-date conservative nationalism, and Jeremiah O'Donovan Rossa, the unstable champion of thus far merely theoretical violence. Both men blocked the path down which Devoy wished to lead the American Irish and the Irish at home. They would have to be dealt with.

Beginning in November 1877, and continuing into mid-December, Devoy wrote a series of long, painstakingly argued letters to the *Irishman*, a nationalist daily newspaper in Dublin, in which he dismantled Butt's gentle agitation for a federal-style arrangement between Ireland and Britain. The letters were signed simply "An Exile," but one Dublin resident thought he recognized the hardheaded arguments and straightforward prose. In a letter to his son, William Devoy mentioned that the *Irishman* had published correspondence from an anonymous American exile. "They are good letters," William wrote with an obvious wink. "[The] writer understands the subject and puts his ideas in the clearest light." With tongue in cheek, William described the letters as "splendid productions for the son of a peasant."

Devoy's arguments betrayed the still-burning embarrassment of his session with the Russian ambassador. "As far as the outside world can judge . . . the Irish people, or a large portion of them, would seem to be engaged in an agitation for something called 'Home Rule,' and which is explained rather vaguely to mean the substitution of some kind of 'Federal connection' with England," Devoy wrote. If, he continued, "the Irish people have accepted Federalism—that is, if a complete revolution has taken place in their feelings and convictions, let us see the proof of such a sudden and sweeping change. Until such proof is forthcoming the Irish people in America will continue to believe that the heart of the old land is still, as of old, fondly bent on the attainment of complete self-government." Once again a simple but ever-so-complex phrase crept into the debate: *self-government*. What did Devoy mean when he said "complete self-government"? After all, having pledged as a young man to serve an Irish republic, was he not obliged to demand nothing else, and nothing less? Couldn't self-government be interpreted as something other than total independence from Britain?

The *Irishman* letter offers a glimpse of Devoy's pragmatic side, a sharp contrast with his image as the Irish-American movement's sternest ideologue. He could easily have insisted that the "Irish people in America" were "fondly bent" on the attainment of an Irish republic. Instead, he chose to emphasize "self-government," a less threatening phrase. It was over such phrases that Irishmen would go to war with each other in the 1920s.

Devoy concluded his letters to the *Irishman* with a challenge to Parnell, wondering if the young leader and his allies had "thoroughly studied the national Question and thought it out." He asked, "Do they really believe that the battle for Ireland's rights is to be fought on the floor of the House of Commons?"

No, Parnell had not thoroughly studied the national question; in fact, he knew little about Irish history. But he did indeed believe that he could battle for Ireland on the floor of the House of Commons.

And Devoy, seemingly the fire-and-brimstone revolutionary, would soon approve of the unorthodox strategy.

The timing of Devoy's letters was well calculated. In mid-January 1878, shortly after the last letter with its challenge to Parnell was published, the Irish parliamentarians and other activists met at a conference in Dublin. The aging Butt was reelected as head of the Home Rule movement, but Parnell's proposal that the party adopt a more aggressive stance in the House of Commons passed. It was less of a defeat for Butt than it was a message: times and circumstances were changing. Indeed, they were changing ominously, faster than either Parnell or Devoy realized. In the Irish countryside, far from the meeting rooms of Dublin—or those of New York, for that matter—agricultural output was in decline. The potato harvests of 1877 and 1878 were poor. Evictions doubled, and soon the specter of starvation would haunt the country.

In the middle of Devoy's letter-writing campaign against Butt, Rossa was once again scandalizing public opinion in America. In his column in the *Irish World*, Rossa took to discussing the latest innovations in chemical poisons, and the means by which such products could be introduced on the very House of Commons floor where Parnell hoped to fight Ireland's battle. On December 2, 1877, Devoy and his colleagues sent a letter to the *Irish World*'s Patrick Ford, demanding that they be given the right to review Rossa's column before publication. Ford apparently refused. But after Rossa justified the assassination of Canadian politician Thomas D'Arcy McGee, a one-time Fenian who became a critic of Irish militants, Devoy resigned as a trustee of the National Fund, saying that he didn't "propose to fritter my life away in endless squabbles nor do I think it safe to go into serious revolutionary work with men who can't keep a secret. Neither will I have my name associated with the childish rigmarole which appears in the *Irish World*."

Devoy reconsidered and withdrew his resignation when Rossa sent a penitent letter, but peace lasted only a few weeks. In late March, Rossa was on a deep bender. He walked out on his third wife and talked about changing his name and moving to Australia. His hotel had failed, and Devoy was receiving reports of Rossa staggering in and out of saloons along Park Row, near the *Herald*'s office. His col-

umn disappeared from the *Irish World* for a month. In going through
Rossa's Skirmishing/National Fund records, Devoy discovered that re-
ceipts were missing and money was unaccounted for, and he feared
that "any vindictive man who has subscribed even $1" would com-
mence a lawsuit and place the funds beyond the trustees' reach.

Indeed, one such suit had already been filed by a Clan na Gael
man who charged the fund owed him money for a trip he had made
to Ireland. He sought an injunction that would have placed the funds
under the supervision of New York's state courts. More than $43,000
was at stake. On March 25, Devoy met with Rossa, found him sober
(which, Devoy said, made matters worse), and then vowed to go public with charges of mismanagement of the fund if Rossa continued to
withhold money from the trustees. The threat worked. As for Rossa,
Devoy arranged to have him put away in a convent in Madison, New
Jersey, for rehabilitation. Devoy's action was decisive, ruthless, and
probably necessary for the health and well-being of the cause and of
Rossa himself. Still, it was a delicate business, for Rossa not only was
an old friend and a man who had suffered mightily, both during the
Famine and in prison, but he had also loaned Devoy money in the
mid-1870s. While Rossa was recuperating, Devoy forwarded payments
on his debt to Rossa's wife in the not-insubstantial sum of $10 a week,
although there were weeks when he had to skip a payment. In a letter
to Mary Rossa dated July 26, 1878, Devoy apologized for missing a
payment and gave a hint of his dire finances: "I have been unable to
send any money, as I know no one who has any to spare. I enclose
twenty dollars, which is all I have left after paying my board and a
couple of small bills."

Nine days after dispatching the letter to Mrs. Rossa, Devoy was
at his desk at the *Herald* when a tall, one-armed stranger appeared in
the newsroom. He was looking for James J. O'Kelly, who had sorted
out his personal affairs in Europe and had returned to New York and
the *Herald*.

The stranger's name was Michael Davitt, a Fenian convict newly
released from Britain's hideous Dartmoor Prison, one of several penal
institutions he had served in for nearly seven terrible years. During a
stretch in Millbank prison, he spotted the name of John Devoy carved
out in block letters on the wooden doorframe of his cell.

Davitt was a London-based operative for the Irish Republican

Brotherhood when he was arrested in 1870, and he had immediately rejoined the movement upon his release from prison. He was thirty-two years of age, a native of County Mayo whose family was driven off their rented land during the Famine. From the horrors of the Famine, the Davitts entered the cauldron of Britain's Industrial Revolution, equally cruel. They found a home in an Irish ghetto in the textile town of Haslingden, near Manchester, where they again suffered the ignominy of eviction.

When he was nine years old, Michael went to the local mills to work, as was the fashion in Victorian Britain. He worked twelve hours a day, six days a week, for eighteen months, until on May 8, 1857, he was ordered to work on a piece of processing machinery. Half an hour into the assignment, a piece of cotton became lodged in the machine, and eleven-year-old Michael, standing on his tiptoes, tried to clear it. His right arm became tangled in the machine. It was amputated a week later, after infection had set in.

Davitt's appearance at the Herald on a Sunday evening came after a long day of taking in the city before heading off to see his mother and sister, now living in Pennsylvania. O'Kelly was the only person Davitt knew in New York, the two having met in Dublin the previous January. After O'Kelly and Davitt renewed their friendship in the Herald's office, O'Kelly immediately introduced Davitt to Devoy. The two men had an instant rapport, and when Devoy's shift ended at 4 A.M. Monday morning, they piled into a train to Philadelphia and a scheduled meeting of the Clan na Gael executive in Dr. Carroll's house.

So was born a memorable but short-lived partnership that would shake British rule in Ireland to its foundation and create in America for the first time a disciplined, effective, and broad-based movement on behalf of the Irish people. The American Irish were about to stride down the path whose briers and brambles Devoy had spent nearly a year clearing.

CHAPTER EIGHT

For Erin's Sake

IF JOHN DEVOY HAD DIED IN 1882, HIS CAREER OF CEASELESS AGI-
tation cut short by nearly a half century, he would nevertheless have
earned a prominent place in the history of America's fight for Irish
freedom. The years 1878 to 1882 produced in Ireland one of the
nineteenth century's greatest social revolutions, and it was founded,
to a great extent, upon the partnership Devoy formed with Michael
Davitt in America during the summer and fall of 1878.

Devoy's two years of self-reflection and strategic maneuvers had
prepared the Irish-American revolutionary movement for a change
that was, in a word, revolutionary. Irish independence itself was not
enough, he decided, because mere independence would be pointless
without sweeping social change In a society where the vast majority
of people farmed land they did not own and lived in constant fear of
eviction, the most important social change was land reform.

Many scholars have attributed Devoy's conversion to agrarian
revolution and social reform as little more than transparent oppor-
tunism, a hard-line revolutionary's determination to grasp any weapon
with which to crack British skulls. That is too simple a view.

Clearly, Devoy never wavered in his goal of ridding Ireland of
British rule. And he would one day condemn with characteristic invective those Irish and Irish-American reformers who seemed, in his
view, more concerned about saving humanity than with fighting for
Irish freedom. But the philosophy he expounded in late 1878 demonstrated that he was keenly aware that genuine freedom required
more than an exchange of political leaders, Irish for English. "The

best friend of the national cause . . . is the man who . . . does his best to lift his countrymen out of the slough of poverty, degradation and despair," he wrote. His experience in Gilded Age America, with its vast social inequities, surely had taught him that. In rejecting mere revolution and conspiracy, he was leading Irish-American nationalism into the wider world of social protest and progressive reform.

In 1878, the Clan na Gael had fewer than ten thousand members at a time when the Irish born population in America was approaching two million. Of course, as a secretive, oath-bound organization pledged to support violent revolution in Ireland, the Clan had no intentions of becoming a mass movement. Still, it was in danger of becoming insignificant as thousands of discontented, working-class Irish-Americans joined the fledgling labor movement and hundreds of thousands joined mainstream fraternal organizations that would have nothing to do with those who talked flippantly about sending skirmishers into British cities.

All the while, as Irish-Americans came to dominate such cities as New York and Boston, the laws of democracy and ethnic politics were taking effect. In 1880, New York elected its first Irish-Catholic mayor, William Grace. In 1882, Boston sent the first Irish-Catholic to Congress, Patrick Collins. The possibilities for Irish nationalists in wider American life were personified by Terence Powderly, the son of Irish immigrants who worked the bleak coal mines of northeast Pennsylvania. As a young man, Powderly helped found the heavily Irish-Catholic Knights of Labor, was elected mayor of Scranton, and served several years as the national treasurer of Clan na Gael. Powderly's career suggested an intersection of Irish nationalism with the broader currents of American life.

In Devoy's mind, the time had come for what he would soon call a New Departure in Irish politics. As other historians have pointed out, the phrase New Departure had been used before, and in fact, Devoy's strategy of bringing radical nationalists into the political mainstream was not original. Parnell, as he told Devoy's friend O'Kelly, was already trying to arrange a marriage between constitutional reformers in Ireland and revolutionists like Devoy in America.

What was utterly original about Devoy's proposition, however, was the way in which he applied it to American politics. Once he opened the blinds on America's fight for Ireland, priests, politicians, reformers, and the rank and file turned the Irish-American movement from a cult of conspiracy into a mass movement reflecting not only the exiles' concern for those they left behind, but the larger discontents of American workers.

The new terms of engagement unfolded slowly, city by city, as Michael Davitt toured the United States under the sponsorship of Devoy and Clan na Gael. In New York, Boston, Philadelphia, and other centers of Irish America, Davitt spoke not only about Ireland's claim to nationhood—and Davitt, like Devoy, certainly remained committed to the possibility of violent revolution—but also about the Irish peasant's claim on the land he tilled and from which he drew his sustenance. Here, then, was evidence of Devoy's influence on Davitt and the movement itself. When Davitt returned to New York on September 23, 1878, after a brief holiday in Cape May, New Jersey, and a quick swing through New England, he met with Devoy and other Clan leaders at Sweeney's Hotel on Chatham Street, near the heart of Five Points. Devoy proposed a series of resolutions to which, he said, the assembled leaders ought to agree. The first resolution, that Ireland had a right to national independence, was not extraordinary, considering the makeup of the crowd.

The next few resolutions, however, showed the extent to which Devoy sought to change the parameters of Irish America's patriot games. One resolution declared that the land of Ireland belonged to the people of Ireland alone. A second, companion resolution stated that "the only final solution of the Irish Land Question is the abolition of landlordism." Until now, radical agrarian reform was never a part of the Fenians' emphasis on political revolution.

Public evidence of Devoy's influence as the theorist of a new Irish movement came three weeks after the conference in Sweeney's Hotel. On October 13, Davitt was scheduled to lecture in Brooklyn before heading out for the western swing of his tour. Again, Davitt met with Devoy and other Clan members before the lecture to discuss a draft of his speech. Davitt's draft, with its approving references to a mild land-reform program, was far too tepid for Devoy. Davitt rewrote his speech to make it more in line with Devoy's suggestions.

Once at the podium, however, Davitt realized to his horror that he had brought the wrong speech. Distracted, he delivered a disjointed hodgepodge, some of it from the draft Devoy had rejected.

Davitt's left hand shook as he held his notes, and he abruptly stopped speaking and left the stage. From the crowd rose a cry for Devoy, who was not prepared to speak and had, at this point, only limited experience as a public speaker. Congressman William Robinson, the evening's chairman, brought Devoy to the podium. The reluctant speaker glanced down at the front row and saw a thundercloud forming on the face of Patrick Ford. America's most influential Irish editor, who had identified land as the essential Irish question years before, was not a happy man. A bad review in the *Irish World* could have put a quick end to Davitt's lecture tour, the proving ground of Devoy's new nationalism.

Devoy started gingerly, making a few weak jokes and offering a tactful endorsement of Davitt's lecture. He added, however, that "there are some portions of it that require further elaboration and plainer speaking." Devoy strengthened Davitt's muddled argument with a veiled reference to his embarrassment at the Russian embassy two years before. "I think we have remained in the background too long and allowed the country to be misrepresented," he said, referring, of course, to Ireland. What would happen, he asked, if England and Russia were to go to war over Afghanistan, the latest crossroads of imperial ambition. "In that event—or rather before that event—it would be the duty of the national leaders, if they know their business, to appeal to Russia for help and recognition. What answer do you think they would get from the Russians . . . ? [The Irish leaders] would be talked to in this way: 'Gentlemen, we have no doubt of your sincerity, but you are only a small party, you don't represent Ireland.' " The only solution for nationalists, he said, was complete participation in public life.

Davitt had said as much, but without Devoy's passion. And Davitt had barely touched on the land question, the issue closest to the heart of chief onlooker Patrick Ford. So Devoy moved on to amplify:

"The land question is the question of questions in Ireland, and the one upon which the national party must speak out in the plainest language." Until now, the establishment of a republic was, in Fenian circles, deemed the "question of questions" in Ireland, and indeed it remained so with the aging revolutionaries in Ireland itself. "I think the only true solution of the land question is the abolition of land-lordism," Devoy continued.

Voices from the crowded shouted, "That's it!"

Devoy went on, "The landlord system is the greatest curse inflicted by England on Ireland, and Ireland will never be prosperous or happy until it is rooted out. The land of Ireland belongs to the people of Ireland and to them alone, and we must not be afraid to say so. . . . I believe in Irish independence, but I don't think it would be worthwhile to free Ireland if that foreign landlord system were left standing."

Such sentiments would set off a firestorm among Devoy's allies in the Irish Republican Brotherhood. John O'Leary, the IRB leader in exile in Paris, told Devoy that "it seems to some people in Ireland that in this matter ye have been led astray now by Mr. Davitt." O'Leary had it exactly backward.

"I regret beyond measure what you have said," O'Leary added, saying that the matter required "a few hours' talk," which was a broad hint to Devoy to begin packing his bags and booking a ticket on the next ship to France. On the American side of the Atlantic, however, observers were far more sanguine. The *Irish World* reported that Devoy's speech concluded "amid a storm of applause," and that the audience was "highly pleased." Clearly the *World*'s editor was. As Devoy left the platform, he crossed paths with Ford, who said that after listening to Davitt, he had been fully prepared to condemn both speaker and cause. Devoy's hard line, however, convinced him otherwise.

Did Devoy mean what he said? There is little reason to think otherwise, especially considering Devoy's genuine identification of landlordism as one of the tools with which Britain had battered Ireland, and his hazy belief that somewhere in the misty past there was a Gaelic Ireland untainted by grubby Saxon hands, where, as he said in Brooklyn, "the land belonged to the people, the land belonged to the clan." Peasant proprietary, that is, peasant ownership of the land, was to become the social question around which Devoy would rally Irish America.

Devoy now set out on a path he hoped would lead to an alliance with, ironically enough, the aristocratic Anglo-Protestant landlord who was creating such a stir in Ireland.

Just over a week after Devoy's Brooklyn speech, the Home Rule Confederation of Great Britain, a moderate Irish nationalist group, reelected Parnell as its president despite Isaac Butt's public objections. According to accounts of the meeting that Devoy monitored as they crossed the *Herald*'s foreign desk, the confederation's action amounted to a public split between the ambitious Parnell and the aging Butt. It was nothing of the sort, but Devoy thought a decisive moment had been reached. After hurried conversations with his Clan colleagues, he composed a telegram to be sent to Parnell through Charles Kickham, the deaf and blind novelist at the head of the moribund Irish Republican Brotherhood.

The telegram of October 24, signed by the leaders of Clan na Gael, including Devoy, read:

Nationalists here will support you on following conditions:

(1) Abandonment of federal demand [and] substitution [of] general declaration in favour of self-government;
(2) vigorous agitation of land question on the basis of peasant proprietary, while accepting concessions tending to abolish arbitrary eviction;
(3) exclusion of all sectarian issues from platform;
(4) [Irish] members to vote together on all imperial and home questions, adopt aggressive policy and energetically resist all coercive legislation;
(5) advocacy of all struggling nationalities in British Empire and elsewhere.

The five-point program was a heavy-handed assault on Butt, the chief advocate of a federal-style solution to Ireland's national demands, who sought moderate solutions to the land question, who was willing to fund Catholic-only schools (although he himself was Protestant), and whose Irish colleagues in Parliament formed an undisciplined and divided party. But the specific positions were less important than the general policy, for Devoy was proposing nothing less than a coming together between men Britain regarded as terrorists and a man pledged to constitutional politics.

Devoy arranged to have the telegram published in the *Herald* on October 25, and two days later, the paper's Sunday edition carried a long story on page 1 bearing the headline: "An Irish New Departure."

The story had no byline, common practice in American newspapers at the time, but there was little doubt about the author's identity. The story consisted of interviews with Devoy's allies, all of whom, rather unsurprisingly, thought the New Departure was a terrific idea. "The *Herald* reporter found everywhere a desire to unite with the advanced Home Rulers . . . and grapple with the land question," the account read. (If Devoy found this sentiment everywhere, it was because he knew where to find it.) The article concluded, "The feeling against Irish landlordism the reporter found to be very intense, and a desire almost universally expressed that the whole system should be swept away. . . . Fenianism, as people will persist in calling the extreme form of Irish nationality, seems really to be about to take a 'new departure' [and] the reporter was assured that lively times are ahead."

In the Midwestern swing of his tour, Davitt was appalled when he read press acounts of Devoy's action. He wasn't opposed to any of the principles enunciated. He simply thought such a public appeal to a member of parliament from a band of American revolutionaries was intemperate at best and the possible ruin of Parnell at worst.

The telegram's contents and the debate it inspired on both sides of the Atlantic were the talk of the Irish press, thanks to the publicity Devoy gave it in the *Herald*. The phrase New Departure would soon become affixed to Devoy's name in the Irish press. Parnell's breezy pose when asked a decade later about Devoy and the New Departure is revealing for its lawyerly language. "The New Departure, I understand to mean, if I ever heard the meaning, I understand the term New Departure to mean the formation of the Land League movement, combining the agrarian and political question," Parnell told a government commission in 1889. When the government's lawyer suggested, correctly, that the New Departure was in fact meant as a combining of the physical force nationalists in America with constitutionalists like himself, Parnell replied with practiced outrage: "Certainly not. My definition of the New Departure, as far as I ever heard the expression used in Ireland, and I cannot say I ever heard it used frequently in Ireland, if at all, is that it was a combination of the political with the agrarian movement."

If Parnell hadn't heard the expression used much, if at all, in Ireland, he wasn't reading the newspapers in late 1878. In a letter to the *Freeman's Journal*, Devoy noted that his name had been mentioned frequently "in connection with the so-called New Departure." Two widely read Dublin-based dailies gave it prominent and constant coverage. The *Freeman's Journal* tentatively embraced it, while the *Irishman*, owned and edited by a nationalist journalist named Richard Pigott, denounced it regularly as a betrayal of Irish nationalism. Pigott's sentiments reflected the opinions of Kickham, O'Leary, and other top IRB leaders.

The possibility of a disastrous split between the Irish and American factions arose in late November, when the Clan na Gael's executive board approved Devoy's program. The Clan and the IRB were supposed to act in concert, which was why the two groups had a joint Revolutionary Directory. The situation demanded, as O'Leary hinted in his letter, prolonged discussion. Davitt decided to return to Ireland to champion the new program to the IRB's governing body, the Supreme Council, of which Davitt himself was a member. Davitt urged Devoy to come with him.

Devoy was in line for a promotion at the *Herald*, and a prolonged absence, as this promised to be, would do neither his career nor his finances any good. He decided to go with Davitt anyway. The Clan designated him an envoy to the IRB, and plans were made for him to join the IRB's executives at a conference in France, far from the eyes of British intelligence. The Clan further authorized him to determine the strength and competency of the IRB in Ireland and Britain. This set of instructions carried with it even greater dangers than a stalled career. Under terms of his amnesty agreement, Devoy was barred from entering Ireland until the expiration of his fifteen-year sentence in February 1882. If he was spotted in Ireland, he would be subject to immediate arrest and imprisonment.

He asked for a three-month unpaid leave of absence from the *Herald*, telling his bosses that he planned to visit his brother Michael, who had recently emigrated from Ireland to New Mexico. The paper's managing editor didn't believe him. "Going to Ireland?" he asked in a whisper. Devoy denied it. The editor merely smiled and winked.

Devoy met often with Davitt in early December 1878 as they plotted out the next phrase of their partnership. Davitt, they decided, would go to Ireland, gather information, then meet Devoy in France in mid-January, when the two of them would state their case to the IRB's Supreme Council. Davitt then joined O'Kelly and Carroll in escorting Devoy to his ship, the French steamship *Canada*, as it set sail for Le Havre on December 11, 1878. On his way across the Atlantic, he drafted a long letter to the editor of the *Freeman's Journal*, lashing back at Ireland's critics of the New Departure. "All intelligent Irishmen feel that the entrance in the everyday political life of the country of a large class of men with strong opinions and habits of organizations . . . who have hitherto held aloof from it . . . would be an event that would largely influence the future of Ireland," he wrote from his cabin. He described the program as a "combination between all sections of Irish nationalists"—the very description Parnell would later reject as a definition of the New Departure. And he again sounded the theme of land reform, saying that no party could win the support of Ireland without pledging itself to "radical" reform.

In closing, he acknowledged that many of his opponents objected to the New Departure because it had been formulated in America, not in Ireland. The complaint of "dictation from America" had been raised in the hostile Irish press, he noted, and to that complaint Devoy answered simply, "These gentlemen must pardon me if I respectfully refuse the honour of being classed as an American." In his own eyes, he remained an exile, defiantly unassimilated, but willing to use American politics and American public opinion to achieve his ends.

He arrived in Paris a few days before Christmas, checking in and out of two hotels under assumed names to throw off any secret pursuers. He mailed his letter to the *Freeman's Journal*, cashed a check with the help of a fellow passenger he had befriended while aboard the *Canada*, and finally checked into the Hôtel des Missions Étrangers under his real name. He had stayed at the hotel, which he described as a haunt of priests and poor aristocrats, when he was in Paris in 1861 to join the Foreign Legion. Davitt joined him on January 10, looking weary. Devoy suggested he take a glass of wine, but Davitt had what Devoy called a "morbid" fear of alcohol, believing that one drink would turn him into an alcoholic. Devoy countered by pointing to the healthy Parisians who looked none the worse for their wine-drinking. The argument was irrefutable, and Davitt agreed to drink wine with his meals. In two weeks, Devoy noticed a marked improvement in Davitt's health and appearance.

The leaders of the Irish Republican Brotherhood assembled in a private room in Paris on Sunday, February 19, for what promised to be a historic session. The Supreme Council consisted of eleven members, seven of whom represented various geographic regions in Britain and Ireland. Davitt, for example, was the member for northern England. Devoy was the only nonmember present; he was allowed to sit in on the meetings as the accredited envoy of the IRB's brother in revolution, the Clan na Gael.

Charles Kickham, as president of the IRB, was chairman of the meeting. He was much beloved, mostly for his sentimental novel *Knocknagow*, but his presence in the chair only made for great confusion. His vision and his hearing were so poor that the proceedings had to be conveyed to him by spelling out words on the fingers of his left hand. One member of the council, John O'Connor, was skilled in such translations, and Devoy, who knew the power translators could wield, immediately set out to learn what was called, in the less sensitive nineteenth century, the deaf and dumb alphabet. After one night's instruction, he was able to communicate his own thoughts to Kickham. Davitt similarly tried to learn the language, but with only one arm to use, he was handicapped himself and gave up in disgust.

In the midst of one increasingly tense session, Davitt's remarks were either taken out of context or otherwise misinterpreted in translation. Kickham immediately clenched his left fist, which cut off O'Connor's communications, and lit into Davitt. Kickham's allies on the council did likewise, "with more zeal than discretion," Devoy reported, and Davitt burst into tears and ran from the room. Devoy tried to explain to Kickham that there had been some sort of misunderstanding, but Kickham refused to release his fingers. Devoy gave up and went after Davitt. It was midnight, and the two men walked to their hotel, talking over the crisis. In the morning, a message arrived from John O'Leary, imploring the two men to return to the sessions. They did, and in Devoy's words, they discovered that the "thundercloud had passed."

The council was in session for a week, and when it was over, the IRB decided that it would not, after all, participate in parliamentary elections, nor would it participate in agrarian agitation. It seemed to be a devastating defeat for Devoy and Davitt, yet neither man considered it so at the time. They had won a small point—the IRB did agree that a public body was necessary to carry on public agitation—although nothing would come of the proposal.

As if to demonstrate that he had not given up on revolution entirely, Devoy proposed, and the IRB ratified, the joint financing of a gunrunning scheme designed to put modern rifles in the hands of the IRB's twenty-five thousand members with American help. The plan called for individual IRB members to purchase rifles from the Clan na Gael for one pound apiece, although they would cost the Clan, Devoy figured, about two and a half pounds each. To make up the deficit, Devoy wrote to his Clan brethren, urging that they "put [their] shoulders to the wheel" to raise funds. Of the one-pound charge, he wrote, "That price is really as much as the men can pay, on the average, and many can't pay at all, so that somebody must pay it for them or they will never get them." Carroll, head of Clan na Gael, put out a call for $25,000 to help pay for the weapons. But the key, Devoy said, would be finding somebody to manage the smuggling of so many guns into Ireland, probably from Britain itself.

After the meeting broke up, the French-speaking Devoy indulged himself in several weeks of wine, cigars, and sight-seeing in and around Paris. "The work has been difficult in many ways," he wrote to his friend James Reynolds in New Haven, "but of course the life I lead is a great improvement to that I spent in New York. Personally it has done me a great amount of good." Devoy joined Kickham and O'Leary, both of whom stayed on briefly in Paris, for a train ride to Dieppe that turned into an unscheduled tour of the cathedral towns of Amiens and Rouen. (The amicable trip with two men who opposed the New Departure demonstrates a magnanimous side to Devoy that he rarely showed.) And O'Leary and Devoy together spent several days touring the countryside, with O'Leary often mistaken for an Englishman in his tweed suit.

When Devoy returned to Paris on February 11, 1879, after seeing Kickham off at Dieppe, Devoy found a letter awaiting him from Davitt.

Parnell, Davitt said, wished to cross the Channel to meet Devoy.

CHAPTER NINE

Hark, a Voice Like Thunder

TALL AND BEARDED, WITH THE BEARING AND MANNER OF THE landed aristocrat that he most certainly was, Charles Stewart Parnell was about the become the latest unlikely vehicle for the passions of Irish-American nationalism. He admittedly knew little of the Irish history that Devoy was raised on like mother's milk. He was educated in Britain, he was Protestant, he was a landlord, he was a model of a Victorian squire, and he was a member of parliament.

For all those reasons, the British came to regard him as far more dangerous than any Irishman who had preceded him in the House of Commons. He could not be caricatured as an emotional and unstable Celtic chieftain. He spoke the English language like an Englishman, yet wore his Anglophobia like the heirloom it was. His grandfather, U.S. Navy commodore Charles Stewart, had sunk two British warships off the coast of Portugal near the end of the War of 1812, and his great-grandfather had fought in the American Revolution. The commodore's daughter, Delia, was born in America and married a British-born squire named John Parnell.

Though there was nothing Celtic about him, Charles Stewart Parnell was reminiscent of a figure from Celtic mythology, a shapeshifter. He was a parliamentarian on one hand, a man with whom William Gladstone decided he could do business. Yet he traveled with American Irish revolutionaries and was a man with whom John Devoy decided to do business. Which was the true Parnell? In fact, he was both.

He was thirty-three years old in 1879, and not yet fully in command of the legions of Irish and Irish-Americans who would rally to his banner. Isaac Butt was still the putative head of the Irish Parliamentary Party, but his days on earth were numbered. As Parnell crossed the English Channel to Boulogne for his appointment with Devoy, he clearly was the heir apparent to the leadership of a party that had grown out of touch. Parnell, in O'Kelly's words, wasn't sure where he was heading, but he knew he wanted to go somewhere.

Parnell and a fellow member of Parliament, Joseph Biggar, stepped off a steamship in Boulogne sometime in early March. Devoy and John O'Leary—the adamant opponent of Devoy's New Departure—were at dockside to greet them.

After a few minutes of small talk, the foursome repaired to a local hotel, where they engaged a private room for dinner and negotiations. From the parliamentary side, Biggar did most of the talking while Parnell remained characteristically silent. Biggar was once a member of the Irish Republican Brotherhood. He also was once a Presbyterian, but now was both a member of parliament and a Roman Catholic. Devoy seized on the latter conversion with a wink:

"Mr. Biggar, I am sorry you turned Catholic. You were a great deal more use to us as a Presbyterian. Now your conversion will be pointed to as a warning to young Protestants of Nationalist leanings to keep away from us, lest the Pope should get hold of them."

Biggar, in the way of converts, launched into a long theological dissertation, the gist of which was that he couldn't abide the Presbyterian belief in predestination. And besides, he asked of the Catholic Devoy, what of his immortal soul?

"Oh, I'd be willing to see you damned for the sake of Ireland," Devoy replied.

During the rest of the dinner and at breakfast the following morning, the revolutionary journalist and the squire-politician exchanged views in a manner Devoy would later describe as "candid."

While no formal agreement was reached, Devoy claimed that the talks cleared the way for Clan na Gael's support for Parnell and for the Clan to provide the Irish with what were called, invariably, the "sinews of war," meaning money and arms. And, Devoy said, Parnell said he would "go with the Irish people to the fullest limit in breaking up the existing form of connection with England."

The "Cuba Five" pose just after landing in New York in 1871. From left to right: John Devoy (at age 28), Charles Underwood O'Connell, Henry Mulleda, Jeremiah O'Donovan Rossa, and John McClure.

In a photograph taken on the roof of the Waldorf-Astoria, John Devoy sits in front of Eamon De Valera. To Devoy's left are Harry Boland and Liam Mellows. To his right are Diarmuid Lynch and Dr. Patrick McCartan.

(COURTESY OF THE AMERICAN IRISH HISTORICAL SOCIETY)

Tom Clarke, John Devoy's former assistant.

(COURTESY OF THE NATIONAL MUSEUM OF IRELAND)

John Boyle O'Reilly was a journalist, poet, and intellectual in Boston. He was a close ally of John Devoy until his untimely death in 1890.

(COURTESY OF THE NATIONAL MUSEUM OF IRELAND)

Patrick Egan, the onetime treasurer of the Land League, became John Devoy's bitter enemy. After the Easter Rebellion, Egan said that Devoy should have been shot.

(COURTESY OF THE NATIONAL MUSEUM OF IRELAND)

Michael Davitt, John Devoy's ally at the time of the New Departure and the Land War.

(COURTESY OF THE NATIONAL MUSEUM OF IRELAND)

John Devoy (left) and his friend John Daly in 1898.

(COURTESY OF THE AMERICAN IRISH HISTORICAL SOCIETY)

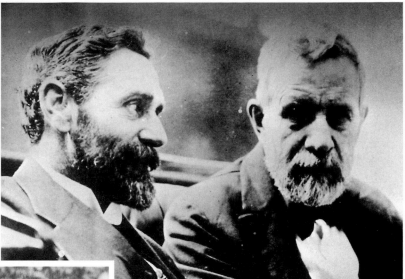

Roger Casement and John Devoy in 1914.

John Devoy with three-year-old Charlie
McLoughlin in the mid-1920s.

The American flag that flew from the mast of the *Catalpa* in 1876.

British troops in action in Dublin in 1920.

After the 1916 Easter Rebellion, John Devoy helped organize a bazaar in Madison Square Garden to raise money for families of prisoners and those who were shot.

POBLACHT NA H EIREANN.

THE PROVISIONAL GOVERNMENT
OF THE
IRISH REPUBLIC
TO THE PEOPLE OF IRELAND.

IRISHMEN AND IRISHWOMEN: In the name of God and of the dead generations from which she receives her old tradition of nationhood, Ireland, through us, summons her children to her flag and strikes for her freedom.

Having organised and trained her manhood through her secret revolutionary organisation, the Irish Republican Brotherhood, and through her open military organisations, the Irish Volunteers and the Irish Citizen Army, having patiently perfected her discipline, having resolutely waited for the right moment to reveal itself, she now seizes that moment, and, supported by her exiled children in America and by gallant allies in Europe, but relying in the first on her own strength, she strikes in full confidence of victory.

We declare the right of the people of Ireland to the ownership of Ireland, and to the unfettered control of Irish destinies, to be sovereign and indefeasible. The long usurpation of that right by a foreign people and government has not extinguished the right, nor can it ever be extinguished except by the destruction of the Irish people. In every generation the Irish people have asserted their right to national freedom and sovereignty; six times during the past three hundred years they have asserted it in arms. Standing on that fundamental right and again asserting it in arms in the face of the world, we hereby proclaim the Irish Republic as a Sovereign Independent State, and we pledge our lives and the lives of our comrades-in-arms to the cause of its freedom, of its welfare, and of its exaltation among the nations.

The Irish Republic is entitled to, and hereby claims, the allegiance of every Irishman and Irishwoman. The Republic guarantees religious and civil liberty, equal rights and equal opportunities to all its citizens, and declares its resolve to pursue the happiness and prosperity of the whole nation and of all its parts, cherishing all the children of the nation equally, and oblivious of the differences carefully fostered by an alien government, which have divided a minority from the majority in the past.

Until our arms have brought the opportune moment for the establishment of a permanent National Government, representative of the whole people of Ireland and elected by the suffrages of all her men and women, the Provisional Government, hereby constituted, will administer the civil and military affairs of the Republic in trust for the people.

We place the cause of the Irish Republic under the protection of the Most High God, Whose blessing we invoke upon our arms, and we pray that no one who serves that cause will dishonour it by cowardice, inhumanity, or rapine. In this supreme hour the Irish nation must, by its valour and discipline and by the readiness of its children to sacrifice themselves for the common good, prove itself worthy of the august destiny to which it is called.

Signed on Behalf of the Provisional Government,

THOMAS J. CLARKE.

SEAN Mac DIARMADA,   THOMAS MacDONAGH,
P. H. PEARSE,   EAMONN CEANNT,
JAMES CONNOLLY.   JOSEPH PLUNKETT.

The Easter Proclamation. Tom Clarke, John Devoy's former assistant, was the first to sign it.

DEVOY NOW TURNED HIS attention to the work of revolution. He prepared for his risky tour of Ireland and Britain to determine the fitness and strength of the various IRB brigades that he hoped to outfit with weapons. He decided that the Clan na Gael should consider manufacturing its own weapons in America, rather than rely on store-bought varieties from various agents.

He sailed from France to England in late March 1879, beginning a four-month stay in Britain and Ireland. He attended IRB meetings in London and Newcastle upon Tyne and came away impressed with the fervor of men he called "half-breeds"—the products of Anglo-Irish marriages who had been drawn into the Irish revolutionary movement. He toured the Irish brigades in Scotland, where he assured IRB members that the New Departure did not mean an end to the work of revolution.

On April 1, he boarded a boat that took him to the Irish port city of Waterford. His first order of business was a reunion with his father. Devoy took a circuitous route up the Irish east coast from Waterford to Dublin as a precaution against detectives, and he arrived at a prearranged hotel in Dublin in early evening. He knew better than to lodge in his father's home. The police, after all, had almost caught him there once before.

He had not seen the city of his childhood since 1867, and he took the opportunity to stroll to the center of town, where nostalgia overtook him. Thirty-year-old memories of his mother came to him as he walked along Dublin's main thoroughfare, Sackville Street. "I had stood there [in the center of the street] with my right hand firmly in my mother's in 1849 on the night before Queen Victoria paid her first visit to Dublin, and my mother turned away in disgust at the blaze of illuminations," Devoy wrote. The Queen's visit had come after millions had died or been exiled during the Great Famine.

Devoy recorded nothing of the reunion with his father, save to note that he and his father invited Davitt to share an Easter Sunday meal with them on April 13. The week before, on Palm Sunday, Devoy and Davitt dined with Parnell at Morrison's Hotel. Parnell's two guests arrived separately and by different routes as a precaution against surveillance. When Devoy suggested that they dine in a private room to spare Parnell the scandal that would ensue if anybody recognized Devoy, Parnell insisted on the public dining room, saying that a private meeting would suggest conspiracy where none existed.

Davitt came to the meeting with urgent news about deteriorating conditions in the traditionally poor counties in the west of Ireland, particularly in his native county of Mayo. As Devoy listened intently, Davitt explained that agrarian agitation could help the national cause. Parnell declined to commit himself.

Devoy's agenda consisted strictly of widening and enlarging the New Departure program of enlisting nationalists of all kinds into the constitutional ranks of conventional politics. Devoy knew the IRB had rejected such participation, but, he told Parnell, the nationalists in America were all for it. The point could not have been lost on Parnell, for it was becoming clear that America and American money were becoming the driving force in the new Irish politics the three men were trying to shape.

They parted with nothing concrete to show for their discussions except a solidified relationship and the assurance that they would meet again. Parnell invited Devoy to join him for a few days at one of his hunting lodges in the Wicklow Mountains—an act of hospitality that the local constabulary might have described as harboring a fugitive—but Devoy tactfully declined, explaining that his work would keep him on the run. His work, of course, consisted of organizing the forces of insurrection throughout Ireland and Britain. Did Devoy tell Parnell the nature of the "work" with which he was so busy? Did Parnell ask what sort of urgent work required Devoy's presence and all the risks it entailed? The records are discreetly silent.

Devoy, Davitt, and Parnell made plans to meet again June 1. By then, everything had changed. The New Departure's marriage of the politician and the revolutionist would be swept aside, and Devoy's long and exhausting tour of the IRB's various strongholds would be irrelevant. "The forces of nature intervened," Devoy wrote with apparent regret. An insurrection was about to begin, but it was hardly the kind Devoy and the American revolutionists envisioned.

Meanwhile, Devoy continued to meet with IRB leaders throughout Ireland. He slipped back to France via England four times to send letters back to Dr. Carroll in Philadelphia—the journey was necessary to keep the letters far from the prying eyes of British detectives. Carroll himself was writing to John O'Leary in Paris to complain, no doubt based on information from Devoy, that the Clan na Gael had sent the IRB $17,000 in 1878 and was preparing to send over another $25,000 for "agricultural implements"—guns—and yet "not one hoe" had arrived in Ireland. A great deal of Devoy's consultations were devoted to setting up an efficient program of turning the Clan's money into rifles for IRB members.

He also held several conferences with Davitt and other agitators in Davitt's Dublin flat, where the group outlined a strategy of agrarian agitation in the west of Ireland. Davitt was shuttling between Dublin and Mayo, where agrarian distress was about to boil over. The meetings in Dublin produced plans for a great rally of angry and anxious farmers in Irishtown, a village in Mayo, on Sunday, April 20. Just before Easter, nearby towns were plastered with notices of the coming meeting. The placards announced that the cry of "Down with invaders! Down with tyrants!" was echoing from the cabins of Ireland's impoverished west to "the wigwams of North America."

When the day arrived, as many as twelve thousand farmers, some on horseback, showed up to hear angry speeches condemning landlords and those tenants who settled on land where a previous tenant had been evicted. ("Land-grabbers," they were called.) The farmers cheered a set of resolutions Davitt wrote, one of which stated that "the land of Ireland . . . was intended by a just and all-providing God for the use and sustenance of those . . . to whom he gave inclination and energies to cultivate and improve it."

All the while, Devoy was meeting with local IRB leaders and getting both a head count and an arms count. He would later report that the IRB had 30,162 members, and that the members had a high regard for the organization's aging leaders. Devoy estimated that the Revolutionary Directory had about $13,600 on hand, and he was able to report that rifles were beginning to arrive in Ireland at last after Devoy restructured the Clan-IRB gunrunning program. Devoy's report indicates that he did his job thoroughly and well.

Rifles, however, had no power over nature. Throughout the spring heavy rains fell ("I never saw a blue sky," Devoy wrote), and farmers were facing ruin. The land was all that mattered now. In the west of Ireland, nearly half the population, some 421,000 people, would soon be in extreme distress.

◈

BEFORE RECONVENING WITH PARNELL on June 1 at Morrison's Hotel, Devoy and Davitt held a long conference to define their goals. Devoy understood that the New Departure had been swept away in the ceaseless downpours of springtime. Desperate farmers were taking events into their own hands in an agitation that threatened to become the premature insurrection Devoy feared. The new movement required a leader, and both Devoy and Davitt agreed only one man was suited for the job—Parnell.

The June 1 meeting became the most controversial of the three at which Parnell and Devoy were both present. Devoy would later insist that Parnell agreed to a series of conditions in exchange for the support of the American Irish revolutionaries. Davitt adamantly denied Devoy's insistence that he and Parnell agreed to a formal alliance with the American militants, but it is entirely likely that Parnell transformed himself into exactly what Devoy wished to see.

Politically, there was no reason for Parnell to formalize his relationship with Devoy. The New Departure telegram publicly pledged Devoy and the American revolutionaries to Parnell. Tactically, too, Parnell had every reason to keep his relationship with Devoy and the Americans informal, and to allow himself every bit of wiggle room— he would need it all—in case the unpredictacle Americans proved to be an embarrassment. He knew Devoy was a revolutionary, and when questioned by a government commission years later, he would rather breezily say that he had never dicussed Fenian business with Devoy. This seemed to make it all right, at least in Parnell's view.

Still, Devoy's rabid insistence that Parnell agree to four conditions, none of them breaking ground that had not already been plowed and fertilized, at the June 1 meeting requires more than the simple dismissal it has received. In Devoy's account, Parnell agreed that Irish members of parliament would do or say nothing to hurt Fenianism or to discredit the notion that physical force might be necessary to win independence; that "the demand for Self-Government" should not be publicly defined; that the final solution of the land question was peasant ownership; and the Irish members of parliament should form their own, independent party.

Devoy's proposals contained nothing to which Parnell would have objected, and it may be that Devoy's belief that they had struck a deal could simply be traced to a nod from the ever-inscrutable Parnell. Devoy certainly had every reason to tell his American colleagues that Parnell was with them, because it was Devoy himself who sought to link the American nationalists to Parnell's star.

Nevertheless, Parnell did not follow through on the principles Devoy outlined at Morrison's Hotel. Eventually, the parliamentarian would accept home rule, rather than complete separation from Britain, and Parnell did nothing to further the cause of peasant ownership, although he did pay lip service to it. Nevertheless, Devoy remained intensely loyal to Parnell to the end, a claim not even Davitt could make. Such magnanimity was not Devoy's style, and it indicates some unbreakable bond, if not a working alliance, between these two vastly different and complicated men.

The exact nature of the Parnell-Devoy relationship would consume hours of testimony when the English government, ten years after the Boulogne-Dublin meetings, attempted to link Parnell and the land movement to violent Irish-American agitators like Devoy. The exercise required some double-talk from Parnell, but the essential truth seems beyond dispute. Parnell willingly worked with a man he knew to be a revolutionary and who, in fact, was conducting revolutionary business all the while. How much did Parnell know and when did he know it? Nobody will ever know. More than a century after his death, his shape continues to shift.

As SPRING RAINS CONTINUED to fall, Devoy set out for the west of Ireland to check on conditions for himself. On July 13, Davitt and his allies held a protest meeting in the Mayo town of Claremorris. Devoy set out by train from Dublin the day before the meeting, despite warnings from Davitt and other allies that the rally figured to draw a huge contingent of police, putting Devoy at greater risk of recognition and arrest. Devoy, understandably, was determined to see for himself the great movement that Davitt had put together. He put on his best Irish tweeds and made arrangements to travel by train from Dublin under the assumed name of Doyle.

As he arrived in Claremorris, he noticed two constables on the platform. They were within earshot when he was approached by a young stranger, who asked if he was "Mr. Doyle." The young man probably was an emissary from Davitt or one of the local IRB leaders Devoy was scheduled to meet with after the Claremorris land meeting. Devoy said he wasn't Mr. Doyle, but the constables' attention was aroused. Rather than walk away in as discreet a fashion as possible, Devoy chose to ask them if they would recommend a hotel in town, explaining that he was a reporter from the *Irish Times* dispatched to Mayo to cover the great meeting. The constables promptly escorted Devoy—their possible quarry—to his destination. Devoy rewarded them with a round of whiskey at the hotel bar.

The meeting the next morning was the largest yet in the series Davitt was orchestrating, and Devoy was impressed by the crowd's size and enthusiasm. Davitt and a young politician named John Dillon both gave fiery speeches, with Davitt demanding that the "soil of Ireland . . . be returned to the people of Ireland," and Dillon bemoaning the fact that the Irish peasantry had no rifles. Listening to the speech, Devoy might have raised an eyebrow. He, after all, was seeing to it that rifles were becoming more plentiful.

Devoy finally left Ireland to return to New York shortly after the Claremorris meeting. Greater agitations were to come, but Devoy had been given a sense of the anxieties of the Irish farmer, and the extent to which Irish politics was being transformed. There was a lesson for his American colleagues: they could talk all they wanted about military preparations, but they could not ignore the new situation in Ireland. Not long after Devoy's return, the *Irish World*'s front page featured a frightening headline: "Famine in Ireland." A generation of Irish-Americans with vivid memories of the Great Famine had vowed, like Jews would after the Holocaust, that such a calamity would never again occur. In a sense, Devoy's New Departure was not dead. But its shape was about to shift.

DEVOY RETURNED TO NEW York in early August and almost immediately hustled to Wilkes-Barre, Pennsylvania, to present a report on his travels to a Clan na Gael convention that began August 9. The delegates heard nothing of the New Departure, nothing of the increasingly desperate situation of Ireland's farmers. Instead, they heard from Devoy a meticulous recitation of the IRB's strength on a county-by-county and even a town-by-town basis. The convention's committee on foreign affairs reported optimistically that "the doubts, diversions and rivalries of the past are being dispelled" and that it detected an "earnest desire to work as brothers and patriots for the common cause," a sentiment that would qualify as precedent-setting news if true. The Clan's treasury reported that $26,500 had been sent to the IRB, and another $10,000 had been dispatched from the Skirmishing Fund. Nowhere was it mentioned that while Devoy was in Ireland, the Clan had loaned Patrick Ford, editor of the *Irish World,* $12,000 to cover his expenses. When Devoy found out about the loan and complained about it, the money was repaid, but the ensuing controversy would lead to something a great deal less than an "earnest desire to work as brothers and patriots."

The Clan's General Military Board reported little growth in recruitment for the American wing of the Irish Liberating Army and recommended that members infiltrate local National Guards, form their own brigades, elect their own officers, and then get the training the Clan could not provide. F. F. Millen, the self-styled general in charge of the Clan's military board and a British spy, reported the findings of his own trip to Ireland, which overlapped Devoy's by several weeks. Millen was happy to report that he saw small groups of men training, although they often were using sticks rather than rifles. He estimated that the Clan could smuggle two hundred rifles per week into Ireland.

The secret reports, including Devoy's meticulous accounting of IRB members, were soon delivered into the hands of the British government.

The proceedings in Wilkes-Barre had an unreality that only Devoy could have appreciated. It was summed up, after the fact, in a letter from Dr. Carroll to Devoy: "Good as the land question is, it should not cause us to lose our heads about it to the neglect of the only ultimate means to our end." The only ultimate means, in Carroll's view, was violent revolution.

Days after the Clan dispersed from Wilkes-Barre, satisfied that their military plans were back on track, an astonishingly more important meeting took place in Castlebar, County Mayo. There, Michael Davitt established a new organization called the Land League of Mayo. He wrote to Devoy shortly after its formation, saying he was eager for Devoy's views on the new turn the land war was taking. There was also a hint about the havoc Davitt's zeal was wreaking on his finances. "You are aware that I have borne my own expenses so far in this Western war against landlordism, and this together with forty-five pounds bad debt—lent to struggling people who can never pay me—has reduced my little capital pretty considerably," Davitt wrote. Devoy took the hint and, with the assistance of the *Irish World*'s Patrick Ford, dispatched $2,000 in National Fund money to Davitt. At the time, the gesture seemed a mere act of generosity, but it would haunt Davitt when he was portrayed as a tool of Irish-American terrorists.

In the fall of 1879, with farmers more distressed by the day, Davitt persuaded Charles Parnell to assume the post of president of the new Irish Land League. The parliamentarians were now officially wedded to agrarian agitation, and the battle for the land of Ireland had begun in earnest. Parnell was about to bring it to America.

DEVOY LEARNED IN LATE October that Parnell would be leaving for New York shortly, with the intention of raising money for the Land League through a series of lectures in the States. "The wealthy Irish-American class who holds aloof from the other National work could . . . be got to move on this one to free the land of Ireland from landlord grasp," Davitt wrote of middle-class Irish-Americans who looked with horror on such efforts as the Skirmishing Fund.

As the man who had championed Parnell among Irish-American nationalists, Devoy understood that his own credibility was about to be tested. If Parnell made a favorable impression, he would prove Devoy's contention that parliamentary agitation need not compromise the Clan's hard-line position on eventual Irish independence, and that the land was, in fact, the "question of questions" in Ireland. If Parnell could quiet the skeptics and win over new converts, bringing Irish nationalism into the mainstream of American political life, Devoy's hand would be that much stronger in setting the Irish-American agenda. The Parnell tour would determine if the confluence of reform, agitation, and conspiracy in America was enough to carry the movement over the jagged rocks that lurked just below the surface.

Shortly after receiving word of Parnell's imminent departure, Devoy arranged for Clan na Gael's backing for the tour, putting the organization's nationwide network at his disposal. Devoy's work in preparation for Parnell's visit earned the praise of Boyle O'Reilly in Boston, who told him that "this is the way to work, Devoy, to accomplish things." But even as he was preparing the way for a member of parliament, Devoy was making plans to send his friend O'Kelly eastward to Ireland to establish a gun-smuggling operation to be funded with $10,000 from the Clan's treasury. This was yet another curious activity about which Parnell, who would soon form a genuine friendship with O'Kelly, knew to know nothing.

Just before Parnell was to set sail for New York, Michael Davitt and several other land agitators were arrested, touching off a round of indignant demonstrations throughout Ireland and forcing Parnell to postpone his visit. The overly excited *Irish World* published a headline announcing the start of "The Revolution!" A *World* correspondent was dispatched to solicit Devoy's opinion of the arrests. "I think the government has done more for the land agitation by the arrest of these men than Parnell, Davitt . . . and the rest of them could do for the next six months," Devoy said. "No movement of this kind amounted to much 'till it had its martyrs."

The British government came to the same conclusion, and Davitt and his colleagues were released in early December. Parnell set sail for New York just before Christmas and arrived on January 2, 1880, after an eleven-day journey across the Atlantic. He immediately announced that in addition to raising money for the Land League, he would begin a second, separate appeal for money to help the tenants of Ireland, whose plight had worsened dramatically as winter set in. The announcement ensured scathing notices for Parnell from Devoy's employers at the *Herald*, who were themselves soliciting contributions designed to "defray the expenses of emigration" from Ireland, thus "relieving the Irish labor market of a surplus."

The *Herald* regarded Parnell as a dangerous radical who had no business bringing his agitation to America—a situation that put Devoy in a difficult position. He was, after all, organizing the very agitation his employers found so distasteful. "The land system of Ireland is a British, not an American, question," the *Herald* thundered just after Parnell set foot in New York. "It is hardly decent for Americans

to organize a crusade for dictating the legislation of a foreign government." The *Herald*'s campaign against Parnell grew so intense that
eventually the bank that had agreed to handle Parnell's funds, Drex-
ell, Morgan and Co., announced it would withdraw its services and
return donations. A Boston bank came to the rescue and agreed to
handle Parnell's money.

Devoy and the Clan rented Madison Square Garden for Parnell's
first speech. Devoy was there, along with a crowd he estimated at
between four thousand and five thousand "of the very best Irish people in New York City." Parnell appeared onstage with his mother and
his three sisters, all of whom were playing an active role behind the
scenes during his tour. In his speech, which was greeted with "wild
tumult," according to the *New York Times*, Parnell acknowledged the
role that America was playing in the Irish national drama. "The
American people occupy today a proud position," he said. "They are
virtually the arbiters of this Irish question."

Reaction was immediate and gratifying. Parnell was invited to
address the members of the New York Stock Exchange and was well
received, although the *Herald* was quick to note the presence of several hostile brokers, who hissed as Parnell was introduced after the
trading bell sounded. Soon, he was invited to address the U.S. House
of Representatives and various state and local legislative bodies. In
all, he visited sixty-two cities, including such places as Des Moines,
Cincinnati, Wheeling, West Virginia, and Columbus, showing that
Ireland's cause need not be confined to the Northeast's ghettos of
conspiracy. In Cincinnati, Parnell delivered his most controversial
speech, saying, at least according to two newspapers, that his goal was
the destruction of the "last link" between Ireland and Brtain.

While Parnell was out West, Devoy was spending his free time
in the newly opened offices of the Irish Famine Relief Fund on Park
Place in Manhattan, just west of the *Herald*'s office. His work on the
relief committee put him in constant touch with Parnell's mother and
sisters, all of whom were strong-willed, independent, and a touch
eccentric. Devoy was flabbergasted when Fanny Parnell, a poet, asked
him to steal a black cat belonging to his boss, James Gordon Bennett,
the *Herald*'s owner. The black cat, Fanny Parnell insisted, brought the
Herald's proprietor good luck. Somehow Devoy managed to duck the
task.

As an editor with the hated *Herald,* Devoy's moments of discomfort were not restricted to strange requests from Fanny Parnell. Her brother wired Devoy several times at the relief office and at the *Herald* concerning the rivalry between the *Herald*'s relief efforts and Parnell's. Even the crafty Devoy found it difficult to balance the interests of his employers and the man to whom he had linked his star and his cause. Before the year was out, Devoy was fired.

Parnell's cross-country tour ended abruptly in early March, when Parliament was dissolved and a new election ordered. On March 11, 1880, just before he left New York, Parnell and his supporters from twenty-eight Irish organizations, including labor unions, met at the New York Hotel and resolved to form an American Land League organization with independent branches grouped according to state, with each state organization dispatching money directly to the Irish Land League in Dublin.

It seemed an innocuous enough proposal, but for Devoy, it was nothing short of a disaster. Without a central organization in America, control, discipline, and autonomy would be impossible, threatening Clan na Gael's position as the arbiter of Irish-American nationalism and certainly making Clan infiltration of the league's leadership more difficult. Though he argued that the League ought to have a strong American executive to shield it from unforeseen events in Ireland, such as the arrest of the Irish Land League leaders, Devoy's intentions were spelled out on a Clan circular sent to members just after Parnell left. "No pains should be spared to secure the control of these [Land League] movements," the circular told Clan members. Devoy's obsession with control and discipline was evident: "Lest these [Land League] organizations may at any time prove dangers rather than assistants to our work, we should so secure control of their management as to be able to disband them if that should ever become necessary." The League, then, was to serve at the pleasure of the Clan, whether it realized it or not.

Devoy saw the dispersal of Land League branches as a formula designed to keep the American movement subservient to dictation from Dublin. Iron-willed, Devoy would not allow such an erosion of his autonomy. Eventually, the fledgling League agreed to send all contributions to a priest, the Reverend Lawrence Walsh of Connecticut, who would turn the proceeds over to Dublin. Patrick Ford, however, decided to raise money on his own through the *Irish World*, which had done so much to encourage contributions to the Skirmishing Fund.

Parnell sailed home having raised hundreds of thousands of dollars. It was a historic and wildly successful tour, and with the official formation of the American Land League, the embattled Irish farmers now had the resources to carry out the land war's biggest battles. Parnell's tour had shown the enormous amounts of money America could generate for the cause of Irish nationalism. That lesson would not be lost on a century's worth of Irish agitators.

Devoy had every reason to take great pleasure in Parnell's success. Still, things were not nearly as smooth. O'Donovan Rossa, for one, was voicing his dissent. Sensing that the Clan was moving away from pure, violent revolution in Ireland, Rossa formed his own group, the United Irishmen of America, and began publishing a newspaper whose pages were filled with casual talk of the kinds of terror that Irish-Americans might inflict on Britain's cities. Clan members, who had taken to calling Rossa "O'Dynamite" and "O'Donovan Assa," wearily expelled Rossa from the organization.

But Rossa was hardly the only cause of Devoy's headaches. In Ireland, Devoy's friend O'Kelly met with little but hostility from IRB members, who rejected his offer to take charge of smuggling weapons into Ireland. His mission a failure, O'Kelly returned the $10,000 Devoy had given him and then, to Devoy's astonishment, not only renounced his membership in the Clan, but ran for and won a seat in Parliament himself. Devoy was furious, in the main because he considered O'Kelly, rightly, to be one of the Clan's best men. Still, the two old friends remained in touch, with O'Kelly often writing to Devoy on House of Commons stationery about their shared interests—such as the brand of weapon best suited for illicit importation into Ireland.

Meanwhile, Devoy's friend and ally Dr. Carroll was becoming increasingly suspicious of the Land League's strategy and ambitions. In fact, Carroll was so suspicious of Parnell, and so fixated on violent insurrection, that he objected to raising money to help the impoverished and starving Irish farmers.

Carroll decided that the League's ambitions would serve only as "a club to break the heads" of Clan na Gael and the IRB. He announced his intention to resign as chairman of the Clan in a series of "Dear Sir" letters to Devoy. The Clan's Executive Board decided to debate the role the organization should play in Land League agitation during a two-day conference beginning June 28. Carroll invited John O'Leary, the IRB Supreme Council member who shared his doubts, from his Paris exile to argue against the Clan's participation. Michael Davitt would make the case in favor. Devoy, though not a member of the Executive Board, was invited to participate as secretary of the joint Clan-IRB Revolutionary Directory.

Sunday, June 27, 1880, was a sweltering early-summer day. Devoy's apartment on Barrow Street was only a short walk from the Clan's meeting rooms on East Fourth Street. On his way there, Devoy picked up a fresh copy of the *Irish-American*, a conservative weekly newspaper. Devoy devoured the paper page by page, scanning even the obituary notices from Ireland. There, in small type, he found his father's name. William Devoy, whose prayerful wish to see his son one more time had been answered, had died on May 31. Nobody from home had cabled him with the news.

Devoy would later describe the steamy morning of June 27 as one of the worst days of his life. Shocked and grief-stricken, he continued on his journey to the Clan's meeting rooms, but was in no position to take an active role in the discussions. After some routine business, which included the appointment of a committee to gather information about "a new explosive compound," O'Leary and Davitt debated the merits of Clan participation in the League. Eventually, by an eight-to-five vote, the Executive Board voted down a resolution that would have banned Clan officers from serving as officers of the League's branches. Instead, they passed a motion that simply reminded Clan members that they shouldn't neglect the work of revolution. Davitt was ecstatic. "O'Leary . . . came from Paris to upset my Land League endeavors, but he will go back a wiser though sadder man," he wrote.

Carroll's resignation was accepted, and Devoy's friend from New Haven, James Reynolds, was elected the Clan's chairman. Devoy, now given a chance to keep the Land League within the Clan's orbit, became president of the Land League's branch based on Manhattan's First Ward. A Clan ally of his, Dr. William Wallace, became president of New York's statewide organization.

For the next year to eighteen months, the Land League in America was among the best-organized and most vociferous critics not only of landlordism in Ireland but of nineteenth-century capitalism in America. In just over a year, the main body of the American Land League established more than fifteen hundred branches across the country, and within two years more than $500,000 (in 1882 dollars) was raised to fund Parnell's land agitation in Ireland.

Just as important, the American Land League accomplished exactly the goal Devoy had sought when he proposed to raise the Irish-American movement from its ratholes. The Land League soon attracted the likes of Henry George, who went to Ireland as a correspondent for the *Irish World* and would be arrested, and James Redpath, the onetime abolitionist who adopted the cause of Ireland's tenant farmers as a natural extension of his work against slavery. "The Land League," noted historian Eric Foner, "was the first nationalist organization to unite the Irish-American community. The land issue had an impact no other could rival."

With the farmers in Ireland increasingly brazen, the Land War was fully engaged thanks to the funds flowing freely from America. Landlords fought back with evictions—some 2,110 families, with nearly 10,000 people, were evicted in 1880, nearly double the number in '79. The figures soon doubled, and then some. Incidents of agrarian crime, including shootings, assaults, intimidation, and livestock mutilations, skyrocketed in the last quarter of 1880, to 1,696, which was more than any single year since 1845, the first year of the Famine. In August, the Land League urged tenants to withhold payments of unjust rents and to continue to shun those who occupied land from which the previous tenant had been evicted. The tactic would become known as boycotting—named for one such "land-grabber" named Charles Boycott. The League set up special land courts to decide on fair rents.

Ireland seemed on the verge of rebellion. The new English secretary for Ireland, W. E. Forster, conceded that "we might pour in thousands of soldiers and occupy the disturbed districts as though they were an enemy's country, but these [agrarian] outrages are as difficult to deal with as guerrilla warfare. I fear no troops will prevent them." On November 3, 1880, Parnell and thirteen other Land Leaguers were indicted on charges of conspiring to prevent the payment of rent. The government was considering calls to suspend civil liberties in Ireland.

Davitt returned to Ireland in late 1880 after spending the spring and summer setting up the American Land League. In a letter to Devoy, he could hardly contain his pleasure at the transformation he saw in the Irish countryside:

"It would take me a week to give you anything like an account of the immense growth and power of the [Land League]. It now virtually rules the country. . . . The courage of the people is magnificent. All classes are purchasing arms openly."

Was the time to strike approaching? Irish nationalists in America, particularly Dr. Carroll, had discussed the possibility of fomenting a rebellion in 1882—the one hundredth anniversary of the formation of a separate (and soon abolished) Irish Parliament under the Anglo-Protestant nationalist Henry Grattan. Now, with 1882 just twelve months away, indications were that the Land War could become a real war. When Michael Davitt was arrested on trumped-up charges of violating his parole in early 1881, Ireland seemed on the verge of outright rebellion.

Devoy, after tacking so hard in favor of land agitation, was already veering back to a more familiar course. Dismissed from the Herald in September, he sent notices to Clan camps across the country that he was setting out on a lecture tour for which proceeds "shall either go to the Revolutionary Fund . . . or to the National Fund, so that we may be better prepared to meet any emergency that may be forced upon us by England." The Land League, he said, "has now enough money for present purposes, and . . . that state of things prevailing in Ireland demands that all money that can be got from our people here should be devoted to revolutionary purposes." Devoy had expended great effort in moving the Irish national movement into the political mainstream. Now, with Ireland seemingly on the brink of rebellion, he was prepared to return to revolutionary conspiracy.

As 1881 began, two explosions rocked the movement on both sides of the Atlantic. One was very real; the other was rhetorical.

On January 14, 1881, a small bomb exploded at a military barracks in Salford near Manchester. A seven-year-old boy was killed, and three people were injured. O'Donovan Rossa's skirmishers had drawn blood.

On January 16, John Devoy spoke at a meeting of the New York branch of the American Land League. He took note of the government's possible crackdown in Ireland. "The people, goaded into a frenzy by studied injustice, may rise against some constituted authority," he was reported to have said. "A local eviction, a collision with the soldiers may ensue, and our people be shot down in multitudes. It is here that the offices of the American Land League will be called into requisition. Will we, then, stand idly by and see our people and country devastated, and content ourselves with enthusiastic resolutions and sympathies? . . . No, for every Irishman murdered we will take in reprisal the life of a British Minister. For every hundred Irishmen murdered we will sacrifice the lives of the entire British Ministry. For every two hundred Irishmen killed we will reduce to ashes the principal city of England. For a wholesale massacre of the Irish people we will make England a smouldering ruin of ashes and blood."

Suddenly, John Devoy sounded a lot like Jeremiah O'Donovan Rossa.

CHAPTER TEN

Pay Them Back, Woe for Woe

IN PARIS IN THE EARLY WEEKS OF 1881, A YOUNG, WIRY NATIVE OF
Cincinnati named William Mackey Lomasney was startled when he
heard details of John Devoy's Land League speech. Lomasney was a
Civil War veteran who had journeyed to Ireland in 1867 to join the
Fenian Rising. He was arrested, imprisoned, and then set free in 1871.
He and Devoy had become friendly while sharing chores in Millbank
prison in the late 1860s, and they had remained in touch, particularly
in recent months.

Lomasney believed Devoy's speech was out of character with the
man he knew and concluded that his friend must have been mis-
quoted. He told associates in Paris that Devoy could not have made
the "alleged speech."

As an accredited agent of Clan na Gael, Lomasney was in France
to make a withdrawal from the Irish Republican Brotherhood's treasury. After having done so, he was to proceed to Ireland to prepare
for a possible rebellion, according to a plan he had devised after long
consultations with Devoy.

Lomasney was, in Devoy's words, a desperate man—a "fanatic of
the deepest dye" whose calm demeanor made argument with him all
the more difficult. But he was not so desperate, and not so wed to
orthodoxy, that he did not see the merit of Devoy's New Departure.
He also supported the Land League agitation, describing its work as
"splendid" and condemning the opposition of Rossa and the IRB leadership as "senseless." As Rossa's men began arriving from America to
set off bombs in Britain in the early weeks of 1881, Lomasney de-

plored their actions as "farcical," though he took some comfort in knowing that the bombers' own incompetence prevented terrible loss of life.

Lomasney understood that the Irish-American militants could do nothing that would turn public opinion against them. "Before we begin to do anything we must feel that we can justify that act, not only to ourselves in moments of excitement, but before the world [and] in the dock," he wrote to Devoy. "But could we act so if we were now to commence a series of desperate acts . . . No! Plainly no! We cannot, must not begin this way."

What was clear in Lomasney's letter was the suggestion that he and Devoy were about to begin *something*. If not desperate acts, then what? Lomasney and Devoy had discussed the merits of what Devoy called "bloodless terrorism" that would frighten the British ruling class, but cause no injuries or deaths. But with Rossa trying to seize the initiative while taunting the Clan na Gael for its apparent inactivity, Devoy allowed Lomasney to make his preparations in France as conditions in Ireland took on all the character and anxiety of wartime. And if war was indeed coming to Ireland, Devoy was determined that a disciplined and well-prepared Clan na Gael would have a critical role to play.

London, too, seemed to be on a war footing. In the aftermath of the Salford bombing, Britain's security forces were on high alert in anticipation of more American-sponsored bombings. The Metropolitan Police in London posted extra constables at Buckingham Palace, this after the lord chamberlain complained that the tradesmen's entrance to the palace was not protected against Fenian invaders. A railway executive, panic-stricken, wrote to the home secretary's office in London, concerned that "a single dynamite cartridge" placed in a gasworks plant "would land us in a state of chaos and disorder." The government immediately ordered a security survey of all London gasworks. The London press reported stories of American-sponsored plots to blow up Windsor Castle.

British politicians knew exactly who was causing all the trouble. The British ambassador to Washington, Edward Thorton, wrote the foreign secretary, Lord Granville, that "it is pretty certain that the [American] Fenians are anxious to do something." Thorton noted that the British consul in New York, Edward Archibald, was negotiating for the services of Allan Pinkerton, private detective to the stars of American commerce, in hopes of further penetrating Clan na Gael.

Devoy's speech in New York did nothing to calm British fears, and while Lomasney may have been willing to give Devoy the benefit of the doubt, Britain's home secretary, William Harcourt, was not so charitably disposed. Devoy gave Harcourt an opportunity to begin what would become a years-long campaign to smear Parnell as an ally of Irish-American terrorists who hid behind the seemingly respectable veil of the American Land League. On February 22, three weeks after Davitt's arrest threatened to spark a general uprising in Ireland, Harcourt found himself engaged with Parnell and his aide Timothy Healy in an exchange over yet another Coercion Bill, which the government so desperately wanted and Parnell was doing his best to obstruct. When Healy suggested that the government was overreacting to reports of American-inspired plots against British targets, Harcourt took the floor in full dudgeon:

"[T]here was a speech . . . by a man well-known in this country, a man who certainly received the grace of the Crown—John Devoy, who was a convict and, unfortunately, [was] allowed to go at liberty before the expiration of his sentence," Harcourt said. After summarizing Devoy's speech in a manner designed for maximum shock value ("He says he will assassinate a single minister, and then he will assassinate the whole Cabinet . . . and then he says he and his friends intend to accomplish a conflagration of the whole city of London"), Harcourt neatly linked Devoy's name to Rossa's, describing them as allies intent on using the now-infamous Skirmishing Fund for the activities he had so luridly described.

Harcourt's speech enraged the Irish members. One of them, Thomas Sexton, asked if "the speech of Devoy" in New York was to be used as an argument for the suspension of civil liberties in Ireland.

It's uncertain why Devoy spoke in such Rossa-like terms. Only a few weeks before the New York speech, he told an audience in Holyoke, Massachusetts, that land was the critical question, and that revolution would be a long time coming. Two explanations for Devoy's rhetorical pyrotechnics are likely. He may simply have overreacted to Rossa's labeling of Devoy and the Clan as do-nothings, or, as a man on tour looking to make money from his lectures, he was simply trying to generate publicity. Whatever the reason, his speech continued to earn citations of outrage on the Commons floor, with Harcourt, on February 24, moving closer to the heart of his attack. "I would like to explain . . . who and what Mr. Devoy is," he said as he launched into a brief and skewed history of the American Land League, suggesting that it was designed to finance the sort of operations Devoy spoke of in his New York speech. Harcourt could hardly resist pronouncing Parnell guilty by association: "Therefore, we have the Irish-American Land League, founded under the auspices of the well-known names of Parnell, Dillon [one of Parnell's aides], Davitt, and Devoy, and here they are all in action together."

The raucous proceedings in Parliament continued for several more sessions, with Harcourt finally announcing that it was the government's duty to stamp out conspiracies in Ireland. When Devoy read an account of Harcourt's speech, he flew into a rage. He fired off a telegram to Harcourt, saying: "Two can play at stamping; the greatest sufferers are those who have the most to lose. The day when you can stamp with impunity has passed forever."

Within days, the London press reported that Harcourt had received a cabled death threat from the American Fenian John Devoy. When the reports surfaced, Parnell was in Paris, where the Land League's funds had been transferred to keep them out of the British government's hands when the inevitable crackdown was ordered. On February 28, he dispatched a telegram to Devoy in New York: "You are reported to have sent threatening telegram to Home Secretary. If true your action most censurable. If untrue should cable contradiction."

The next day, when Harcourt took the Commons floor, a friendly colleague asked whether it was true that "he has received a telegram from Mr. Devoy . . . threatening him with assassination, and, if so, whether any and what representations have been made to the Government of the United States on this subject?"

Harcourt replied with practiced resignation that he thought the matter wasn't "worthy of notice in the House of Commons." Despite these heartfelt reservations, Harcourt then confirmed that he did indeed receive a telegram from John Devoy. "It was somewhat of a menacing character," he said. "It promised to stamp me out, but it did not explain the . . . method in which the operation was to be performed."

John Dillon, one of Parnell's aides, rose on the House floor two days later to speak on Devoy's behalf. Referring to Devoy as a friend, Dillon described him as an "obscure man" who "had spent his whole life—who had spent the best years of his manhood— arguing, sometimes in the direst poverty, against a hateful and atrocious government." Even if Devoy had in fact threatened Harcourt, Dillon said he would prefer Devoy's company to that of the "sleek and contented Home Secretary." If that weren't impertinent enough, Healy rose and called Harcourt a liar, leading to his ejection from the House. Parnell, finally back in the House after his trip to France, rose on March 4 and announced that Devoy had sent him a telegram denying that he threatened Harcourt's life. Parnell continued the assault on Harcourt: "The right Honorable gentleman was not satisfied with . . . misrepresenting the meaning of the cablegram which he received from Mr. Devoy, but he tried to fix an additional stigma on the character of that gentleman. He spoke of him as a convict. But this is not the first time for Irishmen who have sacrificed their all for what they believed to be in the good of their country, and have cheerfully faced the horrible punishment of penal servitude for their opinions, to be stigmatized in the House as convicts."

Small wonder that in the many quarrels to come, Devoy never launched personal attacks on Parnell. But the government's men, Harcourt included, had a point. Parnell and his party were keeping company with some Americans of radical intent.

These months of crisis found Devoy living the life of a road lecturer, staying in cheap accommodations or the homes of friends as he traveled from New England to the Midwest to the West Coast in search of paying audiences. His drawing power was something less than expected in the Irish population centers in the Northeast, but he found, oddly enough, bigger audiences as he moved away from them. He spent St. Patrick's Day and the following few weeks in and around Chicago, where the atmosphere was so welcoming he considered looking for a full-time job in the city.

Among the Chicago-area people he found most hospitable was a surgeon and a local Clan na Gael officer with the unlikely name of Henri Le Caron, who was the senior guardian, or chief officer, of a Clan camp in Braidwood, Illinois. He was also president of the local chapter of the Land League, indicating the extent to which Clan members were infiltrating the League, a development Sir William Harcourt would have delighted in bringing to the notice of his colleagues in Parliament. Devoy addressed both the Clan and the Land League chapters in Braidwood and spent several days in Le Caron's company, sharing dinner with him in the doctor's apartment above the town drugstore.

Le Caron, though obsequious in Devoy's company, later wrote an unflattering portrait of the man he introduced to friends and allies in Braidwood:

"Devoy . . . was at once seen to be a man of weighty influence. Forbidding of aspect, with a perpetual scowl upon his face, he immediately conveyed the idea of being a quarrelsome man, an idea sustained and strengthened by both his manner of speech and gruffness of voice. . . . [H]is friendships were few and far between, and had it not been for his undoubted ability . . . he could never have reached the prominent place which he subsequently attained in the Fenian organization."

Le Caron claimed to be a French-Canadian whose mother was Irish, and if he seemed an unlikely Irish nationalist, he certainly had an impressive record. He fought with the army of Irish-Americans that invaded Canada in 1870, the last of the three Fenian invasions. And he apparently had the full confidence of a rising Chicago Clan member named Alexander Sullivan, a lawyer, politician and all-around man on the make.

In mid-April, Devoy was accused, on the front page of the *Irish World*, of doing nothing to seize the moment in Ireland. It was time, the paper said, to use the Skirmishing Fund to "strike at England's pocket. . . . Strike! Strike! Strike! And keep on striking!" The *World* demanded an explanation for Devoy's apparent lack of interest in setting off explosions in London. Devoy fired off a letter to Patrick Ford, threatening to publicize the $12,000 loan the *World* received from the Fund in 1879. Thus began a feud that would last for nearly a half century and would be resolved in a court of law long after Patrick Ford was dead and when John Devoy was nearly blind, nearly deaf, and nearly dead himself.

Around the time of the *World*'s assault, Devoy met again with Le Caron, who announced that he would soon be heading to Europe. Would Devoy provide him with any letters of introduction to Irish nationalists in France? Devoy later said he reluctantly provided Le Caron with letters for John O'Leary, the crabby IRB exile in Paris, and Patrick Egan, the Land League treasurer who also was in Paris with the League's treasury. Le Caron left for Europe shortly after getting the letters from Devoy. France was not his only destination, for he arranged to meet with Parnell and James J. O'Kelly, now Parnell's chief male confidant, in the lobby of the House of Commons. Le Caron would later claim that Parnell told him that he no longer believed that anything but violent revolution would resolve Ireland's problems. Furthermore, according to Le Caron, Parnell said he wished to meet again with Devoy in France to discuss the explosive situation in Ireland and Britain.

Details of Le Caron's conversations with Devoy and Parnell were duly reported back to the British government, for Le Caron was a British spy and had been since the Fenian invasions of Canada.

AS HIS TOUR TOOK him to such outposts as Denver, Des Moines, and Laramie, Wyoming, Devoy was keeping tabs on Lomasney's mission. In a letter to James Reynolds, the new chairman of Clan na Gael, Devoy noted with satisfaction that guns were arriving in Ireland at "a better rate" than they had been, with one shipment of 160 arriving in a single week. He also was trying to negotiate the purchase of artillery—it isn't clear of what sort—for shipment to Lomasney's growing arms depots.

But even as Devoy prepared for a rebellion in Ireland, the moment of crisis passed. Had Parnell and his Irish colleagues walked out of the House of Commons and set up their own legislature in Dublin after Davitt's arrest, the rebellion for which Devoy was so carefully planning would probably have erupted. But Parnell took no such course, and the moment of maximum danger passed without a shot fired in anger. In the fall of 1881, the Land League was suppressed, and Parnell, O'Kelly, and several colleagues were arrested and sent to prison. Rather than leading to violence, the crackdown led to a peace pact between Parnell and the British government. As a condition for their release in May 1882, the Parnellites agreed to halt the Land War and would then turn their energies toward a campaign to win a limited form of self-government called home rule.

In America, though, men with dynamite and a historic grievance were determined to bring the battle to England. A bomb was discovered at London's Mansion House—the residence of the lord mayor—on March 16, 1881, three days after Czar Alexander II was assassinated in Russia, shocking Europe and particularly its royal families. The would-be bombers at Mansion House were Rossa's men, and if nothing else they succeeded in frightening Queen Victoria. On March 18, Her Majesty expressed concern for the safety of Buckingham Palace.

Lomasney, who told Devoy that he was building his arms and ammunition depots quietly, was aghast that Rossa's men had nearly succeeded. In a distinction that the British might not have recognized, Lomasney and Devoy believed they were preparing for a day in which the Irish could take the field themselves in legitimate warfare, armed with American-supplied weapons and perhaps fortified with an army of exiles from America. Rossa's bombers, Lomasney wrote, were "reckless fools" whose projects were "wholly, or nearly so, unjustifiable." Lomasney was deputized to find and stop Rossa's men before they struck again.

He was unsuccessful, because the British got there first. In June, two Irish-Americans were arrested in Liverpool after lugging a dynamite-laced cast-iron pipe from London. The dynamite, it was discovered, had been smuggled into Britain directly from the United States. Two weeks later, British customs authorities discovered six dynamite bombs, which the British dubbed "infernal machines," aboard the SS *Malta* when it docked in Liverpool after a trip from New York. Scotland Yard men were ordered to keep an eye out for Irish-Americans lurking in British ports.

At the same time, British agents in America were keeping watch over a curious vessel under construction in the Delamter Iron Works on Manhattan's West Side. John Holland, the Irish-born grammar-school teacher who had met Devoy just after the *Catalpa* rescue, was building something for which there was not yet a word in the English language. The cigar-shaped vessel would later be called a submarine, and it actually was Holland's second working model. Two more vessels, the last of which would serve as a prototype for the world's first submarine fleets, would follow.

Assisting Holland with construction was Devoy's friend John Breslin, who had played the key role of coordinating the *Catalpa* rescue on the ground in Australia. Through Breslin, Devoy was funneling tens of thousands of dollars from the Skirmishing Fund to the submarine project, eventually reaching the startling sum of $60,000. Devoy entertained visions of attacks on Royal Navy warships, and for the moment anyway, Holland shared the vision. The press, which was watching the proceedings with mounting curiosity, would soon dub Holland's vessel the *Fenian Ram*. The vessel was towed across the Hudson to the Morris Canal Basin in New Jersey in spring of '81, and in June, Holland himself took it underwater for the first time. The experiment lasted only a few minutes, but two days later, Holland and an engineer submerged themselves for nearly three hours. Tests continued throughout the summer.

Before long, British diplomats in Washington were imploring the American government to stop or seize what they called the "Fenian Torpedo Boat." In a letter to U.S. secretary of state James Blaine, a British diplomat named Victor Drummond asked that the American government monitor the vessel's progress. "You will see that the Torpedo appears to have most wonderful powers as a destructive machine," Drummond wrote.

It had long been Irish-American policy to find ways to heighten tensions between Britain and America, and if nothing else, Rossa's dynamite campaign and the submarine experiments were accomplishing just that. But Britain's diplomats in Washington feared that their complaints were falling on deaf ears. When the new president, James Garfield, appointed Blaine as secretary of state in 1881, the British diplomatic corps did not hide its sorrow. British ambassador Edward

Thorton told Lord Granville, the foreign secretary, that Blaine "dislikes England and pretends to think, or perhaps does think, that she is in her decadence."

Convinced that diplomatic pressure would be to no avail, Thorton was devising a plan to plant "judicious articles" designed to "create a hostile feeling against the Irish among Americans." Thorton wrote that he was convinced that most American politicians "hate the Irish no less than the majority of their countrymen [do]."

DEVOY'S JOURNEYS TOOK HIM back to Chicago in early August, 1881, for the Clan's annual convention. All signs pointed to war preparations. The National Fund, formerly the Skirmishing Fund, was officially shut down, with $38,000 in cash on hand (and nearly $90,000 having been raised since it began in 1876). Lomasney briefed members on the results of his illicit activities. Alexander Sullivan, the Chicago lawyer, was elected the group's new chairman, and he pushed through a resolution pledging the Clan to what it called, not very subtly, "active work." The Clan's executive shrank from eleven members to five for security reasons. (All for naught—the spy Le Caron was in attendance as a delegate from his camp.)

Exhausted by his travels and preparing to reenter the newspaper business, Devoy submitted his resignation as a member of the Revolutionary Directory. It was accepted. Devoy was now without a position of authority in the Clan for the first time since 1873. The National Fund, which he oversaw as a trustee, was closed, the Directory had three new members, and he was not a member of the Clan executive. As he prepared to start a new Irish-American weekly newspaper with the proceeds from his lecture tour, Devoy had relegated himself to the equivalent of a backbench member of parliament, with no formal power in the Clan na Gael. Once out of Devoy's control, the new Clan executive almost immediately set out on a course that would lead to a bitter, and finally deadly, feud with Devoy and his allies. Proprietorship, as Devoy ought to have known—and would later never forget—has its privileges.

Devoy returned to journalism in November when his newspaper, *The Irish Nation,* began publishing from an office on Park Place in

Manhattan. The *Irish Nation* followed the standard formula of the day, with modest, single-column headlines on page 1 and an entertaining jumble of short and highly opinionated essays on page 4. (Once such essay denounced cigarette smoking, saying the habit was turning America into "a nation of idiots." Devoy himself was fond of an occasional cigar.) To build circulation, the paper carried a weekly announcement offering a free rifle to readers who sold twenty subscriptions. A drawing of the weapon ran horizontally down half a column.

When the *Irish Nation* opened for business, Devoy was putting the finishing touches on his first book, *The Land of Eire*, which purported to tell the story of the Land League movement in Ireland and in America. As a piece of contemporary history, it is enlightening but far from complete. This was long before the age of confessionals; Devoy wrote nothing about his secret visit to Ireland, his meetings with Parnell, and the Clan's role in the League's leadership.

Devoy's entry into the crowded and raucous world of Irish-American journalism meant that now he, Rossa, and Patrick Ford were competitors in addition to being political enemies. Devoy wasted little time with his new-found power. A story about Rossa was introduced with the headline "Eleven Years of Fraud and False Pretenses Exposed." Another headline informed readers of Rossa's "Drunkenness and Dishonesty." Rossa's speeches were described as "rambling and disconnected . . . the weak attempt of a beaten man." Another Rossa speech bore the headline "More Stupid Anger Than Wit."

When Ford broke bitterly with Parnell in 1882, after Parnell called a halt to the Land War, Devoy compared Ford's arguments unfavorably with those of a "raving lunatic." "Is Mr. Ford mad, or does he take the Irish people for idiots?" Devoy wondered.

The most stunning event Devoy's newspaper reported in its first few months of existence took place forty-eight hours after Parnell, O'Kelly, Davitt, and the others won their release from prison. On May 6, in the Dublin dusk, the new chief secretary for Ireland, Lord Frederick Cavendish, and his secretary, Thomas Burke, were hacked to death while walking through Dublin's Phoenix Park. This sensational and cold-blooded act so unnerved Parnell that he offered to resign his seat. (Gladstone dissuaded him.) Coming as they did after a year of bombings, near-bombings, and numerous false reports of bombings in Britain, the Phoenix Park murders stunned Britain and Ireland and changed the political situation overnight. No longer could Parnell stand in the House and obstruct government security measures, and in America, no responsible spokesman could justify the murders. The British diplomatic corps in Washington was convinced the murderers had been dispatched from American shores.

The *Irish Nation* gave straightforward accounts of the murders, but on its editorial page, it said—in what surely were Devoy's words— that any "level-headed Englishmen" would understand that the murders were "the fruit" of their government's "blundering tyranny." Worse, the paper stated that the "Irish race" should not offer sympathy for those "on whom the penalty of the sins of their countrymen has fallen. . . . Why should our voices be raised in [a] wail over the fate of an English lord and recreant Irishman?" Devoy's reaction to the atrocious murders exhibited his considerable powers for invective at their worst, and they would serve him poorly during the *Irish Nation*'s short life. Alexander Sullivan dispatched several letters to Devoy, pleading with him to keep his personal quarrels out of the paper. "I don't like to intrude advice, but . . . the people don't want to read of personalities," Sullivan wrote.

But with Sullivan in control of the Clan, invective was the only power Devoy had left.

SOMETIME IN EARLY 1882, Sullivan journeyed to New York to discuss a startling proposal with Devoy. Sullivan said he planned to go to France to meet with Patrick Egan, the Land League treasurer, and would demand that the League turn over to the Clan half its funds, some twenty thousand pounds (or $100,000 in 1882 currency). In the future, Sullivan said, the League would give the Clan half the money it raised.

Devoy was aghast. Sullivan's proposal would confirm the worst slanders the British had flung at the Land League and Parnell—that he and the League were partners with Irish-American terrorists. But Sullivan made it clear that the decision was made, and that he was on his way to France. Devoy's objections were for naught. Sullivan left for Paris and returned with the money he wanted.

When the American Land League met in Philadelphia in April of 1883, Clan na Gael infiltrators helped elect Sullivan president. Devoy again objected, arguing during a caucus of Clan delegates that such an audacious move would damage Parnell if the British realized that Sullivan headed not only the public League movement but the shadowy Clan as well. (Parnell sent a telegram of support to the convention, asking it to frame a platform that would "enable us to continue to accept help from America.")

Once again, Devoy's objections went unheeded. Sullivan was elected president, and the Clan's penetration of the League was now nearly complete. Five of the seven national executives were Clan members.

The League's eminently respectable members had no idea of the dangerous game Sullivan was playing through his power over the Clan. Three weeks before the League convention, six Clan na Gael members had been arrested in various locations in Britain. The roundup also hauled in five hundred pounds of dynamite. Led by a physician named Thomas Gallagher, who had been conducting dynamite experiments on deserted Long Island beaches, and ably assisted by an Irish immigrant named Thomas J. Clarke, the Clan members were under Sullivan's orders to begin setting off bombs in London. A few months after the arrests, the Clan executive sent a circular to its members:

"We cannot see our way to an armed insurrection in Ireland this side of some great Foreign War with England. But in the meantime we shall carry on an incessant and perpetual warfare with the power of England."

The Clan had declared war on Britain in the name of Irish freedom.

THOUGH DEVOY OPPOSED THE bombing campaign, he continued to supervise the gun-smuggling operation he had put into place when he was in Ireland in 1879. The identity of his partners is not clear, nor is the method by which the guns were brought into Ireland. What is certain is that he was receiving critical advice on the subject from his friend James J. O'Kelly, member of parliament.

As the Land War in Ireland gave way to a constitutional crusade for home rule, the relationship between Devoy and O'Kelly took on an intriguing significance. O'Kelly was Devoy's oldest friend, and by the early 1880s, O'Kelly enjoyed the full confidence and friendship of Parnell. In the view of historian Robert Kee, if any of Parnell's colleagues were privy to their leader's affair with Katherine O'Shea, it was O'Kelly. That suggestion becomes all the more likely in light of O'Kelly's own messy personal life, tainted by divorce and an out-of-wedlock child.

If the two men did share confidences with each other, it is fair to wonder whether O'Kelly acted on his own or with Parnell's quiet or unspoken consent when he dispatched a series of letters to Devoy on illicit weaponry.

In September 1882, four months after Parnell and his colleagues agreed to restore peace to rural Ireland, O'Kelly advised Devoy to tell his "friends" that they "ought to secure" twenty thousand rifles in London and suggested that they look into buying "some 50,000 breach-loading Springfield rifles" from U.S. Army arsenals. (O'Kelly explained that the Springfields were good choices because "soldiers could fire buckshot out of them effectively at short range." This would give "raw men" confidence and "render their fire really effective.")

To be sure, O'Kelly goes on to advise what Parnell's biographer Conor Cruise O'Brien called a "moderate course." In the September letter to Devoy, O'Kelly noted that he had heard rumors of an Irish-American plot, led by Lomasney, to blow up Dublin Castle, the seat of British rule in Ireland. "I hope there is no truth in this rumour, or, if there should be, that the projectors will abandon their intention," he wrote.

But in ensuing letters, O'Kelly's immoderation is evident. In October, writing from Berlin, O'Kelly tells Devoy that "when writing to me about Irish affairs, you should use a secret ink—a weak solution of yellow prussiate of potash, I think, is the best because the safest. . . . You must take care to write with a quill pen." O'Kelly said he, too, would occasionally write in invisible ink, telling Devoy to soak the letters "with a solution of copperas."

O'Kelly had good reason to keep his ink invisible. "With regard to the arms you are buying," he wrote to Devoy in October, "I consider the Colt revolver antiquated. Though a good shooting weapon . . . no man could reload the Colt during a fight—while the Smith and Wesson . . . could be easily and rapidly reloaded by even men new to the business." O'Kelly was nothing if not well-informed on the subject: "The price you are paying, 42 shillings, is excessive. The Belgians are making very good imitations of the Smith and Wesson . . . which could be purchased in large numbers for probably one pound. They are sold retail in Turkey for 36 shillings. . . . The arms could be delivered in London or Liverpool."

This is a rather intriging bit of advice, coming from a member of parliament and man judged to be Parnell's confidant. Cruise O'Brien, in examining the same letters, says simply that O'Kelly employed a "Fenian tone." Indeed.

So the question arises: As he prepared to launch a spectacular, if ultimately vain, campaign to win Ireland a measure of self-government, was Parnell aware that his second-in-command was conspiring with John Devoy to bring arms into Ireland? A better question might be this: How could he not have known? Why would he not want to know?

ON JULY 3, 1883, another of Devoy's projects got under way, literally. From its moorings in the Morris Canal, John Holland's submarine slipped into New York Harbor. Holland, who had begun experimenting with projectile torpedoes in the Morris Canal basin, wanted to test the vessel in the harbor's deep waters. Throughout the summer, the extraordinary vessel entertained and frightened onlookers as it disappeared from the water's surface in a great, clumsy dive, reappearing minutes later. During one such journey, Holland heard a scuffling noise overhead. He opened the hatch to find a young, frightened boy sitting astride the turret. On another occasion, a ferryboat captain plying from Staten Island to Brooklyn brought his vessel to a stop when he spotted the strange, cigar-shaped submarine floating nearby. When Holland's vessel disappeared below the surface, the captain immediately turned his boat and headed back to shore in a panic.

Other developments were taking place below the surface, too. The *Irish World*'s story accusing Devoy of wasting Skirmishing Fund money specifically pointed to the submarine experiments as a failure. The story confirmed publicly Britain's private complaints that the submarine experiments were the work of Irish-American fanatics intent on destroying British shipping. At the same time, a lingering lawsuit from Rossa's days at the Skirmishing Fund promised even more public embarrassment. The plaintiff, a physician named Denis Dowling Mulcahey, was seeking a claim on the submarine in lieu of expense payments he had never received while on a Clan mission to Ireland. Devoy and the other trustees of the Skirmishing Fund were listed as defendants in the suit.

Making matters worse, Holland himself was upset about expenditures, and he, too, threatened to bring a lawsuit. John Breslin, Devoy's ally who served as a liaison to Holland (and who now was business manager of the *Irish Nation*), decided to bring matters to a dramatic close. Rather than risk losing possession of the submarine in a court action, Breslin and a few confederates—Devoy was not among them, but he must have given his approval—decided in late November 1883 to kidnap the sub from its dock. Under cover of darkness, they maneuvered a tugboat next to the sub, tossed a line around her, and towed her to New Haven, out of the New York courts' jurisdiction. The Holland-Devoy partnership, which so worried the British, came to an end. The *Fenian Ram* never sailed again.

But John Holland, the visionary from County Clare, eventually sold his plans to the U.S. government and built two more submarines. The first U.S. Navy submarine, based on Holland's design, was christened the USS *Holland*.

THOUGH HE WAS FINANCING the submarine project, John Devoy was not among the gawking onlookers who gathered on the shores of Bay Ridge and Staten Island to watch Holland's summer-long exercises in 1883. He spent the bulk of that summer in a steamy Manhattan courtroom, the defendant in yet another lawsuit. His passion for vitriol had landed him in the Court of General Sessions, where he was prosecuted on charges of criminal libel against August Belmont, the aging and politically connected banker who was among the most powerful men in New York in the 1880s.

In yet another arcane battle that found its way into the *Irish*

Nation, Devoy charged, incorrectly, that Belmont had made off with funds that the American Fenians had deposited with his partner's bank just after the Civil War. For this alleged treachery, Devoy urged his readers to vote against Belmont's son, Perry, who was running for Congress from Manhattan in 1882.

The legal proceedings lasted nearly a year, draining the finances of both Devoy and the *Irish Nation*. The first trial ended in a hung jury on June 18, 1883, four weeks after he had become an American citizen; the second found Devoy guilty of criminal libel. He was sentenced to sixty days on the prison colony of Blackwell's Island in Manhattan's East River, from which, in the distance, he could see the expanse of the harbor where Holland was testing the submarine Devoy had financed. He was released on August 17, with the *Irish Nation* reporting that its editor was "unrepentant."

Devoy's case was a minor cause célèbre among his colleagues, with newspapers around the state demanding that Gov. Grover Cleveland, a Democrat, intercede to keep Devoy from prison. Devoy's lawyer filed a motion for executive clemency with Cleveland's office. But Cleveland did nothing, no doubt because Belmont was the Democratic Party's treasurer and one of its top fund-raisers.

The case lifted eyebrows across the Atlantic as well. Perry Belmont, on a visit to London, was cornered by his father's onetime business partner Baron Rothschild, who berated the Belmonts for proceeding with their suit. The prosecution of Devoy, the baron said, would serve to strengthen the intemperate hand of O'Donovan Rossa, a shrewd interpretation of the differences in the American Irish movement. Rothschild told Perry Belmont that his father's crusade against Devoy had damaged the elder Belmont's chances of one day becoming American ambassador to Great Britain—the British, Rothschild suggested, might block such an appointment.

EIGHT WEEKS AFTER DEVOY became a free man again, on October 30, 1883, two bombs exploded in the London underground system within minutes of each other. The first, just before 8 P.M., injured seventy-two people, most of them working class, riding in third-class coaches. The second caused no injuries. William Mackey Lomasney, who had been horrified by O'Donovan Rossa's bombers, was on the job. After midnight on November 21, the Home Office in London received a message from a British agent in America "describing the machine with which and the manner in which" Queen Victoria's train was to be blown up on its way to Balmoral Castle in Scotland.

The underground explosions took place after months of correspondence between London and Washington, during which frustrated British diplomats asked Washington to close down what it called the "dynamite press"—by which they meant the *Irish World*, Rossa's paper (the *United Irishmen*), and a new entry on the scene, the Brooklyn-based *Ireland's Liberator and Dynamite Monthly*. British diplomats told their American counterparts that they would hardly stand by if the London press were calling for the murder of an American president. The argument was meant to touch a nerve—President Garfield had been assassinated in 1881.

But the new British ambassador, Lord Sackville-West, reported back to London that Garfield's successor, Chester Arthur, was "afraid of doing or saying anything to offend the Irish faction." Sackville-West described the United States as a "safe refuge for murderers and their accomplices." In despair, Prime Minister William Gladstone complained to Queen Victoria that "no other civilized country in the world would tolerate the open advocacy of assassination and murder." An explosion rocked the luggage room at Victoria Station on February 26, 1884. Security forces were immediately dispatched to other large railway stations, where three more bombs were found.

Devoy's onetime tormentor, Home Secretary William Harcourt, wrote to Her Majesty that "the origin of these devilish schemes is certain. They are planned, subsidized and executed by the assassination societies of American Fenians, who announce their intentions and advertise them openly in newspapers published without the smallest restraint in the United States." Harcourt complained that Washington had responded only with a message of "a most unfriendly character." Three more bombs were detonated on May 30, one of them outside Scotland Yard, an astonishing breach of security. The blasts caused no deaths, and only a few minor injuries.

Word was dispatched to Britain's ports to be on the lookout for men who "from their appearance" might be Irish-American. The vigilance paid off with the arrest of John Daly, who was caught in a rail station with bombs in his pockets. A police informer claimed that

Daly had planned to throw the bombs onto the House of Commons floor from the building's public gallery.

Daly had been in Britain for weeks and was so low on money that just before he was arrested, he pawned his only possession that could fetch a decent price. It was the watch John Devoy had given him when he was in New York.

What did Devoy know about the Clan bombings, and when did he know it? Given that the Clan had recently reduced its executive further, from five members to three, and that Devoy was distant from the new center of Clan power—Chicago—it seems likely that he knew little, if anything, about the bombings, even if he did know some of the bombers. The Clan's three executives, led by Sullivan, soon became known simply as the Triangle, a symbol of identification they used on Clan circulars.

Devoy's newspaper was conspicuously silent during the bombing campaign. Though Devoy opposed the Clan's new tactics, the *Irish Nation* was a failing business, and Devoy was taking handouts from Sullivan and the Revolutionary Directory. Even Devoy didn't dare attack his benefactors.

He chose instead to concentrate on American politics. In 1884, the contenders for the presidency were James Blaine, the Republican and former secretary of state, and New York governor Grover Cleveland, the man who had refused to use his power to keep Devoy out of prison. That Blaine was widely thought of as a pro-Irish secretary of state and bore the considerable burden of having a Catholic mother (there was some whispering about *his* religious upbringing) made Devoy's choice that much easier. He became a founding member of the Anti-Cleveland Union, an organization of Irish-American supporters of James Blaine.

Devoy turned the *Irish Nation* into a virtual campaign organ for Blaine, hailing the Republican candidate's opposition to free trade, which Devoy and other Irish-Americans saw as a British plot to prevent American economic growth. Britain watched what appeared to be an Irish-American defection from the Democratic Party and Cleveland with growing unease. "There is no doubt that if the nomination of Mr. Blaine results in his election to the Presidency . . . our relations may become uneasy," wrote Ambassador Sackville-West to Lord Granville. Sackville-West's fears were well-founded. A New

York Clan na Gael camp published a meeting notice summoning the presence of "all dynamiters who favour the election of James G. Blaine for president of the United States." Blaine, the advertisement said, was "a true friend of the Irish."

All was going according to plan until Blaine had the bad luck to meet with several Protestant ministers in New York, perhaps as a means of fending off rumors of his closet Catholicism. In an immortal phrase, and one that displayed little knowledge of what was actually happening in the campaign, one of the ministers promptly announced that Blaine would protect the nation from "rum, Romanism and rebellion."

Blaine lost by twenty-five thousand votes out of 10 million cast, after the Catholic defection to the Republican Party reversed itself. Devoy quickly learned the hazards of playing partisan politics. His readers began deserting the paper, and Devoy published what amounted to an apology for its support for Blaine. "To those who disagree with us in American politics we would say that the paper had enough to recommend it, irrespective of American affairs, to all who are in sympathy with . . . its unwavering course toward Mr. Parnell and the movement of which he is the honored head." A public stock offering, at ten dollars a share, didn't help much (although Mayor Grace of New York bought several shares).

On April 22, 1885, at ten o'clock in the morning, the office furniture and equipment—including 1,100 pounds of type—belonging to the *Irish Nation* were put up for auction in a sheriff's sale. The paper was dead, and Devoy was once again out of work. Now he had neither standing in the Clan nor a forum for his ideas.

IN THE EVENING HOURS of December 13, 1885, Devoy's friend William Mackey Lomasney, accompanied by two other men, gently guided a rented rowboat along the Thames. The three men attached a bomb to an iron grating underneath London Bridge. The bomb exploded prematurely, causing little damage to the bridge. When police arrived, they found only a section of the boat the bombers had used. No bodies were ever recovered. Lomasney, Devoy wrote, "exploded into atoms."

Five weeks later, on January 24, two teams of Irish-Americans set off bombs at the Tower of London and in the Houses of Parliament. The attacks had London in a panic.

The guerrilla war between Britain and Irish-America, however, was about to come to an end. Ireland's nationalists in America were about to go to war with each other.

CHAPTER ELEVEN

The Ould Triangle

ALEXANDER SULLIVAN WAS A TOWERING, ROUGH-HEWN FIGURE
in Chicago politics, a well-connected lawyer who was the unelected,
self-appointed boss of an independent political machine that placed
hundreds of Clan na Gael men in dozens of government agencies,
especially the police department. Thanks to his rather flexible political allegiances, his contacts were bipartisan, reaching as high and as
far as Washington itself.

As president of the Land League and chairman of the Clan na
Gael, Alexander Sullivan was the most powerful Irishman in America
in the mid-1880s, a man whose crude glamour made him an attractive
figure to visiting Europeans. In their eyes, Sullivan was a character
from a Wild West story, complete with cowboy boots and an ever-
present pistol. He had killed a man who had insulted his wife (the
victim called Mrs. Sullivan a "tool of the Jesuits"). He successfully
argued that he had acted in self-defense. He shot and wounded a
political opponent in New Mexico. And he had fled a job as a postal
official in the Southwest when his books didn't add up. A one-man
metaphor for the forgiving powers of America and particularly the
West, he moved to Chicago and reinvented himself as a sophisticated
and respectable man of the law. Handsome, with a fine head of dark
hair and strong jawline, he was married to a journalist named Margaret Buchanan, and the two of them reigned as Chicago's unofficial
first couple, partners as well as husband and wife—a rare arrangement
in nineteenth-century America.

His dual role at the head of the Irish-American nationalist movement gave him control over hundreds of thousands of dollars earmarked either for Parnell's use, in the case of the League money, or for terrorism, in the Clan's case. The sums in question were enough that Parnell had little choice but to send obsequious telegrams, along with duly appointed envoys, to the League's various conventions. Between 1884 and 1886, the American National League (the successor to the American Land League) raised $314,000 to assist Parnell in a general election campaign and his crusade for home rule. The Clan's treasury was nearly as flush. At its convention in 1884, it reported raising $253,000, with $128,000 spent on what it called "active work." During the stormy years of 1881 to 1888, Devoy estimated that the Clan raised a half million dollars.

Sullivan was a natural leader, and he moved with ease in the most elevated circles of American politics. It was Sullivan who led an Irish-American delegation to the White House in 1883 to ask President Chester Arthur to crack down on, of all things, Irish immigration. The early 1880s had seen an upsurge in immigration from Ireland, the result of the poor harvests of the late 1870s and the Land War evictions that followed. When the British began a policy of what it called "assisted emigration"—offering Irish families money to leave Ireland for America—Sullivan, Devoy, and other Irish-Americans predictably and perhaps understandably suspected a plot to depopulate the Irish countryside. A less charitable explanation had it that the new immigrants were an embarrassment to the growing Irish-American middle class.

In 1884, with his power over Chicago's machine nearly dictatorial and his leadership of both the public and the secret Irish-American movements unquestioned, Sullivan embarked on the course that would lead to a brutal falling-out with Devoy, the virtual dismantling of Clan na Gael, and his arrest on murder charges in a case that shook Chicago politics and made national headlines. At the Clan's 1884 convention in Boston, Sullivan and his two top aides in the Clan—the other sides of the so-called Triangle—formally dissolved the organization's fraternal link with the Irish Republican Brotherhood because of the IRB's opposition to the Clan's terrorism campaign. The IRB insisted that the Clan had no right to conduct operations on the Brotherhood's territory of Ireland and Britain; Sullivan and the Clan denied the Brotherhood's right to dictate policy to America. The Land War had given way to the Turf War.

Sullivan's actions constituted a very real, and decidedly new, departure from Devoy's patient efforts to build up a conventional arms arsenal in Ireland—always in conjunction with the IRB—in preparation for the moment when Britain would be engaged in some military adventure elsewhere. But Sullivan's radical change of course should not have surprised Devoy, for as early as 1880, Sullivan made it clear that he was impatient for a fight: "I fear our work and money are wasted, while the I.R.B. is under control of men who lack activity and brains," he wrote to Devoy. "Unless a change is made, my judgment is that the home connection ought to be dropped. We could do something if alone."

Devoy had thus far managed to avoid a confrontation with Sullivan and the Clan leadership, but after the Boston convention, it was clear that another sort of explosion was imminent. Devoy regarded the IRB as Ireland's provisional government, with the absolute right to determine policy within its sphere of conspiracy. When the New York delegates returned from Boston, they gathered for a convention of their own and passed a Devoy-authored resolution condemning the Clan leadership's action and demanding a restoration of the Clan's relationship with the IRB. According to Devoy, when Sullivan heard of the resolution, he denounced its author—anonymously—as a tool of Scotland Yard.

Even as he cleared the way for the Clan's continued assault on the heart of the Empire, Sullivan was quietly negotiating with Democratic Party leaders in hopes of winning the party's vice presidential nomination in the 1884 election. Sullivan's past, including the possibility that he was born in Canada and thus ineligible for national office, made his ambitions seem scandalously arrogant. (Then again, that year's Democratic presidential nominee, Grover Cleveland, managed to win the White House despite revelations that he had fathered a child out of wedlock.)

When his proposal failed, Sullivan immediately entered into negotiations with Blaine and the Republicans and reregistered as a Republican after, according to Devoy, extracting the promise of a cabinet post from the Republican nominee. He resigned as president of the National League, which had pledged to stay out of American partisan politics, but he was careful to choose a pliable successor. His choice was Patrick Egan, newly arrived from France after serving as the Irish Land League's treasurer.

The Blaine campaign became a testing ground for the war that was to come. Though they wore they same Republican uniform, Devoy and Sullivan circled each other warily, each taking the measure of the other's leadership and support. When Sullivan spoke on Blaine's behalf at a rally in New York's Academy of Music on Fourteenth Street, Devoy saw it as an incursion by a hostile force and pointedly refused to take a seat on the platform. He was delighted to see some of his allies walk out during Sullivan's speech. Not long afterward, Sullivan's allies set up an anti-Cleveland organization in New York to compete with Devoy's Irish-American Anti-Cleveland Union.

Devoy himself traveled to twenty-eight cities and towns throughout New York and New Jersey to speak on behalf of the Blaine campaign and was in such demand in his home territory that he could not accept Henry Cabot Lodge's invitation to tour Massachusetts. His speeches were carefully constructed to avoid criticism of the Democratic Party, to which many Irishmen owed their jobs and prospects. Devoy's cautious approach did not always have his listeners on the edge of their seats, as he discovered one night during a rally in the upstate New York town of Schaghticoke.

On this Saturday night during the campaign's last few weeks, the tiny hall's stove was turned up full blast to keep out the midautumn cold. The heat did nothing to arouse the crowd's enthusiasm, and Devoy's speech only added to the general malaise. As he spoke of the great qualities of candidate Blaine, Devoy noticed a man with "an unmistakeably Irish face" nodding off, snapping out of it, then nodding off again. If Devoy adjusted his remarks accordingly, it was to no avail, as the man eventually surrendered to sleep. Unfortunately, the poor man's face pitched forward into the head of the man sitting in front of him. Perhaps sensing a chance to add some excitement to the campaign rally, the man who had been knocked on the head decked his sleeping assailant, touching off a brawl. A woman sitting in the front row fainted. Long after the incident, Devoy described it, with resignation born of intimate knowledge, as "the old Irish story of hitting a fellow first and finding out the reason afterwards."

AFTER BLAINE LOST THE presidency and Devoy lost his newspaper, the divisions in the Clan began to harden. Sullivan suspended the Clan camp to which Devoy belonged, the Napper Tandy Club, when it continued to criticize the Clan leadership's break with the IRB. Wholesale suspensions of clubs in New York and New Jersey followed, leading to a rump convention that renewed contact with the Brotherhood in Ireland. The stage was set for a disastrous and bloody split.

The internecine battles in America came just as Parnell was about to bring Ireland's cause to the forefront of British politics. In mid-1885, Parnell formed an alliance with the Conservative Party to bring down William Gladstone's Liberal government, and as a reward for Irish support, the Conservatives ended coercion in Ireland and introduced mild land reforms. In the general election that fall, Parnell negotiated with both parties over the merits of a home-rule bill for Ireland. Two days before the election, Parnell announced his support for the Conservatives. When the votes were counted, neither major party could mount a majority without the support of Parnell and his bloc of eighty-six members. Parnell turned his back on the Conservatives to support Gladstone, and the way was cleared for the introduction of a historic bill that would grant Ireland a form of self-government—that slippery phrase Devoy used in the days of the New Departure.

The enthusiasm for Parnell in Ireland, where he was at the peak of his reign as Ireland's uncrowned king, was noticeably absent among some of his erstwhile allies in America. Margaret Buchanan Sullivan, the Clan and League leader's wife, traveled to London in the spring of 1886, possibly to tell Parnell that his party would receive no further financial assistance from the National League unless he pushed harder for complete independence. Whether or not she actually delivered such a message, it is clear Parnell knew who she was and what she represented. According to Parnell's colleague William O'Brien, Parnell spotted Mrs. Sullivan in the Strangers Gallery of the House of Commons during the debate over home rule. He was instantly gripped with the fear that she was about to throw a bomb onto the House floor.

His fears had some justification. In March 1886, as the home-rule bill worked its way through the House—the bill would eventually fail—Sullivan and the Clan voted to renew the dynamite campaign when the debate reached its conclusion. Britain was making ambitious plans for Queen Victoria's fiftieth anniversary as monarch in 1887, and the Clan wanted to be part of the fireworks. A dynamite offensive was planned to coincide with the jubilee festivities.

AN OUT-OF-WORK, financially pressed John Devoy left New York for Chicago in August 1886, for an American National League convention that brought together all of the contending forces of Irish-American nationalism. Parnell himself was supposed to attend, but he feared that Sullivan and the Clan firebrands would embarrass him with violent speeches and demonstrations. His judgment was impeccable.

As a preliminary to the promised convention drama, the delegates and the mainstream Chicago Irish planned to gather for an annual picnic in Ogden's Grove on August 15, an event sponsored by a front for the Clan na Gael called the United Irish Societies. On the eve of the festivities, Devoy received a message from Michael Davitt, whom he had not seen nor heard from in four years. The two men had split in 1882 when Davitt took up the cause of land nationalization as the solution to Ireland's problems, a formula Devoy's friend O'Kelly denounced as "communistic." Devoy was similarly put off, and he regularly criticized Davitt in the pages of the *Irish Nation*. Davitt, in Chicago for the convention, proposed a reunion with his New Departure partner, and Devoy agreed. The two men gathered for what must have been a bittersweet lunch. They had helped change the Irish and Irish-American political landscape and thus touched off a social revolution. Their rapport had been instantaneous, and their partnership historic. They helped each other redefine the goals of an Irish revolution. Now, just a few years later, they were estranged.

Devoy was an unsentimental man, so he probably agreed to meet Davitt not for the sake of old times but in hopes of winning an ally in his increasingly contentious dispute with Sullivan. Devoy spent the meal outlining his complaints and his charges of financial corruption. Davitt, in Devoy's account, listened carefully, but made it clear that his sympathies were with Sullivan. "We parted as friends," Devoy later wrote, "but with a wide gulf between us, and we never met again."

The tragedies that were about to visit Irish nationalists on both sides of the Atlantic were foreshadowed as delegates gathered in Ogden's Grove for the preconvention picnic. In Davitt's presence, a speaker read a series of resolutions asserting that constitutional means alone could not free Ireland, a clear slap at Parnell's home-rule crusade, which Davitt supported. Another speaker, a fiery and slightly unbalanced former congressman named John Finerty, defended the Irish-American dynamite campaign. This was exactly what Parnell had feared. Davitt could not remain silent; he rose to reply to Finerty:

"The fight for Irish national self-government looks, perhaps, different in Ireland to what it does in Chicago. It is very easy to establish an Irish republic three thousand miles away from Ireland by patriotic speeches. I assure you it is no easy task, though, to do it in old Ireland."

Davitt and Finerty were not finished with each other. When the League convention opened formally, Davitt delivered an unremarkable speech on behalf of Parnell's home-rule crusade, which pleased the moderates in the house but not Sullivan's sizable Clan na Gael contingent. Finerty, apparently egged on by Sullivan, took the podium and delivered yet another fiery speech in praise of, in Devoy's words, "unrelenting war against England with any available weapons, using the fires of hell if they could be got at."

Once again Davitt could not remain silent. He rose from his seat on the speakers' platform, and grasping the chair with his left (and only) hand, he announced that he and Finerty had "crossed swords before . . . and I don't think I have come out second best."

If Parnell's men and the lawyers, priests, and semirespectable politicians in the audience were not already embarrassed, they soon would be. When Davitt finished, Finerty sprang out of his chair and charged across the stage in Davitt's direction. Davitt, hardly in a position to fend off a wild man, stood his ground as Finerty approached. A one-sided brawl between a former congressman and a disabled messenger of peace seemed inevitable, but Finerty was wrestled to the ground by the convention's chairman and others before he could further demonstrate the subtle points of his argument.

Devoy, watching the proceedings from the convention floor, saw in Finerty's outbursts the hand of his own protagonist, Sullivan. He was convinced that Sullivan and his allies were preparing to overthrow Parnell as leader of the Irish Parliamentary Party, perhaps by cutting off his American funds through the National League, a body that remained very much under Sullivan's control. The fiery speeches, Devoy believed, were meant to send a message.

With no prospects to return to in New York, Devoy decided to stay in Chicago. Thanks to his political connections, he found a job at the Cook County Elections Commission and began watching Sullivan's every move. He took a room in a lodging house where Finerty lived and soon formed an alliance with another prominent Chicago Clan member, a physician named Patrick H. Cronin. He, too, was determined to free the Clan from Sullivan's grasp. His efforts would cost him his life.

DEVOY JOURNEYED TO BROOKLYN in early 1887 to form a separate Clan na Gael organization, one that the Irish Republican Brotherhood immediately recognized as its authorized partner in America. Devoy was dispatched on a recruiting mission that took him through the Midwest, close to Sullivan's base of operations. His mission proved successful enough that Sullivan's wing soon dispatched messages offering terms. A joint convention was arranged and scheduled in Chicago to coincide with the Republican National Convention of 1888, for the Clan's two sections were united on at least one issue— the removal of Grover Cleveland from the White House.

What was billed as a Union Convention of the Clan in June of 1888 should have marked the end of the story of the Clan na Gael's division. Sullivan, who had once seemed so powerful, resigned before the convention met, unwilling to face Devoy's questions about the organization's finances. Devoy was allowed to present his accusations, and on June 13, 1888, he formally accused Sullivan and his lieutenants of misappropriating Clan money. An ally of Devoy's, Luke

Dillon—who had participated in dynamite attacks in Britain and returned to tell about it—charged that Sullivan and the Clan leaders
had lied about spending money for rifles and had neglected the families of his fellow dynamiters in British prisons.

In a very real sense, Devoy already had his victory. Sullivan had
been forced from power, and a new, nine-member Executive Committee had been formed, with four of Devoy's allies included. His own
prospects had improved considerably. In a sure sign that he understood the significance of Sullivan's resignation, he left his monitoring
post in Chicago and moved back to New York for a reporter's position
with the *Evening Journal* newspaper.

Nevertheless, Devoy was not satisfied. Sullivan, he decided, had
to be discredited and crushed. Devoy demanded that the new Clan
executive appoint a committee to investigate his charges and those
of Dillon. The executive agreed, and the panel returned a decision
that neither confirmed nor denied Devoy's charges, but chastised Sullivan and his cronies for mismanagement. Again, Devoy had a chance
to simply end the proceedings. Instead, he demanded a full, in-house
trial for Sullivan and his coconspirators. Devoy's ally, Dillon, wanted
to drop the matter, but Devoy was not to be denied, and a trial
committee was duly appointed. Dr. Cronin, Devoy's strongest ally,
was among six members appointed to the tribunal, which spent the
summer of 1888 looking into Devoy's and Dillon's charges.

Devoy's timing was as deplorable as his obstinacy. Even as he
pressed his crusade beyond the limits of discretion, Charles Stewart
Parnell was fighting for his political life, arraigned before a government commission investigating charges published in the *Times* of
London that he not only approved of the infamous Phoenix Park
murders, but that he was working hand in glove with Irish-American
terrorists and bombers who financed his party through the American
National League and its predecessor, the American Land League. The
charges were so close to home that Devoy would have been advised
to accept the Clan committee's finding of mismanagement and allow
all concerned to lower their profiles as their names were bandied
about in a London courtroom. And yet Devoy persisted.

Parnell clearly was not comfortable with the turn of events in
America. He dispatched James J. O'Kelly across the Atlantic in the

vain hope that his chief lieutenant could persuade Devoy to postpone the Clan trial until after Parnell's own ordeal was over. Parnell had good reason for his unease. He feared that Devoy, in his mania to crush Sullivan and his lackey Patrick Egan, was prepared to reveal that Egan had turned over to Sullivan and the Clan $100,000 in Land League money during the Clan's dynamite campaign. This was exactly the link the government hoped to make. The revelation could have finished Parnell.

Devoy told O'Kelly that he could not and would not postpone the trial, but he assured his old friend that the smoking-gun transfer of funds would remain a secret. As passionate as Devoy was about his crusade, he understood how high the stakes were for Parnell.

THE TRIAL STARTED IN Buffalo in late August, then moved to a saloon hall in New York City. The first two sessions gave an indication of what was to come: Sullivan demanded that Devoy be barred from the proceedings because he was a British spy. When the trial resumed in September after a short break, both Sullivan and Devoy brought revolvers.

The proceedings were extremely tense, and Devoy and Sullivan were not the only men bearing arms in the room. According to Devoy, one of Sullivan's men predicted that "Aleck [Sullivan] would make a morgue" of the room. Devoy was convinced that he was marked for assassination. On one occasion, in a restaurant near City Hall, Devoy believed he was being set up by his onetime friend Tom Desmond, who had become a Sullivan ally. Desmond brought a friend with him, and Devoy grew suspicious when the man's accent didn't match the part of Ireland he claimed as his home. According to Devoy, a few of his newspaper colleagues were seated at an adjacant table and later told him that the stranger "had murder in his eyes." Desmond's friend showed up at Devoy's apartment some days later and stalked away when he was told Devoy wasn't home.

The court adjourned on September 16, a Sunday, to allow Sullivan, Devoy, and their warring allies to put away their sidearms and spend the next six weeks working on the common cause of electing Benjamin Harrison president. Devoy had been hired to serve as president of the Irish-American Anti-Cleveland and Protective League, which the Republican National Committee funded. As he did for Blaine, Devoy traveled throughout the New York area giving speeches for Harrison and was startled to find voters in the Hudson Valley region who expected to collect a fee of $2 in return for their votes. Harrison won the election, helped by a stunning victory over Cleveland in New York. Devoy claimed Harrison's critical win in New York was directly attributable to the votes of thirty thousand Irish Democrats who switched party lines to support the Republican.

Apparently Harrison thought so, too. Devoy and several of his Irish-American friends, including the former Clan chairman Dr. William Carroll, were invited to dinner at the president-elect's home in Indianapolis shortly after election day. Devoy described his conversation with Harrison as pleasant, although he found the incoming president somewhat aloof when the Irish-American guests offered advice about candidates for cabinet posts.

THE DAY AFTER THE Clan tribunal adjourned its saloon-hall proceedings, judges, barristers, and an eager press gathered in London for a preliminary session of the special commission charged with investigating Charles Parnell's links to American terrorists.

The Parnell Commission's most immediate concern was an accusation, printed in the *Times* of London, that Parnell approved of the Phoenix Park murders, raising yet again the specter of the Irish parliamentarian plotting with terrorists and assassins. The *Times'* charge was based on a letter allegedly written by Parnell to an associate in 1882, in which he said that one of the Phoenix Park victims, T. H. Burke, had gotten what he deserved. The *Times* got hold of the letter and printed it, along with a front-page article bearing the lurid headline "Parnellism and Crime."

But it was clear from the beginning that the government was prepared to broaden the investigation much wider. During the first day of testimony, October 22, the attorney general revisited Parnell's trip to America in 1880, asserting that when Parnell hurriedly left the States in March, he placed his affairs in the hands of American Fenians. Three days later, on October 25, Devoy's name was mentioned for the first time, as the government linked Devoy and Davitt as partners in conspiracy. The attorney general quoted word for word the resolutions Devoy had written and introduced in September 1878 before Davitt's first speech in New York. The resolutions not only called for the abolition of landlordism but the "complete overthrow of British domination." Striking a theme that would be repeated constantly in the coming months, the attorney general said, "Now, my lord, will you just consider for a moment what the starting point of this organization was. It was working with the knowledge of Mr. Parnell." That was not true; neither the New Departure nor the Land League had been launched at the time of Davitt's lecture tour. But the government was on a mission.

The commission sat for more than a year. In the middle of the proceedings, Richard Pigott, the man who had provided the *Times* with the letter incriminating Parnell, took the stand. Pigott, the editor of the since-closed *Irishman* newspaper, appeared before the commission on February 20, but failed to show the next day. Indeed, he never showed up again. He was found in Spain, his throat cut by his own hand. Pigott had forged the letter.

Pigott's death should have ended matters, for it utterly discredited the *Times* stories that had prompted the government's investigation. But British officials were determined to crush Parnell. Two weeks before Pigott's disappearance, a man with whom Devoy had shared several conspiratorial conversations appeared on the government witness stand. He gave his name as Thomas Beech, but said he was known in America as Henri Le Caron, the physician from Braidwood, Illinois. He portrayed himself as a man at the heart of the conspiracy the government was intent on uncovering. Not only had he met with Devoy and Parnell, he claimed to have carried messages between them. He provided the commission with dozens of documents, including correspondence with Devoy and secret Clan memos.

The disclosure of a spy at the highest levels of the Clan's leadership was stunning. But Le Caron's appearance on the witness stand coincided with increasingly more explosive events in America.

THE CLAN TRIBUNAL, BY a vote of four to two, cleared Sullivan and his allies of the most serious charges against them. It found, however, that large sums of money had been wasted—though not stolen—and that Sullivan and his friends had neglected the families of Clan members who were killed or imprisoned during the bombing campaign. Devoy's ally Cronin voted in favor of conviction on all counts and issued his own report declaring Sullivan and company guilty of fraud and of wasting $110,000. Cronin refused to turn over the notes he had kept of the proceedings, despite an agreement that all evidence would be destroyed after the verdict.

The verdict infuriated Devoy and Cronin. Devoy would later charge that Sullivan had lost tens of thousands of Clan dollars speculating on the Chicago Board of Trade. Certainly something was wrong with the Clan's accounts for the period, but by the time of the unsatisfactory verdict, Sullivan and his immediate allies no longer held any power in the Clan and very likely never would again. Their extravagance, if not their alleged criminal behavior, had been exposed and condemned. It was highly unlikely Sullivan could recover from his disgrace.

Nevertheless, Cronin returned to Chicago and submitted his findings to Clan camps throughout the area. His attacks won the notice of the local press, and he published a pamphlet suggesting that Sullivan's party might try to murder him.

In London, Henri Le Caron, or Thomas Beech, was on the stand, testifying that four other British infiltrators were in the ranks of the Clan na Gael. Sullivan's allies began spreading word that Cronin was one of the spies.

Cronin disappeared on May 4, 1889. His battered body, naked save for the religious scapular that hung around his neck, was discovered in a storm sewer on May 22. His funeral, on May 26, was described as Chicago's biggest and most impressive since the death of Stephen Douglas, the Illinois senator and failed presidential candidate in 1860.

The murder created a national sensation. For nearly a quarter century, the Clan had operated without public attention. Now, with its feud turned deadly, members of both Clan sections were forced to appear before a coroner's jury to explain the Clan's internal workings, including the rivalry between Sullivan and Cronin. In June, the jury declared that the murder was the work of a Clan na Gael feud and directed that Alexander Sullivan, along with three other men, including a Chicago police detective, be placed under arrest for murder. The jury, in a scalding report, declared that the Clan na Gael was "not in harmony with and [is] injurious to American Institutions." Devoy's section of the Clan took out newspaper advertisements to explain that Clan na Gael was not "a murder society."

Eventually, Sullivan was freed and the charge of murder dropped. But Devoy believed his rival was responsible, at a minimum, for spreading the rumor that Cronin was a spy. The tenuous unity of the Clan dissolved in the scandal. Devoy quit his job in New York and moved back to Chicago, where he spent the next four years serving as the avenging ghost of his friend Dr. Cronin. When Cronin's accused murderers were on trial, Devoy attended every session, and in speeches to his section of the Chicago Clan, he continuously named Sullivan as the crime's mastermind.

Such obsession took no shortage of personal courage, for Devoy later said he was threatened with death several times while living in his enemy's home city and working at various newspaper jobs. He carried a revolver at all times and nearly used it one afternoon when he and Sullivan crossed paths in a Chicago restaurant. Devoy intentionally walked past Sullivan's table, keeping his right hand in the coat pocket that held his weapon. "I knew that he always carried a revolver," Devoy wrote of Sullivan, "and if he had made a motion to draw it, I would have shot him before he could reach his hip pocket."

The organization that had carried off the *Catalpa* rescue and created a movement of exiles that struck fear—and terror—in the heart of the world's most formidable empire had been reduced to little more than two rival factions led by men with revolvers in their pockets.

CHARLES PARNELL ENTERED THE House of Commons on February 13, 1890, and was greeted with a great, collegial ovation. The special commission's final report had been made public, and the Irish leader had been exonerated. The uncrowned king was triumphant.

But even as Ireland celebrated and prepared for the next battle, another court action was making its way through the British legal system. William O'Shea, Parnell's parliamentary colleague, had begun a divorce proceeding against his wife, Katherine, who had given birth to three of Parnell's children. Parnell was named as a respondent.

The case was brought into court on November 15, 1890. The *Times*, inhaling the scent of revenge, published a lurid account of the accusations of adultery that were heard in the courtroom. Neither Mrs. O'Shea nor Parnell were in court to mount a defense. Their silence spoke volumes.

The English press and some Protestant clergymen in Britain called for Parnell's resignation. His party, however, seemed solidly behind him. Timothy Healy declared that the Irish Party members would not join "with this howling pack." By the end of November, the howling pack included the aging British statesman William Gladstone. He told Parnell's allies that the Liberal Party was doomed to lose the next general election if Parnell remained at the head of the Irish Party. Gladstone had married his party and prestige to the cause of home rule and Parnellism. A nudge from Gladstone was not meant to be taken lightly, and it wasn't. Without Gladstone, the Irish Party was nothing but a powerless rump group. The Parnell Split, tragic and embittering but only the latest such division among Irish nationalists, was beginning.

As Gladstone's gambits caused the first hints of dissent in the previously closed ranks of Irish Party members, Devoy dispatched a telegram to O'Kelly:

"If Parnell yields to English clamour [it] will destroy American movement. No other man or men can keep it together. Retirement means chaos, leaving Ireland at mercy of English whims and Irish cranks. . . . Assure him [that he] may count on unswerving support and increased financial aid of American Irish, with or without Liberals."

Devoy's telegram contained fine sentiments but an odd grasp of reality. With Cronin dead, with Devoy accusing Sullivan of murder, and with the Clan bitterly divided, the American movement had already been damaged, if not destroyed. No action Parnell took could heal the divisions in America, and the action Devoy advised Parnell to take would do nothing except export division to Ireland.

The Irish Party gathered in Committee Room 15 in the House of Commons on December 1, 1890, for what would a wrenching, weeklong debate over Parnell's fitness as the party's leader. On Saturday evening, December 6, the seventy Irish members prepared for a final vote. John Redmond, one of Parnell's supporters, argued that to depose Parnell was to do Gladstone's bidding. Gladstone, he said, would be "master of the Party."

Tim Healy rose and sneered, "Who is to be the mistress of the Party?" It was Healy who only weeks before had pledged not to join with the "howling pack."

When the night was over, there were two Irish parties, Parnellite and anti-Parnellite. Parnell's party consisted of twenty-six members; the anti-Parnellites numbered forty-four, including Healy and John Dillon. The movement was bitterly and tragically divided.

With heartbreaking bravado, Parnell refused to give up and spent the early months of 1891 campaigning for his supporters in by-elections throughout Ireland. Devoy received a telegram from him in March, announcing the impending arrival of O'Kelly along with three colleagues dispatched to America to collect funds for the shattered "national movement." Losses in a series of elections piled up.

Devoy, horrified by the turn of events, offered himself as a broker between the two sides. He was an unlikely person for such a role, but though a Parnellite, he was on good terms with the anti-Parnellite John Dillon, the man who had risen in Devoy's defense on the House of Commons floor years before. He contacted Dillon in July, just after Parnell married his now-divorced mistress, Mrs. O'Shea. Dillon replied on August 6 and told Devoy that "one of the great misfortunes of your life has been that you are far too ready to take notice of 'charges' against you. . . . It is a miserable characteristic of our people that they seem to be utterly unable to differ on a political question without immediately becoming ferocious personal enemies. You were born for better things, but I must confess it was with the deepest pain that I saw you giving up your life to this wretched quarrel in Chicago." Dillon proceeded to say that Ireland would never again unite under Parnell's leadership.

Despite Dillon's position, Devoy believed he could bring the two sides together. He wrote Dillon and Parnell on August 30 with a series of propositions aimed at reuniting the Parliamentary Party and "putting an end to the deplorable strife which has brought the national movement to the verge of ruin." However much he had contributed to the "deplorable strife," it is hard not to sense Devoy's grief. Everything he had worked for was disappearing.

Devoy's plan called for Parnell and the leader of the anti-Parnell party, Justin McCarthy, to resign their leadership positions, for Parnell to be elected chairman of a reunited Irish Party, and for Parnell to then resign the post. Dillon would be elected as Parnell's successor, and Parnell would be dispatched to America, Australia, and Canada to raise funds for the reunited party.

"I want peace. I want union," Devoy wrote, before adding, significantly, that he wanted "a Home Rule Bill that Ireland can accept without loss of dignity."

It was no use. Dillon sent a respectful letter in reply, rejecting Devoy's peace pact and laying the burden for the split on Parnell's insistence on leading a "faction."

Two weeks later, on October 4, Parnell spent a restless Sunday night in London. The months-long campaign to regain his party and his good name had broken his health. He soon seemed delirious and could not get out of his bed. To Katherine, he said, "Hold me tight, then . . . so I can fight those others."

He died the next night. He was forty-five.

Parnell's colleagues sent Devoy a telegram thanking him for his support. Devoy does not record his emotions, but surely even so hard-hearted a man as he must have been shocked and grief-stricken. In something of a tribute, he would continue to call himself a Parnellite.

After Parnell's death, Devoy took a job with the *Chicago Herald*, where Margaret Sullivan, wife of his great antagonist, was one of his colleagues. He continued his obsession with Cronin's death, forming a committee to erect a monument to his slain friend. Anger and invective continued to flow in great, raging rivers. He fired off a telegram to his onetime dinner companion President Harrison when Harrison named Sullivan ally Patrick Egan as ambassador to Chile. The previous ambassador was William Roberts, who had helped plan the second Fenian invasion of Canada in 1866. Devoy wrote candidly that Harrison felt obliged to appoint an Irish-American to succeed Roberts in Chile. This may be the first documented case of diversity politics at the White House.

Most tragically, Devoy attacked Michael Davitt when Davitt announced his candidacy for Parliament in early 1892. In a circular addressed to "Members of Parliament, the Bishops and Clergy and the people of Ireland," Devoy charged—with some reason—that Davitt was among those who had suggested Cronin might be a British spy. For that reason, the circular stated, Davitt was responsible "for a portion" of Cronin's fate. "He stands today as the avowed champion of the men who are notoriously chiefs of the murder conspiracy," the circular concluded. It was signed with the names of Devoy and several of his allies.

It had been only a dozen years since Devoy, Parnell, and Davitt had discussed the future of Ireland and of Irish America's role. Now all was in ruins.

After two more aimless years in Chicago, Devoy was asked to return to New York to serve as secretary of the empty shell that was Clan na Gael. His ally and friend Luke Dillon (no relation to the parliamentarian John Dillon) thought Devoy could perform some miracle of organization before the cause disappeared, driven off the stage by scandal and apathy. Dillon's plan was simple. He would send Devoy on a cross-country tour to regroup and reorganize for the next battle.

Devoy was fifty-two years old in 1894, nearly ten years older than Parnell was when he died trying to heal a split. The work promised to be painstaking. The journeys promised to be long and exhausting. The assignment would test men much younger than Devoy.

Nevertheless he went to New York to see Dillon.

CHAPTER TWELVE

Darkest Just Before the Dawn

INCLUDED AMONG THE BURDENS JOHN DEVOY CARRIED WITH HIM aboard the train that took him back East was his role as the surrogate head of his scattered family. It was odd that he would become the stand-in for his dead parents. During the first twenty years of his exile, he maintained only limited contact with his siblings. His brother in New Mexico, Michael, gently chastised John for his long silences between letters back home.

Of the seven Devoy children, only two married and only one had children. Catherine, known to her family as Kate, had wed an aspiring businessman named Jack McBride in 1872. They had no children, and Jack, though ambitious, was something of a ne'er-do-well, a failure barely tolerated by his in-laws in Ireland. He tried to make a living in Ireland as a cork-cutter, without success, and soon gave up and set sail, with Kate, for America, arriving in 1889.

Like his elder brother John, Joseph had fallen in love with a woman who shared their mother's name, Elizabeth. Joseph and Elizabeth, whom he called Eliza (as his mother and as John's onetime fiancé were called), had in quick succession four sons—William, Peter, John, and James—and a daughter, Eileen. Joseph's household also included his two unmarried sisters, Bridget and Mary. The youngest Devoy sibling, the impetuous James, named for the ill-fated prodigy who died of Famine cholera in 1849, had left Ireland to find work in Britain.

Thanks to William's insistence on an education for his children—including his daughters—the poverty that remained the lot of the average Irish-Catholic had passed over the Devoy family. However, the persistent curse of emigration obviously had not. Four of the seven siblings lived overseas, joining the tens of thousands of Irish who continued to stream into Britain and America in search of work. There was no famine in Ireland nor was there a threat of one, and political affairs had reached a peaceful status quo, but still the Irish left for foreign shores, with hundreds of thousands passing through the newly opened immigrant facility at Ellis Island in the 1880s and 1890s. By 1900, the population in Ireland reached a low of 4.5 million, just about half of what it was before the Famine.

Once Kate and her husband crossed the Atlantic in the late 1880s, the far-flung Devoy siblings reestablished, in their middle years, the ties of kinship that were formed in childhood. While none was as deeply immersed in the ancient cause of Irish freedom as John, they followed nationalist politics—and their brother's career— closely. Before long, Kate became something of an adjunct for her brother. She was well suited for the work, for she had tended to the needs of Fenian prisoners and their families in the aftermath of the Fenian rebellion of 1867, and during her brother's years in prison, Kate had kept him informed of news from Ireland through coded messages in the few letters Devoy was allowed to receive. Both Kate and her younger sister, Mary, were eager soldiers in the Land War, signing up as members of the Ladies Land League under the direction of Charles Parnell's mother and sisters.

Kate was a handsome woman, dark-haired like her brother. And she was a fine argument for the fledgling women's movement that was taking hold in America and parts of Western Europe: she was strong-willed, well-informed, a writer of fine, thoughtful sentences. She would need all of her strength and character in the terrible test to come.

Not long after her arrival in America in 1889, she began sending John heartbreaking accounts of the steady disintegration of her marriage. She complained of Jack's "irritating ways," which included long absences and a failure to make good on debts.

Through the early months of 1890, John, still living in Chicago, regularly sent his sister money, usually in increments of five or ten dollars, to pay bills that were piling up while McBride's prospects and his sanity eroded. "He [Jack] seems indeed almost to have lost his mind," Mary Devoy wrote to John as she monitored her sister's dilemma from afar. From Britain, James Devoy wrote John that "the news about poor Jack is terribly serious, but under the circumstances hardly surprising. That terrible time in Dublin when he worked day and night without either profit or hope of profit would be quite enough to account for this breakdown." James wrote that he was prepared to give up his life in Britain if it meant helping Kate and John. With Kate thinking about joining John in Chicago, James wrote, "I propose that we complete the present Chicago programme by adding my name to it. Let John look around for some employment for me . . . All he [John] need say is resign and come, and if I go I will undertake to make things pleasanter all around." John could hardly ignore this selfless offer. He gave the word, and James was soon on his way across the Atlantic and half a continent.

Kate began taking typewriting lessons in preparation for a life she could not have imagined when she married Jack. With her husband still away and providing little financial support, Kate left the apartment they shared on West Forty-sixth Street in Manhattan and moved into a boardinghouse on Manhattan's Lower East Side. "My room is small but very clean and comfortable and has a window," she wrote to John. The noises from the raucous neighborhood, however, penetrated that window and kept her awake at night. Still, she was determined to follow the consequences of her decision to strike out on her own. "I did not tell Jack of the change [of address], and I don't think I will, either," she told John.

Kate moved from the boardinghouse to Chicago in July, followed soon by James. Jack McBride soon disappeared from the family correspondence, and he would die, alone and forgotten, in 1898. Meanwhile, the three Devoy siblings shared a roof for the first time since they were young adults. Though the arrangement was better than the boardinghouse Kate had bunked in, they were living on the edge of the poverty they had avoided in Ireland. Only John was bringing home a paycheck, thanks to a job with the *Chicago Evening Post*, but his work never was, and never would be, his first priority. Their life together was a far cry from the relative comforts of their childhood home in Dublin, and as Kate took over management of the household's finances, she soon had to choose between the landlord and the coal company during the vicious Chicago winters.

While Kate had found, in Mary's words, a "protector" in her elder brother, the life she led must have been joyless and painful. The help she received from John was more material than emotional, for all of his energy and spare time were spent on his campaign against Sullivan and the renegade Clan members he blamed for the murder of his friend. John was a protector all right, but probably not much of a comforter. And when Luke Dillon summoned him back East in 1894 to serve as the decimated Clan's secretary, he didn't hesitate to leave behind Kate and James for a job that paid him about $1,000 a year. For that lowly sum, he was about to begin what he would describe in his diary as "the slowest work I ever did."

It was unseasonably cold when Devoy began his journeys with a stop at the seaside resort of Atlantic City in late October. From Chicago, Kate advised John to stop sending her money, since she and James had managed to pay the rent on time and cover an unusually large gas bill. "Instead . . . I wish you would get yourself a good overcoat, for you need it so badly," she wrote.

As Devoy set out on his critical mission, his work apparently was not all-encompassing. His long years of bachelorhood may not have been as solitary as his friends and colleagues seemed to believe. "Try and have the overcoat and make yourself as nice as possible before meeting that widow as first impressions go a long way," Kate wrote to her brother. "I wish to goodness you could secure one of them— a well to do one, of course. You are not such a bad-looking fellow when you are fixed up, anyhow some women seem to admire you, though James says they have bad taste not to prefer him."

Devoy got himself the overcoat, but came home empty-handed in the search for a well-to-do widow.

The winter of 1894–95 was but a season in a long life, and a blink of an eye in a struggle that spanned centuries, but the record Devoy left of his battle with apathy, disorganization, and the elements is a testament to his fortitude. His base of operations was the Vanderbilt Hotel on Forty-second Street in Manhattan, chosen for its proximity to the rail lines that would take him to the Irish-run cities of the Northeast and Midwest.

A preliminary organizing jaunt to Yonkers on October 25 served as a warning of how difficult Devoy's task would be. The would-be rebels Devoy hoped to recruit stayed away from the meeting in droves, for it was raining outside. Devoy "got back to the Vanderbilt at 2 A.M. drenched," wondering, no doubt, what manner of man would allow a cloudburst to interfere with the work of Irish freedom.

More humiliations were to come. Devoy set out for Albany on November 2, and he spent the next day in search of a contact who never showed up. Across the Hudson in Troy, Devoy met another contact who told him he was wasting his time. He trudged back to Albany, where another potential recruit told Devoy that he was "disgusted" and "didn't feel like touching Irish affairs again." After midnight on a night of sleet and rain, Devoy brought his crusade to the home of yet another potential recruit, only to be told that the notion of a united Irish-American movement was impossible. He returned from that meeting at 4:30 A.M., "through sleet and slush, weary and somewhat exhausted." With what he called an "ulcerated throat" and a fierce cold, he continued to shuttle between Troy and Albany, tramping through a two-day snowstorm and shrugging off broken appointments. He spoke at a meeting in Troy that drew just six people. At other meetings, he endured suggestions that his murdered friend Dr. Cronin was a British spy. The ultimate indignity took place on November 10. As he prowled snowbound Albany with his sore throat and miserable cold, a pack of five dogs attacked him, "one of them a big fellow." He tried fighting them off, but only the intervention of police officers broke the attack. Devoy wrote in his diary that he had never seen anything like the assault he had just endured.

He persisted nevertheless and met with anybody who would meet him, at any hour. It was not uncommon for him to return to his hotel room in Albany just before dawn, cold, tired, and often disgusted. Still, his sister Kate observed that "the roving life seems to suit you admirably." She was pleased to learn that her brother had taken her advice about his outerwear. "I cannot tell you how glad I am that you have got . . . new clothes. You were such a ragamuffin in that old overcoat." As a reminder of her own precarious condition, Kate dropped a gentle hint: "If you are able to send the full

amount of December's rent, I shall consider myself very well off."
The landlord, she noted with relief, "has not come" yet. Devoy
promptly dispatched a money order for $50, which Kate used to pay
the rent and buy coal.

In the weeks between Thanksgiving and Christmas, Devoy journeyed back to New York, then to Pittsburgh (a trip that took eight
hours by an overnight express train), Scranton and the Pennsylvania
coal country, Binghamton, Rochester, back to Pittsburgh (where his
rivals took to calling him an "emissary from Scotland Yard"), and
finally, on Christmas Eve, to Chicago and a reunion with Kate and
James. Though the tour had started with little promise, by the holiday
season he was well pleased with his efforts. Clan groups in Albany,
Troy, Pittsburgh, and several other cities were successfully reorganized, and his enemies in the Sullivan wing in those cities put to
flight.

Kate was especially pleased to see her brother again, for she had
spent a lonely and cold season since John had left for New York.
James, who was working for Chicago's vast political machine, had
taken to the city's nightlife, often keeping the same sort of hours
John kept, but in a far different pursuit. "It is rather lonesome [with]
you away and James being out til long after midnight, as usual," she
wrote to John before his return. Meanwhile, even as the three siblings
toasted the holiday in their cold apartment on Seminary Place, Kate
was fretting about the next month's rent.

Devoy returned to his nomadic life before New Year's Eve, and
in fact, he would not rest for the next five years. His efforts produced
remarkable results. In 1894, his section of the Clan numbered just
over 4,000 members; by 1896, membership had grown to 9,702.
Though it seemed dormant, the Clan by 1900 was prepared to resume
its place at the center of the international conspiracy to win Ireland's
freedom.

But life spent with a packed suitcase and an empty wallet took
a heavy toll. Kate, lonely and disturbed by James's increasingly er-
ratic behavior, abandoned America for Dublin and the shelter of
her brother Joseph and his family, who were mourning the death of
an infant daughter, Eva Mary, dead after four months. Left on his
own, James became ever more rootless and lonesome. By the spring
of 1898, John had checked his little brother into a lunatic asylum

in New York, visiting him when he was in town and patiently feeding him grapes, James's favorite fruit, by hand. That same year, during an organizing tour of Chicago, John himself became gravely ill, so much so that Clan leaders and John's brother Michael seemed to believe that John was near death. He recovered, but James did not. The impetuous immigrant who gave up his life in Britain to come to the aid of his sister and brother died in New York in the fall of 1898. John spent $15 to buy James a grave in New York's sprawling Calvary Cemetery.

Not long after James's death, Kate returned to America, and brother and sister found an apartment together on East Ninety-ninth Street in Manhattan. But there was no respite from family tragedy. In the first year of the new century, Eliza Devoy, Joseph's wife, died at age thirty-four, less than a year after the death of her infant daughter. Like William Devoy before him, Joseph was left alone with a young family and unimaginable grief. Though they had never met their uncle John in person, Joseph's children, particularly Eileen (who was called Eily) and Peter, soon began to regard him as a second parent, regularly sending him affectionate letters and politely acknowledging money John and Kate began sending home. Young Eileen, Joseph wrote to John, "says you are like a older brother, and that she loves you. You can take that any way you wish." It melted John's heart. Eileen and John's sister Mary came to New York to visit in 1905, and decades later Eileen would recall jumping aboard the back of her now-graying uncle for a ride around the apartment on East Ninety-ninth Street.

Perhaps because he preferred to keep his emotions and his personal life private, and certainly because he was a master of insult and vitriol, Devoy has long been portrayed as a hard-hearted, hardheaded ideologue with emotional attachments to nothing save his work. The Devoy who emerges from the family correspondence bears little resemblance to the man whose caustic and quarrelsome ways were often his own worst enemy.

THE LONG NIGHTS SPENT in search of recruits and converts, the hours spent aboard loud, clanking trains, and the tedious years of performing the grunt work of reorganization soon paid off. In 1899, at a series of meetings in Boston, Philadelphia, and Atlantic City, Devoy and nine colleagues—five from each of the Clan factions—agreed to reunite after fifteen years of bitter and murderous division. Delegates from the two sides gathered in fraternal brotherhood in Atlantic City in July 1900 to begin again the work of Irish freedom in America. After a couple of days devoted to bits of arcane detail (such as passwords and hailing signals), Devoy, feeling all of his 57 years, returned to his hotel room and fell asleep fully clothed. Before long, however, he was awakened by a knock on the door. Several colleagues were outside, deputized to tell him that he had won election as the reorganized Clan's secretary. Suddenly, he later wrote, he found himself shaking hands with men he thought he would never have a civil word with, or for, again. The job paid $100 a month.

The reunification of the Clan and its hoped-for reemergence as a political and revolutionary force in America took place as Ireland was beginning to shake off the trauma of Parnell's downfall and death. Another Gladstone-sponsored home-rule bill had been passed by the House of Commons and vetoed by the House of Lords in 1893, but the exercise generated no great excitement. The Irish had tired of revolutionary politics for the time being; a disillusioned generation began to look in another direction, albeit one filled with nationalist possibilities. Douglas Hyde, an Anglo-Irish Protestant barrister, founded the Gaelic League to promote the study and speaking of Ireland's native language and its culture. An obscure economist named Arthur Griffith was formulating a theory of economic independence that would one day be encapsulated in a two-word label: Sinn Fein—Gaelic for "ourselves." A young poet steeped in the mists of ancient Irish mythology had burst onto the literary scene to become Ireland's national poet. William Butler Yeats was the most prominent member of a glittering array of Anglo-Irish Protestant artists who sparked a cultural renaissance rooted in Celtic mythology and Irish folklore. The new century was greeted with the works of the playwrights John Millington Synge, Lady Gregory, and George Bernard Shaw, all of whom regarded themselves as distinctly Irish.

Politically, though, the movement remained moribund. In a curious coincidence, the Parliamentary Party that had been split apart by Parnell's divorce reunited under the leadership of John Redmond even as the Clan's two factions were coming together in Atlantic City. Redmond had little of Parnell's charisma, but he shrewdly understood how much of the late leader's power flowed from his control over the American Irish and their money. With extremists like Devoy seemingly out of the picture, Redmond successfully rallied moderate Irish-American opinion behind him, as Parnell had done before and during the Land War. Redmond and his allies established the United Irish League of America as a respectable vehicle for assimilated Irish-Americans to work for the respectable goal of home rule. In its first ten years of existence, beginning in 1900, it raised thousands of dollars for Redmond's party and claimed the loyalty of Irish-America's political leadership. Men such as the great New York orator Congressman William Bourke Cockran flocked to its banner, and its advocacy of home rule won the support of non-Irish leaders such as Theodore Roosevelt, William Howard Taft, and Woodrow Wilson, men who were in a position to let their opinions be known to their British colleagues.

When a constitutional crisis in Britain in 1911 broke the veto power of the House of Lords, a new home-rule bill was inevitable, and the Lords could do nothing to stop it. Redmond and his American allies seemed to have the field to themselves as they prepared public opinion on both sides of the Atlantic for an Ireland that, if not completely free, at least had a measure of self-rule. Among the politicians who expressed their delight was Theodore Roosevelt, who wrote that "Home Rule . . , would be of very great importance in removing one source of friction between the United States and Great Britain." Such a removal was becoming urgent as the European powers drifted toward war.

But others in Ireland, not yet prominent and operating far from the reaches of government power, would not be content with mere home rule. And John Devoy, on behalf of the American Irish who cared little about middle-class respectability, already was in touch with them.

THOMAS J. CLARKE WAS one of the hard-liners who had no use for Redmond and his party. A newlywed in 1901, gaunt, stooped, and balding, he looked much older than his forty years. His appearance was but one manifestation of the cruelties of his youth, for he spent the years 1885 to 1899 in a British prison, a casualty of the Clan na Gael dynamite war. One of his bomber colleagues, the Irish-American physician Thomas Gallagher, had gone insane while in prison and was released and sent back to America, where the Clan cared for him until he died in a sanatorium. Clarke's mind suffered no such wounds, and his soul remained defiant. After his release from prison, he returned to New York, where he had lived and worked in the early 1880s and had even become a naturalized American citizen in 1883. During his first stint in America, he took the oath as a member of Clan na Gael, joining the very camp, the Napper Tandy Club, to which Devoy belonged. He had volunteered to go to England on a "special mission," but was arrested before the mission could be carried out. Now, all these years later, Clarke turned to Devoy in hopes of not only finding work in New York, but of picking up where he had left off when he was arrested.

Tom Clarke and John Devoy were similar in temperament: they were hardheaded revolutionaries who suffered neither fools nor dilettantes (and the Irish movement was burdened by both) gladly. Devoy was a guest at Clarke's marriage to twenty-three-year-old Kathleen Daly in New York in 1901, and for the first seven years of the new century, Clarke served as Devoy's trusted lieutenant and coconspirator. Later, after he moved back to Ireland, Clarke addressed Devoy in letters as "Uncle." Though a code name, it hinted at the genuine intimacy between them.

Just after the new century debuted, Clarke began working as Devoy's personal assistant for $15 a week, a salary that forced him to work a second job to support the family he was starting. But his prospects and salary improved in 1903, when Devoy asked him, on behalf of the Clan, to help start a New York–based weekly newspaper to be called the *Gaelic American*. Devoy was determined to get back into the journalism business to spread the Clan's word and consolidate his own power, even though it meant taking on a second full-time job to go along with his work as the Clan's secretary. The first issue was printed and distributed in September 1903, with Devoy as the paper's editor and Clarke as business agent and managing editor.

The *Gaelic American* had all the trappings of the many other ethnic weeklies in the nation's immigrant cities, but its goal was quite different. Devoy's paper would not be an immigrant's guide to assimilation; it would not cover the tragedies, triumphs, and struggles that were a working-class Irish-American's lot. It would not crusade for better housing, safer working conditions, and an end to child labor.

Instead of trying to turn the Irish into better Americans, the paper existed to propagate the gospel according to Clan na Gael. Its readership was not to be the great mass of Irish America. With its erudite analyses of European politics and dispatches from various lands struggling under Britain's yoke, the paper was written and edited for educated and highly literate leaders of Irish America. A solicitation for classified advertising noted that the paper circulated in "the homes of people who needed servants." Priced at five cents, with subscriptions available for $2.50 a year, it was distributed throughout the country, attaining an influence beyond its circulation of about thirty thousand.

The *Gaelic American* would serve as Devoy's base of power for the rest of his life, and from its cluttered offices in downtown Manhattan, he not only set the terms of debate for radical Irish nationalists in America, but also carried out his arduous secretarial duties for Clan na Gael. The double assignment would have been difficult for a man half his sixty years, and though he occasionally toyed with the idea of giving up one job or the other, he never did.

In fact, Devoy often managed to meld the two jobs into one. As the Clan's secretary, Devoy was the organization's ideological whip, and from his editor's chair, he was able to dictate what would be discussed, what issues were to be seized upon, what enemies villified, and what rivals dismissed. But what served both the Clan and the newspaper best was Devoy's genius at identifying issues that stoked the cultural insecurities and resentments of second- and third-generation Irish-Americans who had never seen Ireland, had no memories of the Famine, and perhaps had little or no opinion about Ireland's place in the world. To be sure, Great Britain served as the *Gaelic American*'s great Satan, but during these years when Ireland itself seemed apathetic about its claim to nationhood, Devoy was shrewd enough to cast Englishmen and English interests as the enemies not of Ireland, but of America and American institutions. His readers didn't have to remember the pain of eviction or the indignity of the workhouse to become enraged at, for example, slick British attempts to trick America into a military alliance or Anglophilic educators rewriting American history to suit British sensibilities. ("The amount of English money spent in organized efforts to Anglicize the American people must be enormous," began a typical lead story in the paper.)

Such charges, made with a fair amount of evidence and wildly overdone rhetoric, fit Devoy's vision of an Irish-American community still very much at the mercy of an ancient enemy who was perfectly capable of crossing the Atlantic to subvert the American republic in general and Irish-Americans in particular to suit the needs of empire. In the world presented to *Gaelic American* readers, "Anglomaniacs" were behind all sorts of un-American schemes.

Even a proposal to bar the "Star-Spangled Banner" in New York's public schools and replace it with "America" (which, as Devoy noted, was sung to the air of "God Save the King") was offered as evidence of British interests seeping into American classrooms. And it didn't stop there. A seemingly innocuous peace organization founded and funded by the Scots immigrant Andrew Carnegie was roundly condemned as nothing more than a front for British sympathizers intent on dragging America into a European conflict on Britain's side. (And when Carnegie scheduled a huge rally in Manhattan's Cooper Union, Devoy and his allies stormed inside the hall and nearly broke it up. It was, Devoy wrote shortly afterward, "the greatest night's fun we ever had.")

Irish-Americans were, in the *Gaelic American*'s pages, constantly under attack from hostile newspapers, robber barons, and double-dealing politicians, all of whom acted as they did to please their social betters across the Atlantic. "The anti-Irish crusade takes various forms and is conducted through many channels, but it never ceases its attacks," Devoy informed his readers. "The stage Irishman, the vile newspaper cartoons, the deliberate misrepresentation of Irish action and sentiment, the suppression of Irish news are all part of the same campaign inspired from England and carried on in this country by English agents, subsidized or volunteers."

Devoy deployed similar language when the topic turned to the parliamentarian John Redmond and his American allies in a new and solidly middle-class organization called the United Irish League. As the league expanded throughout the country, becoming the agenda-setter for moderate Irish-American opinion, Devoy used the *Gaelic American* to portray Redmond as prepared to sell out the dream of a republic for the unacceptable compromise of home rule—even though Devoy's sainted partner, Parnell, was willing to do the same. The United Irish League of America was portrayed as a dupe of Britain and its scheming, un-American allies.

To serve his own purposes and reflect a reality far removed from the respectable achievement of the United Irish League's members, Devoy advised his readers that their aspirations for assimilation were doomed thanks to the dark forces of Anglo-American plutocrats. In lecturing his brethren, he cited American Jews as role models for Irish-Americans. There is some irony in his expressions of admiration, because Devoy railed about Jewish businessmen with the same ferocity that he condemned British politicians, Irish turncoats, and the Anglo-American establishment. "Irish-American parents could profitably take a lesson from the Jews in the training and education of their children," he wrote. "In spite of every obstacle, in spite of ridicule itself, most of the children of Jewish parents remain true to the faith, customs and language of their fathers. . . . Unlike the Jews, Irish-Americans have broken with the traditions of their race. The ancestral speech has been lost, and to the bulk of Irish-Americans, Irish history is a closed book." To Devoy, of course, the book was very much open and would not be closed until he himself turned the last page.

The twin themes of Irish-American insecurity and British perfidy inspired several memorable crusades in the *Gaelic American*'s first decade as Devoy attempted to rally the Clan and Irish America to the tattered flag of identity politics and nationalism. Most memorable, but least flattering, was his campaign against Synge's play *Playboy of the Western World*, which featured characters that were somewhat more earthy than those with whom the old bachelor was familiar. Beginning with the play's controversial launch in Dublin in 1907 and continuing to its New York debut in 1911, Devoy called it a "vile libel on Irish womanhood and a gross misrepresentation of their religious feelings." When William Butler Yeats, who had met with Devoy while passing through New York in late 1903 and shared a platform with him in early 1904, defended Synge, Devoy denounced him as "foul, gross and vulgar." Various Irish societies were encouraged to pass sharply worded resolutions condemning the play, the author, and their supporters. When the play opened in New York in late 1911, Devoy was among those in attendance who disrupted the first act despite a heavy police presence. He stood up at one point in the performance and shouted, "Son of a bitch, that's not Irish." He, of course, had not been in Ireland in more than thirty years.

More edifying was Devoy's crusade against a proposed arbitration treaty between Great Britain and the United States during the Taft administration. Beginning in 1907, Devoy began warning his readers that British diplomats such as Ambassador James Bryce meant to lure Washington into a military alliance with Britain to help fend off the growing threat from imperial Germany. And when a formal pact, known as the Root-Bryce Treaty, was negotiated and sent to the Senate in early 1911, Devoy spared nothing. Week after week in the *Gaelic American*, often in several stories, he denounced what he called the Anglo-American alliance. The treaty, he assured readers, was bound to increase America's risk of being dragged into a European war.

As the Clan's secretary and as an increasingly visible spokesman for Irish America, he organized a multifront offensive against the treaty, using the power of Irish America's numbers to meet with senators, organize Clan-led opposition throughout the country, and deliver lectures throughout the country. It seemed yet another quixotic effort. The British and the Taft administration had spent years negotiating the pact, and the Anglophobia that had characterized post–Civil War politics had quickly given way to an upper-class consensus that the two English-speaking nations shared a common destiny.

Devoy devoted large chunks of time, at one point six straight weeks, to his Washington lobbying effort, buttonholing friend, foe, and those of undetermined loyalty in an effort to persuade them that this was an issue at the core of American—and not Irish—politics. At one point during his campaign, he met with Sen. John Sharp Williams of Mississippi, who complained that the treaty's opponents were "hyphenated Americans." Devoy tried biting his tongue, to no avail.

"Aren't the Anglo-Saxons hyphenated?" he asked tersely.

"Yes, but I'm not an Anglo-Saxon," Williams said. "I'm a Welshman. But my people have been in America for a hundred and fifty years."

"Judging by that standard," Devoy replied, "Sitting Bull has a better record."

Back in New York, Devoy met with local leaders of the Central Federated Union of New York, the largest group of unions in the world, and helped inspire a revolt against Samuel Gompers, president of the American Federation of Labor and a key supporter of the treaty and a member of Andrew Carnegie's pro-treaty Peace Society. The union informed Gompers that "Mr. Devoy, of the Irish-American Societies, made a clear-cut statement as to the purposes of this [treaty]. . . . He quoted newspaper articles and dispatches from Washington and London to show the underlying motives to be not international peace but an Anglo-American alliance." Eventually, four hundred unions passed resolutions calling for the treaty's defeat.

Devoy created an alliance of his own, collaborating with German-American societies throughout the country that were equally opposed to the treaty. The two groups, cheered on by the *Gaelic American*, held a joint rally at New York's Cooper Union on Sunday night, February 19, 1911, attended by leaders of both ethnic groups, including Devoy and a German journalist named George von Skal, who worked out of the German consulate downtown. The two men knew each other from their days of organizing American support for the Boers in their futile but bloody war against Britain. With a European war seemingly inevitable, they understood they could be useful to each other.

Devoy was among the Cooper Union rally's featured speakers, and he made a deliberate argument against the treaty on the basis of American, and not Irish, principles. "We love America more than we hate England, and it is our love for America which governs our actions in this matter," he said. "We are here tonight to ask the Senate to stand by George Washington's policy of no entangling alliances and to demand that closer relations with England amounting to a virtual alliance shall not be established."

On the eve of the full Senate's vote in early March 1912, Devoy played a card he had placed up his sleeve years before. Unlike most of the senators who were about to pass judgment on the Root-Bryce Treaty, Devoy had read a book Bryce had written about American politics, entitled *The American Commonwealth*. In it, he seemed to belittle the Senate's role in confirming treaties, sniffing that unscrupulous senators often "sucked out" political advantage as part of their deliberations. "The treaty-confirming power of the Senate opens a particularly easy and tempting door to such [electioneering] practices," Bryce wrote.

Devoy and others had argued all along that the treaty's proposed establishment of an arbitration commission to settle disputes between the two countries effectively curtailed the Senate's power over foreign affairs. Now Devoy proposed to hang Bryce with his own words. He and a clerk copied excerpts of Bryce's unkind analysis of the Senate and sent them to the offices of every senator. In the early-morning hours of March 7, 1912, after prolonged debate, the Senate rejected the treaty. Devoy, probably more exhausted than any of the combatants on the Senate floor, wired statements to daily newspapers in Ireland. It was, he wrote, Irish-America's greatest political victory over England. After the Clan's convention a few months later, Devoy and other leaders quadrupled a proposal to raise and spend $5,000 on recruitment and organizing activities.

From the ashes of division and dissension, the movement was being reborn, and an identity was being revived. The timing was fortuitous. Although John Devoy's eyes and ears were beginning to fail him, he could see the clouds that were gathering over Europe, and he could hear a distant and terrifying thunder.

JOHN DEVOY WAS A few months shy of seventy when the Senate turned down Root-Bryce. His dark hair and whiskers had turned a soft gray, and time and insomnia had carved deep pockets under his eyes. He remained thick around the middle, and the three-piece suits he often wore exaggerated his solid bulk. But the years and his many battles had done nothing to dampen his enthusiasm for a fight. The

Gaelic American remained, if not "America's Finest Weekly" (as the paper so modestly claimed to be), then certainly one of the nation's most vitriolic journals.

If Devoy seemed especially contentious in what proved to be just the beginning of his protracted old age, few but his closest friends (and he didn't have many) knew of his private sorrows. In his hour of victory in 1912, John Devoy was as lonely as he had ever been in his life.

Kate McBride's health had never been the same since her ordeal with her husband. Still, she managed to play what Devoy would call, in words he meant to be flattering, "a woman's part" in the male-dominated world of Irish-American nationalism. He kept few secrets from her, and that alone attested to Devoy's hardheaded regard for her judgment and discretion. She was her brother's roommate, his sounding board, and his companion, appearing at his side on social occasions such as Tom Clarke's wedding and at the endless rounds of fund-raisers for Clan na Gael and other Irish organizations.

On Satuday, August 29, 1908, John and Kate boarded a train in New York bound for Atlantic City for a late-summer getaway with a few friends and other Clan officials. Kate had only recently returned to the United States, having crossed the Atlantic again to visit her brother Joseph, his family, and her two sisters, Bridget and Mary. She came back from Ireland looking healthier than she had in years. But John and Kate had barely checked in at the St. Charles Hotel in Atlantic City when she began feeling ill. A doctor and a nurse were summoned, and then a priest, who performed the Catholic Church's rites for the ill. John, distraught, wrote hurried letters to his brother and sisters in Dublin, telling them of Kate's sudden illness. The priest returned on Monday morning to offer Kate Holy Communion. In this state of grace, she died just before sundown on September 1. She was sixty-three.

The affection Kate inspired was evident on the train that bore her body from Atlantic City to St. Raymond's Cemetery in the Bronx. More than a dozen of the Clan's top leaders joined their grieving ally on his sorrowful journey. The extent of the blow is clear in a letter from Mary to John in which she begged him not to give in to the strain. "You have work to do . . . you mustn't leave your life's work uncompleted," she wrote. "If [Kate] is not already in heaven . . . may God in his mercy bring her soon there. If ever there was an unselfish being in the world, it was our poor Kate." After Kate was buried, John gave up the apartment they had shared on East Ninety-ninth Street and moved in with his assistant at the *Gaelic American*, James Reidy, a young redhead with a large and rambunctious family. The arrangement was probably meant to be short-lived, but Devoy stayed with Reidy until moving into a hotel room on Forty-second Street around 1914.

Fewer than three months after Kate died, Mary was taken ill in Dublin, but Joseph told John that there was no cause for alarm. "She is quite upset by poor Kate's death, for there never were two people more attached to each other," Joseph wrote. Mary was dead four weeks later. "People here said you would be the greatest sufferer by poor Kate's death, but it hasn't turned out so," Joseph wrote to John when Mary died. "I don't think she cared to live after Kate's death. They are together now."

Upholding the Devoy family tradition, Joseph's sons were taking their first, tentative steps down the broken and dangerous path of Irish nationalism. Joseph took obvious pride in reporting back to John that his oldest son, William, had become an "out and out Sinn Feiner" while James was "an uncompromising little patriot . . . [he] goes into a shop for goods and when they are parceled up he asks if they are Irish made, and if they are not [he] won't take them." Three of Devoy's nephews Gaelicized their names—William to Liam, James to Seamus, and Peter to Peadar. (Their brother John, named for their rebellious uncle in America, had more immediate concerns. Plagued by tuberculosis, he was sickly and unable to work.) Meanwhile, Joseph reported that Eileen, the youngest, was beginning to win prizes in Irish-dancing competitions.

A thousand such little dramas were being played out in Ireland's cottages and flats, particularly among families that could afford the luxury of indulging in a language that had only the faintest pulse, and in a folk culture that had been thought crushed by famine and emigration. While the Irish Republican Brotherhood was showing only slight signs of life (there were but fifteen hundred members by 1912), young Ireland was rediscovering its cultural identity through literature, dance, language, and athletics. But even for Joseph's family,

the language lessons and dancing competitions and political activism were soon overshadowed by real life. Joseph Devoy, father and
mother to his young family, died suddenly in 1909 at fifty-six, com-
pleting a dreadful twelve months during which John lost three of
his five remaining siblings, all of them younger than he. Joseph's six
children were orphans, consigned to the care of John's elder sister,
Bridget. Whatever money John could afford to save from his $25-a-
week salary was now dispatched in regular installments to his
brother's children, who never failed to acknowledge Uncle John's
kindness with a letter and an annual sprig of shamrocks to com-
memorate St. Patrick's Day.

Through his friend and assistant Tom Clarke, who had returned
to Dublin and was running a tobacco shop, Devoy knew that more
was stirring in Ireland than language and dance classes. Whatever the
IRB lacked in numbers, it was attracting talented, young members.
Clarke soon wrote that "it is worth living in Ireland these times—
there is an awakening. . . . [The] slow, silent prodding and the open
preaching is at last showing results."

Even still, the IRB was but one of several manifestations of an
Irish awakening, and to most people—including those in government
positions—it was the least consequential. As an adversary of John
Redmond's constitutional nationalism, the IRB existed in the shadow
of a new, public movement named Sinn Fein. Though Sinn Fein was
not committed to a republic, as the IRB was, its membership was
peppered with revolutionaries, and Devoy helped establish an American wing to raise money and provide public support in the States.
Meanwhile, the Gaelic League and the Gaelic Athletic Association,
innocent enough in their pursuits of Irish language and sports, inevitably inspired fledgling nationalists, just as Devoy's own Gaelic lessons so many years ago had preceded his swearing the IRB oath. And
a newborn labor movement, though it renounced nationalism as an
ideology, was shaking Irish workers.

Only a minority of nationalists, however, took a militant approach. John Redmond stood astride Irish politics as a new Parnell,
that is, committed to constitutional change and prepared to use an
alliance with the British Liberal Party to advance Ireland's cause.
British politicians prepared for the introduction of a third and final
home-rule bill for Ireland, one the House of Lords could do nothing

to stop. The bill was introduced in 1912 amid much acclaim in Britain, Ireland, and America. A New York judge sent Redmond a letter of congratulations, telling him, "You have the race at home and abroad solidly, sincerely and almost unanimously with you."

The telling phrase was "almost unanimously." Devoy and the Clan remained adamantly opposed to home rule and feared that its inevitable success would mean the end to their dream of an independent Irish republic, the republic to which Devoy pledged his loyalty in 1861. Dr. William Carroll, the aging former head of the Clan, now retired, called home rule a "betrayal" in a letter to Devoy, while one of the Clan's current leaders, John Keating, said bitterly that after all his and the Clan's work, "we are reaching what seems to be the end." Keating noted Devoy's contention that the Clan had to do something other than simply oppose home rule, but, he conceded, "I can see no alternative within our reach."

As luck would have it, however, the Clan in America and the IRB in Ireland were not the only opponents of home rule. As the bill made its torturous way though the House of Commons, some men in Ireland would see to it that answers would not come easily, cheaply, or bloodlessly. Protestant Irishmen whose families had been in Ireland for centuries clung desperately to the Union Jack, and they pledged undying opposition to home rule. They referred to it sneeringly as "Rome rule." A quarter million Irish Protestants, most of them crowded into the province of Ulster, signed what they called a Solemn League and Covenant in 1912, pledging to resist home rule with a private army, called the Ulster Volunteer Force. It was nothing less than a declaration of treason. The Ulster Volunteers then backed up their solemn pledge with something more tangible. With German help, they smuggled into Ireland tens of thousands of guns and millions of rounds of ammunition. The British, however, did nothing as the gun was introduced into twentieth-century Irish politics.

The Loyalists found themselves arguing that so intense was their devotion to Britain that they were prepared to rise in arms against the British government in order to remain British. But when the government seemed ready to crack down and disarm the Loyalist army, British officers in the Curragh barracks—just a few miles from Devoy's birthplace—resigned en masse. The government backed down in the face of mutiny and disloyalty. Responding to the formation of a private Loyalist army, nationalists formed an army of their own called the Irish Volunteers. The organization grew to more than one hundred thousand members; by the time it did, the IRB had infiltrated its leadership in a brilliant and well-planned silent coup.

The stakes were getting higher, and government leaders were beginning to whisper about the inevitability of partition, a possibility that Protestant Loyalists and Irish nationalists both rejected as nothing more than yesterday's compromise, and a failed one at that. Even Irish-American moderates such as Congressman William Bourke Cockran and John Quinn, the men who helped fund Redmond and his party, rejected partition.

ALTHOUGH, OR PERHAPS BECAUSE, Devoy was nearly a half century older than some of the IRB's emerging leaders, many had taken pains to introduce themselves to the man they saw as the link between the Fenians of 1867 and the nascent revolutionaries of the early twentieth century. By 1912, he had met many of the new men in person. His relationship with Tom Clarke, of course, was long-standing. During the early 1900s, Devoy was introduced to a labor organizer and devout socialist named James Connolly, who endured a painful and poverty-stricken eight-year exile in America with his family before returning to Ireland in 1910. Though they were hardly more than acquaintances, the trust between the two men was immediate; Connolly would later deputize his daughter, Nora, to deliver messages from Ireland to Devoy in New York.

Others whose names would soon find a place in Irish history books also passed though Devoy's office in the years before World War I. John McBride, no relation to Devoy's misbegotten brother-in-law, and his future bride, Maude Gonne—Yeats's great love—both crossed Devoy's path at various times, with McBride making a better impression. A young physician from County Tyrone named Patrick McCartan emigrated to America in 1900 and enlisted in the cause of Irish nationalism. He joined the Clan na Gael at the urging of his fellow Tyrone exile, a Philadelphia businessman named Joseph McGarrity, who had become an important Clan leader and a confidant of Devoy's. McCartan, imbued with revolutionary fervor, decided in short order to return to Ireland to stir up revolution, and when he did so, Devoy signed him up as a correspondent for the *Gaelic American.*

Not long after the fateful year of 1914 began, yet another of the IRB's new leaders presented himself at Devoy's newspaper office. His name was Patrick, or Padraig, Pearse, a dark-haired, 35-year-old poet and schoolteacher who had only just joined the Brotherhood. Pearse's visit was twofold. Not only was there revolutionary business to transact, but Pearse was also looking for American money for his down-at-the-heel school for boys, St. Enda's, near Dublin. There, Pearse, taught from the gospel of Irish nationalism, and in the Irish language. Devoy, Joe McGarrity, and an up-and-coming Irish nationalist named Judge Daniel Cohalan saved the school from bankruptcy.

On the morning of February 21, 1914, Pearse and his traveling companion, Bulmer Hobson, an IRB member and correspondent for the *Gaelic American,* convened a meeting with Devoy in the newspaper's offices on William Street. Hobson presented Devoy with a document that outlined what the American Irish might do for Ireland if Britain and German went to war. The document's author, Hobson said, was Sir Roger Casement, an Anglo-Irish Protestant who had been knighted for his work exposing the slavelike conditions of workers in the Belgian Congo. Casement himself would soon be in America to see Devoy on revolutionary business.

McGarrity walked in as the meeting was winding up. Devoy, squinting through spectacles, handed Casement's paper to his confidant from Philadelphia. It was, Devoy said, "an able document." It was high praise indeed from Irish America's sternest taskmaster.

Before the first shots were fired on the battlefields of Europe, blood was flowing in the streets of Dublin. In late July 1914, the Irish Volunteers, in flattering imitation of the Ulster Volunteers, staged a successful gun-smuggling operation in the port town of Howth. The haul was not nearly as large as the Ulster group's. Only about nine hundred rifles were brought in, along with hollow-tipped ammunition that Pearse would later declare, in a letter to Devoy, to be unfit for "civilized warfare." As the gunrunners arrived in Dublin, they were confronted by British soldiers near the banks of the river Liffey. The troops opened fire, killing three civilians.

Days later, the lights went out over Europe.

CHAPTER THIRTEEN

Impatient for the Coming Fight

IN AUGUST 1914, THE ARMIES OF EUROPE BOARDED TROOP TRAINS and were led, herdlike, to late-summer fields that would serve as a continent's abattoir. Nearly forty years earlier, John Devoy had seen in Bosnia the tinderbox that might light the Irish sky, but the crisis of the 1870s had passed without incident, simmering resentments doused in a shower of imperial diplomacy. Now, however, a murder in Sarajevo had set king against kaiser, cousin against cousin, in a family feud that would drench Europe in the blood of men, women, and children who knew little of international politics and of the great games that nations play.

For Devoy and his colleagues in America and in Ireland, the moment of deliverance was drawing close. A generation of Britain's muscle and brains was assembling in France to face the challenge of upstart Germany. Fenian doctrine had it that Britain's difficulty was Ireland's opportunity, and America's neutrality presented Devoy with a chance to exploit that opportunity.

Even as the guns of August fired their first salvos, Devoy emerged from his two-bed, $1.50-per-night room in the Ennis Hotel on Forty-second Street to lead a delegation of Clan na Gael leaders uptown for an appointment at the plushly appointed German Club on East Fifty-ninth Street. Awaiting Devoy and his colleagues were the German consul general in New York, Count von Bernstorff, and a handful of aides and hangers-on, including Devoy's friend from the anti–Boer War demonstrations, journalist George von Skal. The ambassador and his staff were eager to hear what these Irish-Americans had to say, for Devoy and his colleagues claimed to speak for revolutionaries in Ireland, and it hardly took a tactical genius to understand that Ireland, the storm forever gathering off Britain's west coast, was the Empire's Achilles' heel.

Unlike in the memorable meeting with Russia's ambassador during the Balkan crisis of the 1870s, Devoy did not act as the Clan's spokesman, an indication that his hearing problems precluded participation in delicate negotiations. At the *Gaelic American*'s office, the recent installation of a telephone had caused Devoy no end of frustration; though designed to make news-gathering and conspiracy-mongering more efficient, the phone was useless in his hands. He couldn't hear his callers and was often forced to use middlemen to conduct telephone conversations. He was similarly at a loss when he and his coconspirators met to plan such initiatives as this very interview with the German ambassador. Muffled conversation passed him by, forcing him to rely on his colleagues to provide unheard details after the meetings adjourned. He complained to his ally McGarrity that his impairment was "an awful handicap at a time when important matters were being discussed."

Devoy and his colleagues were ushered into a private room at the German Club, where von Bernstorff greeted them. The Clan delegation formally proposed to align the Irish-American movement with Germany on behalf of the Irish Republican Brotherhood in Dublin. For the revolutionaries of Irish America, the war in Europe in 1914 posed none of the moral imperatives that the Second World War would pose. Absent the evil that Germany would unleash in Europe some quarter century later, Devoy and his comrades adopted the traditional strategy of befriending the enemy of their enemy. Ireland's liberty, he wrote in the *Gaelic American*, would best be served by a German victory. American neutrality offered them a chance to agitate on Germany's behalf without anyone questioning their loyalty as American citizens.

The Clan delegation told von Bernstorff bluntly that a revolt would take place in Ireland sometime soon, while Britain's soldiers were occupied on the Western Front. They had come not to ask for money—the American Irish would provide cash—but for the promise of German arms and officers when the time came for the IRB to rise and strike their preoccupied foe.

When Devoy had made a similar request to the Russian ambassador all those years ago, when his beard was dark and his hearing sharp, he was told that he and his colleagues were dreamers. This time, however, the credentialed men of state listened with care to these civilians without portfolios, although the ambassador diplomatically made no commitments.

The German government embraced the Irish-Americans' offer. Cables to and from Berlin soon described Devoy as a "confidential agent" of Germany. Sinister though the title sounds, it's not clear exactly what he did on Germany's behalf beyond organizing and addressing pro-German meetings and turning the *Gaelic American* into a propaganda arm of the kaiser's armed forces. (The paper's front page often featured heroic sketches of Germany's top military commanders.) While Devoy was unsparing in these efforts, it is highly unlikely that he participated in anything remotely seditious, though the same would not be said for some of the men he worked closely with during the war years. He soon became a cochairman of an innocent-sounding, New York–based group called Friends of Peace, which organized huge antiwar demonstrations in New York, Chicago, and other heavily immigrant cities. The Friends of Peace, however, were not entirely dovelike in their intentions, for the group's founder was a German spy—and an associate of Devoy's—named Albert Sanders.

In aligning the Irish-American nationalist movement so publicly with pro-German societies and acting, in effect, as an unpaid agent for Germany, Devoy had no illusions that President Woodrow Wilson would be persuaded to enter the war on the side of the Central Powers. Rather, the mass rallies and fiery pro-German editorials were designed literally to neutralize the undisguised pro-British sentiments of the American ruling class, that bastion of Protestant, Anglo-American power, which Devoy held in no higher regard than the genuine article in London. If the combined political clout of the nation's two largest immigrant groups, the Germans and the Irish, could be massed together, pro-British politicians might think twice before committing U.S. troops to the Western Front.

New York was to be the base of the German-Irish-American triangle, the place where the IRB met the German General Staff through the intervening power of John Devoy. But Irish-American agitation had another, equally important, component. With the Irish-parliamentary leader John Redmond proclaiming support for Britain, leading his allies among the establishment Irish in America to do the same, Devoy and his colleagues sought to emphasize—loudly and repeatedly—their contention that Redmond did not speak for them. Ireland had no quarrel with Germany, Devoy insisted, and the young manhood of Ireland should stay at home and out of His Majesty's bloodied uniforms.

When war broke out in August, John Redmond was on the verge of bringing to Ireland all that even the great Parnell had failed to do. All that stood between Ireland and self-government within the United Kingdom was the signature of King George. But in a late development, the British decided to suspend home rule for the duration of the war emergency.

Still, Redmond pledged his loyalty to Britain. His support was applauded in Britain, adding to the appearance of a reconciliation between the two islands. During a speech in Woodenbridge, County Wicklow, he vowed that the Irish Volunteers would fight wherever needed—in other words, alongside British troops in Flanders' fields. For the militants in America and in Ireland, this was the height of hyperloyalty to the Crown.

Some months before the Woodenbridge speech, Redmond had gained effective control over the burgeoning Irish Volunteers—the private militia formed in reaction to the founding of the anti-home-rule Ulster Volunteers. The Irish Volunteers were 170,000 strong when the war broke out. After Redmond's speech, however, the militants among the Volunteers would tolerate Redmond no longer. Among those militants were members of the Irish Republican Brotherhood who had infiltrated the Volunteers' ranks. The organization split, but with the vast majority of the movement remaining loyal to Redmond and thus to Britain's war effort.

Not surprisingly, Devoy regarded Redmond's actions as traitorous, and the Clan formally condemned Redmond at its annual convention in fall of 1914. On August 9, ten thousand Irish-Americans assembled in Celtic Park in New York to hear speeches denouncing Redmond's pledge of cooperation with Britain. Five days later, Devoy traveled by train to Newark, New Jersey, with a friend named Jeremiah O'Leary— who would be indicted in New York on treason charges in 1918—to address a meeting of German societies. The intent was clear: whatever

Redmond said and whatever his followers in America chose to believe, the Irish-American revolutionary party did not support Britain's war effort.

Ironically, though, Devoy actually concurred with Redmond's assessment of Irish public opinion, although the old Fenian was decidedly less pleased about it. In one of his almost daily letters to McGarrity, Devoy bemoaned "the moral rottenness" in Ireland, the chief symptom being the pro-British sympathies Redmond identified. "I have no doubt a few more German victories will make a big change," Devoy wrote, "but still the moral rottenness will remain. What can you do with a people which doesn't know its own mind . . ."

Devoy complained of lack of sleep during these months, and his health was poor—he developed bladder problems that required at least three doctor's visits in a four-week period. He was, in the words of his hardy antagonist from the Land League days, Patrick Egan, a "sleepless demon," an insomniac rushing from work to meetings and from meetings to rallies and fund-raisers, all the while corresponding regularly with Tom Clarke, McGarrity, and other conspirators privvy to the secrets of the IRB and the Clan. During business hours, Devoy was a regular visitor to the German consulate on Wall Street, a short walk from both the *Gaelic American*'s offices and the office of the Friends of Peace, while at night, when he wasn't at a meeting or a rally, he often stopped by the palatial uptown home of Judge Daniel Cohalan, one of several Clan members who walked a tightrope between respectable and revolutionary politics.

Cohalan was forty-nine in 1914 and was on the verge of becoming one of Irish-America's most influential spokesmen, a title on which he clearly had designs. The son of immigrant parents from County Cork, Cohalan was the embodiment of American success. He was a lawyer and a jurist, but his education and experience took place within the world that Irish America had created for itself, a world separate from mainstream America. He had attended Manhattan College, found his place in the Irish-Democratic world of New York politics, and now was, in effect, the in-house counsel of Clan na Gael. In 1914, he also was but two years removed from a bitter battle to block Woodrow Wilson's presidential nomination, an act neither judge nor president had forgotten.

In the midst of this furious activity, Devoy received a telegram on September 3 telling him that yet another sibling, his brother Michael, had died in New Mexico. Michael's death was not nearly as shattering as Kate's, for there is no record of the two men having seen each other in all the years they were in America together. Devoy left for the long rail journey to the Southwest that afternoon, and meetings and plans requiring his input were put on hold. Devoy clearly resented the intrusion, complaining to McGarrity that "it [Michael's death] comes at a most inconvenient time." He was in New Mexico for at least a week, but he came back a man of substantially greater means. His brother's estate was valued at some $20,000, and John was Michael's only heir. The money eventually made its way to John's orphaned nephews and niece in Dublin.

Before leaving for New Mexico, Devoy sent a $3,500 check to McGarrity, who sent it on to the IRB in Dublin. As in the days of the Land League, American cash was the fuel that kept the flame of Irish revolution burning, and Devoy and McGarrity, who made a fortune in the retail liquor business, saw to it that Clan branches thoughout America pressed harder for money from their members. On November 6, 1914, Devoy reported in a letter to McGarrity that another $15,000 was soon to be on its way. A succession of IRB couriers—including Sean T. O'Kelly, future prime minister of Ireland—brought the cash back to Ireland, though in at least one case there was a complication. In the spring of 1915, Devoy found himself in possession of some gold, the value of which he didn't give, though he indicated that this was not his preferred currency of conspiracy. "It is heavy and inconvenient," he complained to McGarrity, the former adjective suggesting something of significant value.

Money, however, was not the only commodity Devoy had to move across the Atlantic. In early August, Roger Casement and Devoy were in Philadelphia together for a rally called to protest the British Army killings in Dublin following the IRB gunrunning in Howth. The two men shared a ride in an open car after the rally, and a newspaper photographer captured the scene—Devoy glaring into the camera, his beard gray and fluffy; Casement looking away, every hair of his well-trimmed, dark beard giving off the image of an aristocrat. The picture, published in Philadelphia newspapers, was an intelligence blunder for Devoy and the Clan, for while Casement's

name was famous—he had won world acclaim and a British knight-
hood for his humanitarian work in the Belgian Congo—his face was
not. And the secret business Casement was about to propose would
now be all the more difficult.

Soon after their afternoon together in Philadelphia, Casement
told Devoy that he wished to go to Berlin to act as the Irish movement's ambassador and lobbyist, and to raise a brigade made up of
Irish soldiers in the British Army who had been captured and sent
back to prison camps in Germany. Devoy thought the plan was the
work of a dreamer. Whatever affinity these two dissimilar men had
for each other in the beginning of their tempestuous relationship,
Devoy clearly harbored doubts about Casement's judgment. It's possible the prudish Devoy suspected Casement's homosexuality. More
to the point, Devoy had a natural distrust for anybody not a member
of the secret societies—the Clan and the IRB—that were pulling the
strings of Irish nationalism. Then again, the gruff Devoy never held
much regard for romantics, which Casement surely was. Though he
was willing to place his life in jeopardy for Ireland and was an enthusiastic founder of the Irish Volunteers, Casement remained outside
the counsels of the shadowy revolutionary movement.

Nevertheless, Devoy put aside his doubts and introduced Casement to his contacts at the German consulate in New York. They
were more than happy to accommodate Casement. He was, after all,
a knight of the British Empire—a trophy convert to Germany's cause.

After several meetings in Casement's room at the St. George
Hotel in Brooklyn Heights, Devoy and other Clan leaders agreed to
sanction the German trip and pay Casement's expenses (in addition
to giving Casement $1,000 for expenses already incurred in Amer-
ica). The Clan supplied Casement with a passport bearing the
name of a New York businessman named James Landy, who was
not only privy to the deception but an instigator. (Landy even supplied a pair of his own glasses, while Clan members friendly with
Landy taught Casement his mannerisms in case he had to act out
his role as the businessman.) Other shadowy friends of the Clan
also helped out; Casement was given a letter attesting to his, that
is, Landy's character, on State Department letterhead. The letter
was probably supplied by a Philadelphia lawyer named Michael F.
Ryan, who was a friend of both Secretary of State William Jennings

Bryan and a high-ranking Clan member named James K. Maguire, a onetime mayor of Syracuse, New York. The Clan's power extended to the most unlikely places.

Casement was booked on the Norwegian liner *Oskar II* bound for Copenhagen, and from there he would travel to Germany overland. Perhaps because of his ill-timed appearance in the Philadelphia newspapers, Casement shaved his beard and bathed his face in buttermilk, a process, he told Devoy, that he believed would give him a lighter complexion and further deceive customs agents.

Devoy, Casement, McGarrity, and Judge Cohalan gathered in the judge's home on East Ninety-fourth Street on the evening of October 13, 1914. The atmosphere was decidedly congenial as the three top Clan leaders made some final preparations before taking leave of their ill-fated companion and coconspirator. For Devoy, the meeting was yet another cause for intense frustration, as he sought to make sense of a jumble of sounds. He heard enough to agree to sending a messenger to Dublin with another $10,000 for the IRB-infiltrated Volunteers, and he heard that Casement had proposed—with his colleagues' consent—to bring along a friend for the journey to Copenhagen. The friend's name was Adler Christiansen, a Norwegian sailor Casement had met two weeks before. Devoy didn't hear the latter detail, and he later said that if he had heard it, he would have objected.

The meeting ended with Cohalan pulling McGarrity aside, asking for reassurance. "Have you absolute confidence in this man?" he asked, referring to Casement.

"I will trust him with my life," McGarrity replied, saying the Irish had not seen a leader like Casement since Wolfe Tone.

If Cohalan asked Devoy a similar question, Devoy's reply is unrecorded.

McGarrity and Devoy left Cohalan's home together, and after Devoy mailed several letters that required shipment on a certain boat—such was the precision of mail service in those days—they retired to Devoy's room in the Ennis Hotel. Before settling into the room's two beds, the two men drank warm milk and chatted about the state of the war and of the conspiracy. Devoy indulged in some gloating over Germany's battlefield victories since the war began.

"We've waited a long time for this," he said with obvious glee. McGarrity steered the conversation to Casement and the mission he would begin in less than forty-eight hours. McGarrity confessed that he feared for Casement's success.

"I envy him," Devoy replied.

Casement left America on October 15. Before doing so, he shared a meal with McGarrity, and the two men talked about Devoy and the old man's long and often-solitary struggle for Ireland. "What a wonderful man!" Casement said. "What a heroic figure!" Just before boarding the ship that would take him to his fateful rendezvous in Europe, Casement wrote a note to Devoy, a man he clearly considered a dear friend and trusted ally:

"Without you there would be nothing, and if success [comes], or even a greater hope for the future, it will be due to you and your life of unceasing devotion to the most unselfish cause on earth. . . . I am only sorry now I did not talk much louder . . . for you to hear our final words. But please God we meet again—and meantime we work and plan."

By the time rebellion came to Ireland, Devoy was doing all in his considerable power to keep Casement in Germany and far removed from battle.

THE CONSPIRACY IN IRELAND, America, and Germany grew stronger with each month.

The winter of 1914 and the whole of 1915 found Devoy in constant touch with the German consulate on Wall Street, where he parleyed regularly with his friend von Skal and the embassy's military attaché, Capt. Franz von Papen. The IRB in Dublin had not yet decided on what form German aid should take; it was Devoy's job to make certain that the Germans remained sympathetic and willing to help. Ever the linguist—despite his hearing loss—Devoy taught himself German, no doubt to impress his would-be allies of his sincerity.

He continued his agitations for Germany, through rallies and editorial commentaries on page 1 of the *Gaelic American*, even after a German submarine attacked and sank the *Lusitania* in May 1915, an act that nearly drove the United States into the war and certainly made it that much harder for Devoy and other pro-Germans. The *Lusitania* incident did nothing to chasten Devoy; indeed, the *Gaelic American* immediately took the offensive, charging on page 1 that the ship was a "floating arsenal" in the surreptitious service of Britain. Obviously concerned that the attack might engender sympathy for Britain, Devoy hurriedly placed a story in the paper reminding readers yet again of Britain's Confederate sympathies during the Civil War, and the paper commenced a campaign against a New York State Board of Education resolution mandating school celebrations of the seven hundredth anniversary of the signing of the Magna Carta.

Any fears Devoy may have had about wavering public opinion were put to rest on Thursday evening, June 24, 1915, when he and other Irish- and German-Americans marshaled their greatest political show of strength yet in a monster rally at Madison Square Garden. Devoy estimated that one hundred thousand people attempted to gain entrance to the arena; the Police Department put the crowd inside and outside the Garden at seventy-five thousand—an impressive figure all the same. Even more impressive was the rally's featured speaker: William Jennings Bryan, who had just resigned as Woodrow Wilson's secretary of state. George von Skal, Devoy's journalist friend who worked out of the German consulate, called the meeting to order, and other speakers included Devoy himself and Jeremiah O'Leary, destined to be charged with treason three years later.

The propaganda value of the Garden rally was immense, thanks to the massive turnout and the prestige of Bryan's presence. But five days after what the *Gaelic American* called, in bold headlines, "the greatest meeting ever held in New York," an even greater opportunity presented itself.

Jeremiah O'Donovan Rossa, who once had personified Irish-American militancy in all its anger and all its bluster, died a feeble man of eighty-four on June 29, 1915, on Staten Island. He had spent most of the preceding two years in a hospital and in a haze, unable to recognize his own daughter and often raving in the Irish language at all hours of the night—leading a rather unfeeling chaplain to refuse him Holy Communion because, as the priest explained to Mrs. Rossa, the patient was "an imbecile."

Just before he took his first, confused steps along a last, dark journey, Rossa had reunited with Devoy after decades of bitter estrangement. Devoy and Rossa had declared their separate paths during the Land War and dynamite campaign of the 1880s and hadn't spoken since, something that required a great deal of effort given that both men traveled in the small circle of New York's Irish-American revolutionaries. Mary Rossa pleaded with Devoy to put the past aside and come to Rossa's bedside in the winter of 1913. "I think if you could come and talk of your earlier hopes and labours together . . . it would do him a world of good," she wrote. "He has a simple loving heart and you were very dear to it long ago." Included with Mrs. Rossa's letter was a short note from Rossa himself: "I am home and in bed every day. I got a fall a few years ago and cannot walk out. 'Tis a lonesome kind of life."

Though often hard of heart and head, Devoy could hardly ignore his old friend's plight. He was a regular visitor to Rossa's bedside until the day the old Fenian, whose memory of the Famine and his father's death by starvation had colored everything that came later, died. If Devoy paused for grief or reflection, it was not for long. The very day of the old Fenian's death, Devoy sent a telegram to Tom Clarke in Dublin: "Rossa dead. What shall we do?"

"Send his body home at once," came the reply.

After a funeral mass in St. Peter's Church on Staten Island on July 13, Devoy arranged for Rossa's body to be shipped to Queenstown, County Cork. Devoy was no stranger to transatlantic shipments in these hectic months, but this was one transaction that wasn't carried out under a conspirator's cover. And it was, in a mystical sense, among the most valuable gifts America presented to the revolutionaries in Dublin.

The IRB, working through the infiltrated Irish Volunteers, arranged for an armed escort as Rossa's funeral procession made its way through the streets of Dublin to Glasnevin Cemetery, final resting place of Ireland's dead heroes. At the graveside, Padraig Pearse, clad in the uniform of the Volunteers, moved forward from a column of similarly dressed men, paper in hand. In an oration by turns romantic and fiery, he summoned forth the conqueror's tongue and unleashed its formidable powers:

"Life springs from death, and from the graves of patriot men and women spring living nations. The defenders of this realm have worked well in secret and in the open. They think they have pacified Ireland. They think they have purchased half of us and intimidated the other half. They think they have foreseen everything, think that they have provided against everything. But the fools, the fools, the fools. They have left us our Fenian dead, and while Ireland holds these graves, Ireland unfree shall never be at peace."

The thousands who filed out of the cemetery after Pearse's speech carried with them a special program published for the occasion. Pearse had contributed an essay in Rossa's honor, and in it he also paid tribute to the man who had sent over Rossa's body. "When his biography is written," Pearse said of Devoy, "it will say that he was the greatest of the Fenians." The *Gaelic American*, in its lavish coverage of Rossa's funeral, did not record Pearse's tribute to its editor.

Throughout the summer and fall of 1915, the pace of the three-way transatlantic negotiations among Germany, the IRB, and the Clan in America picked up, with Devoy at the center. So voluminous was his correspondence during these weeks that his writing hand protested, forcing him to dictate his letters to a secretary. Casement sent word from Germany—where he would soon take refuge in a sanitarium as the pressure on him grew—that Devoy should send him $500 a month and American officers to help train the few dozen Irish-born prisoners of war he had recruited for his brigade. Devoy's letters to McGarrity during these critical months reflect a growing impatience with Casement (at one point Devoy reports that German embassy staff burst out laughing when told of one of Casement's requests). But Devoy's candor was wasted on McGarrity, who still regarded Casement as the second coming of Wolfe Tone. McGarrity soon grew distrustful not of Casement, but of Devoy. When Devoy asked McGarrity to send a copy of a treaty Casement negotiated in 1915 between himself and representatives of the German government, McGarrity refused, writing in a note on Devoy's letter, "This was an attempt to secure from me the last copy of the treaty, I believe to suppress it and kill Sir Roger's efforts for Ireland."

Even as he continued to send money to Ireland, Devoy discovered that the *Gaelic American* was running out of money. In July 1915, the newspaper's board informed him that the paper had only "$22 and a few cents" in the bank. He was stunned. "They [the newspaper's board] should have told me long ago, but I was so absorbed in other work that I paid no attention to business," he wrote. Worse, by the time of Rossa's funeral, the Clan was nearly as cleaned out as the *Gaelic American*'s coffers. In addition to the money sent to Ireland, the Clan, through Devoy and McGarrity, had sent nearly $8,000 to Casement for his stillborn recruiting mission. Before learning of his newspaper's dire financial status, Devoy loaned the Clan $3,340 from the money he had inherited from his late brother's estate and another $1,000 to several colleagues.

209

It's not clear how the paper managed to right itself financially, but the crisis passed. The Clan rebuilt its treasury the old-fashioned way, through assiduous collection of dues and fees from members and their camps. Planning for the rising, meanwhile, went forward in the three capitals of conspiracy. Sometime around the time of Rossa's death, Irish labor leader James Larkin, on a long organizing tour in the American West, asked Devoy to help arrange a meeting with German diplomats. Larkin, who was living on strong tea and little else, was prepared to take a German offer of cash in exchange for his support of the German war effort. Larkin clearly wanted Devoy to be party to the deal so he could be a witness in case of trouble.

Sure enough, the Germans implored Larkin to help organize sabotage in American ports. One of Devoy's contacts at the consulate in New York, Wolf von Igel, took Larkin on a tour of Germany's secret sabotage center in Hoboken, New Jersey, just across the Hudson from Manhattan. Von Igel showed off an assortment of nasty devices designed to ruin the rudders of transatlantic ships. Larkin refused a formal offer to supervise sabotage operations on the American East Coast, but he agreed to continue to stir up labor trouble. How much Devoy knew of Larkin's involvement isn't certain. Devoy's letters from the period often refer to Larkin, usually under the code name Longfellow. And when Larkin was in New York, he often sat in on meetings with Devoy, Cohalan, and McGarrity and was thus privy to the deliberations of Clan na Gael's top leaders.

IN SEPTEMBER 1915, JOSEPH Mary Plunkett, one of the poets who would command Ireland's insurrection, arrived in New York Harbor to see Devoy with urgent news. Plunkett, twenty-eight years old, was a man of steely determination but a wasted body. Dying of tuberculosis, he nevertheless threw himself into the tactics and strategy for the coming fight and would eventually be named the IRB's director of military operations.

Fresh from a trip to Berlin, Plunkett was to inform Devoy that the German General Staff was cooperating and a rebellion would take place soon. But his mission was nearly stopped at the border, for the young poet's tuberculosis was so advanced he was denied entry into the United States when he disembarked at Ellis Island. Devoy was summoned to the island to find some way of getting Plunkett into New York. For a time, it seemed an impossible task, and Devoy didn't hide his annoyance. "The law forbids the landing of tuberculosis cases and his is of a most pronounced type," he wrote to McGarrity. "It was folly to send him."

Devoy used his influence with New York senator James O'Gorman to get Plunkett into the country, giving him a chance to spend ten days in the company of the poet Joyce Kilmer and other American writers. Devoy, now apparently flush with cash, supplied $1,000 to cover a bond the government insisted on before allowing Plunkett to set foot in America. Plunkett was the last of the rebellion's emerging leaders to come to America, and he was the last Devoy would meet in the flesh.

On January 26, 1916, Berlin advised the German embassy in Washington to contact three Irish-Americans who could be of assistance to the German cause. The telegram named names: Joseph McGarrity of Philadelphia, John P. Keating of Chicago, and Jeremiah O'Leary of New York. All were deemed "suitable for carrying out sabotage in the United States." Devoy's name is conspicuous by its absence, for he was the only member of the Clan na Gael's Revolutionary Directory not listed. O'Leary was eventually indicted. Keating died before the telegram was written, indicating that German intelligence in America was not what it might have been. McGarrity escaped prosecution after publicly challenging the government to haul him into court.

The Germans had ambitious plans for their American allies: "In the United States sabotage can be carried out on every kind of factory for supplying munitions of war," the telegram from Berlin to Washington said. But the German Foreign Ministry was well aware that such a campaign must restrict itself to military targets: "Railway embankments and bridges must not be touched," it warned.

When the telegram was made public more than a year later, Devoy's allies forcefully denied that they had ever contemplated such actions against the United States. But in the early months of 1916, there was no denying that Germany and Irish America were battlefield allies, and that Devoy had helped form the delicate alliance.

On February 5, 1916, a young Irishman named Tommy O'Connor showed up unannounced at John Devoy's cramped newspaper office on William Street, around the corner from City Hall in downtown Manhattan. O'Connor was a ship's steward for the Cunard steamship line, working the transatlantic route between Liverpool and New York, with a stopover in Queenstown, Ireland. It was dangerous work in 1916, for the Germans were putting John Holland's invention to the sort of use Devoy and the Fenians envisioned in the 1880s, when the *Fenian Ram* was the only submarine in existence. But O'Connor believed the risk was worthwhile. A member of the Irish Republican Brotherhood, O'Connor was a courier between the IRB and John Devoy. He brought messages to Devoy; he returned home with cash Devoy raised for the IRB's treasury. In the past few months, O'Connor and several other couriers had carried $100,000 to the IRB, money Devoy had been quietly withdrawing in $5,000 and $10,000 sums from his accounts with the Corn Exchange Bank.

Some hours before O'Connor's arrival, Devoy had scrawled a note to McGarrity concerning a matter that had grown to a near obsession. Casement's companion, the Norwegian sailor Adler Christiansen, was back in New York after a short stay with Casement in Germany. The old man, whose patience with Casement's dithering in Berlin had worn thin, was convinced that Christiansen was a British agent or might become one. Christiansen's pleas for money to pay his rent and other expenses in New York also drove Devoy to distraction. Nevertheless, he gave Christiansen the money, fearing perhaps that the Norwegian would turn to another paymaster.

When O'Connor arrived, Devoy brought him around the corner for lunch at Haan's Restaurant on bustling Park Row. The East Side streetcar lines came to a clanging halt outside the restaurant, delivering passengers to downtown New York's financial and commercial district. A fair portion of John Devoy's life had been spent in this busy intersection of commerce, politics (City Hall was just across the street), and journalism (the *Times*, *Herald*, and *Tribune* had been based here, although they had already started the journey uptown). Devoy had started his newspaper career in the *Herald*'s old Park Row office, and now, forty-two years later, he still filed his copy and conducted his business over the din of the streetcar bell.

O'Connor got down to business, passing Devoy a sealed envelope from Dublin. The old man opened it immediately. Contained within was a message written in code, which had become standard practice for both the IRB and Devoy, ever mindful of the leaks that had foiled many a Fenian plan before. So sensitive were the conspirators to security leaks that they spurned the telegraph and relied instead on transatlantic couriers such as O'Connor, who were reliable but could move only as fast as a steamship could take them, generally a week.

Devoy stared hard at this new message. Oddly, it was written in a cipher he didn't know. He handed the paper to O'Connor, who recognized the code and started to translate. Devoy ordered him to stop when he deciphered the second sentence: "This message is to be read only by members of the Revolutionary Directory." Devoy was one of the directory's three members; O'Connor was not, and so the young steward was sent away while Devoy hustled back to the office to translate the rest of the message. Once deciphered, Devoy understood the urgency. It was from the Supreme Council of the IRB:

"We have decided to begin action on Easter Sunday. We must have your arms and munitions in Limerick between Good Friday and Easter Saturday. We expect German help immediately after beginning action. We might be compelled to begin earlier."

Easter Sunday was less than three months away. Though he was well aware of the IRB's military preparations and its infiltration of the Volunteer movement, Devoy thought the great day of liberation was at least a year away, when, he believed, the Germans would have the upper hand on the Western Front.

There was an astonishing amount of work to be done. Not for the first time, the task of publishing the *Gaelic American* fell to Devoy's assistants while the old man scheduled endless rounds of meetings. The first was convened the following morning, in Judge

Cohalan's home. There, he briefed Cohalan and McGarrity on the contents of the message and its request for German assistance. Both men were as surprised as Devoy was, but they were not in a position to argue, nor was it their job to do so. "They [the IRB] did not ask our advice; they simply announced a decision already taken, so . . . our plain duty was to accept it and give them all the help we could," Devoy wrote.

John Devoy had been waiting for this moment for a half century.

CHAPTER FOURTEEN

A Flag of War

As JOHN DEVOY'S PARTNERS IN CONSPIRACY, GERMANY'S DIPLO-
mats in America lacked a sense of urgency in this matter of a rebellion
on their enemy's western flank. Cables and memos with highly confidential information, some of them bearing John Devoy's name, were
scattered carelessly on desks in the New York consulate's inner offices.
The German embassy in Washington dispatched wireless messages
from Devoy to Berlin in the same code it had been using since the
war broke out.

The day after Devoy met with his Irish-American colleagues to
discuss the IRB communiqué, he visited the German consulate in
downtown Manhattan. For months, Devoy had been warning both
von Igel and his colleague Franz von Papen to be more careful with
correspondence relating to the American-Irish-German conspiracy in
case the U.S. Secret Service paid an unannounced visit. Von Igel
told Devoy he was being overly cautious, for such an invasion would
be a violation of international law and diplomatic courtesy, and the
Wilson administration wouldn't dare contemplate such a breach.

"They don't care a damn about international law or American
law," Devoy growled, his eyes ablaze. "They want your papers . . . and
will get them if they can, law or no law."

Von Igel ignored Devoy's outburst and his suggestions that he
keep the door to his inner office locked. When Devoy arrived at the
consulate on February 7 with his message from Dublin, diplomatic
papers still lay carelessly on desks spread out across the four-room
office. Devoy, no doubt after surveying the mess with some disgust,

showed von Papen a copy of the decoded message from the IRB and gave them a message to be forwarded to the German embassy in Washington for transmittal to the General Staff in Berlin. The message, labeled "Most Secret," was dispatched from Washington on February 10, in Devoy's own words: "Unanimous opinion that action cannot be postponed much longer. Delay disadvantageous to us. We can now put up an effective fight. Our enemies cannot allow us much more time. . . . We have therefore decided to begin action on Easter Saturday. Unless entirely new circumstances arise we must have your arms and munitions in Limerick between Good Friday and Easter Saturday. We expect German help immediately after beginning action."

For reasons Devoy never explained, his message to Berlin said the rising would take place on Easter Saturday, rather than Sunday. It was, in any case, a minor oversight, because the more critical time frame, as far as the Germans were concerned, was the plan for the arms delivery. Here again, though, Devoy apparently made an adjustment in the timetable. In his memoirs, he stated that the IRB's original communication specifically called for an arms delivery between April 20 and April 23, a four-day interval from Holy Thursday to Easter Sunday. Yet records from his correspondence with Berlin clearly show him requesting the delivery in the narrower time frame of Good Friday to Easter Saturday. To add to the confusion, on April 12, Devoy's colleague on the Revolutionary Directory, Joseph McGarrity, received a message from Padraig Pearse in Dublin requesting an arms delivery "between Good Friday and Easter Sunday." As events transpired, the timing of the arms delivery was to become the Rising's biggest might-have-been.

In an addendum to Devoy's message to Berlin, the German diplomats in America noted that "the confidential agent"—Devoy—would, at the consul's request, advise his colleagues in Dublin "to wait, and [he] will point out the difficulties in the way of our giving help." It is unlikely that Devoy ever did so. The IRB, after all, made those kinds of decisions.

A week after Tommy O'Connor's visit, another courier turned up in Devoy's office. She was Philomena Plunkett, daughter of a distinguished papal count and sister of IRB leader Joseph Plunkett, the tubercular poet who had visited Devoy in August 1915. She handed Devoy another message from the IRB, written in the same code as the previous week's. This one provided more specific details about the IRB's plan and requested the presence of a submarine in Dublin Bay.

Devoy trooped to the German consulate with the IRB's more detailed plan of action. On February 18, the Germans in Washington surreptitiously attached a memo to an otherwise long dispatch relating to German-American negotiations over the *Lusitania* sinking. The memo, from the German ambassador von Bernstorff, noted that "the Irish leader, John Devoy, informs me that a rising is to begin in Ireland on Easter Saturday. Please send arms to Limerick, west coast of Ireland, between Good Friday and Easter Saturday. . . . Let me know if help may be expected from Germany." Once again, Easter Saturday, rather than Easter Sunday, is given as the date of the proposed rebellion, and the time frame is narrower than what Devoy said he was originally given. It's hard to imagine that Devoy was so careless that he got the date wrong twice, which suggests that the date was jumbled in translation or that somehow Devoy's extremely faulty hearing was to blame for not catching the mistake in his conversations with his allies.

Two days before this latest dispatch from Washington to Berlin, Devoy presented the Germans with a long memorandum outlining the relative strength of the rebel army as well as the British troops and the local constabulary in Ireland. To drive home the point that an Irish rebellion would help Germany's cause, the Devoy memo estimated that the planned action would mean the transfer of five hundred thousand British troops from the Western Front to Ireland. No doubt based on reports from Tom Clarke, the memo asserted that of the forty thousand British troops in Ireland, thirty thousand were "poorly trained, [with] few competent officers, no trained noncommissioned officers, little artillery and a few machine guns." Devoy put the number of Irish Volunteers at forty thousand, and with no evidence other than his own certainty, Devoy claimed that fifty thousand of the National Volunteers—the forces under the control of the parliamentarian John Redmond—would join in the rebellion. While Devoy's estimate of British troop strength in Ireland and the quality of their training and equipment was on target, his estimates of friendly forces were worse than exaggeration. It was the sort of wishful thinking reminiscent of the Fenians of old.

The actual strength of the Irish Volunteers was about twelve thousand, and they were under the command of a college professor and Gaelic scholar named Eoin MacNeill, who was blissfully unaware that his wing of the Volunteer movement was under the effective control of the secret, oath-bound IRB. The Volunteers' Military Council was made up entirely of sworn IRB men.

Another person seemingly at the heart of the conspiracy was unaware of what Devoy and the IRB leaders were planning. Roger Casement was lying in bed in a German sanitarium, his plans to raise a brigade among Irish prisoners in Germany come to nothing. Devoy intentionally withheld information from his supposed agent in Berlin.

Devoy's trust in Casement's judgment and ability, never particularly strong, now was nonexistent, and with good reason. Even before he left for Germany, Casement had shown himself to be indiscreet—in the summer of 1914, he told Congressman William Bourke Cockran and attorney John Quinn of his plans to go to Berlin, a breathtaking breach of security. Both Cockran and Quinn were vehemently pro-British in the European conflict and were not the sort to be entrusted with the revolutionary conspiracy's secrets. Nevertheless, the two men apparently kept their knowledge to themselves.

Ultimately, though, it was Casement's embarrassing failure to achieve the purpose of his mission—the formation of an Irish Brigade in Germany, which consisted of a pathetic fifty members—that led Devoy to conclude that he was a liability. Devoy, with the support of Clarke and other IRB leaders, instructed Berlin to keep Casement in Germany "as Ireland's accredited representative" when the rebellion broke out. Devoy wanted Casement as far away from Dublin as possible.

In early March, Devoy was summoned back to Wall Street to receive Germany's reply to the IRB's request for military assistance: "It is possible to send two or three small fishing steamers, with about ten machine guns, twenty thousand rifles, ammunition and explosives, to Fenit Pier in Tralee Bay. Irish pilots should wait north of Inishtooskert Island from before dawn of April 20, displaying at intervals three green lights. Disembarkation must be effected immediately. Let us know if this can be done." The date selected was Holy Thursday, a day earlier than Devoy's request. The clear designation of April 20 as the earliest possible date for the arms delivery, however, should have cleared up whatever confusion there might have been.

Devoy had been hoping for one hundred thousand rifles, batteries of artillery, and the commitment of experienced German officers to lead the untried Irish troops. He wrote to McGarrity in his usual barely disguised language: "I have received an answer to my application for the position. . . . It is favorable, but the salary is not as big as I expected, but it is a living wage and I am certain I would get a raise soon when they [see] I could make good." Devoy signed the letter with one of his many aliases, James Digby. A week later, the Germans told him they would send the weapons in one large mercantile ship, rather than in three fishing vessels. There was no mention of a submarine.

On March 12, 1916, the embassy in Washington sent Devoy's reply to Berlin: "Irish agree to proposition."

In the midst of these tense negotiations, Devoy decided that, as in the days of the American Land League, a public organization was required to organize support in America—a public organization that the Clan, of course, would control. Devoy understood the importance of recruiting mainstream politicians, writers, clergy, and other Irish-American leaders to a seemingly nonrevolutionary, reform-minded organization. He discussed the idea with Cohalan, Jeremiah O'Leary, and via letters, with the former American consul in Munich, an Irish-born diplomat named Thomas St. John Gaffney, with whom Casement had been in touch.

The public organization born of Devoy's consultations came into existence in early March. Called the Friends of Irish Freedom, its foundation was the carefully planned outcome of a two-day gathering of about twenty-five hundred Irish-American leaders held in New York on March 4 and March 5. Of course, the convention had an unspoken agenda. With the rebellion in Ireland a mere six weeks away, Devoy and the three other men who knew of the planned insurrection—McGarrity, Cohalan, and a Buffalo lawyer named John T. Ryan—sought to remind the Wilson administration of Irish America's political influence at a time when events were about to explode.

Devoy's stage-managing of the convention displayed Irish America in all its newfound influence and power—the chief speakers were Congressman William Bourke Cockran, whose eloquence had captured the imagination of Winston Churchill; Judge Cohalan; and the composer Victor Herbert. In size, scope, and influence, it was among the most important gatherings of the Irish in America since the Land League days, and even those meetings didn't contain the range of political and commercial accomplishment. Devoy himself spoke to the convention, but he offered only a bland speech about the importance of Irish unity while warning against what he called "imprudent speech." The convention's closing document was a great deal more militant. It demanded that "in the name of liberty and of the small nationalities . . . that Ireland may be cut off from England and restored to her rightful place among the nations of the earth." Shrewdly, the newly formed Friends of Irish Freedom named the eminently respectable Victor Herbert as president, but of the seventeen people chosen as the group's trustees, fifteen were Clan na Gael men, including Devoy.

The FOIF's executive committee assembled in New York's Murray Hill Hotel on March 15 to issue an urgent appeal for donations to give "Ireland the help which she so badly needs in this hour of her danger and her opportunity." That very day, Devoy walked to the Corn Exchange Bank's offices on Forty-second Street and cashed a check he wrote to himself for the sum of $10,000. The money was converted into pounds sterling and transmitted to Ireland under the name "J. Digby."

DEVOY WAS UNDER NO illusions that his agitations for Ireland were passing without the notice of the pro-British Wilson administration, nor did he believe that a respectable front group like the Friends of Irish Freedom shielded him from prying eyes. His letters and newspaper writings from this critical time are filled with references to the U.S. Secret Service, and he would later write with confidence that a government agent was residing in a room adjacent to his when he took up residence in the Ennis Hotel. The extent to which the Wilson administration was monitoring his activities and those of his allies was made evident on April 6, when a federal subpoena was delivered to the *Gaelic American's* offices, demanding Devoy's presence in Manhattan's federal court building the following day. A grand jury was investigating pro-German activities in America, and it already had heard testimony from Devoy's colleague John T. Ryan, another member of the Clan's Revolutionary Directory. Clearly, the Wilson administration knew it was on to something.

Devoy showed up as ordered on April 7, a Friday, and was questioned about an alleged plot to blow up the Welland Canal in Canada. The supposed existence of such a plot, and several others, was revealed by a German spy captured in Britain who had agreed to cooperate with authorities in both London and Washington. Devoy said he knew nothing of the Welland plot. But he was also questioned about the activities of von Papen and von Igel, two of the German diplomats with whom he had been conspiring since the war began. With the Germans about to deliver the arms and ammunition shipment, he helped arrange through those same diplomats, Devoy must have been rattled as he stepped down from the witness box.

As the grand jury sifted through Devoy's testimony, a 1,400-ton steamer slipped out of the German port of Lübeck. Flying the flag of neutral Norway, the ship, named the *Aud*, was under the command of Karl Spindler, a captain in the Imperial German Navy. Spindler's vessel carried the arms shipment Devoy had arranged—twenty thousand rifles, a million rounds of ammunition, and ten machine guns. But Spindler, a thoroughly professional officer and an admirer of the Irish revolutionaries, was troubled, for he believed the cargo he was carrying was inadequate for the task at hand. The rifles were nearly fifteen years old and were quite literally leftovers—booty the Germans captured from the Russians on the war's Eastern Front. And the *Aud* itself was hardly state of the art. Among the amenities it lacked was a wireless, rendering it incommunicado from the moment it left its berth. Nevertheless, the captain skillfully steered a circuitous course that took him north, nearly to the arctic circle, then south and west, in an effort to avoid British war vessels.

On April 12, three days after the *Aud* set sail, a distraught Roger Casement climbed into a German submarine bound for Ireland, accompanied by two allies, Robert Monteith, an emissary from Devoy sent from New York in late 1915 to assist Casement, and Daniel Bailey. Devoy wanted Casement to remain in Germany, ostensibly to serve as a liaison between the provisional government the rebels intended to establish and the German government. In fact, Devoy knew that Casement had become disillusioned with the Germans and had been making increasingly vocal demands for greater assistance. Indeed, so critical had Casement become of the German military that one high-ranking officer threatened to notify Devoy that Germany was withdrawing its offer of support. If Casement were transported to Ireland, Devoy thought, he might try to stop the rebellion in its tracks.

In Dublin, the would-be revolutionaries were beginning to be overwhelmed by logistics. It occurred to them that the German arms might arrive too early, unwittingly giving the British advance warning of the rebellion. Philomena Plunkett was again dispatched to New York with a new message for Devoy. She boarded her steamship on April 7, the day of Devoy's grand jury testimony, and arrived in Devoy's office on April 14, a Friday, two days after Casement left Germany. She handed Devoy another coded message, and he hurried to a quiet office and spent hours decoding it. He was shocked when he finished:

"Arms must not be landed before night of Sunday, 23rd. This is vital. Smuggling impossible. Let us know if submarine will come to Dublin Bay."

The Germans had said that the landing could take place as early as April 20. The change in plans was stunning. Worse, by the time he decoded the message it was past five o'clock, the time the German embassy on Wall Street closed for the day. After spending an especially sleepless night, Devoy showed up at the embassy the next morning. He was told that the arms ship had already left for Ireland and, incredibly, that it was was not equipped with a wireless. There was no way to pass the message to Spindler, but Devoy, in desperation, handed over to the consulate staff a copy of the IRB's request, hoping for the best.

After a frenzied consultation with McGarrity and Cohalan, Devoy dispatched a messenger to Ireland with instructions to find Pearse and tell him the bad news. The courier, however, never reached Pearse. On Tuesday morning, April 18, the German military attaché von Igel was sifting through papers on his desk at the consulate, awaiting the arrival of James Larkin. Von Igel still held out hope that the Irish labor leader would cooperate with Germany's plans to disrupt American shipping.

A mass of papers was on von Igel's desk, some of them taken from his safe, which was open. In the time he had before Larkin's arrival, von Igel was sorting through his correspondence, setting some of the most sensitive letters aside for removal from the office. The door to his inner office was closed but unlocked.

In an adjacant office, George von Skal, the German-American journalist who doubled as an intelligence agent for the embassy, was seated at his desk. Like his friend Devoy, von Skal had urged von Igel to be more cautious in his work and in particular to keep his door locked at all times. Von Igel ignored the advice.

As von Igel continued to pore through his paperwork, a half dozen well-dressed American men entered the consulate's outer office, asking for the young attaché. The men drew revolvers, pushed open von Igel's unlocked door, and grabbed hold of the German's arms. Hearing shouts from von Igel, von Skal rushed to his colleague's aid, digging his foot into the abdomen of one of the armed men. Von Igel squirmed free and slammed the door to the safe while von Skal and one of the intruders grappled over a telephone. Eventually, the two Germans were subdued.

The armed men identified themselves as agents of the U.S. Secret Service, acting on orders from Woodrow Wilson's Department of Justice. With the consulate staff held off at gunpoint, the agents rifled through the papers spread across von Igel's desk. One agent came upon copies of messages dispatched to Berlin via Washington. Covering the copies was a note reading, "This was handed in by confidential agent John Devoy." Underneath was a copy of Devoy's request that the German arms be landed no earlier than Easter Sunday night. Also attached was a memo from Judge Cohalan that outlined plans for a coordinated Irish-German strike at Britain. "There would be an air raid on England and a naval attack timed to coincide with the rising [in Ireland], followed by a landing of troops and munitions and also of some officers, perhaps from an airship," Cohalan suggested, anticipating airborne assaults by a quarter century. "It might be possible to close the Irish harbours against England, set up bases for submarines and cut off food export to England. A successful rising may decide the war."

The Secret Service agents scooped up the papers, arrested von Igel, then informed reporters that they had uncovered a secret Irish-German plot against the United States. One of those reporters was a friend of Devoy's. He called the old man and told him of the security disaster.

The following day, Devoy showed up at the German consulate even as the morning newspapers offered lurid accounts of the alleged plot to bring the war to America. None of the papers had specific details, and there was no mention of the Devoy and Cohalan telegrams. As Devoy entered an elevator that would take him to the fourth-floor consulate office, an elevator operator, who had come to know Devoy through his frequent visits, winked broadly and motioned to a crowd of strangers in the lobby. They were Secret Service agents monitoring the aftershocks of the raid. Devoy ignored them.

After a private briefing at the consulate, Devoy was strangely calm, relieved to hear that the American agents had found only one of his telegrams to Berlin. He wrote McGarrity in thinly veiled code: "I know you will be anxious after hearing of the fire in our home to learn if we all came out safe. I am glad to be able to inform you that all the papers relating to the property were saved except for one little scrap, and that will not be much of a loss. The sale will come off on time and everything looks all right. We were very anxious for a whole day, but when the firemen got through with their work of salvage we found we had no excuse for worry." Devoy signed the note David Jones.

Devoy either was misinformed about which telegram the Americans had seized or he was trying to delude himself, for the raid and seizure were a devastating breach of security. His reassurances seem oddly tranquil, considering that the "one little scrap" now in the possession of American intelligence consisted of nothing less than the date of the planned rising in Ireland, along with clear evidence that an arms shipment—arranged with the help of Devoy himself in a clear breach of American neutrality—was on its way.

What Devoy didn't know is that months before, the cream of British intelligence had cracked the German diplomatic code, and every one of Devoy's messages to Berlin was read first in London. British intelligence could hardly believe its luck, for the usually efficient Germans hadn't changed their codes regularly. They wondered how the Germans could be so stupid.

Dublin was unaware of what was happening in New York, Berlin, and London. Plans for the rebellion moved ahead in accordance with the IRB-led Military Council's strategy. The rising would take place under the cover of military maneuvers that were part of daily life in Ireland. The country in 1916 lived not only with the presence of forty thousand regular British soldiers, but the thousands more who were members of the three Volunteer armies—the Irish Volunteers, the National Volunteers, and the Ulster Volunteers—that were indulged by an uneasy government. Nobody would notice the activities of large groups of armed men parading around the country. It was perfectly normal.

Unfortunately for the would-be rebels who would soon be summoned to action, the IRB's strategy was no more innovative than that of the British generals on the Western Front who ordered charges on machine-gun nests. The IRB and the Irish Citizen Army, James Connolly's small cadre of trade unionists turned revolutionary nationalists, would seize five strongpoints in Dublin, each one commanding a strategic portion of the city. There, they would proclaim the Republic and await the inevitably furious British response. The plan was as suicidal as a stroll across no-man's-land, for even the poets knew they could not maintain a static defense against overwhelming firepower. Still, the leaders believed a show of force, however futile, would help ensure Ireland a place at the peace talks when the war on the Continent finally ended.

The fulcrum of the Rising was to be the General Post Office on Sackville Street, a Romanesque structure with fine marble columns. Pearse, Connolly, and the other leaders would make the GPO the Republic's command post. The site's only strategic value lay in its position in the heart of Dublin's city center, just a few hundred feet

from the Marlborough Street School where the young rebel John Devoy had struck his first blows for liberty. Among those in training for
the assault on the GPO was a young soldier named Peter, or Peader,
Devoy, John Devoy's orphaned nephew. Only weeks ago, on March
18, Peter Devoy's older brother had died after a lifelong battle with
tuberculosis. Named for his uncle John, he was but thirty-five at his
death, and he was buried in Dublin's Glasnevin Cemetery in a plot
with his baby sister, Eva, dead at four months, his mother, Eliza, and
his father, Joseph. Now, Peter was preparing himself to be part of a
poetic sacrifice. With his comrades, he would march gladly toward
Ireland's Golgotha.

By Holy Thursday, John Devoy had resigned himself to a reluctant place on the sidelines while the great drama was played out in
Dublin. For some weeks, Devoy had been trying to arrange for false
identity papers so he could board a ship that would take him to
Dublin, where he would join in the fight he had worked so hard to
bring about. For a time, it appeared as though the old man, half-deaf
and troubled by poor vision, would get his wish. One of his contacts
was arranging to get the papers of a dead man who was approximately
Devoy's age, size, and weight. Just how serious Devoy was about this
romantic plan is indicated in a letter he received from O'Donovan
Rossa's widow. Dated April 6, Mrs. Rossa wrote, "I feared you were
gone to Ireland until I went [home] a few days ago and Eileen [her
daughter] showed me a letter she had from you. I hope you will remain
at this side to direct . . . the forces you have marshaled for the assistance of the men at home. To throw yourself into the midst of things
in Ireland would be the fulfillment of a beautiful dream to you, I am
sure, but while you can be of more practical benefit here, I hope you
will regard the dream as a temptation." Mrs. Rossa's letter did nothing
to change Devoy's mind, but the arrangement fell though a week or
so before Easter; otherwise the old Fenian might have taken a place
beside the poets, romantics, and dreamers—and his nephew—in the
GPO.

Late in the evening of Holy Thursday, Eoin MacNeill, the putative chairman of the Irish Volunteers, discovered not only that the
IRB had taken over leadership of his organization, but that a planned
drill of the Volunteers on Easter Sunday was, in fact, a cover for a
rebellion. After a long and heated meeting with Pearse, MacNeill

vowed to do all he could to stop the rising. Later, on Good Friday morning, the rebels persuaded him to do nothing for the moment. An arms shipment from Germany was on the way, he was told.

Even as MacNeill was arguing with Pearse, the *Aud* was lying offshore in Tralee Bay. As far as Spindler knew, all was going according to schedule. He arrived at his assigned spot late in the afternoon on Holy Thursday, April 20. In a feat of expert seamanship, Spindler had managed to slip past British ships that were ordered to the Irish west coast after Devoy's messages to Berlin were intercepted and decoded. From his rendezvous point, Spindler flashed signals to the shore, expecting the Irish to be at the beach waiting for their guns.

No answering signals replied. There was nobody waiting.

Incredibly, the IRB military council had nobody watching for what it considered a premature delivery. With British ships on the lookout for a suspicious vessel, Spindler ordered the *Aud* to hunker down through Thursday night while lookouts searched the shore for flashes of green—the answering signal.

The *Aud* was not the only German vessel off the Irish coast that night. The submarine carrying Roger Casement and his two colleagues surfaced off Banna Strand in County Cork in the predawn darkness, and Casement and his two aides shoved off in small boat and headed for the Irish shore. After a terrible struggle through stormy waters, the small party stumbled onto shore near dawn. Casement, weakened by the ordeal, had to be helped onto dry land. They tried to scuttle their small boat, but failed and then headed inland, looking for help. When a passing constable discovered the boat floating along the beach, he found it contained a knife and a thousand rounds of ammunition. An alert was issued, and Casement was found and arrested by Good Friday afternoon. Bailey, too, was soon in custody, and he told constables what he knew of the arms shipment. Monteith remained a fugitive.

The conspiracy was collapsing.

In Tralee Bay, Spindler gave up and decided to make a run for freedom. Before long, however, a Royal Navy gunship caught up with the *Aud*. The British captain ordered the trawler to proceed to Queenstown Harbor for inspection. As it entered the harbor, Spindler ordered his men into lifeboats, and the *Aud* blew itself up in the harbor, taking the IRB's arms shipment to the bottom.

Devoy's years of careful planning had come to this: Casement was under arrest, the arms shipment was at the bottom of Queenstown Harbor, and the conspiracy itself had unraveled. When word of the disasters got back to Dublin, MacNeill canceled orders for the Volunteers' maneuvers on Easter Sunday and placed an advertisement to that effect in the Sunday *Independent* newspaper. The countermanding order meant that hundreds, even thousands, of Volunteers would not show up for what was planned to be the start of the rebellion. The IRB's military council, faced with chaos on one hand and the near certainty that the government, alerted by Casement's arrest and the capture and scuttling of the *Aud,* would soon break the conspiracy, hurriedly decided to go ahead with the Rising after a twenty-four-hour postponement.

At precisely noon on Easter Monday, approximately 1,500 green-shirted Volunteers assembled throughout Dublin, along with 150 members of the Irish Citizen Army. The lead column marched up Sackville Street from the River Liffey, drawing broad double takes from tradesmen, strollers, and shoppers. As they approached the GPO, Pearse shouted, "Charge!" The army of the Irish Republic established its headquarters without a shot fired, and Pearse strode out to the GPO's facade to read a proclamation to anyone who chanced to be in the neighborhood:

"Irishmen and Irishwomen, in the name of God and of the dead generations from which she receives her old tradition of nationhood, Ireland, through us, summons her children to her flag and strikes for her freedom. Having organized and trained her manhood through her secret revolutionary organization, the Irish Republican Brotherhood, and through her open military organizations, the Irish Volunteers and the Irish Citizen Army, having patiently perfected her discipline, having resolutely waited for the right moment to reveal itself, she now seizes the moment, and, supported by her exiled children in America and by gallant allies in Europe, but relying first on her own strength, she strikes in full confidence of victory."

The first signature on the proclamation was that of Thomas J. Clarke, John Devoy's former assistant and a naturalized American citizen.

While the rebels dug in for the inevitable British onslaught, Plunkett arranged for an IRB party to seize the telegraph office on Valen-
cia Island off the west coast of Ireland. The rebels did so, then
dispatched a message in code to Devoy and his allies in America:

"Tom successfully operated today."

CHAPTER FIFTEEN

Yonder Waits the Saxon Foe

THE EASTER RISING, WITH POETS MANNING COMMAND POSTS AND
plotting strategy while the might of an empire cranked up its engines
of destruction, has about it, even after all these years, an aura of
perfect sacrifice, the act of selfless men and women who volunteered
for death so that generations unborn would know freedom. When it
was over, even the unsentimental John Devoy described it as an act
that saved the soul of an Ireland on the verge of becoming no more
than a cultural annex of Britain.

While the battle was raging in the streets of Dublin, however,
Devoy was engaged in a very different but related fight, this one for
the mind and sympathy of American public opinion. It was a decidedly less romantic battle, and defeat would bring no glory, no claims
to moral authority. When the great powers of Europe finished slaugh-
tering each other's young, there would be a settlement, Devoy knew,
and the power of American opinion could achieve for Ireland at the
peace table what its poets could not on the battlefield.

As the de facto spokesman and chief propagandist of the Irish
revolution in America, Devoy's enemy was the mainstream, pro-
British press. The fight for Irish freedom was replicated in America
as a fight for public opinion, with Devoy at the head of the rebel
column.

Most mainstream American dailies heaped contempt not only on
the rebels, but on their allies in the United States as well. The *New
York Herald*, Devoy's former employer, referred to the rebellion's supporters in America as "Gaelic sympathizers and pro-German propa-

gandists." The *New York Times* described Pearse, Connolly, Clarke, and their colleagues as something "like forward children, causing untold annoyance to others, but themselves suffering the heavier penalties of misbehavior." The *Christian Science Monitor* dismissed the rebellion as little more than a riot, an opinion the *Times* shared in a headline that reflected wishful thinking as well as poor information. "Troops Crush Revolt in Dublin; Take Post Office Seized by Rioters," the *Times* announced on Wednesday, April 26, when the rebellion was at its fiercest (and when the tricolor of the Irish Republic still flew defiantly over the GPO). This sort of coverage tended to confirm Devoy's insistence that most American newspapers, particularly those in New York, were reflexively pro-British.

During the first few days of the rebellion, the *Gaelic American*'s offices were bombarded with reporters seeking Devoy's comment. A *Herald* reporter showed up on April 26 and elicited a remark from an unnamed Gaelic American staff member, probably Devoy. The staffer reported, with a touch of indiscretion, that "we were not surprised [by the rebellion]. I can't answer the question of whether any preparations were made in this city." The *Herald* ran the comment under a headline that read, "Irish Leaders Here Had Secret News of the Revolt."

When it hit the newsstands on April 27, Devoy's *Gaelic American* offered a different version of the story in Dublin. Its headline read, "Ireland, in Arms, Fighting for Freedom." But a series of small subheadlines betrayed Devoy's uncertainty: "No Matter What the Immediate Outcome May Be, the Revolt Must Exercise an Important Influence on the Result of the War—Ireland Puts in Her Claim for Recognition at the Peace Conference."

By midweek, Devoy clearly held out little hope for the rebellion's success. Like the IRB leaders in Dublin, he considered the German arms shipment vital. Without additional rifles and ammunition, he knew all was lost, and the rising would go down in history as yet another glorious failure. His life's work had been a struggle to rebuild the movement after ruin. Now, all would be in ruin again, but at age seventy-three, John Devoy seemingly had run out of time. In his bitterness and frustration, he lashed out at the Wilson administration with an accusation that created a sensation in America. The *Gaelic*

American published an editorial charging that Wilson tipped off the British about the arms shipment based on the documents the Secret Service found at the German consulate in New York. Under the headline "Wilson's Base Act of Treachery," Devoy wrote that "the sinking of the German ship loaded with arms and ammunition . . . was the direct result of information treacherously given to the British Government . . . on the orders of President Wilson. . . . This was America's official expression of gratitude for the splendid services of Irishmen in the Revolution, the War of 1812, the Civil War and the Spanish-American War."

Devoy or one of his colleagues gave advance copies of the editorial to reporters at the New York dailies. Reporters from Newspaper Row by City Hall rushed to Devoy's office several blocks away to ask for comment, but Devoy refused. The accusation was banner-headline news the next day, with the *Herald* screaming, "Irish Newspaper of This City Attacks the President."

The *Times* placed an official White House denial of Devoy's charge on page 1 on April 28. The paper quoted Secretary of State Lansing as ridiculing the accusation, while an anonymous White House official reportedly "indulged in some caustic references to Editor Devoy." The *Herald* quoted Wilson's private secretary, Joseph Tumulty, saying of the charge that "it's a lie, and the man who wrote it knew it was a lie." Tumulty may have thought Devoy's charge was false, but Wilson administration records indicate that Devoy was at least half-right. Internal documents from the Division of Military Intelligence note that the State Department adamantly denied Devoy's accusation, but intelligence officials conceded that Justice Department officials probably slipped word to British authorities in America. Ultimately, though, the British needed no help from Washington in penetrating the conspiracy. Britain's code-crackers and their superiors knew about the arms shipment long before the American raid on the German consulate.

Having served as a witness in a government investigation of subversive German activities in America, Devoy was especially vulnerable to the White House's inevitable counterattack. Even as the fight was nearing its end in Dublin, the *Times* reported that the government was probing reports that the rebellion had been organized in

233

New York, which, the paper noted, would constitute a violation of American neutrality. Copies of the *Gaelic American* were in the hands of prosecutors, the paper reported, although "beyond private expressions uncomplimentary to Mr. Devoy, there was no disposition in official quarters to pay attention to his editorial."

But by the time the *Gaelic American*'s subscribers had a chance to read Devoy's charges against Wilson, the fight in Dublin was nearly over. After a few successful skirmishes early in the week, as the weekend approached, the rebels were being pounded and picked apart, and there was nowhere to hide, no line of retreat.

The poets and dreamers in the GPO held out for five days. They surrendered on Saturday morning, and among those who were alive to lay down his arms was Peter Devoy. The rebellion had cost the lives of 450 people, most of them civilians. The center of Dublin was a smoking ruin. The makeshift army of the Irish Republic had been written off in the court of public opinion as mere rioters. Still, it had been the fiercest and most prolonged revolt in Ireland since John Devoy's grandfathers took the field with the United Irishmen in 1798. Pearse, the poet, schoolmaster, and commandant general of the rebel army, had told one of his students that he fully expected the Irish people's condemnation after the rebellion was over, and he was not mistaken. The ragged troops were jeered as they were marched to holding areas throughout Dublin. The rebels had claimed to act on behalf of Ireland, but Ireland wanted no part of them.

Militant Irish-Americans, however, embraced them, despite the nearly unanimous condemnations from the press, politicians, and moderate Irish-American nationalists. "The men of Dublin have redeemed the honor of Ireland and restored the lost prestige of the Irish race," Devoy wrote. "They have brought back the soul of Ireland and made a new epoch in Irish history." In New York, Irish-American nationalists gathered in the Cohan Theater near Broadway on Sunday, April 30, for a rally that had been scheduled earlier in the week as a show of support for rebels in the field. Now, with the rising crushed, the rally went ahead anyway, to mourn the loss and praise the sacrifice. A *Times* reporter at the theater noted that the tenor of the evening was subdued, "not a single reference was made to President Wilson or the U.S. government. Even John Devoy, editor of the

Gaelic American, which last week contained an editorial making scurrilous references to the President, failed to voice further views of this nature."

When Devoy was introduced, he stepped forward to deliver his remarks but was stopped short when a band, on cue, struck up "The Star-Spangled Banner." The hyphenated Americans in the audience stood and sang the words of what was then the nation's unofficial national anthem, then settled back into their seats for Devoy's speech. He claimed he had received death threats from "cowardly Englishmen posing as Irishmen. One of these English curs tells me that I am to be assassinated and that this meeting will be broken up," he said, adding, in what he no doubt intended as a joke, that "I must add that there is a coroner here ready to hold an inquest." He then launched into an attack on the American press, asserting that most American editors were "unnaturalized Englishmen."

Referring to the possibility that the rebellion's leaders would be executed, Devoy said, "If I had my way, I would shoot two Englishmen to one Irishman they put to death." John Redmond, the Irish parliamentary leader, would be first on his hit list, he said.

The executions to which Devoy referred began in early May. Tom Clarke, Padraig Pearse, and the poet Thomas McDonough were the first to die. The night before his final dawn, Pearse wrote to his mother: "We have done right. People will say hard things of us now, but later on they will praise us." Clarke told his wife, "I'm glad it's a soldier's death I'm getting. I've had enough of imprisonment." They were executed on May 3; not long afterward, Padraig Pearse's brother Willie, a member of the rebel army but by no means a leader, was shot, too, simply because he was Padraig's brother.

The executions, stretched over ten days, shocked the pro-British American press. The *New York Times* sought reaction from prominent Irish-Americans and got more than it bargained for when it interviewed Patrick Egan, the aging onetime treasurer of the Land League who had emigrated to America and sided with Alexander Sullivan in the Clan na Gael split years before. He told the *Times*, "My heart goes out to those men who had to face the firing squad today. . . . I do not think that England should have had them shot. Ninety-eight percent of all Irishmen were not in sympathy with the revolt, and

England has nothing to gain by shooting people after it is over. . . . If anyone were shot it should have been John Devoy, who hatched the whole nefarious scheme here in New York and was personally responsible for it." Devoy fired back in reply, revealing for the first time the damaging fact that Egan, while entrusted with Land League funds collected by Charles Parnell, had agreed to give money to Sullivan to fund dynamite operations in London in the mid-1880s.

Meanwhile, the executions continued. As Pearse predicted, the tide of popular opinion changed, though even he could not have foreseen how quickly he and his colleagues were transformed from rioters to patriots. Devoy and the Clan whipped up American opinion, with the *Gaelic American* labeling the executions cold-blooded murders. Soon the leading newspapers in New York and Washington were calling for an end to the executions, and American politicians were questioning the wisdom of their shadow ally, Great Britain. Woodrow Wilson's foreign affairs adviser, Col. Edward House, predicted that the executions would "come back to haunt us." Devoy had a prediction of his own: the Irish would reorganize and resume the fight, he wrote, "and will capture many British soldiers and officers [who] will be . . . duly tried and executed by a firing squad. That is the law of war." In New York's Central Park, a group of poets and writers convened on behalf of the poets in Dublin and read their protests aloud.

Still, the executions went on. James Connolly, the labor leader, was shot on May 12, strapped to a chair because he could not stand. He had taken a bullet in the foot at the GPO and had declined proper medical treatment while in prison. Two days after Connolly's death, some twenty thousand people gathered in and around Carnegie Hall in New York for a demonstration to protest the executions. The extent to which public opinion in America had changed was summed up in the presence of so many utterly respectable and now utterly outraged American political, cultural, and religious figures. Father Edward Duffy, soon to win fame as the Fighting Sixty-ninth's chaplain, addressed the crowd, as did the composer Victor Herbert and the distinctly non-Irish future secretary of state, Bainbridge Colby. But the presence and words of Congressman W. Bourke Cockran, until now an Irish-American nationalist of the mildest sort, turned the demonstration from a lament to a rallying point. Cockran was the sort of polished, well-educated, and thoroughly upper-middle-class politician who mixed easily with diplomats and cabinet officials, and his moderate views on Ireland were no bar to friendship with prominent Englishmen like Winston Churchill.

Now, however, with firing squads doing brisk business, Cockran was prepared to concede the error of his past, conciliatory ways. "I am here to make a confession," he said. "For thirty years I have been one of those who had believed . . . that it was the part of prudence for Irishmen to forget—aye, seek to forgive and try to forget—the wrongs of the centuries in the hope that better days were dawning. . . . And now, behold the consequences of this attempt. The vilest murders ever committed in Irish history are fresh before our eyes. The noblest Irishmen that have ever lived are dead, dead by the bullet of British soldiery, shot like dogs for asserting the immortal truths of patriotism!"

From his place among the throng, John Devoy stuggled to hear Cockran's words. They were eloquent and passionate and everything Devoy might have said himself. The rebellion had failed, but now everything was changed, in Yeats's words, changed utterly. On both sides of the Atlantic, men and women who had regarded the rebels as fools and the rebellion as a fool's errand, people like Yeats and Cockran, now saw the rising as the sacrifice of martyrs.

THE EXECUTIONS STOPPED WITH Connolly. Gen. Robert Maxwell, the commanding officer of the British garrison in Ireland, had heard the outcries, particularly those from America. In any case, the next execution on his list figured to cause an international incident. New York–born Eamon De Valera was to follow Connolly in front of the firing squads, but with the war on the Continent hanging in the balance, American public opinion was not to be trifled with. The tall mathematics professor was spared. The *Gaelic American* hailed De Valera's survival (taking pains to point out that De Valera was "not Italian") and proclaimed the Carnegie Hall rally to be a propaganda and political victory for the American Irish.

The transformation of American public opinion took the spotlight off Devoy. Before the executions, he found himself on the defensive, assailed in the press—much like the rebellion's leaders, although with far less lethal results. But for British bungling, Devoy might have been forced to take cover as charges of Germany sympathy pounded around him, like massive shells from siege guns. However, with the British now on the defensive in the battle for public sympathy, Devoy and his allies wasted no time in taking the initiative, staging a huge rally at Madison Square Garden to raise money for relief operations in devastated Dublin. Showing yet again a deft appreciation for symbols and the power of continuity, Devoy and the Clan featured as the event's showpiece attraction the thirty-year-old tub of iron that was once known as the *Fenian Ram*. John Holland's invention was brought out of mothballs to deliver a message: the struggle did not begin nor did it end with Easter Week.

Throughout the ensuing months, Devoy used the influence of the *Gaelic American* and his own financial resources in an effort to save the life of the one rebel whose fate remained uncertain, Devoy's ally and nemesis Sir Roger Casement. As a peer of the realm, Casement was entitled to a better hearing than the pro forma military courts that had been set up in Dublin for the likes of Pearse, Connolly, and the rest. He was transported to London to stand trial in open court for treason. Casement's guilt was obvious and the ending just as certain, but Devoy was determined that Clan na Gael stand by Casement in his most desperate hours. Dipping into the money he had made through the sale of his late brother Michael's estate—money set aside for his orphaned nephews and niece in Dublin—Devoy sent $5,000 to the imprisoned Casement to help pay for his legal fees. The money was delivered by Michael Francis Doyle, the well-connected Philadelphia lawyer who had helped Casement get out of America and into Germany in 1914. When Doyle presented the check to Casement, the prisoner burst into tears in his cell.

With Woodrow Wilson's reelection campaign under way, Devoy and Cohalan attempted to use the political muscle of Irish America to persuade the president to intercede on Sir Roger's behalf. The British, hoping for American intervention in the war, could hardly ignore a plea from Wilson, or so Devoy believed. In the weeks before the Democratic National Convention, a group of friendly congressmen presented a petition on Casement's behalf to the president through Joseph Tumulty—Wilson's chief of staff and a Catholic with informal ties to the upper crust of Irish-American society. But a memo from Tumulty to Wilson outlining Sir Roger's case brought a curt reply: "It would be inexcuseable for me to touch this," Wilson wrote. Wilson was equally blunt when he received a written message from Jeremiah O'Leary, the angry New York pamphleteer who had been mentioned in German messages as a possible candidate to carry out sabotage in the United States. O'Leary warned Wilson that that he would lose votes if he didn't advocate more forcefully for Ireland; Wilson replied with a magnificent dismissive: "Your telegram received. I would feel deeply mortified to have you or anybody like you vote for me. Since you have access to many disloyal Americans and I have not, I will ask you to convey this message to them."

Roger Casement was found guilty of treason and was hanged in the Tower of London on August 3. In the days before the execution, the Wilson administration declined to pass along to London a Senate resolution calling for clemency. Devoy wrote that "President Wilson hates the Irish with the implacable hatred of the Ulster Orangeman— the stock he comes of." In a masterful example of Devoy's invective, he cast aspersions not only on Wilson, but on the president's Southern antecedents, in particular, his father, a Presbyterian minister: "Mr. Wilson has never missed an opportunity of repeating his false accusations of disloyalty against a race that proved its loyalty on the bloody battlefields of the Civil War fighting for the Union, while his [Wilson's] relatives were fighting to destroy it and his father was desecrating a Christian pulpit by railing in favor of human slavery."

With the election a mere three months away, Wilson's advisers feared such venom would stampede the Irish out of the Democratic Party in much the same way that similar attacks by Devoy had helped depose Grover Cleveland in 1888. One sympathetic clergyman wrote Tumulty that the Clan na Gael "is the only organization you have to fear. . . . If you see the Gaelic American, edited by John Devoy, you know what [he] has been saying, in a most scurrilous fashion, against the President. . . . I am told that the man to silence Devoy and his paper [is] the Judge [Cohalan]."

Even if Cohalan had the power to muzzle Devoy, he was not about to do so, not for the sake of Woodrow Wilson. The judge, a Democrat, was about to announce his support for Wilson's Republican opponent, Charles Evans Hughes. It was the second time in four years Cohalan had opposed Wilson, the first coming at the Democratic National Convention of 1912. And Woodrow Wilson hadn't forgotten Cohalan.

In September, a month after Casement's execution seemingly closed the book on the Easter Rising and its aftermath, Devoy convened a meeting of the Clan's executive and Revolutionary Directory in Manhattan's Murray Hill Hotel. There, he proposed dispatching to Germany a formal request for yet another arms shipment, this one complete with German soldiers, as soon as it could be arranged. The motion passed, and Devoy himself drafted a memo to the German General Staff analyzing the rising's failure and its belated but surprising support from the Irish people. The Germans replied that they were willing to try an arms shipment again in February or March, just after launching an all-out submarine offensive in the Atlantic, but they could not supply troops. Devoy wisely turned down the offer, saying "without landing [troops] it would be useless." It was just as well. As before, Devoy's communications to Berlin were being read in London. Britain's code-crackers were on the job again.

Still, the Clan was not ready to give up just yet. The wealthy McGarrity hatched a plan to buy a steamship and run arms to Ireland without German help. At McGarrity's urging, the Clan was looking into the purchase of a five-thousand-ton, British-built ship to carry out the secret assignment. But such dreams were outpaced by great events. On April 6, 1917, the United States entered the war against Germany. Suddenly, John Devoy was on the wrong side, fighting Ireland's battle in alliance with America's enemy. For nearly a century, Catholics in general and the Irish in particular had been accused of dual loyalties, of placing their fealty to the pope and to the cause of Ireland's independence ahead of America's national interest. Here, then, was a decisive moment. An agent of the Dublin Metropolitan Police, in New York to spy on Devoy and his allies, noted coolly that "the extreme Irish" were uneasy "as to whether the [U.S.] government may take action against them for their past performances carried out under their agreement with the German agents."

With stunning dexterity born of cold-blooded necessity, Devoy moved quickly to cover Irish America's exposed flank. Just before

Congress granted Wilson's request for war, Devoy dispatched a Clan circular pledging that "we will remain loyal and will yield to none in devotion to the flag," by which he meant, of course, the American flag. He followed up by calling a rally in the great auditorium named for one of his bitter enemies in battles past, Andrew Carnegie. There, Cohalan repeated the sentiments of Devoy's circular, and Devoy himself read a letter he had sent to House Speaker Champ Clark—but not Wilson—repeating the Clan's pledge of "unswerving loyalty" to the American war cause. Another Clan circular took pains to note that its previous "work" was conducted "entirely within the law and consistent with loyalty to the United States, in which we yield to no class of citizens in this Republic. . . . Our previous activities were always perfectly legal and legitimate, and we have never violated American law."

If these flowery phrases seem a bit overdone, it was because Devoy was indeed protesting too much. In a private letter to McGarrity, he revealed his genuine feelings. Speaking of the circular and the Carnegie Hall rally, Devoy said they were "a cruel necessity which was very irksome to me. . . . We [will] fight for the same thing, simply adjusting our tactics to the new situations." The American war effort might inspire an Irish-American like George M. Cohan to great flights of patriotism, but not the hard old man of the Clan na Gael. Publicly, Devoy insisted that America's alliance with Britain would work in Ireland's favor because Washington, after saving the British from battlefield disaster, would have the power to demand Irish independence once the war was over. Still, while Devoy wished no American doughboy harm, it's hard to imagine that he stopped hoping for a British defeat or at least a negotiated peace. The question he now faced was suggested in his letter to McGarrity: What sort of "new tactics" could he employ to the "new situations"? How to agitate on behalf of Ireland (and therefore, against Britain) while Americans and Britons were fighting side by side in a world war?

Whatever course he decided on, Devoy was shrewd enough to know that his pledges of loyalty to the American war cause did him little good in Washington. He told McGarrity that he believed the Secret Service was watching him day and night, so he "changed [his] lodging place three times." His paranoia was well placed. Wilson's

Division of Military Intelligence was watching Devoy and his allies closely, and the Secret Service had just raided the home of a friend of his in San Francisco, where agents once again managed to come across an explosive letter written over Devoy's signature. In it, Devoy described his relationship with German diplomats in America before the Easter Rebellion and defended the assistance the Germans had given the Irish. He also vented his spleen about Casement, blaming him in part for the rebellion's failure. The letter, which confirmed U.S. government suspicions about the Irish-German conspiracy in America, was forwarded to Washington, where it was added to the files the Wilson administration was keeping on Devoy and his friends.

Devoy spent these volatile months observing events with great care and doing his best—not always successfully—to mind his manners. Prudence forced him and other American Irish leaders to take a lower profile as American troops prepared to join forces with the British. The Clan-infiltrated Friends of Irish Freedom chose discretion over valor and canceled its second annual Irish Race Convention, scheduled to take place in late 1917. On those occasions when Irish dissent was openly displayed, authorities often cracked down quickly. Police in San Francisco shut down pro-Irish-freedom meetings during the summer of 1917, and in New York in late August, a local chapter of the Friends of Irish Freedom saw an outdoor rally in Herald Square come to a quick end when police arrested six people. All the while, though, younger men and a sizable number of younger women concluded that the Clan was too old and compromised to function as the voice of Irish freedom in America. They formed a new group, the Irish Progressive League. One of its moving spirits was a young poet named Peter Golden, who was on staff at the *Gaelic American*. Though Devoy and the IPL occasionally worked in tandem, ultimately he regarded the group as yet another "butter-in" on matters that ought to be the exclusive province of the Clan na Gael.

Devoy's long career was marked by a careful staking out of turf; in his mind, no other revolutionary group in America could speak for Ireland except the Clan. It was, after all, the only group that had an official alliance with the IRB in Dublin, and the IRB was, in Devoy's eyes, the Irish Republic in its gestation. And, beginning in the summer of 1917, those contacts with the IRB began to take on renewed significance as Britain started emptying its prison cells of rebels caught in the Easter net, among them the man who had barely escaped the firing squads' bullets, Eamon De Valera. The IRB promptly dispatched an acquaintance of Devoy's from earlier in the century, Dr. Patrick McCartan, to America as an envoy to Clan na Gael.

The pressure on London to placate Irish-American opinion was building, even after the release of De Valera and his colleagues. In a brilliant publicity stunt, De Valera and another former prisoner, William T. Cosgrave, won election to the British House of Commons as candidates of the Sinn Fein party. It was a death blow for John Redmond's moderate party and a sign of renewed revolutionary spirit in Ireland. British prime minister David Lloyd George made a great show of assembling a special convention to discuss the Irish issue, but it amounted to nothing. It was clear that dangerous times were returning to Ireland. With the election of De Valera and Cosgrave—they abstained from taking their seats—the Ireland that had been awakened after the Easter Rising was making its voice heard.

That voice, however, required assistance from America. Militant Irish America was already making life difficult for President Wilson. Now it was an obstacle to the great transatlantic crusade to make the world, or at least selected portions of the world, safe for democracy. Something had to be done.

Both the Secret Service and the Division of Military Intelligence had been monitoring Devoy and filing reports on Irish-American meetings in New York. Government agents were watching when Devoy and Cohalan met in a Manhattan hotel with Jeremiah O'Leary, who was under investigation for treason. In the fall of 1917, the Wilson administration decided to play the cards it had so carefully gathered.

On September 22, Secretary of State Lansing made public some of the documents the Secret Service had seized in its raid on the German consulate just before the Easter Rising. Included among the documents given to the newspapers was Devoy's memo asking the Germans to change the date of the arms delivery off Tralee Bay and Cohalan's memo asking for a zeppelin raid on London. The documents produced the intended effect on a war-feverish American public, which had already begun to cast out of the culture all things Germanic. A New York Herald headline shrieked, "Justice Cohalan Named as Kaiser's Adviser."

The report left Devoy, Cohalan, and the movement itself in utter frenzy. Wilson no doubt was gleeful as he watched his tormentors struggle for explanations, the most obvious being that their contacts with the Germans took place before America's entry into the war. Months of anti-German propaganda, however, made such distinctions meaningless. Tommy O'Connor, the IRB courier who had passed on the fateful message alerting Devoy to the Easter Rising in 1916, recalled that Devoy was panic-stricken.

Judge Cohalan clearly was the target of the Wilson administration leak—Devoy, in the *Gaelic American*, charged that his friend was the victim of a plot hatched in the British embassy. Cohalan also denied the suggestion that he was working closely with the German embassy at the time of the Easter Rising.

Nevertheless, the New York press called for Cohalan's impeachment as the White House turned up the pressure. On October 8, Jeremiah O'Leary's satirical newspaper, *Bull*, was suppressed, and U.S. authorities arrested Dr. McCartan—the IRB's envoy to America—in Halifax, Nova Scotia, while on his way to Germany. Secret Service agents questioned him about Devoy, Judge Cohalan, and Joe McGarrity. The coup de grâce came two days after McCartan's arrest, when the White House released more documents seized in the raid on the German consulate in April 1916. The revelations contained a copy of the telegram from Berlin that named O'Leary, McGarrity, and the deceased John Keating as possible recruits for pro-German sabotage in the States.

The Wilson administration achieved its goal. Devoy and the Clan were once again placed on the defensive, their loyalty called into question, and their activities placed under new scrutiny. Devoy charged that the White House had "undertaken to create a wave of prejudice against Irish Nationalists." It may also have timed the release of the damning documents to assist the pro-Wilson, pro-war mayor of New York, John Purroy Mitchel, who was fighting a vain battle to win reelection in the face of opposition from Tammany and New York's Irish-American nationalists. Whether the timing was coincidental or not, Mitchel seized the opportunity, making Devoy, O'Leary, and Cohalan—all of whom were supporting Mitchel's challenger, John Hylan—an issue in the campaign's final weeks. In late October, Mitchel attacked Devoy, Cohalan, and O'Leary by name, saying that "behind Judge Hylan . . . you will find . . . every force of enemy intrigue, of sedition and disloyalty that today curses our country. . . . Cohalan, Jeremiah O'Leary . . . Devoy [are] all fighting for the election of Judge Hylan." Devoy launched a blistering counterattack under a headline that read, "Mitchel a Shameless Liar." The feud erupted just a month after Irish nationalists in Ireland, marching under the banner of Sinn Fein, gathered for a pro-freedom rally at the birthplace of one of Devoy's heroes, the journalist and agitator John Mitchel—grandfather of the mayor of New York.

With Mitchel's stunning defeat and a false U.S. government charge that a new Irish rebellion was being planned in America, newspapers throughout the country called on Washington to suppress Devoy's *Gaelic American*. The *Providence Journal* charged that "Devoy's actions have shamed millions of Americans of Irish ancestry who are honest men. His paper . . . should have been closed up long ago." The *New York Sun* reported that the Justice Department was preparing to bring Devoy to the dock for conspiring with the Germans. The *New York Times* reported with barely disguised glee that a federal grand jury was preparing to complete its investigation into Devoy's activities and that officials were carefully examining the contents of the *Gaelic American*, presumably in search of seditious material. Federal investigators interviewed Devoy about the activities of a Germany spy named Hans Bohm, whose existence was a mystery to Devoy. Anticipating the worst, Devoy (referring to himself in the third person) wrote:

"The *Evening Sun* . . . reported that John Devoy would probably be indicted. . . . The statement was probably intended to frighten Devoy into running away, but he will not run away. He will stand his ground and fight this infamous Anglo-American conspiracy against Irish liberty, in court or out of it. . . . And he has unshaken confidence that the fight for Irish freedom will be eventually won, no matter how many hard knocks he and others may be obliged to take, even to the forfeiture of life itself. And it will be won with the help of the American people."

With newspapers themselves leading the campaign against both Devoy and the *Gaelic American*, the government's next move hardly came as a surprise. On Monday morning, January 21, 1918, a notice from the Post Office arrived at the *Gaelic American*'s offices, informing

Devoy that his newspaper had been banned from the U.S. mails. Two other Irish-American weeklies, the *Irish World* and the *Freeman's Journal* (unrelated to the *Freeman's Journal* of Dublin), had also been banned under censorship provisions of the government's espionage law. For a newspaper with a wide circulation across the country and one that considered itself a national, as opposed to a regional, newspaper, it was a deadly blow. While the *Gaelic American* would continue to be available on newsstands in New York, its impact as the voice of Irish-American nationalism had been severely muted. Eventually, a new newspaper called the *Irish Press*, printed in Philadelphia, published by Joe McGarrity and edited by Dr. McCartan, would compete with the *Gaelic American* as the national voice of the Clan na Gael.

IN IRELAND, MEANWHILE, REBELLION once again was in the air. The Volunteers were once again parading in Ireland in full uniform, telegraphing to London and the world that Ireland's discontents remained unresolved. Newly released rebels with names such as Michael Collins and Harry Boland were at liberty to reorganize the nationalist movement in its public manifestation—Sinn Fein and the Volunteers—and its secret, oath-bound arm, the Irish Republican Brotherhood. Collins, who had emerged as a leader of uncommon talents while in prison with his fellow rebels, took up the task of developing an intelligence network and turning the IRB into a guerrilla army.

With the war in Europe becoming increasingly desperate, Britain moved in quickly to break up the beginnings of new trouble in Ireland. Arrests under the Defence of the Realm Act were frequent, and in August 1917, an IRB leader named Thomas Ashe was arrested along with two colleagues. In late September, Ashe joined with other prisoners in a hunger strike to protest their detention. The authorities resorted to force-feeding of several prisoners, including Ashe. The result was not what officials had intended. Ashe, a young veteran of the Easter Rising, died after being force-fed. Once again, the cause had produced a martyr. Ashe's body, clad in a Volunteer uniform, lay in state while thirty thousand people offered their respects. His close friend Collins spoke at the graveside, and from him there was none of the exuberant rhetoric Pearse had employed over the grave of

O'Donovan Rossa in 1915. Collins spoke just after an armed guard of Volunteers fired a final salute over Ashe's coffin. "That volley which we have just heard is the only speech which it is proper to make above the grave of a dead Fenian," Collins said.

In such volatile circumstances, Britain blundered yet again. Ireland had thus far been exempt from Britain's conscription act, but with the bodies of a generation buried in the fields of France, the British Army was running out of men at a decisive hour. A conscription bill for Ireland was introduced in the House of Commons, and in an instant, the agitations of a small group of militant nationalists became the grievance of a nation. Sinn Fein embarked on a massive campaign to resist the draft, recruiting allies in all sectors of Irish society, including the Roman Catholic clergy. Ireland's bishops announced that they believed "that Conscription forced in this way upon Ireland is an oppressive and inhuman law which the Irish people have a right to resist by every means that are consonant with the law of God."

America's Irish nationalists similarly took advantage of the issue. On May 4, 1918, the Irish Progressive League sponsored an anticonscription rally in Madison Square Garden attended by ten thousand people, including clergy and politicians. Devoy was among the speakers and used the occasion to recapitulate the Irish contribution to America's wars and to state his unswerving loyalty to the United States. But, he complained, Irish America's love for its adopted homeland was unrequited:

"The record of the Irish Race entitles it to proper recognition from everybody in America. . . . It is entitled at least to fair play, but it is not getting it. . . . There is a vindictive, ruthless campaign of calumny against us in the American press that is utterly without excuse or justification. . . . The impudent claim is made that it is treason to work or speak for the freedom of Ireland."

Addressing the government's action against his newspaper and the two other Irish-American papers, he asked:

"Why, then, are these papers barred from the mails? The connection between their suppression and the publication of . . . outrageous and untruthful attacks on Ireland and on Irish citizens is not accidental. It is part of an organized campaign. . . . The purpose is clear and definite, that Ireland is to reap no benefit from this war for freedom and democracy. . . . While Belgium and Serbia are to be freed from the grasp of the Central Powers, Ireland must remain under the heel of England."

The authorities on both sides of the Atlantic had heard enough. On May 17, 1918, De Valera and nearly all of his top advisers were arrested and charged with plotting yet again with the Germans to foment a rebellion in Ireland. Newspapers in Britain and America expressed shock at Sinn Fein's treachery, although London produced no evidence of what it called a "German plot." In fact, the British sent to Washington the skimpy evidence they had—most of it a rehash of the conspiracy of 1916—and pressured the Wilson administration to circulate it in the American press. Clearly, the intent was to discredit the Irish cause in America, but Secretary of State Lansing opposed the proposal on the grounds that it would "involve us in all sorts of difficulties with the Irish in this country."

Within weeks of the "German plot" revelations in Britain, similar accusations were directed at two allies of Devoy's, along with an assortment of German agents operating in America. In mid-June 1918, John T. Ryan, a member of the Clan na Gael's Revolutionary Directory, and Jeremiah O'Leary were indicted on espionage and treason charges in Manhattan Federal Court. Ryan fled the country to avoid arrest. O'Leary was already in prison on other charges. Lt. Col. Nicholas Biddle of the Division of Military Intelligence was disappointed that the government didn't produce more indictments of Irish-American agitators. In a "Dear Bill" letter to Assistant Secretary of State William Phillips, Biddle wrote that "from our point of view, it would be most unfortunate for the Government to confine itself to the prosecution [of O'Leary and Ryan] and omit a consideration of the Irish activities in the United States as a whole." Biddle referred specifically to Devoy and the *Gaelic American* in pressing for further government action, noting that the newspaper was barred from the mails and that Devoy's writings hinted of further rebellion in Ireland. America had a duty, he wrote, to protect Britain from Irish rebels.

Biddle was not the only one pressing for action against Devoy. A seventeen-page summary of the Clan na Gael's agitation prepared for the Military Intelligence Division noted that the *Gaelic American* had been "violent in its denunciation of the Administration" and asserted that Devoy had conducted "treasonable traffic with the Germans."

The war ended with without an indictment of Devoy, an indication that officials realized that they could prove nothing treasonous or seditious about his activities since America entered the war. But when the guns were silenced at the eleventh hour of the eleventh day of the eleventh month in 1918, with America, Britain, and France united in victory, it did not signal an end to the government's watch over Devoy. Government agents continued to infiltrate Clan na Gael meetings and report details back to Washington. Irish America had been marked with the scarlet letter of disloyalty.

The extent to which the Wilson administration was trampling over the First Amendment was evident even in the war's closing weeks, when the utterly respectable Jesuit weekly *America* was barred from the mails because of a series of articles it ran on Ireland's future in the postwar world. The author was an Irish-American veteran of the British Army and a rising power in nationalist circles, Dr. William Maloney.

The Irish in America wasted no time in reminding Wilson of his vision of a world made safe for democracy and for the freedom of small nations. On November 12, 1918, the day after the armistice brought an end to the bloodshed in Europe, the Irish Progressive League held yet another mass meeting in New York to demand that Washington recognize Ireland as an independent state. The Friends of Irish Freedom, under the control of Devoy and Cohalan, sent a memorandum to Wilson asking that Ireland be accorded a place at the upcoming peace talks in France. The Foreign Affairs Committee of the House of Representatives began hearings on the question of Irish independence. And prominent Catholic clergy made their voices heard, with the loudest rumbling coming from the conservative archbishop of Boston, Cardinal William O'Connell.

Through a series of delicate machinations, Devoy and Cohalan invited the cardinal to address a Friends of Irish Freedom rally in Madison Square Garden. The cardinal's speech was a milestone, as Devoy pointed out: "It was the first time that a Prince of the Church had appeared at such a meeting and given his [approval] to the movement for the complete independence of Ireland. Cardinal O'Connell blazed the way and others soon followed." To a cheering throng of twenty-five thousand people gathered in the huge hall, decorated in green, white, and orange bunting, the cardinal noted that "this war, we were told again and again . . . was for justice for all, for the inviolable rights of small nations, for the inalienable right, inherent in every nation, of self-determination. The purpose of this meeting tonight is very specific. The war can be justified only by the universal application of those principles. Let that application begin with Ireland."

More than a half century before, Devoy had resolved to never again discuss his politics on bended knee when Roman Catholic clergymen condemned his cause and his methods. Now, from his seat behind one of America's most prominent Catholic clerics, Devoy heard an entirely different message. The old man blinked back tears as O'Connell finished speaking. When Devoy took the podium, he talked of the critical role that his longtime antagonist President Wilson would play at the Paris peace conference:

"We don't know that President Wilson intends to bring the Irish question directly before the Conference. . . . We don't know whether he only intends to bring it privately before the English representatives at that Conference; but we do know that his solemn declarations committed him irrevocably to bringing the case of . . . all oppressed peoples. . . . If he leaves Ireland out I am afraid he will never live long enough to live it down."

Four days later, the Irish people in Ireland went to the polls for the first parliamentary elections since the war's beginning. In a dramatic ratification of the change in Irish public opinion since Pearse, Clarke, Connolly, and the others were executed, Sinn Fein—the party of national independence that had been banned and its leaders imprisoned—captured 73 of 105 parliamentary seats in Ireland. Many of the victors, De Valera included, were unable to receive the tallies in person as they were in British prisons and had been since the German-plot arrests in May. The Sinn Fein result was more impressive considering that the party had no chance at winning any seats in the six northeast counties, the core of hard-line loyalty to the British crown.

Events took on a breathtaking pace. Devoy and his fellow Clan leaders assembled in New York on January 5, 1919, to plan another, perhaps climactic, Irish Race Convention. A hint of the trouble to come, however, was evident in Cohalan's seemingly innocent statement congratulating the Irish people for supporting "self-determination" in the previous month's general election. The following evening, at an Irish Progressive League rally in New York, speakers pointedly referred to the election as the ratification of an Irish republic—and not merely an expression of Ireland's "self-determination." For such distinctions, Irish nationalists would soon come to grips with each other, with lethal results.

In Dublin, Sinn Fein members established an independent Irish Parliament, the Dail Eireann, and adopted a declaration of independence and a provisional constitution. The Irish thus became the first people to challenge President Wilson to deliver on his promise of self-determination for small nations. The Dail emphasized its hopes for a settlement in Paris by appointing a three-man delegation to the peace conference consisting of Eamon De Valera, Count Plunkett, and Arthur Griffith, all of whom were in prison. But not for long.

In the small hours of February 3, Michael Collins and Harry Boland reconnoitered outside the grim walls of Lincoln Prison in Manchester. On the other side of the wall awaited Eamon De Valera, His Majesty's most prominent political prisoner. Collins had a duplicate key to the prison gate, but it became stuck in the keyhole. The resourceful De Valera, however, had a copy of his own. He was out in a flash, and the escape made headlines around the world. The forces of Irish freedom achieved a stunning public relations victory.

In New York, Devoy was working with Cohalan and their allies to organize the third Irish Race Convention, scheduled for February 22 and 23 in Philadelphia. Hard on the heels of the Dail's declaration of independence, an act of war, the convention would be viewed as a test of Irish-American power and resolve as the Irish crisis intensified. Devoy and Cohalan spent long hours attempting to stage a public relations coup of their own. Cardinal James Gibbons of Baltimore was America's foremost Catholic prelate, a man much beloved for his support of workers and their right to join labor unions. He had triumphed dramatically over conservatives in Rome and in America, helping to align the worldwide Church with issues of social and economic justice.

Cohalan was determined to persuade Gibbons to deliver a major address and present a series of resolutions. Devoy was given the responsibility of finding language that Gibbons, who considered Cohalan a radical, would accept. Of course, the wording also had to be

acceptable to the Clan, which would dominate the Convention's proceedings. With two weeks left before the gavel fell, Devoy was still
laboring to find common ground, and he eventually found it in the
loaded, Wilsonian phrase of "self-determination." It was, after all,
what Wilson had promised the small nations of Europe, and it was a
reasonably vague characterization of Irish ambition.

It was not, however, a demand for American recognition of the
Irish Republic, and Devoy knew that some of his allies would accept
nothing less. Gibbons, on the other hand, would endorse nothing
more than self-determination. Devoy was in an impossible situation.

Cohalan prevailed on Gibbons to attend, and his speech was reported as yet another sign that Irish-American demands for a settlement in Ireland were no longer the province of a small minority. "All
Americans should stand as one . . . for Ireland's inalienable right of
self-determination," the cardinal said. The same phrase appeared in
the resolutions he read aloud, calling on the conferees in Paris to
"apply to Ireland the great principle of national self-determination."

Even while Gibbons spoke and the power of Irish America
seemed united as never before, shouting matches were under way in
private hotel rooms near the convention hall. Patrick McCartan, the
physician whom De Valera had dispatched to America as an envoy
to the Clan, was joined by another physician, William Maloney, and
Joseph McGarrity in objecting to Devoy's nuanced resolutions. They
were furious that neither Gibbons's speech nor the resolutions he
presented mentioned the Irish Republic. Devoy lost his temper and
angrily stomped out of one meeting.

The public saw none of this, and Devoy seemingly won his point
when De Valera sent a telegram to America from his hiding place in
Ireland, congratulating the convention and stating that "if England
accepts the principle of Self-Determination for this island it will settle
the Irish question forever."

Not long afterward, with Ireland hurtling toward open warfare,
De Valera decided to return to the land of his birth to present Ireland's case to the court of American public opinion. His decision
shocked allies such as Collins, who believed De Valera, as the elected
chairman of the Dail, should stay home as the army of the Irish
Republic prepared to battle the forces of the British Empire.

De Valera, however, understood that the Irish war of independence would be fought on several fronts. Collins would send the Irish Republican Army into the streets and lanes of Ireland, but in New York, De Valera would be in command of the battle for Irish America's hearts and minds.

That, of course, would mean relieving John Devoy of his duties.

CHAPTER SIXTEEN

Passions Vain and Lowly

As a new generation of rebels in Ireland fired the first shots of what promised to be a climactic struggle with the ancient foe, John Devoy's position as a leader of a great and seemingly united exile movement was unchallenged. He told an audience gathered in the Metropolitan Opera House in New York that "the most striking . . . thing about the present Irish situation is the complete unity that prevails among the race at home and abroad. There was never anything like it in all Irish history, and the chief task . . . before us now is to preserve that unity until the work is done."

With his carefully chosen allies, Devoy shared control of a mass public organization, the Friends of Irish Freedom, and the secretive Clan na Gael, with its historical ties to the militants of the Irish Republican Brotherhood. As Eamon De Valera stepped onto American soil for the first time since he was a toddler, the Friends of Irish Freedom were in the midst of collecting a million dollars for their Irish Victory Fund, the proceeds of which were intended for use in both America (for publicity) and Ireland (for weapons). At this crucial moment—"the most critical time in our history," Devoy wrote—the exile movement in America had the power and the funds to make itself a powerful advocate for Irish freedom through the judicious use of American politics. Between the Friends and the Clan, Devoy and his allies were in a position to put a well-oiled machine at the service of the Irish Republic's chosen leader.

The man who bore the title of *priomh aire* (or first minister) of Dail Eireann was an austere and oddly charismatic leader with a clear understanding that in the renewed fight for Irish freedom, American public opinion would be as critical to the cause as arms and ammunition. Eamon De Valera came to America determined to win political recognition for the republic he represented and to collect funds for the war that had already begun. With an American presidential election year beckoning, he believed no politician dare ignore the aroused emotions of 20 million Irish-Americans. Eamon De Valera, of course, was not the first leader to view America as a vast army of potential recruits for the Irish Republic. It was that very vision, and that very mission, which had inspired another young Irish rebel nearly fifty years before, when John Devoy first caught sight of New York.

De Valera was John Devoy's junior by forty years. He was born in New York in October 1882, the son of an Irish-immigrant mother and a Spanish father, and was dispatched to Ireland to live with relatives in Bruree, County Limerick, after his father died when he was two years old. An American by birth and half-Spanish by lineage, he would one day announce that if he wanted to know what the Irish people wanted, he need only consult his own heart, the repository, he assumed, of all things Irish. Devoy, in his own way, shared De Valera's self-assurance; in his letters and his journalism, Devoy often asserted as a matter of simple fact that all true Irish-Americans agreed with whatever position he took in the long list of controversies that had rendered him sleepless, combative, and ever more determined to prevail against enemies foreign and domestic.

De Valera was the personification of the bond between Ireland and America, or more precisely, between Irish revolutionaries at home and their sympathizers and fellow conspirators in the United States. Devoy surely relished the symmetry: the elected leader of the revolutionary Irish government was an American by birth, and to America he had come in search of support, funds, and political recognition. Devoy could hardly have envisioned a better beginning to what he hoped would be the end of his long crusade.

This singular moment in Irish and Irish-American history was bittersweet, however, for Devoy was nearing the age of eighty, and his body was beginning to betray him. And while he remained extraordinarily busy, often long into the night, his life was ever more solitary. Nearly all of his friends and family were long since dead; he was the last active Fenian, as archaic and, at times, as seemingly harmless as the last of the old American Civil War veterans who still haunted the landscape, living monuments to a time long gone. Occasionally, when he trudged home to his spare hotel room near Grand Central Terminal, his thoughts wandered to the days of his youth, and he would later write that he spent these years grieving for Eliza Kenny, his long-lost fiancée. Years before, even before the Easter Rising, he had been told that Eliza had died, a childless widow who had never left County Kildare. He kept his grief private; his friends knew nothing of the long-ago romance, the broken engagement, and the promise he had not kept.

They were all dead, it seemed—Eliza, all of his brothers and sisters except for Bridget, Parnell, Michael Davitt, John Boyle O'Reilly, O'Donovan Rossa, Tom Clarke and the rest of the Easter martyrs, even James J. O'Kelly, the rebel turned Parnellite. O'Kelly had sided with Britain when World War I broke out—bought off, in his old age, by the honors and privileges of the Crown. With his last public act (he died in 1916), O'Kelly had managed to alienate his boyhood friend Devoy.

Nearly everybody Devoy knew—his coworkers, his fellow conspirators, even the president of the Irish Republic—was young enough to be his child, and behind his back, they called him "the old man." Judge Cohalan was born the year Devoy asked Eliza Kenny for her hand. Joe McGarrity was born while Devoy was organizing the global conspiracy that became the *Catalpa* rescue. And twenty-eight-year-old Michael Collins, the ruthless military genius who was about to launch a campaign in Ireland the likes of which Britain had never seen, was young enough to be Devoy's grandchild.

Devoy's hearing, failing for years, was by now little more than a memory. Proud and stubborn, he tried to fake his way though meetings with his fellow conspirators—those vital young men and women born after he had crossed the threshold of middle age. When the Clan na Gael or the Friends of Irish Freedom convened to discuss business in hotel rooms or, as often was the case, in Judge Cohalan's residence, Devoy made sure he was sitting next to a reliable ally, one who would later tell him exactly what had transpired, what arguments had been made, and what agreements had been sealed. His deafness made participation in meetings extraordinarily difficult, if not impossible, and left him exceedingly frustrated. He was left to argue his positions in writing in the *Gaelic American*, and even this would be-come difficult soon as he began a losing battle with cataracts.

Ireland had begun its war of independence, decades in the making and the final product of John Devoy's lonely years of agitation and sacrifice. But in this dramatic hour, the old man with the white beard and ferocious temper found himself cut off from the whispers of con-spiracy, hostage to the interpretations of friends, particularly Judge Cohalan, who were children or even years from birth when John Devoy was breaking stones in a British jail.

In the half century that Devoy had spent in America, rebuilding the Irish-American exile movement from the ashes of failure and dissension, there had been an unspoken but definite understanding between the two wings of the transatlantic conspiracy. Ireland, or more precisely, the Irish Republican Brotherhood, decided matters on its side of the ocean; Irish America, through the Clan na Gael, gov-erned its own affairs and attended to business in America as it saw fit. It was a delicate but necessary balancing act, grounded in the belief that the IRB knew what was best for Ireland and the Clan understood America. The two organizations could, and did, act jointly, but one did not impose its beliefs, tactics, and strategies on the other.

Respect for each other's turf had allowed the Clan and the IRB to work in harmony in the decades since Devoy had helped broker the partnership in the 1870s. This understanding allowed Devoy pre-cious freedom of action through the years, enabling him to respond to, or effect, changes in American politics and public opinion, and just as important, giving him and the Clan control over money they raised in America. Devoy, like all good Irish revolutionaries, recog-nized the IRB and now the Dail as the legal government of Ireland, but neither the IRB nor the Dail would dare tell him how best to do his business in America. The American fight for Ireland's freedom had become entwined with the battle over American entry into the League of Nations—Devoy and Cohalan were agitating mightily and with great success against the League and had aligned themselves with Republican isolationists determined to crush Woodrow Wilson's dream, a development that would have given the two Irish rebels immense satisfaction. At the same time, both men were lobbying members of Congress from both parties in an effort to write a resolution of some sort—any sort—that would put lawmakers on record in favor of Irish independence. Winning anything more than a resolution of good intentions, however, required flexibility. The devil, as ever, was in the wording.

All of this, Devoy argued, required an intimate knowledge of American sensibilities, something no Irish visitor, however prominent, could match. He and his allies knew best how to win victories for Ireland in America. At the same time, Devoy made it clear to the new generation of Irish rebels that he would never attempt to impose his views on his colleagues in Ireland—after all, he had had his doubts about a rising in 1916, but he never expressed them to the IRB's Supreme Council. "We have never tried to interfere in the slightest degree with the workings of the movement at home," he said in a letter to Harry Boland, one of De Valera's aides brought over to America to help with the fund-raising and propaganda tour. "The men at home decide on their policy and we do our utmost to help them to carry it out. . . . We expect and insist upon the same treatment in regard to the conduct of the movement in America. As long as our policy is to support your policy and our public programme proclaims that support, we here must be the sole judges of the measures to be taken to carry it out. This ought to be self-evident. An American policy in favor of Irish independence directed from Ireland by men with imperfect knowledge of America would be just as sure to fail as an attempt to dictate the policy of Ireland from America."

Devoy wrote those words in a moment of despair, for he had reason to believe that his recitation of ancient dogma was for naught. As Ireland began to fight once again for its freedom, one man with "imperfect knowledge of America" seemed intent on upsetting the delicate understanding between Ireland's rebels at home and those in the United States. Ironically enough, that man had been born in America.

EAMON DE VALERA'S MOTORCADE wheeled around Thirty-third Street in the late afternoon on June 23, 1919, and it slowed to a crawl as a huge crowd surged forward, eager for at least a glimpse of the president of the Irish Republic. John Devoy and Judge Cohalan were awaiting De Valera's arrival outside the entrance to the grand

Waldorf-Astoria Hotel, which was to become the Republic's presidential headquarters in exile. Dozens of reporters gathered to record the thoughts of one of the world's most famous fugitives.

The presidential motorcade pulled up to the Waldorf at 5:30 P.M. Devoy, grasping the green, white, and orange tricolor of the Irish Republic, and Judge Cohalan, carrying the Stars and Stripes, greeted De Valera at curbside and escorted him through the hotel's lobby, an assignment that required sharp elbows as the cheering crowd pushed forward. With some difficulty, Devoy, De Valera, and the rest of the party made their way to an elevator bank for a trip to the hotel's roof, where photographers took pictures of the Irish revolutionary party in America. Somebody found a chair for Devoy, and the young men of the Irish Republic stood behind him, vital and triumphant, the bitterness and tragedy of the very near future unknown and unimaginable. Harry Boland, Liam Mellowes, Dr. Patrick McCartan, and Diarmuid Lynch flanked De Valera, who stood directly behind Devoy, his left hand on the old man's shoulder. Devoy, his stout frame stuffed inside a three-piece suit, looked away from the camera, his eyes seemingly fixed on some unseen object in the distance.

From the roof, the party made its way back down to a suite for a private reception and then to a ballroom for a public rally. Cohalan served as master of ceremonies, Devoy delivered an apparently unremarkable speech—his own newspaper, the *Gaelic American*, quoted not a word from it—and De Valera rose to accept a thundering ovation from hundreds of Irish-Americans, most of whom had probably believed that they would never set eyes on an elected president of an Irish republic. Yet there he was, a man with a distinctly non-Irish surname, a man born within walking distance of this American palace. Devoy later noted that the ovation was "a striking demonstration of the fact that Irish men and women are the same here as in the Old Land and that long years of absence, or even birth in the United States, changes nothing at all." Nothing, indeed; birth in the United States had not prevented Eamon De Valera from becoming the next, great Irish leader, successor to the fallen leaders of ever-present memory: Parnell, O'Connell, Wolfe Tone, and the Easter martyrs.

The celebration went on for hours, and Devoy reveled in every moment. He remained in De Valera's suite until four in the morning, outlasting many of those younger revolutionaries (although he noted in a letter that he was "fit for nothing" the following afternoon). Earlier in the evening, he and Joe McGarrity, his longtime partner on the Clan na Gael's Revolutionary Directory, had a tense discussion over Irish-American policy toward President Wilson, the tormentor of both Cohalan and Devoy. McGarrity apparently told Devoy he believed Wilson could be persuaded to state the case for Irish freedom during the peace talks in Paris. Devoy vehemently disagreed—he still viewed the president as a vindictive bigot who suppressed the *Gaelic American* and tried to smear Cohalan and himself. In Devoy's eyes, anyone who had a good word to say about Wilson, or who believed he would challenge his British colleagues for the sake of Ireland, was not to be trusted. A good portion of the Irish Victory Fund would be spent in outright anti-League, anti-Wilson agitation in the coming months. McGarrity was veering from Devoy's agenda.

The rest of the evening was not nearly as contentious, although there were a few uncomfortable moments when De Valera found himself cornered by a tipsy priest from the president's adopted hometown of Bruree. Devoy watched with some apprehension as De Valera's aides tried to steer the clergyman out of the room. "[B]ut D. V. treated him with the utmost kindness," Devoy wrote. De Valera's handling of the incident impressed Devoy, as did the entire evening, save for the unpleasant conversation with McGarrity. Devoy left the suite for his hotel room persuaded that he was right when, several weeks before, he had told a colleague that De Valera "is the best leader that Ireland has had for a century." In some of his letters, he took to calling De Valera "Fear Mor"—"great man" in the Irish language.

Increasingly, though, Devoy was less impressed by some of his putative allies. The trio of McGarrity, McCartan, and Maloney had formed a clique that Devoy looked on with increasing suspicion. McGarrity and McCartan had moved in to fill a void when the *Gaelic American* was banned from the U.S. mail, setting up the Philadelphia-based *Irish Press*. Even though the ban on the *Gaelic American* had lapsed, the new paper competed with Devoy's as the voice of the militant exiles. The three men had achieved great success in publicizing Ireland's claim to a hearing at the peace conference, and with each success, it seemed, Devoy grew more dubious of their intentions, even though McGarrity had been one of Devoy's most-valued coconspirators for years.

Tension between the two camps predated De Valera's arrival, and De Valera himself apparently was unaware that the movement was riddled with dissension. In April 1919, weeks before De Valera's arrival, Devoy traveled from New York to San Francisco by train to fulfill a hastily organized speaking engagement. Devoy spent most of his waking hours during the five-day trip with a pencil and paper, writing a long and harsh letter to McCartan. When Devoy arrived in San Francisco and found a typewriter, he translated his handwriting into a twelve-page, single-spaced letter that set the tone for what was to come.

McCartan had suggested that Devoy was preparing to settle for something less than a republic; Devoy now accused him of the same. "I am quite satisfied to stake my reputation as citizen of the Irish Republic, to which I swore allegiance in January, 1861, on the writing of those resolutions . . . and I will say further that any man who keeps up a fight about them now, no matter how honest his motives, is doing an injury to the Irish Republic which we are all trying to serve," he wrote. Devoy warned that if McCartan was spoiling for a fight with the organizations Devoy represented, "I'll not shrink from my duty. It can have only one ending."

Devoy certainly did not shrink from slander, and he accused Maloney, McCartan's close friend, ally, and fellow physician, of being a British spy—an accusation Devoy and Cohalan would both make in public settings in the coming months. Devoy offered no evidence for his charge other than the fact that Maloney had served in His Majesty's forces during World War I. Since arriving in America, Maloney had been an aggressive advocate for Irish independence, but he had earned from Devoy nothing save the suspicion of a man who guarded his turf and who never forgot that he had once taken into his confidence another physician, a man who gave his name as Henri Le Caron—the British spy Thomas Beech, star of the Parnell Commission hearings. Devoy put the point bluntly to McCartan in a masterpiece of invective:

"You impugn the motives of Cohalan, who has rendered priceless service to the Cause and whose father was a Fenian, while Maloney's family has been sending members into the British Army in every generation since Waterloo. I was at first half-inclined to believe that Maloney was a sincere convert, though I disliked the expression of his face and his furtive eyes and thin velvety voice, but I am now morally certain that he is a British agent." Devoy's certainty was misplaced; Maloney was one of Irish America's most articulate and successful advocates for Irish freedom.

In the coming months, this distrust, verging on paranoia and evident on all sides, would cripple the American movement. As war raged in Ireland, Irish rebels in America would watch each other with studied care, looking for nuance, hints, and suggestions that the war in Ireland might conclude with something less than the Republic the men of Easter had proclaimed and died for. It was as though they knew that the end would be bitter, that compromise would taint the purity of victory—and that somebody would have to bear the blame.

When De Valera spoke to reporters during that long night of celebration on June 23, he managed to finesse the point, referring to an "Irish Republic established by the will of the Irish people, in accordance with the principles of Self Determination." In a single phrase, he had embraced words that his own envoy, McCartan, had viewed as hopelessly irreconcilable.

Words were about to become the weapons of choice in Irish America's civil war. Wielding them were two experts in the defensive and offensive properties of a well-constructed sentence: John Devoy and Eamon De Valera. Devoy would later write that while he was fond of De Valera, the two of them could never get along because "I had the temerity to insist that words have only the meaning given to them in the dictionary."

It's clear from the public record and from private correspondence that Eamon De Valera came to the land of his birth believing that as president of the Irish Republic he was the spokesman and leader of the Irish at home and abroad. The exile organizations that Devoy had built and rebuilt ultimately existed to serve the Republic and, therefore, in De Valera's eyes, the Republic's chosen representative. The conflict that soon erupted has often been portrayed as one of personalities—De Valera versus Devoy and Cohalan, with the judge described alternately as Devoy's puppet or his puppeteer (De Valera's sympathizers couldn't quite agree on these disparate notions). While not discounting the role that personal characteristics played in this foreshadowing of another, more brutal conflict between Irishmen, it's clear that a conflict over principle was inevitable, and inevitably, that conflict would be bitter, bruising, and tragic.

The principle concerned the role of the American Irish. From the days of Charles Stewart Parnell, Devoy had demanded, and received, the freedom to operate in America as he saw fit. It was why, all those years ago, he had objected to Parnell's proposal for separate state treasuries dispatching money directly to the Land League. Without a central organization in America overseeing the funds, Devoy had successfully argued, Dublin would be in control of the American support and fund-raising apparatus.

Though he paid lip service to it, De Valera never seemed to appreciate fully the notion that Irish-Americans such as Devoy and Cohalan were American citizens, Cohalan by birth and Devoy by naturalization. Indeed, after Wilson's White House mounted a smear campaign against the two men with the implicit charge that they were traitors, they could hardly afford to be anything but American, acting always in America's best interests. It was no easy assignment, after all. America had just fought side by side with Britain on the Western Front, and Irish independence was hardly a popular issue with the British. Framing Ireland's cause as something inherently good for America was a delicate task, one that required kid gloves and, of course, just the right words.

Devoy and Cohalan saw themselves as the leaders best suited to carry on Ireland's cause in America. De Valera thought otherwise. As Devoy wrote to McCartan even before De Valera arrived in the States, such a conflict could have only one ending. De Valera later reported back to Dublin that in his conflict with Devoy and Cohalan, "I held that Ireland's interests should come first." That, of course, was De Valera's job. But if Devoy and Cohalan were viewed as holding Ireland's interests above America's, all the rhetoric about dual loyalty, all the insinuation about their hyphenated Americanism, would be flung at them again. And in 1919, U.S. attorney general Mitchell Palmer was hard at work arresting those of dubious loyalties. Among those caught in his net was Devoy's erstwhile friend James Larkin, the Irish labor leader who, like Devoy, had been in close contact with the Germans before and after America's entry into World War I. Devoy helped bail out Larkin by dipping yet again into his late brother Michael's estate. Devoy put up $5,000 on Larkin's behalf.

The first flashpoint, as it happened, was over money, and it was resolved without too much difficulty. De Valera had come to America to raise funds for Dail Eireann through a bond offering. He asked for $10 million, figuring, correctly, that he'd get about half. But the Friends of Irish Freedom were already shaking Irish America's money trees in an effort to build a war chest for the organization's battle against the League of Nations as well as the inevitable guerrilla war against the British. At such a critical moment, it would hardly make sense to have two competing fund-raising drives under way, so the Friends of Irish Freedom not only announced an abrupt end to its effort, but it supplied De Valera with $100,000 to start up his own campaign. (The Friends, under the effective control of Devoy and Cohalan, also appropriated $26,000 for De Valera's expenses while crisscrossing America.)

Cohalan had won no points from De Valera, however, by at first opposing the bond sale, arguing that American laws prohibited bond sales by governments the United States did not recognize. Eventually, the correct words were found to allow the sale to take place—De Valera was not selling bonds; he was selling bond certificates, which, he noted, were for sentimental appeal "and not an appeal to investors." Before this scheme, which historian Tim Pat Coogan called the "first junk bond flotation," was foisted on Irish America, it was brought before an impartial, outside counsel for his opinion. A young lawyer named Franklin Roosevelt judged it sound.

Devoy shared Cohalan's reservations about the bond drive, though not for any legalistic reasons. His years as a conspirator had taught him to recognize a power grab when he saw one, and that was exactly how he viewed De Valera's decision to create a separate organization to handle the drive and its proceeds. De Valera established the American Commission on Irish Freedom to control the bond sale, neatly bypassing the Friends of Irish Freedom. After a conversation with De Valera, a wary Devoy wrote to Cohalan, "When I talked . . . with D.V. he spoke of establishing a permanent organization to take care of the bonds. . . . This means a rival organization and taking the work out of the hands of the National Council [of the Friends of Irish Freedom], so I [wrote] a note saying D. V. has too much good sense to entertain a suggestion of that kind, that it would breed dissension, etc." De Valera ignored Devoy's attempt at flattery.

The *Gaelic American* as yet reflected none of Devoy's misgivings. Throughout the summer and fall of 1919, Devoy's newspaper recorded De Valera's every move as he traveled throughout the States, a tour designed strictly for publicity purposes—the bond drive would come later. A typical headline in the *Gaelic American* said of De Valera: "He Is Fast Dispelling the Smoke Screen of British Propaganda."

Privately, though, Devoy was becoming increasingly wary of De Valera's intentions and obsessed with the notion that De Valera was falling under the influence of McGarrity and McCartan, and thus, Maloney—the man Devoy suspected of being a British agent. He viewed any private criticisms of Cohalan or the Friends of Irish Freedom as "the propaganda of disruption."

De Valera was back in New York in late August and convened a meeting that Devoy attended, but, as usual, the proceedings took place in an unintelligible murmur. "I could not hear a word of what was said," he later recalled, "but out on the street later I was told all of it." What he was told was that De Valera had apparently criticized Cohalan's handling of the Irish Victory Fund, a substantial portion of which was being spent on the effort to crush Wilson's League of Nations. De Valera's criticism came the night before Cohalan's starring-role appearance in front of the U.S. Senate's Foreign Relations Committee, during which the judge gave a long and masterful presentation of Ireland's case for independence as well as the American case against the League of Nations.

Devoy was quick to see Maloney's hand in De Valera's criticism. Furious, Devoy returned to his hotel room and spent yet another night tossing and turning, in a rage over words he had not heard. A week later, he dispatched a long, typewritten note to Harry Boland, De Valera's aide, complaining that "Fear Mor" had aligned himself with "the little handful who are working might and main to sow distrust and create dissension at a time when absolute unity is more essential than at any time in our history." In a telling aside, Devoy told Boland that it would not have been appropriate for De Valera to address the Senate hearing that had featured Cohalan. "That hearing was for Irishmen who are American citizens," Devoy wrote. Clearly, De Valera and his party resented Cohalan's presence as a spokesman for Irish independence. That was supposed to be De Valera's turf. Devoy's letter, delivered to Boland by hand, prompted a hastily arranged meeting between Devoy and De Valera. "D.V. was straight and he evidently meant every word he said," Devoy reported to Cohalan. "Of course, he defended [McGarrity] and [McCartan], but I think the air will be cleared and that it will be [smooth] sailing in future."

Deaf as he was, Devoy couldn't hear the distant thunder of dissension.

ON SEPTEMBER 12, 1919, British authorities ordered Dail Eireann suppressed and its members arrested. The action came after the Dail took on the trappings of an alternative government, with ministers attending to various portfolios (Michael Collins was minister for finance; Cathal Brugha, defense; and in De Valera's absence, Arthur Griffith served as acting president of the Dail). Just after De Valera left, the Dail established its own court system to hear disputes between tenants and landlords. And a military body that came to be known as the Irish Republican Army moved though the streets and lanes, ambushing members of the Dublin police force and the Royal Irish Constabulary—the forces of the Crown. Collins was already selecting members of the team that would become known simply as the Squad—young men trained to kill at close range, even in front of children and spouses, if circumstances demanded it. The war in Ireland would be fought face-to-face. There would be no trenches, no artillery barrages, no gas attacks—none of the weaponry that Europe's civilized nations brought to bear on each other during World War I.

The Dail's suppression meant an escalation in hostilities in Ireland. What had been a low-intensity conflict involving police officers and gunmen would now become a military operation. Rebellion had become war.

Two days after Britain's action against the Dail, McGarrity, McCartan, and Maloney organized a protest meeting in New York's Lexington Theatre. The meeting was advertised in the city's newspapers, and parish priests mentioned it from the pulpit. Everybody in the city, it seemed, was told about the great rally—everybody, that is, except for Devoy and Cohalan. Devoy took up his pen and filled in Cohalan, who was at his summer home in the Adirondacks:

"The latest development in the effort to sidetrack us was the meeting at the Lexington Theatre on Sunday evg. last. All our men went to it and made it a great success because of the announcements from the altar and the big ads in the paper. It was started, managed and carried out by Joe, Dr. McC. and Maloney, and they sat on the platform together with an unmistakable air of ownership. For the first time we have proof that they worked with Maloney. . . . They did not tell a single one of our men a word about it. I knew nothing at all about it except through a notice in the evening papers."

In protest, Devoy canceled an appointment to accompany De Valera on a short trip to Newark. "The point is that a man on D.V.'s staff [McCartan] was one of the prime movers in the work of shoving us out of the way and parading Maloney as the man to be trusted," Devoy wrote. "This continual recurrence of sudden crises precipitated upon me is a bad blow to my efficiency. It unfits me for serious work . . . I am very, very tired of it all."

Three weeks later, McGarrity presented the Friends of Irish Freedom with a bill for $1,515—the expenses incurred in organizing the rally and hiring the hall. The Friends paid it, grudgingly. McGarrity then proposed that the Friends bear the entire cost of organizing De Valera's bond drive and sending him on another coast-to-coast tour. The estimated cost was put at $1 million. The motion was voted down, and an unmistakable message was sent from one faction to the other. "We have preserved the appearance of unity on the surface for the sake of the big things at stake and through fear of giving comfort to the enemy, but it is only on the surface," Devoy wrote. "It can't remain [that way] for long."

THE YEAR 1920 IS known in Irish history as the Year of the Terror. It was the year the British raised the stakes by sending in shock troops who were so quickly recruited that there weren't enough uniforms for them. So they donned dark trousers and khaki coats and thus became the Black and Tans—named for a pack of hounds with similar hues. The Black and Tans, along with another quickly recruited outfit known as the Auxiliaries, had little doubt about their mission. They were to make Ireland hell for the IRA, for Sinn Fein–elected officials, and for the public at large. It was also the year that Michael Collins and the IRA responded with war as the Irish had never waged it before, a ruthless campaign of ambush and assassination in which information, and not geography, defined the stakes. Collins's theory of war was simple enough: London could replace bodies, but not the knowledge of its military and police officials. With the help of his own spies and informers (traditionally the curse of Irish rebellions), Collins struck with ruthless precision at the brains of British administration in Ireland.

The Year of the Terror saw war fully engaged—in Ireland, and in America as well.

Judge Cohalan had closed out 1919 with another memorable appearance in Washington, this time in front of the House Foreign Affairs Committee. At issue was a bill introduced by Congressman William Mason of Illinois calling for the expediture of $14,000 for the appointment of an American envoy and consuls to the Irish Republic. The bill was a backdoor attempt at winning American recognition of the Republic in a presidential election year and was clearly designed to bypass Wilson—by now incapacitated by the strokes he had suffered in his long and vain effort to win approval of the Treaty of Versailles and its commitment to American membership in the League of Nations. Devoy made sure that Cohalan's testimony—indeed, nearly everything Cohalan said—received prominent coverage in the *Gaelic American*. The effort to portray Cohalan as Irish America's most prominent spokesman was transparent, as was the message Devoy was sending to De Valera. If the war in Ireland was a battle over information, the conflict in America was more traditional. At stake were strategic bits of turf, fiercely held.

The Mason Resolution eventually came to nothing, even when it was watered down to a mere expression of sympathy for Ireland's "aspirations," making no references to the Irish Republic. Congressional leaders and even the stricken president were loathe to express overt political support for Ireland's rebels. The Mason Resolution and its bitter ending offered a lesson in exactly how much American politics could be manipulated for Ireland's sake, but only Devoy and Cohalan seemed to notice.

By mid-February, the revolution in Ireland was under way in earnest. Martial law had been proclaimed in Dublin, and citizens registered their protest in a most democratic fashion. In a series of local elections throughout the country, more than 170 of Ireland's 206 local-government councils returned pro-Republic majorities. Thousands of homes in Ireland were raided. Meanwhile, in America, the long-planned bond drive was inaugurated with a ceremony in New York City at which the mayor, John Hylan, purchased one of the junk bond certificates and presented De Valera with a key to the city. The *Gaelic American* proclaimed, "Greater Unanimity Than at Any Previous Period in the History of the Race in America." Devoy no doubt growled as he wrote those words.

It was at such a moment that De Valera granted an interview with a correspondent from the London-based *Westminster Gazette*, apparently unaware that an American newspaper, the *New York Globe*, regularly reprinted dispatches from the *Gazette*. In the interview, which he had every reason to believe British prime minister David Lloyd George and his colleagues would read, De Valera offered what sounded for all the world like a compromise. Without consulting anyone—and certainly not any American history books—De Valera suggested that Britain and Ireland could coexist in the manner of the United States and Cuba. He noted that in the aftermath of the Spanish-American War, Cuba and America agreed to a treaty in which Cuban independence was guaranteed as long as the island did not become a launching ground for attacks on the United States. "The United States safeguarded itself from the possible use of the island of Cuba as a base for an attack by a foreign power," De Valera said. "Why doesn't Britain do with Ireland as the United States did with Cuba? The people of Ireland . . . would co-operate with their whole soul." Not for the first time, and certainly not for the last, De Valera searched his own heart and found what the Irish people wanted.

Or so he thought. He apparently also thought his idea of equating Ireland with Cuba bespoke an intimate knowledge of world affairs. Those who were better informed, however, knew that Cuba was little more than a vassal state under American domination, and that Washington reserved the right to intervene in Cuban affairs with military force. The Easter martyrs, forever lurking over the shoulders of the succeeding generation of Irish and Irish-American leaders, surely had not died for Ireland to become a North Atlantic version of Cuba. The proposal would also eliminate the possibility of American action on Ireland's behalf—something De Valera, who was on a mission to encourage American interference in Anglo-Irish affairs, clearly didn't consider.

When the interview was reprinted in the *Globe* on February 6, Devoy's anger was matched by that of De Valera's allies—McGarrity and McCartan were outraged, and in Dublin, the Dail was sent into an uproar. Devoy roared back in the *Gaelic American* the following week. Under a headline reading, "De Valera Offers Settlement to England," Devoy reprinted the offending interview and followed it with a rare, signed reply, entitled "John Devoy's Objections." What followed was a stinging and well-written analysis, and, given the anger and frustration that had been building for months, one that was remarkably free of Devoy's blistering invective:

"The effect of the publication [of De Valera's interview] can easily be foreseen. It opens the way for the discussion of a compromise or a change in objective, while England has her hands on Ireland's throat. It will be hailed in England as an offer of surrender. . . . The Britishers will conduct their side of the controversy in the hope of creating a cleavage among the Irish forces in Ireland and America. England's only hope of triumphing over Ireland now lies in the possibility of creating disunion in the Irish ranks. . . . The Cuban precedent is cited . . . but [De Valera] must know that the Cuban Government was kept in a strait-jacket by the United States."

Devoy went on to argue the American case for Irish independence, which asserted that a free Ireland would deprive Britain of its mastery of the seas, therefore allowing the United States to dominate the Atlantic. Devoy concluded by noting that the Dail had endorsed a free and independent Republic, that the Friends of Irish Freedom supported that policy, and that "not even the President of the Irish Republic has authority to change it."

The relentlessly well-argued reply left De Valera battered. McCartan admitted that he agreed with Devoy and later wrote that the interview so damaged De Valera's credibility that he was "no longer an asset" in making the case for American recognition of the Republic. McGarrity, so loyal to De Valera that he named a son after the Irish leader, was equally infuriated, as were members of the Dail. McCartan was dispatched to Dublin to deliver De Valera's rebuttal, a task that must have required a great deal of soul-searching. Before McCartan left, however, De Valera fired off a letter to Cohalan. "After mature consideration," he wrote, he had decided to ignore Devoy's attack. He then proceeded to do anything but. He alone, he said, was responsible to the Irish people—so emphatic was he ("I am definitely responsible to them, and I alone am responsible . . . I cannot divest myself of my responsibilities") that he seemed to be trying to convince himself of his case. Slyly, he sought out Cohalan's position: "I am led to understand that these articles in the *Gaelic American* have your consent and approval," he told Cohalan. "Is this so?" He said it was "vital" that he know "exactly how you stand in this matter."

He got his wish. Cohalan replied, "The *Gaelic American* is edited, as you know, by Mr. John Devoy, for whose opinions and convictions I entertain the highest respect. I control neither him nor them. That he has the right to comment upon or discuss your public utterances or those of any man who speaks for a cause or a people, I assume you will grant. In any event, it is a right recognized by all Americans as one of our fundamental liberties. We have no law of *lèse-majesté* here, nor, so far as I can judge, is there talk of having one in the democratic and free Ireland in which we believe." Cohalan told De Valera that he labored under a misapprehension about the relations between them: "What I have done for the cause of the independence of the Irish people . . . I have done as an American, whose only allegiance is to America. . . . If Ireland were to change her position and to ask a measure of self government that would align her in the future with England as an ally in what I regard as the inevitable struggle for the freedom of the seas . . . between America and England, every loyal American will without hesitation take a position unreservedly upon the side of America."

De Valera did not reply to Cohalan's letter. But he included Cohalan's letter among the documents he sent back to Dublin with McCartan. The president of the Irish Republic complained about the tactics he suffered at the hands of a "tricky police court lawyer."

The lawyer and the editor were prepared to take the battle to another level of ferocity. "All the advantages, except the scandal of a fight, are on our side now . . . we'd be worse off in the end than if we fought it out now," Devoy wrote to a friend, John McGarry. "I am also convinced that [De Valera] meant to fight us all along. . . . He selected the wrong time and the wrong issue, because his judgment is very poor. . . . His motto is the King can do no wrong. . . . We cannot permit the continuance of present intolerable relations." The let-

ter to McGarry wound up in the hands of De Valera's allies, preserved
for use at a strategic moment.

IN THIS PIVOTAL YEAR for Ireland and Irish America, Judge Cohalan
was chosen as grand marshal of the St. Patrick's Day parade in New
York, a sign of the judge's popularity and a ratification of his militant
views on Irish freedom. To be named grand marshal of the Western
world's largest nonmilitary parade was, and remains, a high honor,
but Cohalan graciously allowed De Valera to share the spotlight. The
judge gave up his place on the reviewing stand to the Irish Republic's
president, and later, at the annual banquet of the Friendly Sons of
St. Patrick, he praised De Valera in a speech and asked his audience
to accord the visitor an ovation.

Behind the scenes, Devoy and Cohalan were plotting a coup. Two
days later, on March 19, Devoy and Cohalan convened a secret meeting of Irish-American leaders in the Park Avenue Hotel, a frequent
meeting place for Devoy and his allies. After arranging for De Valera
to be invited to a nonexistent event in Chicago, Devoy and Cohalan
planned to put the president on trial, with the hope that the jury of
Irish-American leaders would find him guilty of arrogance and would
order him transported back to Ireland. De Valera's allies, however,
got wind of what was about to happen and prevented him from boarding a train that would have taken him out of New York. McGarrity
showed up at the hotel uninvited and listened as Cohalan and then
Devoy presented the prosecution's case. Devoy said De Valera's aides
were "the enemies of the leaders of the Irish race in America." He
charged that they were bungling the bond drive, he accused De Valera
of offering the British a compromise settlement, and he defended
himself against charges that he had attacked De Valera personally in
his analysis of the Cuba interview. The leaders of Irish America
seemed impressed, but a voice from the audience broke in: Where,
said Joe McGarrity, was De Valera? Why was he not present to defend
himself?

Some of the gathered dignitaries, notably New York Supreme
Court justice John Goff (a splendid, white-haired lawyer who had
become embroiled in a battle with Devoy during the *Catalpa* rescue

in the 1870s) and Congressman William Bourke Cockran agreed that De Valera ought to be present. An emissary was dispatched to the Waldorf, and before long, the suspect was brought before a jury of his peers. Devoy pressed his attack, assailing De Valera for his Cuban analogy and noting that America had sent troops to Cuba to monitor an election on the island. Did the president of the Irish Republic wish to grant England that power over Ireland?

In a long response to the charges, De Valera paid tribute to Devoy for his long service to the cause, but insisted that he was out of touch with the new, young leaders of Ireland. A testy exchange followed, with Devoy insisting that those young leaders of Ireland agreed with him, and De Valera arguing that Devoy's articles in the *Gaelic American*—tame by the editor's standards—were hurting the cause. De Valera said it had taken him only a month to realize that America was too small for himself and Judge Cohalan, a point the meeting's chairman, Bishop William Turner of Buffalo, dispensed with by pointing out that the judge could hardly leave his own country just because the president of the Irish Republic had arrived.

As the level of rhetoric intensified, De Valera told Devoy that he "did not understand the A.B.C.'s of democracy." Devoy fired back that "the whole alphabet of autocracy" was evident in De Valera's February letter to Cohalan. With tempers at the breaking point, De Valera announced that he had documents that proved Devoy had been plotting to discredit him and have him sent back to Ireland in disgrace. Devoy heatedly denied the charge, but in dramatic and no doubt carefully scripted moment, Boland interrupted with the assertion that not only did Devoy reveal his scheme in a letter, but the man to whom Devoy had sent the letter—John McGarry—was in the room. The letter, Boland said, would show that Devoy had said that De Valera must be defeated. Devoy couldn't hear what Boland was saying, but an ally repeated the charge, and Devoy roared that Boland was lying. Pandemonium broke out, and De Valera gestured toward McGarrity, telling him to produce a copy of the offending letter. McGarrity made a great show of searching his coat pockets for the letter as tension mounted.

In those few moments between vigorous disagreement and an outright split, voices demanded that the two sides make peace. Bishop Turner interceded and demanded that those in the room lower their voices, get on their knees, and pray for peace. They obeyed. There are conflicting accounts about whether Cohalan and De Valera shook hands after the bishop's intercession. There seems to be no suggestion, however, that Devoy and De Valera went through with such a charade.

The first skirmish of Irish America's civil war lasted, incredibly, for ten hours. Afterward, one of the participants, Mayor John Grace of Charleston, South Carolina, wrote to a friend, "I attended a conference at New York on March 19, and I confess before Heaven that President De Valera was that day revealed to me as either laboring under some psychopathic condition or that the evil spirit himself had taken hold of the Irish movement. . . . Justice Cohalan, humbling himself under insults repeated constantly . . . did everything humanly possible or imaginable to bridge the chasm. [We] begged President de Valera on our knees . . . not to persist in his apparent determination to have a public test of strength with Justice Cohalan."

EVEN AS THE WARRIORS in New York trudged home to bed, Ireland was in an uproar. The lord mayor of Cork, Tomas MacCurtain, had been assassinated in front of his wife while Irish America argued in a hotel ballroom. A coroner's jury summoned to investigate the death returned a verdict of "willful murder against David Lloyd George, Prime Minister of England," and other officials. The killers were off-duty police officers, seeking retribution for the killing of a colleague.

Before long, the British campaign of murder, arson, and terror would sicken even some of its own officers. A British general would write, "Law and order have given way to a bloody and brutal anarchy. . . . England has departed further from her own standards and further from the standards . . . of any nation in the world."

In America, the president of the Irish Republic was preparing his next assault against his enemies—John Devoy and Daniel Cohalan.

The American political conventions of 1920 figured to be a test for Irish America's clout. With Ireland in flames, political support from America was critical. While Irish-Americans were a vital part of the Democratic Party's constituency, Devoy and Cohalan figured the Republicans would be more sympathetic. The hated Woodrow Wilson, after all, remained the putative leader of the Democrats, even after his strokes and the subsequent defeat of the League of Nations. Cohalan and Devoy had played key roles in agitating against the League, and in doing so, they had become friendly with Senator Hiram Johnson and Senator William Borah, both Republicans and both extremely sympathetic to the Irish cause. Johnson was a candidate for the Republican nomination in 1920, and Cohalan (though a Democrat) and Devoy threw their support behind him. (It wasn't subtle: an editorial in the *Gaelic American* concluded by advising readers simply, "Go to the primaries and vote for Johnson.") Devoy had apparently been assured that a victorious Johnson would name anti-British Borah as his secretary of state, and the new administration would promptly recognize the Irish Republic. De Valera and his supporters would later sniff that Devoy and Cohalan were playing backroom politics, to which they might have responded: Yes, and what of it?

The Republicans met in early June in Chicago, and Cohalan had an apparently amiable meeting with De Valera in late May to discuss strategy for the convention. Since the fateful ten-hour meeting in March, Devoy and Cohalan had kept their opinions to themselves and had in fact welcomed De Valera as the featured speaker of a Clan na Gael rally at the Lexington Theatre in New York on Easter Sunday night, April 4. Devoy and Cohalan both made speeches after De Valera left—so the visiting president wasn't in the hall to hear Cohalan introduced as the leader of the Irish race in America.

With great fanfare and apparently little concern about either political propriety or fiscal constraint, De Valera set up a headquarters in Chicago as the Republican National Convention prepared to get under way. McCartan was appalled and advised against such a public demonstration of political pressure by a foreign agent. Other Irish-American leaders begged De Valera to back off and allow Cohalan, who arrived in Chicago several days later, to present Ireland's case. De Valera was not about to grant such a request. From De Valera's headquarters streamed press releases, pamphlets, banners, even a daily newspaper. From the looks of things, De Valera himself seemed to be a candidate for the American presidency. McCartan later wrote, "There was no chance of offending America that we did not take."

The spectacle of a foreign and unrecognized government so blatantly attempting to manipulate American presidential politics was distinctly unappetizing, but De Valera was determined to outflank his rivals.

Devoy and Cohalan arrived in Chicago on June 6, two days after De Valera. With their allies, they began the tricky work of drafting a resolution strong enough to send a message across the Atlantic but moderate enough to win mainstream American acceptance. The fate of the Mason Resolution, which never saw the light of day even in a diluted form, was not lost on the two men. But they were determined to get what they could in whatever words were necessary. If the Republicans agreed to an Irish plank in their platform, the Democrats, even in the shadow of Wilson, could hardly ignore the issue when they met a few weeks later in San Francisco.

Cohalan and Devoy submitted a plank to the convention's committee on resolutions committing the party to support "the principle that the people of Ireland have the right to determine freely . . . their own governmental institutions." It was admittedly a mild statement, though Cohalan demonstrated his political agility by avoiding the phrase "self-determination," which was so closely identified with the Democrat, Wilson.

De Valera, in the meantime, was assiduously drawing up a competing resolution, one that expressly committed the Republicans to recognition of "the elected Government of the Republic of Ireland." He submitted it to the convention's resolutions committee and made it clear that he wished to argue on its behalf in front of the resolutions committee. Republican leaders were appalled—this was interference of an astonishing sort. Furthermore, De Valera demanded that the convention drop Cohalan's resolution. Irish-American officials met with De Valera in an attempt to reach a compromise. They labored in vain.

The next day, June 9, De Valera's resolution was rejected by a 11–1 vote, the only vote in favor coming from Cohalan and Devoy's friend Borah, the would-be secretary of state. Cohalan's resolution, however, passed by a 7–6 vote. The Republicans were now on record in favor of Irish self-determination, that purposely ambiguous phrase that Devoy had been using from time to time since the New Departure.

De Valera exploded; this was worse than a defeat. It was a personal humiliation. He publicly demanded that Cohalan's resolution be withdrawn and his own resubmitted for another hearing. The chairman of the committee, disgusted by the infighting, changed his vote on the Cohalan resolution and allowed it to die in committee.

The Irish were stuck with a public relations disaster of monumental proportions. With war in Ireland growing fiercer by the day, the Republican Party made no mention of the Irish—not even an expression of sympathy—in their party platform. De Valera had inserted himself into American politics, a game Devoy and Cohalan knew well, and the result was a faction fight—hardly the sort of image the Irish in America wished to present to the world. All the effort in Chicago had come to nothing. There would be no reason for the Democrats to engage in one-upmanship.

Devoy was livid, for the convention had been doubly disastrous. There was no public expression of support for Ireland, and Devoy's candidate, Johnson, had lost the nomination to Warren Harding, an unknown entity who now set out for the White House with no commitment of support, or even sympathy, for the Irish. Devoy vented on the front page of the *Gaelic American*: "De Valera Prevented Action on Ireland," shouted the lead headline in the June 19 edition. De Valera fired back with a press release that managed not only to denounce the newspaper by name—he called its account a "tissue of misstatements"—but also insulted the American government. "We want action which will end the apparent acquiescence of America in British barbarity in Ireland," he wrote. It was the first time anybody had suggested that America somehow shared the blame for Britain's terror campaign in Ireland.

Devoy and Cohalan decided to let De Valera go it alone at the Democratic Convention, where, it must be said, the two men would not have been especially welcome given their work against the League and their quarrelsome history with Wilson. De Valera came up empty with the Democrats, too, and so the two parties prepared for the presidential campaign with no mention of the war in Ireland. Such blundering had come at high cost, too, for De Valera had asked for and received a budget of $500,000 from the Dail in his efforts to manipulate the American presidential election, and up to $1 million to win official recognition of the Republic. Tim Pat Coogan notes that the sum was extraordinary considering that the Dail's budget for its war with Britain was $1 million.

Devoy and McCartan sparred throughout the summer from their respective press organs. McCartan poured venom on the group he called "Cohalan-Americans" in the pages of the Philadelphia-based *Irish Press*, while Devoy charged that McCartan was "notoriously under the domination of a British Agent." As invective flew, other Irish-American leaders sought to bring the two warring camps together—in one of Devoy's letters to Cohalan, mention is made of a report that De Valera was sounding out Cardinals Gibbons and Hayes to act as mediators. Devoy, who once referred to De Valera as "Fear Mor," now simply referred to him in private as "the visitor." It was clear to Devoy, the veteran of every Irish movement since the 1860s and a student of those that had come before, what was likely to happen. On July 31, the *Gaelic American* featured a long story under Devoy's byline about great moments in Irish history ruined by splits and dissension. As he contemplated the relentless pace of history repeating itself, he lay awake in his hotel room, a sleepless hostage to rage, frustration, and bitterness. His health was turning poor; he complained of diarrhea and dizziness.

"The personal abuse of myself I don't mind," he wrote in his recapitulation of Irish divisions in the *Gaelic American*. "I have been accustomed to it all my life and would feel rather lonesome without it. I am responsible for my own personal action and was doing some things many years before Judge Cohalan was born, or before he could wear trousers, but now the pet theory of the disruptionists is that I am a poor old fogey dominated by Judge Cohalan." In an assessment that proved eerily prophetic, he wrote that De Valera "has many fine qualities, but he is utterly wrong in trying to bend the best and brightest men of the race in America to his will on subjects on which they have more training and experience. He cannot obtain recognition for the Irish Republic now while Wilson is President . . . yet he would smash some Irishmen because he cannot accomplish the impossible and [will] put upon them the blame for his own failure."

Throughout the summer, Devoy wrote nearly every day to Cohalan, who was at his summer retreat in the Adirondacks. The correspondence details the thrust and parry of Irish America's civil war. After failing in an attempt to capture control of the Friends of Irish Freedom's treasury, De Valera tried to take over the group itself by demanding a convention in Chicago—away from Devoy's base of support in New York. When that failed, De Valera sent home to Dublin a report singling out Devoy and Cohalan for not giving "their wholehearted support to the President." The report said that Devoy and Cohalan "attempted to force the President into the position of accepting their dictation in all matters of policy connected with his mission." The criticism was entered into the Dail's official minutes.

After that blast, Devoy, Boland, and other Irish leaders met on August 15 in New York and concluded another tentative peace treaty—this after Devoy characterized De Valera as "the most malignant man in all Irish history" in a private letter to Cohalan. As part of the informal treaty, Devoy agreed to publicly withdraw charges he had made that De Valera had misused funds during the Republican convention in Chicago, and he apologized for his criticism of De Valera over the Cuba interview. The gesture was reported as the *Gaelic American*'s lead story on August 28: "John Devoy Withdraws Charges in the Interest of Irish Unity." It was a remarkable concession on Devoy's part, particularly after his learning that De Valera had arranged to blacken his name and that of Cohalan in the official minutes of Dail Eireann.

For a few weeks anyway, the *Gaelic American* was filled not with news of combat among the Irish in America, but of the war in Ireland. A dramatic personal story was unfolding amid the terror and carnage. The new lord mayor of Cork, Terence MacSwiney, had commenced a hunger strike after his arrest and imprisonment. Like his murdered predecessor, Tomas MacCurtain, MacSwiney was a Sinn Feiner. The world's press focused on this intense showdown, and before long, McCartan wrote, "from the banker in his club to the tramp in the ditch, few ate without at least a passing thought of the Lord Mayor of Cork."

Devoy's private dispatches, however, contain few observations about Ireland. The peace pact with De Valera was holding, but relations continued to deteriorate. In early September, Devoy reprinted in the *Gaelic American* an extraordinary interview with Michael Collins, commander of the rebel forces. The interview had first appeared in the *Philadelphia Ledger*, and in it Collins rejected a peace feeler from Lloyd George, who was pushing through the House of Commons a bill calling for a form of home rule for six counties in the north of Ireland and twenty-six counties in the rest of the country—clearing the way for a dreaded partition of the island. In an editorial note carrying the headline "Michael Collins Speaks for Ireland," Devoy was effusive in his praise for this "calm, quiet, deliberate" commander who was "the recognized leader of the fighting men of Ireland." The unspoken contrast with De Valera was obvious, and just in case anybody didn't get the point, Devoy ran a front-page picture of Collins in the following week's edition. It was an extraordinary bit of bad judgment, for Collins was a man on the run whose face was unknown to British intelligence. Under the picture, a caption read, "Michael Collins, Ireland's Fighting Chief." Of his public praise for Collins, Devoy wrote, with some prescience, "I expect to be told it is an attack on D.V. Well, it is not an attack, but it is a suggestion about Mick. He must have an idea of the ultimate leadership in his Corkonian head." Of course, De Valera had some ideas about ultimate leadership floating about in his head, too.

In late September, after weeks of conflict, Devoy was exhausted, embittered, and ready for a final showdown. It was coming, and as ever, it would involve words. In mid-September, his competitors at the *Irish World* newspaper reprinted an article from 1882 charging that Devoy had made off with Land League money. In a new introduction, the newspaper charged that Devoy was mishandling money collected by the Irish Victory Fund. Devoy hired a lawyer to prepare a libel suit, although he feared the cost would bankrupt him. He had less than $2,000 in the bank, "and that," he wrote, "is a blue [outlook] for my declining years."

De Valera made one last move on the Friends of Irish Freedom, working with allies to introduce a series of amendments to the body's constitution that would split it into a series of state organizations, with no central authority. It was, in fact, the same tactic Parnell had tried at the beginning of the American Land League forty years before. On September 17, at yet another tumultuous meeting, the De Valera amendments failed. De Valera, in fact, wasn't allowed to speak. He turned on his heel and left the meeting.

Devoy was on his way to Grand Central Terminal for an out-of-town engagement on Sunday morning, October 24, when a messenger handed him a letter from Harry Boland. In his capacity at the Irish Republican Brotherhood's representative in America, Boland informed Devoy that the Clan na Gael was being read out of the Irish revolutionary movement. "In the view of the parent organization it is intolerable that the *Gaelic American*, well known here and in Ireland to be the organization organ, should be using its circulation . . . to propagate misrepresentation and falsehood. . . . Speaking with full authority in the name of the Supreme Council of the Irish Republican Brotherhood, I hereby announce that the Clan na Gael organization is no longer affiliated with the Brotherhood." Devoy responded in the paper with typical bravado and defiance, and in fact he did a remarkable job of ignoring Boland's directive, even as his onetime ally Joe McGarrity announced the formation of what was called the "reorganized Clan na Gael." Devoy's private emotions, however, were expressed in a bitter and undated letter to Boland.

"I received your letter . . . but am not in much condition to answer it. I will get a meeting of the [Clan] executive as soon as possible and will resign. . . . My physical defects render me unfit to continue the responsibilities of my position in the midst of the malignant warfare waged upon me and the incessant turmoil in which I am compelled to live. When I am out of the way at least one of the difficulties will be removed and if peace does not follow I shall have peace myself. . . . If I were a younger man I would . . . take whatever is coming to me, but I am too old and cannot endure it any longer. . . . After sixty years of the best work that was in me, instead of dying by an English bullet or the hangman's rope, I am driven out by the chief officers of the Irish Republic."

Terence MacSwiney died on hunger strike the day after Devoy formally received Boland's order. Less than a month later, De Valera announced the formation of his own public organization, the American Association for the Recognition of the Irish Republic. It was designed to replace the Friends of Irish Freedom, with its quarter million members. The Irish-American movement, to which John Devoy had devoted his life, had been split at the very moment of Ireland's greatest peril and greatest opportunity.

De Valera's announcement was made on November 16. Five days later, on a Sunday morning in Dublin, Michael Collins sent his Squad—including a future prime minister of Ireland, Sean Lemass—into action. By the time they were finished, the cream of British intelligence in Ireland was wiped out. Nineteen members of the Crown's forces were slain, some in front of family members. When news of the IRA assault reached the rank and file, the Black and Tans and the Auxiliaries invaded Croke Park, where thousands of Irish civilians had gathered for a football match. The soldiers opened fire on the crowd with machine guns, killing fourteen people. The claim was made that the soldiers were fired on first. Oddly, though, there were no casualties on the British side.

A week later, the IRA attacked a squad of British troops, killing seventeen. In reprisal, British troops burned Cork city.

De Valera left America on December 10. He left behind, in American banks, some $3 million of the more than $5 million he had collected in bond certificates. Ireland, in its fearsome freedom struggle, never saw the rest of the money.

But Ireland, despite De Valera's efforts, had not heard the last of John Devoy.

CHAPTER SEVENTEEN

A Nation Once Again

ONE NIGHT IN EARLY 1921, AFTER EAMON DE VALERA HAD LEFT A divided Irish America to return to war-torn Ireland, three men made their way quietly through the streets of downtown Manhattan until they reached the four-story Reed Building on William Street, a few blocks to the east of City Hall. It was after midnight, so the streets were lonely, and the building was deserted. The men were familiar with their surroundings and moved quickly to the building's top floor once they had broken into the main entrance on the ground floor. At least two of the three burglars had been in the building many times before, walking freely, in the light of day, into the chaotic offices of the *Gaelic American* to consult with their friend and ally John Devoy.

At this hour, Devoy probably was in his solitary hotel room uptown, writing letters or lying awake in his bed, waiting for the embers of his temper to cool. If the double blow dealt him during De Valera's last few weeks in the States had inspired momentary thoughts of giving up the fight—as his letter to Harry Boland indicated—they had passed quickly enough. Though officially written out of the revolutionary movement, his place as the American liaison to the IRB taken by Joseph McGarrity, Devoy remained fully engaged in the fight for Irish freedom. The battle he was fighting, however, was taking place on American soil, and his opponents were his onetime allies and partners, the men who had gone with De Valera into the American Association for the Recognition of the Irish Republic, or who were cooperating with McGarrity in forming what they called a Reorganized Clan na Gael.

The absurdity and tragedy of the split in America infuriated Devoy, kept him tossing from side to side in his bed. Whatever energy had been sapped by Boland's maneuver, whatever bitterness De Valera had inspired, Devoy remained on the job, convinced that his side in the Irish-American quarrel would prevail—as it had done in previous faction fights. The Reorganized Clan had made some inroads in recruitment, but Devoy ran a disciplined organization, and McGarrity had won few converts in and around New York, the heart of the Irish nationalist movement since the days when the Fenians planned their invasion of Canada. Devoy intended to see to it that the Reorganized Clan remained little more than an ineffective cadre of De Valera acolytes, denied a base in the most important Irish city in America, New York. In this hour of Ireland's suffering, Devoy's attention was focused on watching McGarrity and his allies Patrick McCartan and William Maloney.

In the postmidnight quiet in the Reed Building, the burglars made quick work of the lock on the door leading to the *Gaelic American*'s newsroom, and they headed directly to Devoy's office, the very place where, not so long ago, they had gathered as allies to plan for the war under way in Ireland. Now, they rifled the office until they found what they were looking for—reams of paperwork with the names and addresses of those who had remained loyal to Devoy in the aftermath of the Clan's split. For Joe McGarrity, Tommy O'Connor, and Lawrence de Lacy, the break-in was a complete success, and they hustled back down the stairs and disappeared into the New York night.

In their effort to eviscerate Devoy's wing of the Clan, McGarrity and his fellow intruders were trying to win over the organization's old guard, and that meant getting hold of its secret membership rolls. Devoy, of course, was rather reluctant to turn them over to McGarrity and his allies, so the Reorganized Clan leaders chose to take matters into their own hands. Behind the absurd theatrics, however, was a bitter, irreconcilable, and very personal division among onetime friends. McGarrity had been Devoy's colleague on the Clan's Revolutionary Directory in 1916. O'Connor was the transatlantic courier who had shown up in Devoy's office in February 1916 with a coded message from the IRB announcing plans for the Rising. And it was in a candid letter to de Lacy that Devoy had defended the Germans from accusations that they had let down the Easter rebels—the very letter that had been seized by the FBI in a raid on de Lacy's home after the Rising and was among the documents the government had released to blacken Devoy's name after America entered World War I. All three leaders of the Reorganized Clan had so recently been Devoy's brothers in conspiracy; now, however, in the proverbial fashion of civil war, brother was pitted against brother.

With the American movement engaged in internecine battle, the war in Ireland was becoming more desperate. Not long after British troops opened fire on innocent civilians in Croke Park and burned the heart of Cork city, British prime minister David Lloyd George announced that his government had "murder by the throat." Of course, by "murder" he was referring to the activities of Michael Collins, Tom Barry, and the IRA, not to those of the troops he had dispatched to Ireland to restore law and order.

The prime minister's announcement was so much red-meat rhetoric meant to impress the Conservatives, whose support he needed. Behind the scenes, Lloyd George was sending peace feelers to Arthur Griffith, who had been standing in as head of the Dail while De Valera was in America. The talks continued even after Griffith was placed under arrest in December 1920. During Griffith's brief interval in prison, Michael Collins was named acting president of the fledgling Republic; it was then that De Valera decided he had accomplished enough in America and now was the time to reassert his authority at home. Upon landing in Ireland, De Valera asked his greeting party how the war was going. Great, he was told. "The Big Fellow is leading us." The big fellow in question was Michael Collins, the man Devoy had labeled "Ireland's Fighting Chief" in contrast to the other chief—De Valera—who was wreaking havoc in America, three thousand miles away from the Irish battlefields. By the time De Valera returned to Ireland, his quest for American recognition of the Republic having failed, Collins's fame was of mythic proportions. Though his capture was given top priority, the British had been unable to lay a hand on him. In the eighteen months since De Valera had set out for America, the Big Fellow had come to personify the war and the cause itself.

De Valera was not amused to hear his colleague spoken of so highly. "Big Fellow!" De Valera is said to have responded, "We'll see who's the Big Fellow."

Essentially, those were the sentiments of the rival organizations that now sought to speak for the Irish Republic in America.

Rather than accept the humiliation of being publicly read out of the revolutionary movement at the most critical moment in its history, Devoy employed the very tactic Dail Eireann had adopted in fighting the British. He simply ignored the dictates of his tormentors. He acted as though Harry Boland's writ counted for nothing, just as members of the Dail had insisted that they, and not the British Parliament, were the rightful rulers of Ireland. He defied his oppressor, De Valera, challenging him week after week in the one institution neither the IRB nor the president of the Irish Republic could suppress—the *Gaelic American*.

With unseemly glee, and perhaps some wishful thinking, the newspaper featured lurid reports of Devoy's rivals at each other's throat and of meetings broken up by knife-wielding dissenters. "Violence and Rioting Common at Meetings of the Organization Started by De Valera to Destroy the Friends of Irish Freedom and the Clan na Gael," read a typically overheated headline. In his correspondence with Cohalan, Devoy reported the latest intelligence from the battlefields of Irish America—the attempted theft of passwords from a Friends of Irish Freedom chapter in Youngstown, Ohio; the drawing up of affidavits in his libel suit against the *Irish World*; an effort to block McGarrity from receiving a state charter to establish a rival organization in New York (Devoy, as luck would have it, was friendly with New York's secretary of state, who granted charters to private organizations).

The American Association for the Recognition of the Irish Republic (AARIR), the entity De Valera had created in hopes of smashing Devoy and Cohalan, drained members from the Friends of Irish Freedom and inspired much faction fighting and internecine squabbling. The Friends saw their membership dwindle from its high of 250,000 to about 70,000, but De Valera's creation hardly drew strength from its rival's troubles. The AARIR established a national headquarters in Washington and held a successful convention in the spring of 1921, but in its stated purpose it was doomed to failure.

As even some of De Valera's allies in America realized, President Harding was no more willing than Woodrow Wilson to recognize the Irish Republic. Congress might sympathize with Ireland's struggle for self-determination, but that was hardly what De Valera's organization was demanding. And even though the AARIR, which Devoy referred to as Growl because that's what the letters in the acronym sounded like, vowed to fight on for full American recognition of the Republic, De Valera himself told the Dail upon his return to Dublin that "if I were President of the United States myself . . . I could not, and would not, recognize Ireland as a Republic."

In fact, there was no reason for the American president to take such action, not with the vaunted political power of Irish America frittered away on internal squabbling. With Devoy and Cohalan at war with McGarrity and his allies, the American organizations that might have brought some pressure to bear on domestic politics were too weak and too divided to do much of anything for Ireland. They certainly were no longer in a position to fulfill the traditional role of financial agent to the rebels. De Valera had tapped Irish America for more than $5 million, some $3 million of which remained in American banks and under his control. Whatever money the competing organizations had left was being spent in an effort to crush rivals. Neither Devoy nor McGarrity could mount a serious political or public relations campaign on behalf of bleeding Ireland. And yet Ireland was producing no shortage of material for an effective propagandist— when the British condemned an eighteen-year-old student named Kevin Barry to the gallows in late 1920, world opinion demanded that the sentence be commuted. It wasn't, and in the words of a ballad that immortalized the young man's name, "another martyr for old Ireland" was added to a roster that was growing by the day.

It took a decidedly nonpartisan and utterly mainstream organization to bring Ireland's case to the court of American public opinion. A group of nearly 150 distinguished Americans, from congressmen to clergymen, came together as the American Commission on Conditions in Ireland under the sponsorship of *The Nation* magazine. Devoy and Cohalan were not asked to serve on the commission, nor were any of their political allies in Congress.

The commission heard riveting testimony from former members of the Irish police force, from firsthand witnesses to British atrocities in Ireland, and from relatives of Irish civilians murdered by Britain's armed services. The hearings, held in late 1920 and early 1921, were a public relations masterstroke—yet Devoy was suspicious of the panel's motives and wary of its goals. Territorial as ever, he considered the commission's members to be "butters-in"—the epithet he used to describe anybody who hadn't devoted sixty years to the cause of Irish freedom.

Devoy attacked the commission in the *Gaelic American*, but as its hearings proceeded, even he must have realized he was wrong. The panel issued a devastating report in late March 1921, leading the *Manchester Guardian* to note that the British had "landed . . . in the dock, without a defence, before the conscience of mankind. To . . . point out a few excesses in this detestable American report would only advertise its crushing remainder in truth. Our Government had put us in the stocks." On the heels of the sympathy and outrage that the hearings and report inspired, an American Committee for Relief in Ireland was formed, and it eventually raised $5 million for humanitarian work in Ireland. President Harding himself approved of the effort, saying that "the knowledge of distress in Ireland makes quick and deep appeal to the more fortunate of our own land where so many of our citizens trace kinship to the Emerald Isle."

The hearings and the relief effort, neither one of which could be written off as Irish-American political posturing, were a public relations nightmare for Britain. And on a more tangible front, the rebel forces in Ireland were showing no signs of collapse despite massive arrests and a brutal campaign of officially sanctioned terror. With a combination of deadly urban warfare and brilliant guerrilla tactics in the countryside, Collins and the IRA were frustrating the might of the Empire even as they practically counted their bullets before each engagement. Though there was tension within the Irish cabinet as the putative defense minister, Cathal Brugha, raged on about assassinating their counterparts in the British cabinet (shades of Devoy's intemperate remarks during the Land War), the hardheaded Collins had the upper hand. As peace feelers continued to make their way across the Irish Sea in the spring of 1921, Collins gave another newspaper interview to an American correspondent. In it he asserted that the IRA would fight for nothing less than an Irish republic. The British concluded that Collins was a hard man (one British observer wondered wistfully where Collins had been during World War I, when he would clearly have done great things for the Crown) and De Valera was more likely to compromise. It was an opinion John Devoy shared.

By late spring 1921, British cabinet ministers concluded that they had but two choices in Ireland: all-out war, as opposed to a running gun battle, or a truce followed by negotiations. Neither scenario was particularly palatable. The first meant the deployment of thousands of soldiers at a time when Britain was still attempting to recover (and it never did) from the loss of a generation on the blood-soaked fields of France during World War I. The second meant something even more unthinkable—negotiating with men so recently condemned as terrorists and murderers. Worse yet, they were *Irish* terrorists and murderers, and therefore members of a race, an ethnic group, a nation, that inspired little except contempt and loathing in Britain. (An official document drawn up in Dublin Castle, the seat of British rule in Ireland, referred to De Valera as a member of "a race of treacherous murderers.") Lloyd George was inclined to hang tough, but events soon suggested that such a course would require stern stuff indeed. In late May, a former top-ranking British officer publicly criticized the behavior and tactics of the Black and Tans, further embarrassing the Crown. A day later, the IRA attacked and burned the Custom House in Dublin—the heart of Britain's administrative nerve center in Ireland. This daring demonstration of the rebel army's tenacity and courage achieved worldwide publicity. Behind the scenes, however, Collins understood that the set-piece battle, reflecting the sort of strategic thinking that had gone into the suicidal Easter Rebellion, was a bloody disaster for the IRA. Six rebels were killed and twelve wounded in the operation, but more significantly, seventy were captured. It was a devastating loss for a small army numbering in the hundreds.

The Custom House assault, however, gave new impetus to the peace feelers making their way to and from London. Lloyd George, having a choice between terrible war and difficult negotiation, chose to pursue the latter course, though he wondered how the British people would react when they learned that His Majesty's government was willing to sit down with Collins, "the head of a band of murderers," in the prime minister's view.

After a flurry of back-channel messages, Britain's King George V arrived in Belfast in late June for the opening of a new Parliament for the six counties in what was now being called Northern Ireland. London had passed Lloyd George's Better Government for Ireland Act, which decreed that Belfast and Dublin would have separate home-rule parliaments, an action that meant nothing to De Valera, Collins, and the rest of the Irish revolutionary movement that didn't recognize British law in Ireland. In Belfast, however, where the ruling class demanded to be kept within the friendly confines of the British Empire, Britain's offer of limited self-government over the six predominantly Protestant counties in the northeast corner of Ireland was accepted. The partition of Ireland was put into effect, and there was little the rebels could do to stop it.

De Valera was arrested by mistake the day the King spoke in Belfast, June 22. Ordinarily, of course, the capture of the president of a rebel government would have been a great victory for British security forces, but delicate negotiations were under way, and it was in nobody's interest to have De Valera dispatched to prison. He was released in a matter of days and began corresponding with Lloyd George almost immediately. Lloyd George invited De Valera to London for talks; De Valera accepted.

On July 11, 1921, the guns in Ireland fell silent.

All summer long, there had been talk of compromise, of the Irish settling for something less than a republic, for a state that would include only the twenty-six counties of "southern" Ireland. Devoy, ever the pragmatist, realized that the Irish would need to be flexible. But publicly, he continued to assail De Valera for preparing to sell out the Republic, even though Devoy himself privately suggested that such an outcome probably was inevitable, and that it was not entirely De Valera's doing. From his listening post three thousand miles from Dublin, he made the following assessment of Ireland's leaders: "They are all in the Compromise plan and the people will accept anything they get," he wrote, underscoring the word *all*.

Compromise would inevitably demand scapegoats, for the Irish Republic was not some diplomatic negotiating point, but a mystical, martyr-producing organism that could trace its bloody and tragic ancestry to Theobald Wolfe Tone. It was for an Irish republic that

Wolfe Tone died, Tone and Pearse, Connolly, Clarke; it was for a republic that Kevin Barry was hanged. The heroes of Irish nationalism demanded nothing less than a republic, but the Fenians and the poets of 1916 never made it to a negotiating table. Somebody was going to answer to the ghosts of Irish rebellions past.

So even if Devoy believed that everybody from De Valera to Boland to even Michael Collins was a party to the coming compromise, it was clear where blame was to be apportioned. A month before the truce, the *Gaelic American* featured a page 1 headline that read, "De Valera Again Reassures England." By now, Devoy's readers knew that when De Valera was caught in the act of reassuring England, the fix was in. Quoting De Valera's own words, the story noted that the slippery president of the Republic had told reporters that "the principle we are fighting for is Ireland's right to complete Self-Determination." That, of course, was exactly the sort of bland, noncommittal language that De Valera couldn't abide when he heard it in America. "At the last elections," he continued, "the Irish people manifested their will to create an Irish Republic. If they wish to change the Constitution or the form of Government, that is their affair."

If De Valera's statement hinted of compromise—and it surely did—privately Devoy was expressing similar statements. On the day the truce went into effect, he told Judge Cohalan that the president of the Friends of Irish Freedom, Bishop Michael Gallagher of Detroit, should not make a formal, dogmatic statement in support of a republic. "I . . . fear that if we appear to be urging the people of Ireland to continue the fight, without being able to give them the military supplies they need, we'll put ourselves in a very vulnerable position before the public and play into De Valera's hands," Devoy wrote. "It is quite enough, I think, for us to state our own firm adherence to the Republic and our determination to support those in Ireland who favor it." Put another way, Devoy was advocating brinkmanship. Publicly he and his allies would continue to support the ideal of a republic, but privately they knew they could hardly tell the Irish people what form of government they ought to accept, and more to the point, they could hardly take a hard line without the means of supplying the hard-liners with the weapons they would need if the truce failed.

The summer of 1921 is still remembered in Ireland today for its

293

tranquillity. Even the notoriously fickle Irish weather cooperated, and Irish men, women, and children basked in the warm rays of sunshine and peace. The war that had begun in January 1919, that had brought untold misery across the length and breadth of Ireland, finally was over. There was in Ireland the expectation that surely the guns and bombs would be put aside, that something would come of the peace talks in London, and that never again would such creatures as the Black and Tans soil the Irish countryside.

In New York, Devoy followed the proceedings with a great deal more anxiety. Overworked and sleepless as ever, he fretted over those in Ireland and in America who would accept peace at any price. At times he seemed almost contemptuous of the peace talks in London. "It is quite evident that the 'peace negotiations' are to be prolonged indefinitely until the people get used to the truce and become confused as to what it is all about," he wrote only two weeks after the truce was called. He told Cohalan that compromise was inevitable because the IRA was short on weapons thanks to De Valera's "spending of the money that ought to have been available for military supplies in the work of disorganization here."

His anxieties were not limited to Ireland. After several years of legal action, he was finally given back the $5,000 he had posted for James Larkin's bail when the labor leader was arrested in 1919—Devoy's rivals in the Reorganized Clan had tried to claim the money, no doubt thinking it had come from the Clan treasury. In fact, it was part of the settlement Devoy had received from his brother's estate in New Mexico. But with that case finally finished, he was preparing for yet another court battle as his libel suit against the *Irish World* proceeded through New York's legal system. The *Gaelic American* once again was on the edge of bankruptcy and in need of reorganization. And he was convinced that McGarrity's organization had placed one of its members in the hotel room adjacent his to listen in on his conversations. The burdens were piling up, one on the other. "I feel myself failing physically every day," he wrote. "I can't sleep and my legs are getting weak." He blamed it all on De Valera, and he lashed out irrationally and with an appalling dose of anti-Semitism: "This half-breed Jew," he wrote of his tormentor, "has done me more harm in the last two years than the English have been able to do during my whole life." It was an absurd and hateful epithet, but

Devoy, in this hour of hope, often seemed to be a bitter old man. "I am sick at heart and weary of having to deal with men who have no sense of honor," he wrote. At night, with sleep a distant and often unattainable goal, he found himself dwelling on the words of the Irish nationalist anthem, "A Nation Once Again," written by the hero of the Young Ireland of his childhood, Thomas Davis:

> And righteous men shall make our land
> A nation once again!

Where, he asked himself as he lay awake in his hotel room, were those righteous men?

Michael Collins, the mysterious gunman, was about to show his face to the British for the first time. De Valera at first rejected Lloyd George's terms for a compromise (an act that led Devoy to send a telegram to De Valera, offering his congratulations as "the oldest active Fenian" and vowing that Irish America would "bury differences and bring united action"). But he reconsidered, and Collins, Griffith, and three of their cabinet colleagues were dispatched to London as plenipotentiaries of the Irish Republic, charged with the task of either reaching and signing an agreement with the British government or breaking off talks and preparing for renewed warfare. De Valera himself didn't go to London, although he had done so when Lloyd George invited him in July to begin preliminary negotiations. With peace talks about to begin in earnest, De Valera argued that it was best he stay out of the fray as the very symbol of the Republic. Collins and the cabinet were stunned, but De Valera prevailed.

Not long before proceeding to London, Collins met with an ally of Devoy's named James McHugh, a trusted member of the original Clan na Gael. The presence of an emissary from Devoy and Cohalan in Dublin at such a moment was, literally, intriguing. Devoy and Cohalan, after all, had been written out as agents of the Irish Republican Brotherhood and replaced by Joe McGarrity; Collins held the title of president of the IRB—the shadowy secret society that had infiltrated every rebel institution from the Dail to the IRA. Protocol would seem to have demanded that Collins snub anybody claiming to represent Devoy, unless, of course, Collins was anticipating a moment when he would need the old man's support.

In meeting McHugh, Collins was clearly sending a message back to Devoy and Cohalan. What was broken, he seemed to be saying, could, and perhaps should, be repaired. Collins spoke warmly of the judge, though he told McHugh that Devoy's criticisms of De Valera had been intemperate. And despite the growing rift between himself and De Valera, Collins defended his chief, saying that he was "playing the game just as he wants." And the Big Fellow assured his American visitor, and thus Devoy, that the rebels were prepared for another round of war if it came to that.

There was little question in Devoy's mind about what would come next. Even at the time, the terms of the settlement seemed obvious. Collins might have sent Devoy reassurances of the IRA's determination to take to the battlefield again, but it was unlikely he meant it, and just as unlikely that Devoy believed it. The secret army had been exposed, its leader—Collins—transformed from a mysterious outlaw to a diplomat whose face was known to the British prime minister himself. A guerrilla army required the support of the people, and the people, as Devoy had already predicted, were ready to accept a compromise. Collins and the others would get only what the British were prepared to give them, and that meant no republic.

Throughout his career as the fearsome and determined face of Irish-American nationalism, Devoy demonstrated a clear willingness to take what he or the movement could get. It was why he supported Parnell's home-rule movement in the 1880s, and why, in 1919 and 1920, he supported bland resolutions of American support for Irish self-determination rather than demand American recognition of the rebel Republic. Yet Devoy was despondent through the weeks of negotiations during the fall of 1921. His obsession with De Valera, with McGarrity and Boland and McCartan and Maloney, warped his vision and colored his view of this historic, if somewhat unsatisfying, turn in Irish history. He raged on about his tormentors in America and in Ireland and complained even about Collins when he heard second-hand that the Big Fellow had criticized the Clan for some ancient offense. "When the leader of the fighting men talks claptrap like that, what is the use of trying to deal with them at all?" he wrote. What he needed, he told friends, was a long, long rest.

Yet for all his bitterness, and for all his exhaustion, for all the torments that followed him from the office to the courtroom to his hotel room, he found the time to help Kathleen Clarke, widow of his old friend Tom Clarke, get her son Daly to a tuberculosis sanitarium in California from Dublin. It was a small kindness, but at such a moment any such act suggested a soft and generous heart. Mrs. Clarke had entered politics after her husband's execution, and she was a staunch supporter of De Valera. In a letter to Devoy asking for his help, she was candid about the political problems she faced in making such a request: "I would ask you to meet [Daly] not as John Devoy the opponent of [De Valera], but John Devoy, the Fenian, his father's . . . old friend. You can understand my position. I cannot forget old friends, but neither can I allow any act of mine to be construed into taking sides against our elected President." Devoy did what Mrs. Clarke asked of him, and more. He quietly paid for Daly's expenses—the young man later told his mother that Devoy did so "out of bigheartedness."

It was a heart that ached, however, at a bittersweet moment. On December 6, 1921, the five Irish plenipotentiaries in London signed a treaty with the British government that called for the creation of an Irish Free State, a twenty-six-county dominion of the British Empire that would have as much power over its domestic affairs as Canada and Australia. And like those nations, the Irish Free State would accept the monarch of Great Britain as its sovereign, and its elected political leaders would be required to take an oath of allegiance to the British Crown.

It was not, as Devoy knew it could not be, a republic. It was not what Tom Clarke had fought for in 1916. It was not what John Devoy had pledged allegiance to in 1861.

But it was something. It was more than Parnell had sought back in the days when Devoy was his staunch American ally. It was, in the words of Collins, the freedom to win freedom, a stepping-stone to the achievement of a republic. It meant that the British Army would withdraw, although the Royal Navy would maintain a presence in four Irish ports, and that the Union Jack would be hauled down everywhere save in the six counties of Northern Ireland, which would remain under the control of London.

It was a compromise. And it was a tangible measure of freedom.

At first, the *Gaelic American* called it a "surrender." As luck would have it, so did Eamon De Valera, a development that came as a surprise to his American supporters, who initially reacted favorably to the treaty's terms. The president of the American Association for the Recognition of the Irish Republic, a wealthy businessman named Edward Doheny, said that "the accomplishment of the Irish Free State is what I have hoped for." It was a strange sentiment, considering that Doheny and his allies were supposedly stalwart in their insistence on nothing less than an Irish republic. And the Free State, with its oath of allegiance to the British Crown, was no republic.

Three days after the treaty was signed and the document brought to Dublin for debate in the Irish cabinet and in the Dail, Devoy joined with his colleagues in the Friends of Irish Freedom for a two-day convention in the Hotel Astor in New York. The occasion had been scheduled for weeks in advance as a show of force and as a vehicle to demonstrate support for Devoy and Cohalan, but the news from Ireland overshadowed all other purposes, including a resolution to raise and spend $2 million to "combat British intrigue in America."

The terms of the treaty had Irish-Americans groping for the correct position, ever mindful of how others were positioning themselves. The Friends convention featured several points of view, with Devoy sounding resigned to the Free State with its continued connection to king and Empire, while Diarmuid Lynch, a veteran of Easter, 1916, and an ally of Devoy's, fairly shouted his adamant opposition. A resolution restated the organization's commitment to a republic as the "only solution" to Ireland's national aspirations. But in his speech, Devoy seemed to back away from the antitreaty commentary in his own newspaper, perhaps because he realized that De Valera himself was against it.

"I knew a year ago that a compromise like this was going to be effected," Devoy said. "The man they sent out here to represent the Irish Republic, from the day he landed, was so shaping things, so engineering the situation, that it could have no other result. He was undermining the organizations that stood for an Irish Republic, the organizations that had, time after time, beaten England in her efforts to secure control of this country.

"For a time I was under the impression that it might be, perhaps, through some mental defect, through some temperamental defect, some feeling of jealousy, some lack of knowledge, but I have made up my mind now—and I think every man who is familiar with all that has occurred since Eamon De Valera landed in America must have already made up his mind—that the policy he pursued towards the Irish Movement in America was deliberate, intentional and calculated only to bring about a compromise with England."

The settlement, Devoy said, had at least brought to an end "the state of cruel suspense in which we have been for the last two years.... We know where we stand ... and the only comfort I can take out of it is that it marks the disappearance of De Valera as the leader of the Irish people." The last phrase was greeted with a burst of applause; it was as though Devoy had finally hit upon the best reason to support the treaty. The old warrior concluded his address by pledging to continue his fight against British propaganda in America. It was, he figured, the only battle left to fight.

The Dail took up the treaty in the closing weeks of 1921 and, after a break for the holidays, prepared to vote on its terms on Saturday, January 7. Collins and Griffith led the debate in favor; De Valera and Cathal Brugha argued vociferously against it. De Valera presented an alternative to the treaty, which he called Document No. 2, which differed in no meaningful way from the treaty. He trotted out all manner of parliamentary maneuvers to delay a vote, but it was to no avail. In a heart-wrenching, heartbreaking session the likes of which hadn't been seen in Ireland since Parnell's colleagues rejected his leadership so many years ago, the Dail accepted the treaty by a 64–57 vote. There were cheers on the winning side when the vote was announced; there were tears, too. De Valera announced that he would resign as the Dail's leader; Griffith was elected in his place.

Ireland, at last, was free. Shortly after the treaty was approved, a new Provisional Government was formed with Griffith at its head and Collins as the commanding general of its army. The Union Jack was lowered from Dublin Castle. The Irish tricolor of green, white, and orange—the banner that Irish rebels had adopted in the days of Young Ireland in 1848—flew from every flagstaff in the twenty-six counties of the Irish Free State. John Devoy had lived to see an Irish army drive the British out of Ireland. No matter what else the treaty said, no matter what compromises had been reached over words, there was no denying the remarkable achievement. At last, an Irish army had forced Britain to the bargaining table, and there the Irish won terms providing for a British evacuation of its occupying army in most of Ireland.

For De Valera and his allies, the settlement was not enough. Kathleen Clarke was among the Dail members who voted against the treaty. She wrote to Devoy after the vote: "Our cause which seemed so rosy and our hopes which seemed so near realization have been shoved back, possibly [by] a generation. . . . I'd like it if you would tell me why you still distrust De Valera. I thought when he definitely stood for the Republic you would forgive the past."

Mrs. Clarke misjudged her old friend. Devoy supported the settlement, but was not in a forgiving mood. But if he allowed himself a moment of reflection, if he paused to consider how far he and Ireland had come since the day he took his oath to the Republic in 1861, it was not apparent in his letters or in the pages of the *Gaelic American*. Trumpets did not sound the notes of victory; there were not even the bittersweet tones of the pennywhistle. Instead, there was only the loud crash of angry cymbals. De Valera had given away the game, Devoy insisted. De Valera's opposition to the treaty only demonstrated just how unfit he was. Devoy neither rejoiced nor fretted over Ireland's newfound independence. Instead, he conceded the merits of the treaty, resigned himself to compromise, and then lashed out at the man he held responsible for an unsatisfactory end to a long and heroic story.

"Every Irish tragedy has a comedy or a farce in it," Devoy wrote after the Dail vote, "and the recent proceedings in Dublin were no exception to the rule. In fact, they afforded the worst instance of the combination in all Irish history." In a sentence that spoke of his underlying contempt for the settlement, even though he supported it, he continued, "The Dail Eireann met to decide the fate of Ireland—to give an irrevocable decision on the question whether the struggle for complete National Independence and Total Separation from England was to continue, or Ireland should be permanently merged in the British Empire and forever renounce her claim to Nationhood. Yet the discussion was not mainly on that all important question, but turned on the claims of a man who is not Irish to be the leader, or the Autocrat, of the Irish Race—a position for which he is wholly unfit, and for which he demonstrated his utter unfitness by his conduct throughout the long discussions." The first sentence is more interesting than the second. Clearly Devoy saw the Free State settlement as allowing Ireland to be "permanently merged in the British Empire," and clearly he preferred that the "struggle for complete National Independence" should continue. And yet he supported the treaty. Why? The answer seems clear at first: De Valera, whom Devoy described as "not Irish either in blood, character, temperament or outlook," was against the treaty. But that explanation, so often cited in Irish and American histories of the period, ignores Devoy's long history of compromise and moderation.

Because his rhetoric often was harsh, and his condemnation of backsliders and compromisers was unforgiving, Devoy's record often gets lost amid the invective and slander. Yet at nearly every stage of his long life as America's foremost Irish agitator, Devoy demonstrated a flexibility and a moderation not in keeping with his public image as an implacable supporter of the Irish Republic. He settled for what he could get, whether it was in dealing with Parnell's constitutional home-rule campaign or in working with American politicians over the exact wording of sympathetic resolutions. He knew as early as the Land War of the early 1880s that the key to mobilizing American opinion was not through conspiracy but open, constitutional agitation. His acceptance of the treaty, while seemingly at odds with his past, actually was the ultimate expression of Devoy's approach.

So Devoy struggled mightily, and not always successfully, to argue in favor of the compromise. Among its virtues were the removal of British troops from Ireland, and suggestions that the Free State was, in fact, a stepping stone to the great dream of a republic.

Meanwhile, the treaty split apart Devoy's rivals in the AARIR. Devoy and Cohalan kept discipline in the ranks of the Friends of Irish Freedom and their wing of the Clan na Gael. In February, Devoy wrote a two-page, typewritten letter to Collins, telling him that "our best men here, under existing conditions, favor giving the Free State [a] chance to do what it can for Ireland." An increasingly beleaguered Collins welcomed the old Fenian's support as Ireland began to lurch toward a civil war that Devoy saw coming. "My earnest hope is that in such a struggle, you may win," he told Collins, "believing as I do that the defeat of de Valera's selfish campaign is absolutely necessary in Ireland's dearest interests." Collins sent Devoy a letter apologizing for the IRB's action in cutting its alliance with Devoy and his Clan faction during Ireland's most dramatic hours. He explained, weakly, that the IRB and others in Ireland at the time had visions of setting up "a world-wide Irish federation, each separate part working through the Government, and in accordance with the laws of the country where it had its being," a fair summary of exactly what Devoy would have expected and wanted. But Collins added in an aside that must have prompted a rare but bitter smile on Devoy's face, "Unfortunately, some of those we sent to America did not understand the vital principle of that idea." By February 1922, Devoy and Collins were of one mind about Eamon De Valera. Collins then sent a onetime confidant of De Valera's, James O'Mara, to consult with Devoy. In a letter to Devoy, Collins wrote, "your good opinion is of concern to us here [in Dublin]."

It was a concern because Ireland was on the verge of civil war. IRA members who opposed the treaty had taken over the Four Courts building in Dublin. Armed and fully prepared to start a shooting war, the IRA contingent in the Four Courts was a symbolic and daily reminder to the fledgling nation that it did not command the loyalties of some of its staunchest fighters, not even in the capital city itself.

The people of Ireland, however, had had enough. They went to the polls in June and repudiated the hard liners. At that moment, the issue should have been decided. The new democracy of Ireland had been put to the test, and the result was clear. But De Valera had told Ireland that if the treaty was accepted, his supporters "would have to wade through Irish blood, through the blood of soldiers of the Irish government, and through, perhaps, the blood of some of the members of the Government in order to get Irish freedom." There would be blood all right, and it would flow, copiously, on both sides. And just as De Valera had predicted, some of it would flow from members of Ireland's new, independent government. But De Valera didn't spill a drop.

By summertime, Ireland was again at war. This time it was Irishman against Irishman, a violent manifestation of every quarrel John

Devoy had witnessed and been party to during his long and eventful life. And within weeks, Harry Boland, Cathal Brugha, and Arthur Griffith were dead. Griffith died of what might be called, in other circumstances, natural causes—of a brain hemorrhage suffered as his country hemorrhaged the blood of its young soldiers and future leaders. The other two were killed by Irishmen wearing the uniform of the new Irish nation. There was some talk of peace in late August, when Michael Collins set out to his native county of Cork for an inspection tour of the Free State forces he commanded. His party was ambushed on August 22, and the commander in chief took a bullet to the head. Michael Collins was dead at age thirty-one. Yet another fallen leader was added to Ireland's long list; half a million people turned out for his funeral. Soon, the Free State government was ordering summary executions of antitreaty prisoners. In one of the more brutal episodes, prisoners were tied together and blown to pieces with land mines. (Because several prisoners actually survived that ordeal, one group was shot in the legs first and then thrown upon the mines.)

From New York, Devoy could do little but watch the spectacle and curse De Valera again. The Irish Civil War, which lasted less than a year, took the lives of four hundred people and caused millions of dollars in damages to a nation that had already suffered so intensely during the last, bloody years of British occupation. Devoy helped shape American opinion in favor of the Irish Free State, but he did so with only limited enthusiasm. His heart was not in it. He was tired. He was deaf. He was going blind. His friends were dead, and so was the Irish Republic.

As FORMER COMRADES CONTINUED to rip each other to shreds in Ireland, Devoy's friends and allies held a testimonial to the old soldier at the Imperial Hotel in Brooklyn on January 30, 1923. Designed to pay tribute to Devoy in an hour of victory, the event had a harsh edge to it. Devoy himself expressed the emotions of those in attendance. He rose to speak after straining with limited success to hear several speeches testifying to his fine character. His speech carried no note of triumph or satisfaction, but instead recapitulated the history of Irish nationalism from the days of Wolfe Tone. It was a recitation of missed opportunities, of fiascos, and of fatal splits. Of the new Irish government and its battle with fellow Irishmen, Devoy had only these bitter words:

"The present split has developed into a savage civil war which is devastating Ireland, ruining her economic life, breaking the morale of the people, and filling the world with the idea that the old English theory is correct, that when England's firm hand was removed, the Irish would start to cut each others' throats. Can we blame the world for accepting that theory when thousands of Irishmen are busily engaged in proving its apparent truth?"

His conclusion came as little surprise: De Valera, he said, was to blame. "He is a monster who must be punished for his crimes. Eliminate him and the trouble will soon end."

With British troops removed from most of Ireland, with the orange, white, and green flying over Dublin Castle, John Devoy remained unfulfilled and in a blind rage.

The Irish Civil War ended by the summer of 1923, and De Valera was placed under arrest.

It was time for John Devoy to return home, but only for a visit.

CHAPTER EIGHTEEN

A Soldier's Song

THE OLD MAN WITH THE TANGLE OF GRAY WHISKERS AND THE heavy, dark suit stood on the deck of the *President Harding* as it prepared to set sail from Hoboken on July 19, 1924. The green, white, and orange flag of Ireland flew from the ship's foremast, and a corps of bagpipers—cheeks billowing, the harbor breeze flapping their kilts—filled the air with bittersweet melodies as the old man bade farewell to his friends—men in straw hats and women in breezy summer dresses. Children squealed as if on a one-day holiday while their parents wished the old man well. The visitors began making their way down the gangway, their eyes moist after bidding their friend a poignant good-bye, as the ship's officers shouted orders to clear the decks. A voice cried, "Three cheers for John Devoy!" And so they were given, in a roar even the old man could have heard.

The ship set sail at precisely one o'clock in the afternoon, and as it slipped away from American soil, the bagpipers gathered on Hoboken's Pier Four broke into a rendition of "A Soldier's Song," the unofficial anthem of the new Irish state.

> *Soldiers are we*
> *Whose lives are pledged to Ireland*
> *Some have come*
> *From a land beyond the waves . . .*

From that land beyond the shores of Kerry and Clare and Mayo and Galway, from the adopted homeland of some 20 million people of Irish blood, John Devoy was returning to the place he had never stopped calling home. He had not been there in forty-five years, when he put his liberty at risk to meet with Charles Parnell and Michael Davitt at the beginning of the Land War. The Ireland he was returning to was not the same as the Ireland he had left. It was not the Ireland he had dreamed of so many years ago. It was not a republic. It was not united. Its politicians still swore allegiance to the British monarch. Indeed, "God Save the King" and not "A Soldier's Song" remained Ireland's official national anthem, and it was played at state occasions. Perhaps worst of all, just three days before Devoy set sail, Eamon De Valera had been released from prison after serving time for his role in the Irish Civil War. (Devoy would later write that had it been up to him, he'd have had De Valera shot rather than waste the government's time and money with a mere prison sentence.)

Even so, even with the compromises and the partial victories and the oath of allegiance to the foreign monarch, the honor guard that would greet him after his transatlantic journey would wear the uniform of a free Irish government. The politicians who would welcome him as a guest of the nation were the freely elected representatives of the Irish people. The nation was in command of its destiny, and the soldiers of the ancient oppressor had been driven off in a war of liberation that would serve as a model for the many such conflicts yet to come in the blood-soaked twentieth century. Newly free Ireland had survived a brutal war of independence and a horrible civil war. Its very existence was a triumph of sorts, a victory of persistence, determination, and single-mindedness, qualities the nation shared, as it happened, with the man who was now steaming his way to Ireland from America, that fabled land beyond the waves.

The journey's complex mix of the bitter and the sweet was not lost on John Devoy, though he often appeared to dwell more on the former rather than savoring the latter. Two days before he boarded the *President Harding*, he had been the guest of honor at a rousing and splendid testimonial in the Hotel Astor near Times Square. The banquet was organized in a matter of days after Devoy let it be known that he intended to make a pilgrimage to the Ireland he had helped create. The banquet raised enough money to pay his passage and then some. Devoy told the audience what they already knew: "My heart has been in Ireland all the time that I have been in America." After all those years, he was no immigrant yearning for acceptance and assimilation; he was the eternal exile, following his heart across the Atlantic.

New York, the capital of the Irish-American movement, soon faded from view, and the ocean liner made its way through the Narrows, into the lower harbor and finally into the Atlantic itself. Devoy eventually retired to his cabin, where he put pen to paper and wrote a letter of thanks to the friends he had left behind in Hoboken. It was impossible to thank them all personally, so he did so en masse through a letter to the *Gaelic American*. He paid a special tribute to the bagpipers who saw him off. Their music, he wrote, "kept ringing in my ears long after we got out to the ocean, and the memory of the scene will linger during the span of life that may be left to me." The music, however it may have rung, was muffled, and the scene, however memorable, was fuzzy and out of focus. His hearing was worse than ever, and now his eyes were failing. He had undergone surgery to remove a cataract in April, but it would prove to be a losing battle. At age eighty-one, Devoy was increasingly dependent upon the kindness of friends—one of them, an active Irish-American nationalist named Harry Cunningham, accompanied him on this journey, and soon other friends throughout America would raise a subscription to help pay Devoy's medical and living expenses. The old man would be told nothing about it.

Devoy marveled at the accommodations aboard the *Harding*—he compared them to the facilities "that one gets in an American hotel—electric lights, hot and cold water . . . a fine lounge, bureau dressers [and] good beds." He usually ate only two meals a day, but he indulged himself with an extra meal while on board ship. He was several days out to sea when he received a message from Ireland sent to the *Harding* via radiogram: "We on behalf of the Distinguished Visitors Committee . . . have the honor to invite you, John Devoy, an eminent man of your country, to be the guest of our Nation from first to tenth August." It was signed with the name of the chairman of the Distinguished Visitors Committee, William Butler Yeats. The poet's graciousness and hospitality should have put a faint blush on Devoy's pale cheeks. Just before leaving New York, Devoy had put the finishing touches on an article in the *Gaelic American* that accused

Yeats of being a "mouthpiece" for a "reactionary minority masquerading as liberals." Yeats's offense? As a member of the new Irish Senate, he opposed a bill that would have required railway companies to print tickets in the Irish language.

Devoy waited a day before dispatching his acceptance of Yeats's invitation. The delay wasn't a sign of embarrassment, but of the habits of a $25-a-week agitator—he had discovered that, for some reason, waiting a day allowed him to save twenty cents a word off the cost of a radiogram to Dublin.

After a pleasant week's journey across the ocean, the *President Harding* neared the port of Cobh in County Cork on July 26. Before independence, when the port had been known as Queenstown, millions of Irish emigrants had embarked from it, their last glimpse of home being the modest town's oceanfront row of shops. Now it was John Devoy's point of entry.

As the ship edged closer to port, Devoy put on a dark fedora and returned to the ship's deck. There, as a midafternoon sun tore holes in Ireland's gray canopy of clouds, he leaned on a railing with both hands and cast his gaze landward. A pair of seagulls lazily flew by as Harry Cunningham stood with him, pointing out landmarks on the shore. Photographers captured images of the old man looking out on the island of his birth, and caption writers at the *Gaelic American*, caught up in the melodrama, later wrote that this was the moment when Ireland's oldest soldier caught his first glimpse of free Ireland. In fact, he didn't see much more than shadows.

In the distance, on a dock in Cobh, emissaries from the president of Ireland boarded a tender and set out into the harbor to extend to Devoy the greetings of the Irish nation and to escort him from the ship to the shore. A contingent of fifty soldiers, rifles in hand, stood ready to offer the returning exile a welcoming salute. The soldiers, wearing the colors of a free Irish nation, were young enough to be John Devoy's adult grandchildren. Not so many years ago, soldiers in service to the Irish nation were armed in the dead of night, with weapons purchased with funds raised in America, raised by John Devoy himself. But there was no need for intrigue anymore, no need for mysterious transfers of money and midnight arms deliveries. The Irish Army was no longer underground.

The tender docked alongside the *President Harding*, and Devoy and Cunningham were helped into the smaller boat for the short journey to Cobh. In the distance rose the massive walls of St. Coleman's Cathedral, built on a hill and towering over the homes and shops of the port town. As Devoy approached, the cathedral bells rang out in welcome.

Devoy regaled his greeting party with tales of his other transatlantic crossings, noting with some pride that he had never once gotten seasick, a record he kept intact on this journey. He couldn't help but draw a comparison between himself—deaf, stooped, and almost blind—and the officials who greeted him. "You are all such young men," he said wistfully.

An honor guard snapped to attention as the tender tied up to a wharf and Devoy was helped onto dry land. Commands were shouted, a crowd gathered dockside waved, and the tricolor of the Irish Free State danced in the wind. Three of his nephews and a niece—Eileen, whom Devoy had last seen when she came to New York for a vist in 1905, when she was a child—were at the dock to greet him. They and his older sister, Bridget, were his only living family.

They took him to the home they all shared in Dublin, and the following day President William Cosgrave greeted him as a conquering hero in the city's government buildings. Devoy mingled with members of the Free State government for nearly an hour and was photographed with the president. He then departed for a poignant visit to Glasnevin Cemetery north of Dublin's downtown. There, he visited the graves of his parents, his siblings, and other relatives, as well as those of Jeremiah O'Donovan Rossa, Charles Stewart Parnell, and Michael Collins, comrades, allies, and partners who did not live to see an Irish nation free and at peace with itself.

A day later, a letter addressed to Devoy arrived at his nephew's home. The correspondent had read of the old man's homecoming and wished to offer him fond greetings. It was, she wrote, the wish of her life that she might once again see her long-lost fiancé. Eliza Kenny Kilmurry, now a frail, invalid widow in her late seventies, was not dead, as Devoy had been told years before. She was living out what years remained to her in the company of a niece in the small market town of Naas in County Kildare, just a few miles from Devoy's birthplace.

Devoy wrote back at once, arranging for a visit several days later, on August 5, a chilly and rainy afternoon. He made the trip by automobile, and he brought along his nephews, his niece, and Cunningham. The streets of Naas, where Devoy had worked and lived in the mid-1860s, hadn't changed a great deal since the two separated lovers had last seen each other. When he arrived at the Kilmurry house on South Main Street, not far from where he had toiled as a clerk at Watkins Brewery, Eliza greeted them while leaning on the arm of her niece. Victorian discretion and the ravages of age apparently ruled out an embrace, but neither Elizabeth Kenny Kilmurry nor John Devoy attempted to hide their emotions.

"John," she said in a voice loud enough for the deaf old man's ears, "why didn't you write? I waited for you for twelve years."

Devoy said nothing for a moment. Then, at last, he replied, "And I've been waiting for you all my life."

He had done his waiting privately, for none of his friends in America knew of this woman he had left behind so many years ago.

Local legend has it that Devoy proposed to her again later that day, and that a priest even volunteered to perform the ceremony, but she declined. Devoy himself suggested that marriage may have crossed his mind, for when he wrote about his reunion with Eliza, he noted with barely suppressed regret that because of their frail health, "marriage . . . was wholly out of the question." Devoy also noted that at some point during the rainy afternoon, Eliza's niece took him to see the local parish priest, a Father Norris, although Devoy offers no clue about the purpose of the meeting, except to add that the priest invited the entire party to lunch in a convent across the street from Eliza's house.

Devoy spent most of the dreary afternoon with Eliza, then left to visit the site where he was born. The cabin was long since gone, but Devoy delighted his relatives by tracing the outlines of the building's foundation not far from the main Naas-Dublin road.

During the next six weeks, Devoy toured nearly the whole of the Irish Free State, and wherever he went, he received the honors and applause of a free Ireland. The outpouring for this living link to the days of Daniel O'Connell, the Famine, the failed Fenian Rising, and the sacrifice of Easter Week served to rouse a nation only a year removed from its brutal civil war, and recently witness to intense squabbling among its elected leaders. Devoy insisted that his was a purely personal visit, but it was a great deal more than that. The receptions, the local-government proclamations, and the fawning press coverage of Devoy's journeys were not simply about the return of an aged warrior. They were about the Irish binding up their new nation's wounds, saluting a hero from the mists of the nineteenth century, and coming to terms with the bittersweet compromise that was the Irish Free State. They were about rallying the goodwill of the nation for an old man who had helped make the cause of Irish free-dom an American issue, who had fought a ceaseless war for Ireland from American shores, and who, in the end, had recognized what was attainable and what would have to remain, for the time being, a dream.

In taking his first steps on free Irish soil, Devoy was performing yet another service, his last, for the land for which he had sacrificed everything, including, as he now realized, Eliza. His tour was a silent, understated, but quite eloquent effort to bring a divided nation to-gether. That such a mission should be entrusted to so divisive a figure as John Devoy was an irony the old man himself no doubt appreci-ated.

And so newspapers printed odes to the conquering hero, such as this tribute in the Dublin-based *Freeman's Journal*: "Never have his labors relaxed, never have his fires dimmed, never has he ceased to cherish the larger hope. He comes now to see things as they are, and, let us hope, to radiate [a] larger patriotism . . . and by healing our divisions reinforce our strength."

The public responded to the cues. Three days before his reunion with Eliza, Devoy was the guest of honor in Dublin's Croke Park for the opening of the Tailteann Games—a sort of Olympics of ancient Gaelic sports. He was seated next to Ireland's governor-general, Tim-othy Healy, the man who had asked of Parnell so many years before, "Who is to be the mistress of the Party?" The two aging warriors, equally talented in the fine art of invective, were saluted with a stadium-rocking ovation.

Devoy did not venture into that geographic symbol of Ireland's legendary splits—the six Irish counties that remained part of Great Britain—although he addressed the issue of partition in words con-sistent with his cautious nature, that side of him so often hidden by a camouflage of slander, acrimony, and the occasional libel. He condemned the internal boundary and declared his opposition to Ireland's partition, but he was not prepared to shed Irish blood for its removal. "The only solution of the boundary question is the abolition of the boundary by the consent of the people of the Six Counties," he said. "That has been my stand all along. I want it to be done peacefully."

Such sentiments earned him the praise of Ireland's newspapers, one of which noted that although Devoy "is probably looked on by many people in Ireland as a bit of a firebrand . . . he has the advantage of knowing Irish history [and] he has lived long in America, where common sense rules men and movements."

He was careful to say all the correct things, even to praise "how liberal" the Protestants in the Free State were. To be sure, he could hardly avoid taking an occasional potshot at what he called "Tory die-hards" in England, but his visit was a series of domestic triumphs for the infant Free State and personal triumphs for himself. He was feted by politicians, relatives of old friends long since gone, and by Ireland's cultural elite. At a reception in Dublin's Metropole Hotel following the opening of the Tailteann Games, Yeats singled out Devoy during a speech to five hundred athletes and VIPs. "We have many diplomatic representatives, we have famous painters, a famous architect, and two of the most famous cricketers who ever lived," Yeats said of his audience. "I welcome all in the name of Ireland, but I may be permitted to welcome with a more particular and personal welcome Mr. John Devoy, who entertained me many years ago in America." Devoy himself addressed the audience and in a short speech quoted from the Young Ireland poet and philosopher Thomas Davis, whose words Devoy's father had read aloud by the hearth so many years ago:

> We do not hate, we never cursed,
> Nor spoke an angry word
> Against a man in Ireland nursed
> How e'er we think he erred.

Devoy could hardly claim to have lived up to Davis's sentiments during his long life. But now, in the aftermath of Ireland's ultimate faction fight, he could quote them from memory.

For six weeks he maintained a schedule that no doubt exhausted his young nephews and niece. A photographer caught them on a day's drive, with Devoy dressed, as usual, in a jacket and tie, with a homburg on his head and a cane in his hand. He found time to make several more visits to Eliza's home in Naas, including at least one Sunday dinner with his family and hers. She clearly was delighted by the attention and welcomed the company for, she told him, all of her old friends were dead. Weeks later, after he returned to New York, she would write him, "I often think of the good days we had when we were young, but they didn't last long, but I never forgot them."

He turned eighty-two on September 3, and he celebrated his birthday on Irish soil for the first time in more than a half century. To mark the occasion and to wish him a safe return to New York, President Cosgrave and yet another glittering audience saluted him with a banquet in Dublin's Dolphin Hotel. The president once more extended the thanks of the Irish people, saying that "no man deserved better of this nation."

When Devoy was called upon to speak, all of the bitterness, all of the sorrow, and all of the sacrifice found its way past the barriers he had put up for the preceding six weeks. The visit had stirred both pride and memories, and not all of the latter were positive. The reunion with Eliza had conjured images of a life not led, and perhaps to his surprise, the thought of what might have been saddened him. The sight of all the old places of his childhood may have reminded him of the beatings he had endured as a student at the hands of other Irishmen, and surely the recent release of De Valera stuck in his craw. He had kept a civil tongue until now, his last public appearance in the Ireland he had done so much to create. Now there was no holding him back. In his farewell speech to a presidential audience, he indulged in some reminiscences, called on the nation to stand behind Cosgrave, and relived some of Ireland's glorious failures. But in speaking about more recent times, his tongue became barbed, and the fine words of Thomas Davis were forgotten:

"I tried to come over [for] Easter Week . . . by getting the naturalization papers of an old friend who had recently died, and who was very like me, but his nephew refused to give them to me. I have often since then regretted that I failed and was not shot with Tom Clarke. . . . That would have spared me the worst agony of mind I have ever endured when from 1919 to last year, I was called a traitor for standing by the Irish Republic by the man who first lowered its flag and who sent men bribed with money which I had helped to collect to repeat the lie all over the United States and to make the worst split in all Irish history, which he later brought to Ireland to bring ruin and disaster upon her."

The reference to De Valera, so recently released from prison by the very government whose representatives filled the ballroom, was hardly subtle. And for those who may have chosen to forget why the old man still held a grudge, he delivered a pointed lecture: "Fenianism failed largely through incompetent leaders, and yet you sent out a man to America who drenched Ireland in blood and totally destroyed your military and economic resources."

As a valedictory speech, it was heavy-handed and filled with self-pity, and it no doubt left the audience slightly deflated. They had come to salute a man for his success, but Devoy's speech mostly concerned itself with failures. Having achieved his goal, partially anyway, he no longer had a frame of reference. After all, he had known only noble failure during most of his nearly six decades of agitation. Victory was something entirely new. He didn't know what to make of it.

He left for New York on September 6 after a memorable six weeks, delivering a farewell message that condemned Ireland's partition but acknowledged that it would take "time and hard work" to bring about cooperation between Northern Ireland and the Irish Free State. It is, of course, impossible to know what he might have said had he known that partition would remain in place for the remainder of the century. But he did offer a clue, one in keeping with his relentless, and often misunderstood, ability to grasp what was attainable. "The only true solution to the boundary question is the abolition of the boundary," he wrote when he returned to New York. The assertion was not exactly groundbreaking, but his caveat confirmed his moderate, democratic, and entirely reasonable nature: "There are two ways of effecting that solution. One way, and by far the best, is by an agreement based on the will of the people of both sections and entirely satisfactory to both. The other is by waiting for England's next war and . . . securing it by force. Force is . . . wholly undesirable. Therefore the only sane policy to meet the present situation is . . . to bring about reunion by consent."

More than seventy years after he wrote those words, consent had yet to be achieved.

DEVOY HAD TOLD AN audience in New York that for all the years he had spent in America, his heart had always been in Ireland. Nobody who knew him thought otherwise. And yet, when his journey was finished, Devoy returned to America as scheduled. He told an audience that his next visit to Ireland would come in a box. Why did he not stay where his heart was, in the land he had helped liberate? If he planned to be buried in Ireland, why not live out his remaining years there? Perhaps he would have if Eliza Kenny Kilmurry had accepted his second proposal (if, in fact, it was actually offered). Perhaps he couldn't because she hadn't accepted. But perhaps six weeks in Ireland had persuaded him that after fifty-four years in America, he was no longer Irish, but, in fact, an Irish-American.

He settled back into his routine at the *Gaelic American*, and while his mind remained clear, his body—particularly his eyes—continued to betray him. Letters from his niece and nephews are filled with words of comfort for his latest affliction, from sciatica to another battle with cataracts to never-ending insomnia. (His nephew Peter Devoy suggested without irony that he should avoid "anything in the nature of an argument at night.") He moved to rooms in Harlem, on West 107th Street, and there he was looked after by two women, Alice Comiskey and her sister, Lily Carragher. A secret fund Judge Cohalan raised helped pay his rent.

Bad eyes and all, he wrote frequently to Eliza, and she wrote him back chatty letters about the miseries of old age that they shared. He sent her a picture taken when he and O'Donovan Rossa and their three colleagues were not long off the steamship *Cuba* after it had pulled into New York in 1871. On the back of the photo, this famously hardheaded Irish rebel wrote in an unsteady hand, "To Mrs. E. Kilmurry (nee Eliza Kenny), in loving memory of our engagement when she was a fine girl of 20 and with deep regret at the misfortunes which separated us. From John Devoy." The photo is dated July 2, probably in 1925.

She returned the favor, sending a current photo of herself with her niece. Devoy inscribed the back of it: "Mrs. E. Kulmurry of Naas, ne Eliza Kenny of Tipper, County Kildare, engaged to John Devoy at the time of his arrest . . . waiting for him for 12 years after his release in 1871."

With the struggle in Ireland over, he redirected his attentions to American politics, launching a fiery crusade against the Ku Klux Klan, and showing once again his taste for political reformers, he urged Irish-Americans to back the quixotic presidential candidacy of the maverick Republican Robert La Follette in 1924. He quietly raised a subscription for Kathleen Clarke, Tom Clarke's widow, who was living on the edge of poverty. He did so despite the political divide between them, for Mrs. Clarke had been adamant against the treaty and had followed De Valera out of the Dail in 1922. She told Devoy that thanks to his help "I can sleep at night when I go to bed instead of laying awake with the strain and worry of how to keep going. People tell me I am looking years younger and ask what am I doing with myself. I smile but don't let them into the secret."

Inevitably, Devoy found himself caught up in feuds, including one with—of all people—Margaret Pearse, the mother of Patrick and Willie Pearse, two of Ireland's Easter martyrs. He continued to press his libel case against the *Irish World* through the mid-1920s, and at one point his bitter rivals were found guilty and Devoy was awarded a $25,000 judgment. The newspaper appealed the decision, and after a long, drawn-out legal battle, the *Irish World*'s guilty verdict was affirmed, but Devoy's award was reduced to six cents—a penny for every year the case was in court; a penny for every county that remained under British rule. He complained to Cohalan that the jury had been led to believe that the dispute was simply "part of an Irish fight."

Letters from Eliza arrived at regular intervals, their tone changing from tentatively formal to openly affectionate as months passed. Her complimentary closes changed from a stiff "sincerely" to "with best love" over a touching, two-year correspondence. She read the *Gaelic American* regularly, but commented on it only when it contained mentions of Devoy's absences due to ill health, mostly related to his eyes. "It must be a great trial on you when you can't read or write," she wrote. By 1926, he was unable to read anything in his own newspaper except the headlines, and he dictated much of his correspondence.

He promised Eliza in one of his letters that he would pay her another visit in 1927, and the news delighted her. By the fall of 1926, though, Eliza was bedridden. She died on February 20, 1927. Devoy received the news in a letter from his nephew Peter. He canceled his travel plans.

His health rallied for a time, and an operation helped improve his eyesight. Soon he was holding forth during small meetings in his rooms on causes ranging from the World Court, which he was against, to what he perceived to be creeping "imperialism" in the Irish Free State government. He renewed his contacts with the once-hated Dr. Patrick McCartan, now a maverick politician in Ireland and an opponent of the Free State's government. The two shared their uncertainties about the government's direction, but Eamon De Valera's reemergence as an opposition leader in the Dail cautioned Devoy against change. De Valera, Devoy wrote McCartan, "has no qualities of leadership and his record should bar him forever." It didn't. Eamon De Valera, who once refused to recognize the Irish Free State's authority and helped lead a war against it, would become Ireland's prime minister in 1932. Remarkably, the winning side in a civil war peacefully turned over power to its former opponents through the democratic process. This time, there would be no faction fight.

In the fall of 1928, America was on the verge of a historic breakthrough. For the first time in its history, an Irish-Catholic would be nominated for the highest elective office in the land. Alfred E. Smith's rise to national prominence was a symbol of a new age. The old resentments, the bitterness of exclusion, the sense of grievance— all were giving way to something new and as yet undeveloped. Irish America had not yet arrived, but it was clearly going places it had not been before. The problems of Ireland were no longer of great concern. Independence had been won. Irish America had played its part, but the time had come to move on. Triumphs closer to home awaited.

The autumn of Al Smith's history-making candidacy found Devoy immersed in his memoirs. He had written four hundred thousand words, most of them about the Fenian Rising—that glorious failure. His narrative moved from 1867 to 1916 without so much as a stop at the New Departure and the Land War, and he had written nothing about Ireland's victory in 1922. In a chapter about himself, he dwelled on childhood memories of the beatings he and his brother had received at the hands of other Irishmen—his teachers. There was no mention of Eamon De Valera, the mathematics teacher who tormented him late in life.

In the proposed title page for his book *Recollections of an Irish Rebel*, Devoy identified himself as "Chief Organizer for the British Army." It was the title he had sported in 1866, when he was arrested. Judge Cohalan gently pointed out that Devoy's readers would think he was a recruiting officer in Britain's service and not the organizer of Fenians within the British Army. The title page was changed accordingly.

On September 21, 1928, Devoy and his friend Harry Cunningham journeyed to Atlantic City. The sea air often reinvigorated him, but this time he could not shake his assortment of ailments. By week's end he was in bed in his hotel room, and a doctor was summoned. There was little he could do, he told Cunningham. At about 1 A.M. on September 29, Devoy asked to be turned over on his side. He died minutes later.

His body was returned to New York for a funeral mass in Manhattan's Church of the Ascension, where hundreds of mourners forced police to close down adjacent streets. He would not, however, be buried in American soil. Instead, nine months later, he made one final journey to Ireland, once again aboard the *President Harding*. In Dublin on June 16, 1929, John Devoy was accorded the pomp and circumstance of a state funeral, with his casket borne atop a gun carriage and drawn by horses through the streets of the capital. The cortege made its way through O'Connell Street and past the General Post Office, the headquarters of the Easter Rising and birthplace of the flawed but free Ireland he had done so much to create. He was interred in the Patriots' Plot in Glasnevin Cemetery, not far from the graves of Charles Parnell and Daniel O'Connell and Michael Collins, and within a few feet of Jeremiah O'Donovan Rossa and Harry Boland. All of them had lived and died for Ireland; only Devoy had lived to see it free and at peace. At his grave, Kathleen Clarke, who loathed the treaty, stood near the family of Michael Collins, who gave his life for it.

The *Times* of London, the voice of the British establishment, sent Devoy to the next world with something of a salute. John Devoy, the paper said, was "the most bitter and persistent, as well as the most dangerous, enemy of this country which Ireland has produced since Wolfe Tone."

The *Times* could not bring itself to add one more descriptive. John Devoy was not simply bitter, persistent, and dangerous. Unlike Tone and unlike so many of the other patriots who now shared hallowed ground with America's greatest Irish rebel, John Devoy was a success, the greatest of the Fenians, indeed. By sheer force of personality and determination, he had made Ireland's cause a transatlantic crusade, enlisting American public support on behalf of a small and strategically insignificant island in the North Atlantic. All the while, he asked of America only what America demanded of itself: genuine democracy and authentic republicanism.

He never ceased to be disappointed.

But he never surrendered.

National Library of Ireland—NLI

Public Records Office—PRO

Metropolitan Police Records (London)—MEPO

American Irish Historical Society—AIHS

New York Public Library—NYPL

Prison Commission (Great Britain)—PCOM

DPB—*Devoy's Post Bag* (two volumes), edited by William O'Brien and Desmond Ryan. A published portion of the Devoy papers in the National Library of Ireland

SCP—*Report of the Special Commission* (Parnell), 1889, 12 volumes

CHAPTER ONE

A Land Beyond the Waves

1: playing poker—John Devoy, *Recollections of an Irish Rebel*, 330.

1: half-written letter—Devoy papers, NLI, MS 18,004.

3: buildup of toxic silt—*New York Herald*, December 9, 1870.

3: 276,000 to a square mile—Ed O'Donnell, "Henry George's New York" (Ph.D. diss.), p. 144.

4: 20 percent were Irish-born—ibid., p. 135.

4: "How Long Will Protestants Endure?"—Florence Gibson, *Attitudes of the New York Irish.*

4: $300 a year—O'Donnell, "Henry George's New York," 144.

5: 50 percent of the city's worst-paid jobs—Philip H. Bagenal, *The American Irish*, 68.

5: "the atmosphere of the place is death"—Ibid., 71.

6: Joseph I. C. Clarke, a broke, twenty-nine-year-old poet—*Gaelic American*, March 7, 1925.

7: Tammany finishing last—*Irish World*, January 22, 1871.

8: The rookie space man had a scoop—*Gaelic American*, March 7, 1925.

8: "had I grasped the treasures"—Jeremiah O'Donovan Rossa, *Rossa's Recollections*, 7.

8: "Tammany tricksters"—DPB, vol. 1, pp. 4–5.

9: "five years' incarceration"—*New York Herald*, January 21, 1871.

9: "to a hotel to-morrow"—Ibid.

10: "The green flag was flying"—*Herald*, January 22, 1871.

10: undisplayed, but naturally assumed, Irish wit—Ibid., January 31, 1871.

11: Grant's arm looked like a pump handle—Devoy, *Recollections*, 361.

CHAPTER TWO

A Most Distressful Country

15: "lightness in the head"—Devoy, *Recollections*, 372–88.

20: 6.8 million to 8.1 million—Gearoid O Tuathaigh, *Ireland Before the Famine*, 137.

21: "neither man nor pig wanted more"—Cormac O Grada, *The Great Irish Famine*, 80.

22: "its majestic mountains rise to the heavens"—Robert Kee, *The Most Distressful Country*, 204.

22: arrived there before his sons—Devoy, *Recollections*, 376.

23: "demonstrations of . . . peaceful resolve"—John Mitchel, *The Last Conquest of Ireland . . . Perhaps*, 37.

23: "not the Catechism he knows, but theology"—Devoy, *Recollections*, 380.

24: "that ends the day's amusements"—Devoy papers, NLI, MS 18,004.

24: "denationalizing the children of Ireland"—Devoy, *Recollections*, 13.

24: "so much difficulty in writing this"—Ibid., 378.

25: "hunger will reduce human nature"—Rossa, *Rossa's Recollections*, 122.

25: William didn't get the job—Devoy, *Recollections*, 378.

CHAPTER THREE

A Great Hunger

27: 5 million of Ireland's 8 million—R. Dudley Edwards and T. Desmond Williams, *The Great Famine*, 53.

27: "unfit for the use of man or beast"—Robert Kee, *Ireland: A History*, 78.

28: "Death had stricken the potato field"—Rossa, *Rossa's Recollections*, 108.

28: "It had been killed and eaten"—Rossa, *Rossa's Recollections*, 116.

29: "what was intended as a blessing"—Cathal Poirteir, ed., *The Great Irish Famine*, 93.

30: "feeble old man muttering"—Cecil Woodham-Smith, *The Great Hunger*, 300.

30: 3 million were receiving some sort of government relief—Kee, *Ireland*, 95.

31: "perverse and turbulent character of the people"—Woodham-Smith, *The Great Hunger*, 156.

32: to accommodate the overflow—Karel Kiely, "Naas Poor Law Union during the Famine" (Ph.D. diss.).

32: an order for more coffins—Ibid.

32: "filled with such brilliant throngs"—Mitchel, *Last Conquest*, 151.

33: buried in Dublin's Glasnevin Cemetery—Glasnevin Cemetery records.

33: constant kneeling—Devoy, *Recollections*, 379.

34: "one hideous mass of cuts and bruises"—Ibid., 384.

35: Elizabeth Devoy died—Glasnevin Cemetery records.

35: an example young John never forgot—Devoy, *Recollections*, 13.

36: Devoy was a frequent visitor to the O'Kelly. . . . forge—Ibid., 333.

38: "the actual number by five"—Ibid., 26.

39: "That young man is very stubborn"—Ibid., 273.

40: broke down and wept—Ibid., 385.

CHAPTER FOUR
Bold Fenian Men

42: "overthrow a tyrannical government"—Desmond Ryan, *Fenian Chief*, 175.

42: sworn into the French Foreign Legion—Devoy, *Recollections*, 386.

42: rust to gather in his rifle—*Gaelic American*, November 28, 1925.

44: continued on their journey to Dublin—Devoy, *Recollections*, 29.

46: "if you wish it so"—Darley Papers, NLI.

46: engaged to be married—*Gaelic American*, March 12, 1927.

46: "the oligarchy of Great Britain"—Robert Kee, *Bold Fenian Men*, 21.

47: "our being able to hold Canada"—Patrick Quinlivan and Paul Rose, *Fenians in England*, 6.

47: was more than $250,000—Kee, *Bold Fenian Men*, 22.

47: "that time as short as possible"—Darley Papers, NLI.

48: "The ink was still wet"—Devoy, *Recollections*, 131.

48: "rather sullen in appearance"—*Hue and Cry*, September 29, 1865.

48: created a distraction—*Gaelic American*, September 12, 1908.

48: began carrying a revolver—Keith Amos, *Fenians in Australia*, 84.

49: started giving information to the British—Kee, *Bold Fenian Men*, 39.

49: "John Devoy was one"—Fenian Briefs, 3/714, National Archives (Dublin)

49: "to so responsible a post"—Devoy, *Recollections*, 146.

51: routine harassment—*Gaelic American*, March 12, 1927.

51: "The Canadian frontier . . . is assailable"—Sweeny papers, NYPL, letter to William Roberts, October 28, 1865.

52: hardly confined to enthusiastic Fenians—Ryan, *Fenian Chief*, 216.

53: Devoy discussed the IRB's desperate straits—Devoy, *Recollections*, 99–111.

56: The detectives placed John Devoy under arrest—*Gaelic American*, May 23, 1925.

56: There, they said good-bye—Devoy papers, NLI, MS 18,006.

CHAPTER FIVE

On the Cause Must Go

57: the mug shot—Larcom Collection, NYPL.

57: set in a stern challenge—Fenian files, NLI.

57: an acquaintance of Devoy's—*Gaelic American*, March 12, 1927.

58: "the destruction of the Confederacy"—Fenian papers, Catholic University of America.

59: "sympathy . . . for us"—Sweeny papers, NYPL.

59: "St. Albans, Vermont, in the east"—Ibid., report to Fenian Congress.

59: "the burning of London"—William D'Arcy, *Fenian Movement in the United States*, 125.

60: Welles wrote in his diary—Ibid., 129.

60: "the Fenian Society"—*Herald*, March 11, 1866.

60: no violation of American neutrality—Ibid., March 16, 1866.

61: "scowling at each other across tables"—Ibid., April 15, 1866.

61: "spirit of liberty is abroad!"—D'Arcy, *Fenian Movement*, 139.

61: "the disintegration of the organization"—Sweeny papers, NYPL.

62: 2 million rounds of ammunition—Ibid.

63: an assault on Japan—*New York Herald*, May 27, 1866.

64: "you would not interfere"—W. S. Neihardt, *Fenianism in North America*, 72.

64: agreed to pick up the tab—D'Arcy, *Fenian Movement*, 165.

65: torment came to an end—Devoy papers, NLI, MS 19,736.

65: imminent return to freedom—Jeremiah O'Donovan Rossa, *Irish Rebels in English Prisons*, 272.

65: to recalcitrant inmates—PCOM 2/361, PRO.

66: politics while on his knees—Devoy, *Recollections*, 122–23.

66: reorganize the movement—Ibid., 187.

66: "deep, sonorous voices"—Ibid., 193.

68: hungry his entire imprisonment—Ibid., 295

68: Christmas prayers to each other—Rossa, *Irish Rebels*, 185.

68: bread, water, and isolation—Ibid., 178.

69: sent back to Millbank—PCOM 2, PRO.

69: darning endless pairs of socks—Devoy, *Recollections*, 327.

69: "it was for a public one"—Rossa, *Irish Rebels*, 255.

CHAPTER SIX

Bound for Western Australia

71: a sugar trader on Wall Street—Michael Lennon Papers, NLI; and *Gaelic American*, March 12, 1927.

72: "Go into business, old man"—DPB, vol. 1, p. 31.

73: he joined the . . . First International—Ibid., 19–22.

73: "hand over the enclosed letter"—*Irish Worker's Voice*, October 1953.

74: "we are friendless indeed"—Sean O Luing, *Catalpa Rescue*, 57.

75: " 'God Save Ireland' "—*Gaelic American*, July 16, 1904.

75: was make it work—O Luing, *Catalpa Rescue*, 58–67.

75: "the work we are engaged in"—Devoy papers, NLI, MS 18,015.

76: a disappointing $7,000—O Luing, *Catalpa Rescue*, 70.

76: "not a solitary minute to myself"—DPB, vol. 1, pp. 91–92.

77: spent the evening corresponding—Ibid., 105.

78: "bored to death"—Ibid., 111.

79: "appointed to West Point"—Ibid., 92–93.

79: land secretly in Florida—O Luing, *Catalpa Rescue*, 88.

80: "a few thousand dollars"—*Irish World*, March 4, 1876.

80: "the same job in England"—DPB, vol. 1, pp. 142–43.

81: "this chance can never occur again"—O Luing, *Catalpa Rescue*, 112.

83: "You have fifteen minutes"—Devoy, *Recollections*, 259.

84: the telegraph cable . . . had been cut—O Luing, *Catalpa Rescue*, 141.

84: "All credit belongs to you"—DPB, vol. 1, p. 173.

85: "Please send instructions"—Devoy papers, NLI, MS 18,017.

86: carted off to a jail cell—Ibid., MS 18,034.

CHAPTER SEVEN

Fetters Rent in Twain

88: weapons from America—DPB, vol. 1, pp. 408–9.

88: an incomprehensible and querulous place—Stanley Weintraub, *Disraeli*, 564.

89: "ready to send off 5 to 10,000 men"—DPB, vol. 1, p. 208.

89: "She will bluster, and muster"—Ibid., 208.

89: various National Guard units—Devoy papers, NLI, MS 18,015.

90: federal-style relationship—Devoy, *Recollections*, 400.

90: "the whole affair is creditable"—DPB, vol. 1, p. 173.

91: "ratholes" of conspiracy—Devoy papers, NLI, MS 18,136.

91: "simple and unpretentious"—*Irish World*, October 10, 1874.

91: "who will devour our substance"—Ibid., October 21, 1874.

92: "character of a people"—*Field Day Anthology of Irish Writing*, vol. 2, p. 167.

92: "homeless and houseless"—O'Donnell, "Henry George's New York," 153.

92: so much as a dollar—Rossa papers, Catholic University of America, Devoy to Mary Rossa, July 26, 1878.

93: "temporal and eternal welfare"—Devoy papers, NLI, MS 18,004.

93: "that was committing murder"—O'Donnell, "Henry George's New York," 152.

93: sixty thousand gallons of urine—Ibid., 148.

93: The Carpenters and Joiners union—*Irish World*, March 4, 1876.

93: 40 percent of New York's 1 million people—O'Donnell, "Henry George's New York," 136.

94: silk production—*Irish World*, March 4, 1876.

94: "send vengeance back"—Ibid., June 3, 1876.

94: grew to some $23,000—Ibid., April 21, 1877.

94: "the burning of English cities"—Gibson, *Attitudes of the New York Irish*, 337.

94: "requiring strict and inviolate secrecy"—DPB, vol. 1, p. 248.

95: "salt-water enterprise"—Ibid., 230.

96: "no great wrong"—Devoy papers, NLI, MS 18,035.

96: "in the way of progressive action"—DPB, vol. 1, pp. 267–68.

96: "and his co-workers"—Ibid., 270.

97: England itself was obliged—Robert Kee, *Laurel and the Ivy*, 159.

98: "the son of a peasant"—Devoy papers, NLI, MS 18,004.

98: " 'Federal connection' with England"—*Irishman*, December 1, 1877.

98: "the House of Commons"—*Irishman*, January 12, 1878.

99: Evictions doubled—T. W. Moody, *Davitt and the Irish Revolution*, 563.

99: letter to the *Irish World*'s Patrick Ford—DPB, vol. 1, p. 285.

99: "in the *Irish World*"—Ibid., 301–2.

100: "any vindictive man who has subscribed even $1"—Ibid., 319.

100: More than $43,000 was at stake—Devoy papers, NLI, MS 18,051.

100: "a couple of small bills"—Rossa papers, Catholic University of America, Devoy to Mary Rossa, July 26, 1878.

101: Devoy's shift ended at 4 A.M.—*Gaelic American*, June 9, 1906.

CHAPTER EIGHT

For Erin's Sake

104: "degradation and despair"—Moody, *Davitt and the Irish Revolution*, 390.

104: fewer than ten thousand members—Devoy papers, NLI, MS 18,051.

105: "the abolition of landlordism"—Devoy, *Land of Eire*, 42.

107: "were left standing"—*Irish World*, October 26, 1878.

107: "ye have been led astray now by Mr. Davitt"—DPB, vol. 1, pp. 373–74.

107: "a storm of applause"—*Irish World*, October 26, 1878.

107: Devoy's hard line—*Gaelic American*, June 16, 1906.

107: "belonged to the clan"—*Irish World*, October 26, 1878.

108: "Nationalists here will support you"—*New York Herald*, October 25, 1878.

109: "lively times are ahead"—Ibid., October 27, 1878.

109: "with the agrarian movement"—SCP, vol. 7, p. 127.

110: "in connection with the so-called New Departure"—*Gaelic American*, July 14, 1906.

110: "Going to Ireland?"—*Gaelic American*, December 13, 1924.

111: "being classed as an American"—*Gaelic American*, July 14, 1906.

111: marked improvement in Davitt's health—Ibid., July 21, 1906.

112: his own thoughts to Kickham—Ibid.

112: "with more zeal than discretion"—Ibid.

112: "thundercloud had passed"—Ibid.

112: neither man considered it so—Moody, *Davitt and the Irish Revolution*, 282.

113: modern rifles in the hands of the IRB's—DPB, vol. 1, p. 406.

113: "will never get them"—Ibid.

113: "a great amount of good"—Ibid., 404.

113: his tweed suit—Devoy, *Recollections*, 285.

CHAPTER ΠΙΠΕ

Hark, a Voice Like Thunder

116: "damned for the sake of Ireland"—*Gaelic American*, August 11, 1906.

116: "sinews of war"—Ibid.

116: "connection with England"—Kee, *Laurel and the Ivy*, 179.

117: store-bought varieties—DPB, vol. 1, p. 410.

117: "half-breeds"—*Gaelic American*, August 18, 1906.

117: "at the blaze of illuminations"—*Gaelic American*, August 11, 1906.

118: Parnell declined to commit himself—*Gaelic American*, September 29, 1906.

118: his work would keep him on the run—*Gaelic American*, September 29, 1906.

118: "The forces of nature intervened"—Eric Foner, "Class, Ethnicity and Radicalism in the Gilded Age."

119: "not one hoe" had arrived—DPB, vol. 1, p. 430.

119: "the wigwams of North America"—Moody, *Davitt and the Irish Revolution*, 289.

119: "cultivate and improve it"—Ibid., 291.

119: "the IRB had 30,162 members"—Devoy papers, NLI, MS 18,036.

119: "I never saw a blue sky"—*Gaelic American*, November 3, 1906.

119: some 421,000 people—Paul Bew, *Land and the National Question*, 89.

120: one man was suited for the job—*Gaelic American*, September 29, 1906.

120: their own, independent party—*Gaelic American*, October 13, 1906.

122: a round of whiskey at the hotel bar—*Gaelic American*, November 3, 1906.

122: "returned to the people of Ireland"—Moody, *Davitt and the Irish Revolution*, 310.

122: "Famine in Ireland"—*Irish World*, August 30, 1879.

123: "patriots for the common cause"—Devoy papers, NLI, MS 18,017.

123: $26,500 had been sent to the IRB—Ibid.

123: $12,000 to cover his expenses—DPB, vol. 1, p. 457.

123: two hundred rifles per week into Ireland—Devoy papers, NLI, MS 18,017.

123: "means to our end"—DPB, vol. 1, pp. 467–68.

124: "little capital pretty considerably"—Ibid., 452.

124: "from landlord grasp"—Ibid., 456.

125: "to accomplish things"—Ibid., 462.

125: gun-smuggling operation . . . with $10,000—Ibid., 463.

125: "The Revolution"—*Irish World*, November 29, 1879.

125: "it had its martyrs"—Ibid.

125: "of a surplus"—*New York Herald*, January 5, 1880.

126: "of a foreign government"—Ibid.

126: return donations—T. M. Healy, *Letters and Leaders of My Day*, vol. 1, p. 80.

126: "the very best Irish people in New York City"—Devoy, *Land of Eire*, 64.

126: "wild tumult"—*New York Times*, January 3, 1880.

126: "the arbiters of this Irish question"—Kee, *Laurel and the Ivy*, 218.

126: "after the trading bell sounded"—*New York Herald*, January 10, 1880.

126: "last link"—Kee, *Laurel and the Ivy*, 220.

126: Devoy managed to duck the task—Healy, *Letters and Leaders*, 81.

127: "should ever become necessary"—Devoy papers, NLI, MS 18,015.

128: raised hundreds of thousands—Kee, *Laurel and the Ivy*, 223.

128: "O'Dynamite" and "O'Donovan Assa"—Moody, *Davitt and the Irish Revolution*, 389.

128: illicit importation into Ireland—DPB, vol. 2, p. 143.

129: "club to break the heads"—DPB, vol. 1, pp. 517–22.

129: There, in small type, he found his father's name—*Irish American*, June 27, 1880.

129: one of the worst days of his life—*Gaelic American*, January 3, 1925.

129: "a wiser though sadder man"—Moody, *Davitt and the Irish Revolution*, 389.

130: $500,000 (in 1882 dollars)—Foner, "Class, Ethnicity and Revolution," 156.

130: "had an impact no other could rival"—Ibid.

130: some 2,110 families—Moody, *Davitt and the Irish Revolution*, 562.

130: Incidents of agrarian crime—Ibid., 420.

131: "I fear no troops will prevent them"—Ibid., 428.

131: "All classes are purchasing arms openly"—DPB, vol. 2, pp. 22–24.

131: "devoted to revolutionary purposes"—Ibid., 12.

132: "ashes and blood"—Ibid., 42.

CHAPTER TEN
Pay Them Back, Woe for Woe

133: "alleged speech"—DPB, vol. 2, p. 44.

133: "fanatic of the deepest dye"—Ibid., 9.

133: the IRB leadership as "senseless"—Ibid.

134: "We cannot, must not begin this way"—Ibid., 10.

134: "bloodless terrorism"—Ibid., 9.

134: not protected against Fenian invaders—MEPO 3/3070.

134: "chaos and disorder"—Ibid.

134: "Fenians are anxious to do something"—Report of the American Historical Society, "Private Letters from the British Embassy," 114–55.

135: "[T]here was a speech ... by a man well-known"—*Hansard* CCLVII: 1554.

135: "the speech of Devoy"—Ibid.

136: "who and what Mr. Devoy is"—*Hansard* 257: 1694.

136: stamp out conspiracies—DPB, vol. 2, p. 43.

136: "with impunity has passed forever"—Ibid.

136: "should cable contradiction"—Ibid., 45.

136: "to the Government of the United States"—*Irishman*, March 5, 1881.

137: "the operation was to be performed"—Ibid.

137: "sleek and contented Home Secretary"—Ibid.

137: "in the House as convicts"—*Hansard* CCLIX: 338.

138: above the town drugstore—*Gaelic American*, September 8, 1923.

138: "attained in the Fenian organization"—DPB, vol. 2, p. 47.

138: "And keep on striking!"—*Irish World*, April 16, 1881.

138: fired off a letter to Patrick Ford—DPB, vol. 2, pp. 62–67.

139: explosive situation in Ireland and Britain—Kee, *Laurel and the Ivy*, 344.

139: guns were arriving in Ireland at "a better rate"—DPB, vol. 2, p. 59.

140: "wholly, or nearly so, unjustifiable"—Ibid., 57.

140: Irish-Americans lurking in British ports—K. R. M. Short, *Dynamite War*, 69.

141: the startling sum of $60,000—DPB, vol. 1, p. 471.

141: "Fenian Torpedo Boat"—American Historical Society, "Private Letters," 143.

141: "as a destructive machine"—Ibid., 146.

142: "she is in her decadence"—Ibid., 111.

142: "the majority of their countrymen"—Ibid., 115.

142: with $38,000 in cash on hand—*Gaelic American*, January 17, 1925.

143: "a nation of idiots"—*Irish Nation*, February 18, 1882.

143: Rossa's "Drunkenness and Dishonesty"—*Irish Nation*, September 9, 1882.

143: "the weak attempt of a beaten man"—Ibid.

143: "More Stupid Anger Than Wit"—Ibid.

143: "raving lunatic"—Ibid., October 14, 1882.

144: "Why should our voices be raised"—*Irish Nation*, May 13, 1882.

145: "to accept help from America"—*Prince of Spies*, 126.

145: "warfare with the power of England"—Short, *Dynamite War*, 155.

146: "render their fire really effective"—DPB, vol. 2, p. 143.

146: "abandon their intention"—Ibid., 142.

146: "with a solution of copperas"—Ibid., 155.

147: "arms could be delivered in London"—Ibid., 157.

147: "Fenian tone"—Conor Cruise, O'Brien, *Parnell and His Party*, 82.

149: sixty days on the prison colony of Blackwell's Island—*Irish Nation*, August 18, 1883.

149: might block such an appointment—American Historical Society, "Private Letters," 172.

150: on its way to Balmoral Castle—Short, *Dynamite War*, 162.

150: close down what it called the "dynamite press"—American Historical Society, "Private Letters," 174–77.

150: "offend the Irish faction"—Ibid.

150: "open advocacy of assassination and murder"—Short, *Dynamite War*, 173.

150: "the smallest restraint in the United States"—Ibid., 177.

151: the watch John Devoy had given him—Ibid., 181.

151: "our relations may become uneasy"—American Historical Society, "Private Letters," 178.

152: "a true friend of the Irish"—Short, *Dynamite War*, 197.

152: "movement of which he is the honored head"—Devoy papers, NLI, MS 18,096.

152: Mayor Grace of New York bought several shares—Ibid., MS 18,046.

152: up for auction in a sheriff's sale—Ibid.

152: "exploded into atoms"—Devoy, *Recollections*, 277.

CHAPTER ELEVEN
The Ould Triangle

155: "tool of the Jesuits"—*Gaelic American*, December 27, 1924.

156: with $128,000 spent on . . . "active work"—Ibid., February 7, 1925.

157: "We could do something if alone"—Michael Funchion, *Chicago's Irish Nationalists*, 65.

157: a tool of Scotland Yard—*Gaelic American*, December 27, 1924.

158: an incursion by a hostile force—Ibid., December 8, 1924.

159: "finding out the reason afterwards"—Ibid.

160: throw a bomb onto the House floor—Funchion, *Chicago's Irish Nationalists*, 96.

160: O'Kelly denounced as "communistic"—DPB, vol. 2, p. 121.

161: "we never met again"—*Gaelic American*, September 22, 1925.

161: "to do it in old Ireland"—Funchion, *Chicago's Irish Nationalists*, 96.

161: "the fires of hell if they could be got at"—*Gaelic American*, September 22, 1923.

161: "I have come out second best"—Ibid.

162: Cook County Elections Commission—Devoy papers, NLI, MS 20,770.

164: transfer of funds would remain a secret—*Gaelic American*, February 7, 1925.

164: The trial started in Buffalo—Devoy papers, NLI, MS 18,018.

164: because he was a British spy—Funchion, *Chicago's Irish Nationalists*, 102.

164: Sullivan and Devoy brought revolvers—Ibid.

164: "Aleck [Sullivan] would make a morgue"—*Gaelic American*, January 10, 1925.

164: "had murder in his eyes"—Ibid.

165: the Irish-American Anti-Cleveland and Protective League—Devoy papers, NLI, MS 18,136.

165: a fee of $2 in return for their votes—*Gaelic American*, January 5, 1924.

165: candidates for cabinet posts—Ibid.

166: "with the knowledge of Mr. Parnell"—SCP, vol. 1, p. 182.

166: cleared Sullivan and his allies—Devoy papers, NLI, MS 18,018.

167: since the death of Stephen Douglas—Funchion, *Chicago's Irish Nationalists*, 106.

168: "injurious to American Institutions"—Ibid., 109.

168: Clan na Gael was not "a murder society"—DPB, vol. 2, pp. 314–15.

168: "before he could reach his hip pocket"—*Gaelic American*, January 17, 1925.

169: "with this howling pack"—Kee, *Laurel and the Ivy*, 557.

169: "with or without Liberals"—DPB, vol. 2, p. 316.

170: "Who is to be the mistress of the Party?"—Kee, *Laurel and the Ivy*, 585.

170: the shattered "national movement"—DPB, vol. 2, p. 318.

170: "this wretched quarrel in Chicago"—Ibid., 320.

171: "without loss of dignity"—Ibid., 321.

171: insistence on leading a "faction"—Ibid., 326–28.

171: "so I can fight those others"—Kee, *Laurel and the Ivy*, 609.

171: a telegram thanking him for his support—Ibid., 328.

172: "chiefs of the murder conspiracy"—Devoy papers, NLI, MS 18,058.

CHAPTER TWELVE

Darkest Just Before the Dawn

All letters from the Devoy family correspondence can be found in the Devoy papers, NLI, MS 18,004.

173: arriving in 1889—*Gaelic American*, September 12, 1908.

174: the direction of Charles Parnell's mother and sisters—Ibid.

176: "the slowest work I ever did"—Devoy papers, NLI, MS 9,919.

177: "didn't feel like touching Irish affairs again"—Ibid.

177: "one of them a big fellow"—Ibid.

178: "emissary from Scotland Yard"—Ibid.

178: membership had grown to 9,702—Ibid., MS 18,015.

179: in New York's sprawling Calvary Cemetery—Ibid., MS 18,157.

179: the apartment on East Ninety-ninth Street—Ibid., MS 18,004.

180: The job paid $100 a month—*Gaelic American*, May 30, 1925.

181: "between the United States and Great Britain"—F. M. Carroll, *American Opinion and the Irish Question*, 20.

182: Clarke addressed Devoy in letters as "Uncle" DPB, vol. 2, p. 444.

183: "people who needed servants"—*Gaelic American*, April 27, 1907.

183: "efforts to Anglicize the American people"—Ibid., February. 4, 1911.

184: "the greatest night's fun we ever had"—Maloney collection, NYPL, Box 4.

184: "English agents, subsidized or volunteers"—*Gaelic American*, March 16, 1907.

185: "Irish history is a closed book"—Ibid., September 28, 1907.

186: "foul, gross and vulgar"—Ibid., September. 14, 1911.

186: "Son of a bitch, that's not Irish"—Carroll, *American Opinion*, 30.

187: "Sitting Bull has a better record"—*Gaelic American*, March 1, 1924.

187: "but an Anglo-American alliance"—Devoy papers, NLI, MS 18,079.

187: passed resolutions calling for the treaty's defeat—*Gaelic American*, March 8, 1924.

187: organizing American support for the Boers—Ibid., June 13, 1925.

188: "a virtual alliance shall not be established"—Ibid., February 25, 1911.

188: "easy and tempting door"—Ibid., March 1, 1924.

188: Irish-America's greatest political victory over England—Ibid.

188: $5,000 on recruitment and organizing activities—Sean Cronin, *McGarrity Papers*, 34.

190: there were but fifteen hundred members by 1912—Ibid., 32.

191: "at last showing results"—Ibid., 37.

192: "almost unanimously with you"—Carroll, *American Opinion*, 20.

192: "no alternative within our reach"—Ibid., 27.

194: "an able document"—Cronin, *McGarrity Papers*, 41.

CHAPTER THIRTEEN

Impatient for the Coming Fight

197: two-bed, $1.50-per-night room in the Ennis Hotel—Cronin, *McGarrity Papers*, 54.

197: journalist George von Skal—Devoy, *Recollections*, 403.

198: "important matters were being discussed"—Cronin, *McGarrity Papers*, 53.

198: would best be served by a German victory—*Gaelic American*, October 3, 1914.

198: The Clan delegation told von Bernstorff—Devoy, *Recollections*, 403.

199: "confidential agent"—*Documents Relative to the Sinn Fein Movement*, 9.

199: Germany's top military commanders—*Gaelic American*, March 6, 13, 1914.

199: an associate of Devoy's—named Albert Sanders—*Documents Relative to the Sinn Fein Movement*, 8.

200: 170,000 strong when the war broke out—Cronin, *McGarrity Papers*, 49.

200: to address a meeting of German societies—Carroll, *American Opinion*, 46.

201: "which doesn't know its own mind"—Maloney Collection (McGarrity papers), NYPL.

201: three doctor's visits—McGarrity papers, NLI, MS 17,609.

202: "it comes at a most inconvenient time"—Ibid.

202: sent a $3,500 check to McGarrity—Ibid.

202: another $15,000 was soon to be on its way—Ibid.

202: "It is heavy and inconvenient"—Maloney Collection (McGarrity papers), NYPL.

203: in addition to giving Casement $1,000—Devoy, *Recollections*, 417.

204: "I will trust him with my life"—Cronin, *McGarrity Papers*, 53.

205: "I envy him"—Ibid., 54.

205: "and meantime we work and plan"—DPB, vol. 2, p. 408.

206: Confederate sympathies during the Civil War—*Gaelic American*, May 15, 1915.

206: "the greatest meeting ever held in New York"—Ibid., July 3, 1915.

206: the patient was "an imbecile"—DPB, vol. 2, p. 460.

207: " 'Tis a lonesome kind of life"—Ibid., 407.

207: "Send his body home at once"—Kathleen Clarke, *Revolutionary Woman*, 56.

208: "Ireland unfree shall never be at peace"—*Gaelic American*, August 21, 1915.

208: "the greatest of the Fenians"—Ibid.

208: forcing him to dictate his letters—Maloney Collection (McGarrity papers), NYPL.

208: "kill Sir Roger's efforts for Ireland"—Ibid.

208: "$22 and a few cents"—Ibid.

209: loaned the Clan $3,340—Ibid.

209: privy to the deliberations—Emmet Larkin, *James Larkin*, 207–8.

210: "It was folly to send him"—Maloney Collection (McGarrity papers), NYPL.

210: Devoy, now apparently flush with cash—Devoy, *Recollections*, 460.

211: "Railway embankments and bridges must not be touched"—*Documents Relative to the Sinn Fein Movement*, 8.

211: from his accounts with the Corn Exchange Bank—Devoy papers, NLI, MS 18,157.

211: grown to a near obsession—Maloney Collection (McGarrity papers), NYPL.

212: "by members of the Revolutionary Directory"—Devoy, *Recollections*, 458.

212: "We might be compelled to begin earlier"—*Documents Relative to the Sinn Fein Movement*, 9.

213: "give them all the help we could"—Cohalan Papers (AIHS).

CHAPTER FOURTEEΠ
A Flag of War

215: "law or no law"—Devoy, *Recollections*, 466.

216: "after beginning action"—*Documents Relative to the Sinn Fein Movement*, 9.

216: Holy Thursday to Easter Sunday—Devoy, *Recollections*, 458.

216: "between Good Friday and Easter Sunday"—Cronin, *McGarrity Papers*, 60.

216: "the way of our giving help"—*Documents Relative to the Sinn Fein Movement*, 9.

217: a submarine to Dublin Bay—Devoy, *Recollections*, 460.

217: "expected from Germany"—*Documents Relative to the Sinn Fein Movement*, 10.

217: "and a few machine guns"—DPB, vol. 2, pp. 485–87.

218: "as Ireland's accredited representative"—Ibid., 487.

219: "if this can be done"—*Documents Relative to the Sinn Fein Movement*, 10.

219: "I could make good"—Maloney Collection (McGarrity papers), NYPL.

219: "Irish agree to proposition"—*Documents Relative to the Sinn Fein Movement*, 10.

220: "imprudent speech"—Devoy, *Recollections*, 449.

220: "among the nations of the earth"—Ibid., 451–57.

220: fifteen were Clan na Gael men—Charles Callan Tansill, *America and the Fight for Irish Freedom*, 189.

220: "her danger and her opportunity"—*Gaelic American*, April 1, 1916.

220: under the name "J. Digby"—Devoy papers, NLI, MS 18,157.

221: a federal subpoena was delivered—Ibid., MS 18,097.

222: its offer of support—Desmond Ryan, *Rising*, 44.

222: "will come to Dublin Bay"—Devoy, *Recollections*, 463.

223: to disrupt American shipping—Larkin, *James Larkin*, 207.

223: the two Germans were subdued—Devoy, *Recollections*, 467.

224: "may decide the war"—*Documents Relative to the Sinn Fein Movement*, 13.

224: the security disaster—Devoy, *Recollections*, 468.

224: "no excuse for worry"—Maloney Collection (McGarrity papers), NYPL.

226: "Peter Devoy's older brother had died"—Devoy papers, NLI, MS 18,004.

226: buried in Dublin's Glasnevin Cemetery—cemetery records.

226: "the dream as a temptation"—DPB, vol. 2, p. 484.

CHAPTER FIFTEEN
Yonder Waits the Saxon Foe

231-232: "pro-German propagandists"—New York Herald, April 26, 1916.

232: "Penalties of misbehavior"—Carroll, American Opinion, 57.

232: little more than a riot—Ibid.

232: "Ireland, in Arms, Fighting for Freedom"—Gaelic American, April 29, 1916.

233: "the Spanish-American War"—Ibid.

233: "Attacks the President"—New York Herald, April 27, 1916.

233: "knew it was a lie"—Ibid.

233: slipped word to British authorities in America—Military Intelligence Division, War Department papers, 9771-56, National Archives.

234: "attention to his editorial"—New York Times, April 28, 1916.

234: "a new epoch in Irish history"—Gaelic American, May 6, 1916.

235: "further views of this nature"—New York Times, May 1, 1916.

235: "unnaturalized Englishmen"—Gaelic American, May 6, 1916.

235: "one Irishman they put to death"—Ibid.

235: "later on they will praise us"—Max Caulfield, Easter Rebellion, 362.

235: "soldier's death I'm getting"—Ibid.

236: "was personally responsible for it"—New York Times, May 4, 1916.

236: "come back to haunt us"—Carroll, American Opinion, 60.

236: "That is the law of war"—Gaelic American, May 6, 1916.

237: "the immortal truths of patriotism!"—Ibid., May 20, 1916.

238: burst into tears in his cell—B. L. Reid, Lives of Roger Casement, 368.

239: "It would be inexcuseable for me to touch this"—Tansill, America and the Fight for Irish Freedom, 210.

239: "convey this message to them"—Carroll, American Opinion, 84.

239: "railing in favor of human slavery"—Tansill, America and the Fight, 213.

239: "the man to silence Devoy"—Ibid., 212.

240: "without landing [troops] it would be useless"—Documents Relative to the Sinn Fein Movement, 25.

240: "with the German agents"—Cronin, *McGarrity Papers*, 68.

241: "in devotion to the flag"—Ibid., 66.

241: "we have never violated American law"—Carroll, *American Opinion*, 98.

241: "adjusting our tactics to the new situations"—McGarrity papers, NLI, MS 17,609.

241: "changed [his] lodging place three times"—Ibid.

243: "Named as Kaiser's Adviser"—*New York Herald*, September 23, 1917.

244: Devoy was panic-stricken—McGarrity papers, NLI, MS 17,609.

244: Secret Service agents questioned him—Patrick McCartan, *With de Valera in America*, 26.

244: "prejudice against Irish Nationalists"—*Gaelic American*, October 20, 1917.

245: "the election of Judge Hylan"—Ibid., November 3, 1917.

245: "closed up long ago"—*New York Times*, November 16, 1917.

245: "with the help of the American people"—Tansill, *America and the Fight*, 270.

247: "the grave of a dead Fenian"—Tim Pat Coogan, *Man Who Made Ireland*, 74.

247: "with the law of God"—Tansill, *America and the Fight*, 247.

247: "Ireland must remain under the heel of England"—*Gaelic American*, May 11, 1918.

248: "the United States as a whole"—Military Intelligence Division, War Department papers, 9771-56, National Archives.

248: "treasonable traffic with the Germans"—Ibid.

249: "independence of Ireland"—Devoy, *Recollections*, 126.

249: "begin with Ireland"—Tansill, *America and the Fight*, 280.

250: "live long enough to live it down"—Ibid., 281.

251: an expression of Ireland's "self-determination"—Cronin, *McGarrity Papers*, 71.

252: "principle of national self-determination"—Tansill, *America and the Fight*, 300.

252: Devoy lost his temper—McCartan, *With De Valera*, 84.

252: "settle the Irish questions forever"—Cohalan MSS, AIHS.

CHAPTER SIXTEEN
Passions Vain and Lowly

Except where noted, letters and quotations from Devoy in this chapter are taken from the Cohalan papers at the American Irish Historical Society.

255: "until the work is done"—*Gaelic American*, March 29, 1919.

257: his long-lost fiancée—Ibid., March 12, 1927.

260: "changes nothing at all"—Ibid., June 29, 1919.

263: "the principles of Self Determination"—Ibid., July 5, 1919.

264: "I held that Ireland's interests should come first"—Tim Pat Coogan, *De Valera*, 164.

264: $5,000 on Larkin's behalf—*Devoy v. Nelles*, New York Supreme Court archives.

265: $26,000 for De Valera's expenses—Friends of Irish Freedom papers, AIHS.

265: "first junk bond flotation"—Coogan, *De Valera*, 158.

266: "the Smoke Screen of British Propaganda"—*Gaelic American*, October 16, 1919.

269: "The Mason Resolution . . . came to nothing"—Tansill, *America and the Fight*, 156–157.

270: "the History of the Race in America"—*Gaelic American*, February 7, 1920.

270: "co-operate with their whole soul"—Ibid., February 14, 1920.

271: "John Devoy's Objections"—Ibid.

271: "no longer an asset"—McCartan, *With de Valera*, 170.

272: "exactly how you stand in this matter"—Cohalan papers, AIHS.

272: "upon the side of America"—Ibid.

272: "tricky police court lawyer"—Coogan, *De Valera*, 164.

272: "present intolerable relations"—Ibid., 173.

273: "enemies of . . . the Irish race in America"—Ibid.

273: analysis of the Cuba interview—Cronin, *McGarrity Papers*, 173.

274: too small for himself and Judge Cohalan—Ibid., 80.

274: "the whole alphabet of autocracy"—Cohalan papers, AIHS.

274: Devoy roared that Boland was lying—*Gaelic American*, June 26, 1920.

275: "test of strength with Justice Cohalan"—Tansill, *America and the Fight*, 368.

275: "any nation in the world"—Coogan, *Man Who Made Ireland*, 124.

276: "Go to the primaries and vote for Johnson"—*Gaelic American*, April 24, 1920.

276: leader of the Irish race in America—Ibid., April 10, 1920.

276: "offending America that we did not take"—McCartan, *With de Valera*, 190–91.

277: "their own governmental institutions"—Tansill, *America and the Fight*, 375.

277: "Government of the Republic of Ireland"—Coogan, *De Valera*, 180.

278: "British barbarity in Ireland"—Cohalan papers, AIHS.

279: its war with Britain was $1 million—Coogan, *De Valera*, 176.

279: "under the domination of a British Agent"—*Gaelic American*, July 3, 1920.

280: "the blame for his own failure"—Ibid., July 31, 1920.

280: "connected with his mission"—Ibid., August 21, 1920.

280: "the Lord Mayor of Cork"—McCartan, *With de Valera* 199.

281: "Michael Collins Speaks for Ireland"—*Gaelic American*, September 4, 1920.

281: "Michael Collins, Ireland's Fighting Chief"—Ibid., Sept. 11, 1920.

282: left the meeting—Cronin, *McGarrity Papers*, 85.

282: "no longer affiliated with the Brotherhood"—*Gaelic American*, October 30, 1920.

283: "$3 million of the more than $5 million"—Coogan, *De Valera*, 194.

CHAPTER SEVENTEEN
A Nation Once Again

286: disappeared into the New York night—Cronin, *McGarrity Papers*, 98.

288: "We'll see who's the Big Fellow"—Coogan, *De Valera*, 196.

288: "Destroy the Friends of Irish Freedom"—*Gaelic American*, June 11, 1921.

288: a rival organization in New York—Cohalan papers, AIHS.

288: to about 70,000—Friends of Irish Freedom papers, AIHS.

289: "would not, recognize Ireland as a Republic"—Tansill, *America and the Fight*, 161.

290: "had put us in the stocks"—Coogan, *De Valera*, 184.

290: "kinship to the Emerald Isle"—Carroll, *American Opinion*, 167.

291: "a race of treacherous murderers"—Coogan, *De Valera*, 220.

291: "the head of a band of murderers"—T. Ryle Dwyer, *Michael Collins*, 135.

292: "the people will accept anything they get"—Cohalan papers, AIHS.

293: "that is their affair"—*Gaelic American*, June 11, 1921.

293: "those in Ireland who favor it"—Cohalan papers, AIHS.

294: "the work of disorganization here"—Ibid.

294: "This half-breed Jew"—Ibid.

295: as he lay awake in his hotel room—Ibid.

295: "the oldest active Fenian"—Ibid.

296: "playing the game just as he wants"—Ibid.

296: "to deal with them at all"—Ibid.

297: "against our elected President"—Devoy papers, NLI, MS 18,001.

297: "out of bigheartedness"—Ibid.

298: called it a "surrender"—*Gaelic American*, December 17, 1921.

298: "combat British intrigue in America"—Ibid.

299: "as the leader of the Irish people"—Ibid., December 24, 1921.

300: "you would forgive the past"—Devoy papers, NLI, 18,001.

300: "comedy or farce in it"—*Gaelic American*, January 14, 1922.

302: "Ireland's dearest interests"—Cohalan papers, AIHS.

302: "the vital principle of that idea"—Devoy papers, NLI, 18,001.

302: "concern to us here"—Ibid.

302: "in order to get Irish freedom"—Coogan, *Man Who Made Ireland*, 319.

304: "proving its apparent truth?"—*Gaelic American*, February 10, 1923.

304: "the trouble will soon end"—Ibid.

CHAPTER EIGHTEEN
A Soldier's Song

305: "Three cheers for John Devoy!"—*Gaelic American*, August 9, 1924.

307: "I have been in America"—Ibid., July 26, 1924.

307: "may be left to me"—Ibid., August 9, 1924.

307: pay Devoy's medical and living expenses—Cohalan papers, AIHS.

307: "one gets in an American hotel"—*Gaelic American*, August 9, 1924.

307: William Butler Yeats—Ibid.

308: "mouthpiece" for a "reactionary minority"—Ibid., July 26, 1924.

309: "such young men"—Ibid., August 9, 1924.

309: her long-lost fiancé—Ibid., March 12, 1927.

310: "waiting for you all my life"—Ibid.

310: "wholly out of the question"—Ibid.

311: "by healing our divisions reinforce our strength"—*Freeman's Journal*, July 26, 1924.

312: "I want it to be done peacefully"—*Gaelic American*, August 30, 1924.

312: "common sense rules men and movements"—Ibid.

312: "How e'er we think he erred"—Ibid., August 23, 1924.

313: "I never forgot them"—Devoy papers, NLI, MS 18,006.

313: "no man deserved better of this nation"—*Gaelic American*, September 13, 1924.

314: "ruin and disaster upon her"—Ibid., September 20, 1924.

314: "military and economic resources"—Ibid.

314: "time and hard work"—Ibid.

314: "bring about reunion by consent"—Devoy papers, NLI, MS 18,127.

315: "in the nature of an argument at night"—Ibid., MS 18,001.

315: "the misfortunes which separated us"—Private collection, author's copy.

316: "after his release in 1871"—Ibid.

316: "don't let them into the secret"—Devoy papers, NLI, MS 18,001.

316: a $25,000 judgment—*Devoy v. Ford*, New York Supreme Court archives.

316: "part of an Irish fight"—Cohalan papers, AIHS.

316: "when you can't read or write"—Devoy papers, NLI, MS 18,006.

317: "should bar him forever"—Cohalan papers, AIHS.

318: within the British Army—Ibid.

319: "since Wolfe Tone"—*Times*, October 1, 1928.

I · PRIVATE PAPERS

Ireland

National Library of Ireland, Dublin:

The single most important resource for this book was the papers of John Devoy. The collection, with its extraordinary insight into more than half a century of Irish and American history, was brought to Dublin several years after Devoy died. A portion of the correspondence found in these remarkable papers was published in a two-volume collection called *Devoy's Post Bag*. The books were the work of William O'Brien and Desmond Ryan, whose pioneering work made this biography possible. They decoded letters written in the Clan na Gael's cipher and annoted their entries with an extremely helpful narrative.

Other NLI collections consulted were the papers of Frederick J. Allen, J. J. Hearn, Michael Lennon, Patrick McCartan, Joseph McGarrity, Patrick Pearse, Frank Robbins, and the Darley family.

United States

The New York Public Library, Manuscripts Division:

The Maloney Collection, including the papers of Joseph McGarrity, Roger Casement, Dr. William Maloney, and Jeremiah O'Donovan Rossa.

The papers of Thomas Sweeny, William Bourke Cockran, and Frank Walsh.

The Larcom Collection.

The American Irish Historical Society, New York: The papers of Daniel Cohalan and the Friends of Irish Freedom.

Catholic University of America, Washington, D.C.: The Fenian papers and the papers of Jeremiah O'Donovan Rossa.

2 . PUBLIC DOCUMENTS

Ireland

National Archives: Fenian Briefs; correspondence from the Chief Sec-retary's Office

National Library of Ireland: *Report of the Special Commission* (H.M.S.O., 1890)

Hue and Cry

Great Britain

Public Records Office: Metropolitan Police records; Home Office cor-respondence; Governor's Journal, Chatham and Millbank prisons

Documents Relative to the Sinn Fein Movement (London, 1921, Cmd. 1108)

Report of the Commissioners Appointed to Inquire into the Treatment of Treason-Felony Convicts in English Prisons (H.M.S.O., London, 1871)

Hansard

United States

New York Municipal Archives, Court of General Sessions and Su-preme Court

Federal Archives, New York, Citizenship Records

American Commission on Conditions in Ireland: *Evidence on Conditions in Ireland* (Washington, 1921)

Atlantic City:
Bureau of Vital Statistics, City Hall

Washington:
National Archives: War Department, Division of Military Intelligence Files; State Department correspondence
Congressional Record
Foreign Relations of the United States

3 · ΠEWSPAPERS AΠD PERIΘDICALS

Ireland

Freeman's Journal; Kildare Observer; The Nation; Irishman; Irish Freedom; Irish Times; Irish Worker's Voice

Great Britain

Times; Westminster Gazette; Annual Register

United States

America; Boston Pilot; Christian Science Monitor; Gaelic American; Irish Nation; Irish World; Irish American; New York Herald; New York Journal; New York Post; Recorder; New York Sun; New York Times; New York Tribune; New York World
Annual Report of the American Historical Society, 1941, "Private Letters from the British Embassy, 1880–1885"

4 · BOOKS AΠD ARTICLES

Amos, Keith. *The Fenians in Australia.* Australia: New South Wales University Press, 1988.

Baylor, Ronald, and Timothy Meagher, eds. *The New York Irish.* Baltimore: Johns Hopkins University Press, 1996.

Beech, Thomas. *Twenty-Five Years in the Secret Service.* London: Heinemann, 1892.

Bew, Paul. *Land and the National Question in Ireland.* Atlantic Highlands, N.J.: Humanities Press, 1979.

Bourke, Marcus. *John O'Leary.* Tralee, Ireland: Anvil Books, 1967.

Brown, T. N. *Irish American Nationalism.* Philadelphia: Lippincott, 1966.

Carroll, F. M. *American Opinion and the Irish Question.* New York: St. Martin's Press, 1978.

Caulfield, Max. *The Easter Rebellion.* New York: Holt, Rinehart and Winston, 1963.

Clarke, Kathleen. *Revolutionary Woman.* Dublin: O'Brien Press, 1991.

Cole, J. A. *Prince of Spies.* London: Faber and Faber, 1984.

Coleman, Terry. *Going to America.* Baltimore: Genealogical Publishing Inc., 1987.

Comerford, R. V. *Charles J. Kickham.* Portmarnock, Ireland: Wolfhound Press, 1979.

Coogan, Tim Pat. *The Man Who Made Ireland.* Boulder, Colo.: Roberts Rinehart Publishers, 1992.

———. *De Valera.* London: Hutchinson, 1993.

————. *The IRA*. Boulder, Colo.: Roberts Rinehart Publishers, 1993.

Cronin, Sean. *The McGarrity Papers*. Tralee, Ireland: Anvil Books, 1972.

————. *Irish Nationalism*. New York: Continuum Publishing, 1981.

————. *Washington's Irish Policy*. Dublin: Anvil Books, 1987.

D'Arcy, William. *The Fenian Movement in the United States*. Washington, D.C.: Catholic University of America Press, 1947.

Davitt, Michael. *The Fall of Feudalism in Ireland*. New York: Harper and Brothers, 1904.

Deane, Seamus, ed. *The Field Day Anthology of Irish Writing* (3 vols.). Deny, Ireland: Field Day Publications, 1991.

Devoy, John. *Land of Eire*. New York: Patterson and Neilson, 1882.

————. *Recollections of an Irish Rebel*. New York: Charles Young, 1929.

Dwyer, T. Ryle. *Michael Collins and the Treaty*. Cork: Mercier Press, 1981.

————. *Michael Collins*. Cork: Mercier Press, 1990.

Edwards, R. Dudley, and T. Desmond Williams. *The Great Famine*. Dublin: Browne and Nolan, Ltd., 1956.

Ernst, Robert. *Immigrant Life in New York City*. Syracuse: Syracuse University Press, 1994.

Foner, Eric. "Class, Ethnicity and Radicalism in the Gilded Age:

The Land League and Irish America." *Marxist Perspectives* 1, no. 2 (1978).

Forester, Margery. *Michael Collins, the Lost Leader*. London: Sphere Books, 1972.

Foster, R. M. *Modern Ireland*. New York: Viking, 1988.

Funchion, Michael. *Chicago's Irish Nationalists*. New York: Arno Press, 1976.

Gibson, Florence. *Attitudes of the New York Irish*. New York: Columbia University Press, 1951.

Greaves, C. Desmond. *Liam Mellows and the Irish Revolution*. London: Lawrence and Wishart, 1971.

Harmin, Maurice, ed. *Fenians and Fenianism*. Dublin: Scepter Books, 1968.

Healy, T. M. *Letters and Leaders of My Day*. 2 vols. New York: Frederick H. Stokes, 1929.

Kee, Robert. *The Most Distressful Country*. London: Penguin Books, 1972.

———. *The Bold Fenian Men*. London: Quartet Books, 1976.

———. *Ireland: A History*. London: Abacus, 1983.

———. *The Laurel and the Ivy*. London: Hamish Hamilton, 1993.

Larkin, Emmet. *James Larkin, Irish Labor Leader*. Cambridge: Massachusetts Institute of Technology Press, 1965.

Leslie, Shane. *The Irish Issue in Its American Aspect*. New York: Charles Scribner's Sons, 1917.

Levenson, Samuel. *James Connolly*. London: Quartet Books, 1977.

Lyons, F. S. L. *The Irish Parliamentary Party*. London: Faber and Faber, 1951.

————. *The Fall of Parnell*. Toronto: University of Toronto Press, 1960.

————. *Ireland Since the Famine*. New York: Charles Scribner's Sons, 1973.

Macardle, Dorothy. *The Irish Republic*. London: Farrar, Strauss, 1965.

Martin, F. X., ed. *Leaders and Men of the Easter Rising*. Ithaca, N.Y.: Cornell University Press, 1967.

McCaffrey, Lawrence J. *The Irish Question*. Lexington: University Press of Kentucky, 1995.

McCartan, Patrick. *With de Valera in America*. New York: Brentano, 1932.

McEnnis, John T. *The Clan na Gael and the Murder of Dr. Cronin*. Chicago: F. J. Schulte and Co., 1989.

Mitchel, John. *Jail Journal*. Dublin: University Press of Ireland, 1982.

————. *The Last Conquest of Ireland . . . Perhaps*. Dublin, 1861.

Monteith, Robert. *Casement's Last Adventure*. Dublin: Michael F. Moynihan, 1953.

Moody, T. W. "The New Departure in Irish Politics." In *Essays in British and Irish History*, edited by H. A. Cronne and others. London: Frederick Muller, 1949.

————. *Davitt and the Irish Revolution*. Oxford: Clarendon Press, 1982.

Morgan, Austen. *James Connolly*. Manchester: Manchester University Press, 1988.

Morris, Richard K. *John P. Holland*. Annapolis, Md.: U.S. Naval Institute, 1966.

Neidhardt, W. S. *Fenianism in North America*. University Park, Pa.: Pennsylvania State University Press, 1975.

Newsinger, John. *Fenianism in Mid-Victorian Britain*. London: Pluto Press, 1994.

O'Brien, Conor Cruise. *Parnell and His Party*. London: Oxford University Press, 1957.

O'Brien, William, and Desmond Ryan, eds. *Devoy's Post Bag*. 2 vols. Dublin: Fallon, 1948, 1953.

O'Broin, Leon. *Fenian Fever*. New York: New York University Press, 1971.

————. *Revolutionary Underground*. Dublin: Gill and Macmillan, 1976.

O'Connor, Ulick. *Michael Collins*. New York: W. W. Norton, 1996.

O'Doherty, Katherine. *Assignment America*. New York: De Tanko Publishing, 1957.

O'Farrell, Patrick. *England and Ireland Since 1800*. London: Oxford University Press, 1975.

O Grada, Cormac. *The Great Irish Famine*. London: Macmillan, 1989.

O'Leary, John. *Recollections of Fenians and Fenianism.* London: Downey and Company, 1896.

O Luing, Sean. *The Catalpa Rescue.* Tralee, Ireland: Anvil Books, 1965.

O'Neill, Thomas P., and the Earl of Longford. *Eamon de Valera.* Boston: Houghton Mifflin Co., 1971.

O'Rahilly, Aodogan. *Winding the Clock: O'Rahilly and the 1916 Rising.* Dublin: Lilliput Press, 1991.

O Tuathaigh, Gearoid. *Ireland Before the Famine.* Dublin: Gill and Macmillan, 1972.

Pakenham, Thomas. *The Year of Liberty.* New York: Random House, 1993.

Phillips, W. Alison. *The Revolution in Ireland.* New York: Longmans, Green and Co., 1923.

Poirteir, Cathal, ed. *The Great Irish Famine.* Cork: Mercier Press, 1995.

Powderly, Terence V. *The Path I Trod.* New York: Columbia University Press, 1948.

Quinlivan, Patrick, and Paul Rose. *The Fenians in England.* New York: Riverrun Press, 1982.

Reeve, Carl, and Ann Barton Reeve. *James Connolly and the United States.* Atlantic Highlands, N.J.: Humanities Press, 1978.

Reid, B. L. *The Lives of Roger Casement.* New Haven, Conn.: Yale University Press, 1976.

Reidy, James. "John Devoy." *Journal of the American Irish Historical Society* (New York) 27 (1928).

Rossa, Jeremiah O'Donovan. *Rossa's Recollections*. New York: Mariners Harbor, 1894.

———. *Irish Rebels in English Prisons*. Dingle, Ireland: Brandon Books, 1991.

Rutherford, John. *The Secret History of the Fenian Conspiracy*. London: Kegan, Paul and Co., 1877.

Ryan, Desmond. *The Phoenix Flame*. London: Barder, 1937.

———. *The Rising*. Dublin: Golden Eagle Books, 1949.

———. *The Fenian Chief*. Coral Gables, Fla.: University of Miami Press, 1967.

Shannon, William. *The American Irish*. New York: Macmillan, 1963.

Short, K. R. M. *The Dynamite War*. Atlantic Highlands, N.J.: Humanities Press, 1979.

Tansill, Charles Challan. *America and the Fight for Irish Freedom*. New York: Devin-Adair, 1957.

Weintraub, Stanley. *Disraeli*. New York: Truman Talley/Dutton, 1993.

Woodham-Smith, Cecil. *The Great Hunger*. New York: Old Town Books, 1989.

5. UNPUBLISHED SOURCES

Kiely, Karel. "Naas Poor Law Union during the Famine." Ph.D. diss., National University of Ireland, St. Patrick's College, Maynooth, August 1994.

O'Donnell, Edward. "Henry George's New York." Ph.D. diss., Columbia University, New York, 1996.